The History of History Writing

Complied by
Dr. Rajesh Gautam

ADROIT PUBLISHERS

Published by
ADROIT PUBLISHERS
4675/21, Ganpati Bhawan, Ansari Road,
Daryaganj, New Delhi-110 002
Phones : 23266030, 23242552

Distributors
AKHIL BOOK DISTRIBUTORS
e-mail: akhilbooks@yahoo.com
akhilbooks@hotmail.com

ISBN : 81-87392-63-0

Layout
Sudhir Vatsa

Laser Typeset by
Nidhi Laser Point
e-mail: nidhi_vatsa@hotmail.com

Printed in India on behalf of M/s Adroit Publishers by
Arpit Printographers, B-7, Saraswati Complex,
Subhash Chowk, Laxmi Nagar, Delhi-110 092

PREFACE

The Subject History, a systematic presentation of the incessant conversation among facts and historians, links the past and the present. In order to make these facts revealed among the people, historians hold a great significance. Historians make the society aware of the past events, orient them in the current period and guide them for a bright future. The past is the mother of the present, and, of course, its foundation, while the future is dependent upon the foundation of the present. Viewing these critical uses of History, Earnest Renon has said "The persons or the countries who do not remember their historical events have no future at all". It is just because the present is the complete picture of the past. The present scenario of both the person and country can be analyzed only on the basis of past. Thus, history based knowledge is the prime asset of human being. History is the best creation of human mind while the nature is the greatest creation of the god. Thus, the creation of human mind is simply available in contrast to that of the creation of the god. If a man is appropriate for human studies, historians have the commendable capacity to understand the present with reference to the past.

History is the major source of social sciences. Politics, Science, Economics and Sociology are its branches. Nepal's secondary school and university level curriculum include each of these subjects. However, the students of history are not taught about the concept of history and its limitations.

Germany is the most popular centre for the critical study of History. It was natural that the professionals of England,

Italy and France were attracted to historical studies towards the end of 19th century. In no time, the critical Western historians -Hegel, Kroche, Karl Marx, Kalingwood, Tene, Ranke and Karl Baker became famous in the western history. Nepal's education is still founded in the western concept and systems. However, the study of History could not attract Nepal's academicians. This is very much important issue for us. Consequently, no attempt was made in the past neither to study nor to educate the problems associated with History. Till now this issue is yet to be covered in the education levels except at the Master's Level.

Like literary writers historians are also considered as the representatives of the contemporary society and thus are the products of dynamic society. Historians possess a good personality in the society because of a number of following reasons. First, historians perceive the past with reference to contemporary social values and prevailing time and explain them. The sole motive of History writing is to fulfil the contemporary need. Therefore, the need for History writing is felt in each time. A History Book portrays the personality of the writer and contemporary view of the society. The rationality of each history based explanation is given due place in context of a particular location and time. Second, historians link the current social values and approaches with the past events and thereby explain those events. Third, reading of History books provides information about the personality of the historians as well as analysis of the contemporary social trends. In these contexts, critical appraisal of history-based knowledge has been gaining currency in the present period.

Prof. J. B. Buri's quotation of the beginning of 20th century like "History as a science neither possesses a great importance nor a very little place" suggested the historians to consider History as a separate discipline. Some historians pleaded and led the movement to make History as an independent and popular discipline as Science. According to these authors, History is not the means of communication of individual opinion rather a systematic presentation of the past events and mirror of the facts. The study of History is open to all the public. There will be a mistake if History is considered as a subject of entertainment. History contains contemporary events: how society functions and guidelines for improving human welfare in the future.

With reference to History writing, Nebur says, "the soul of historians is just like the soul of honey bee: a collection of sweet honey keeping poison away. Thus, the duties of historians are to collect and disseminate the good aspects of past events among the societies with the disposal of the bad elements of the past events". An appropriate exposure to History can only enable one to understand the real meaning of historical events and distinguish the good and bad ones.

History writing is itself an arduous task. The philosophers have made this task still difficult. The material presented in this book consists of my M. A. class notes, various books, journals and news papers. In one way or other, I am greatly influenced from the published works of a number of authors. Despite the existing legal provision that no part of a publication can be reproduced by any means without the publishers' permission in writing, I have used such publications in this book. Therefore, I want to repent for this. I hope that I would be forgiven because my attempt is to present the opinion and approach of the earlier writers in a simple manner and make them widely disseminated.

My heartfelt thanks go to my respected teacher at Central Department of History, Tribhuvan University: Dr. Professor Krishna Kant Adhikari. I think he has immemorial efforts to incite interest in this subject and encourage me to take a carrier in History. He not only holds deep respect for imparting knowledge and makes me converse on History but also provides me suggestions, assistance and directions in the areas of my interests. Therefore, I owe to him as he is the forever source of inspiration for me.

Many other professors of Tribhuvan University have helped me with references, encouragement, and suggestions, and I am particularly grateful for their good helps: Dr. Tulsi Ram Vaidya, Tri-ratna Mandhar and Associate Professor Mr. Krishna Bahadur Udaya.

I am also benefited from the suggestions and helps of many friends: Mr. Bimal Sharma, Dr. Yagyan Nath Acharya, and Dr. Hari Raj Bhattarai, Trichandra Campus, Mr. Naranath Luintel, Madan Tuladhar, Krishna Murari Adhikari, Sri Ram Shrestha, Mr. Vishwambharlal Pradhan and Mr. Madhuman Pradhan.

My sister Mss Kabita Paudyal, wife Mrs Illa Gautam, sons Mr. Shobhendra Gautam and Mr. Nissim Gautam have a constant source of help.

I also thank the staff of the Nepal American Cultural Centre, Nepal British Council Library, Nepal Bharat Cultural Centre, Kehsar Library, Tribhuvan University Central Library and Trichandra Campus Library for providing various reading materials relevant to this book.

Lastly, I would heartily appreciate the comments and suggestions from the readers.

Dr. Rajesh Gautam
Themel

CHAPTER 1

The Study of History

Modern historians aim mainly at reconstructing an accurate record of human activities and at them. This conception of their task is quite recent, dating only from the development in the late 18th and early 19th centuries of scientific history, cultivated largely by professional historians. It springs from an outlook that is very new in human experience : the assumption that the study of history is a natural, inevitable kind of human activity. Before the late 18th century, historiography (the writing of history) did not stand at the centre of any civilization. History, and it never claimed to provide an interpretation of human life as a whole. This was more appropriately the function of religion, of philosophy, even perhaps of poetry and other forms of imaginative literature.

The article is divided into the following sections :

History of historiography
Ancient historiogrpahy
Early Christian era
Early China
Medieval historiogrpahy
Europe from the 5th to the 11th century
Europe from the 12th to the 14th century
Byzantine historiogrpahy

Historiogrpahy in the 19th and 20th centuries
Source material
Using source material
Ancillary fields
Archaeology
History of archaeology
Fieldwork
Interpretation

Muslim historiogrpahy
Historiogrpahy in the European Renaissance
Early modern histogriogrpahy
Historiogrpahy in the age of the Enlightenment
Indian
Egyptian
Babylonian and assyrian
Jewish
Greek
Roman
Christian
Muslim
Pre-Columbian American
History of the study of documents
Diplomatic method
Development and characteristics of chancenes
Materials and techniques
Inscriptions as historical source material
Descriptive bibliography
Critical bibliography
Chinese
Japanese
Inscriptions as social and cultural records
The use of inscriptions
History of epigraphy
History of genealogical study
Modern genealogy
Types of writing materials
Analysis of texts
Seals in antiquity
Medieval European seals
Modern use of seals
Chinese and Japanese seals
The materials of the investigation
Critical methods
History of textual criticism

HISTORY OF HISTORIOGRAPHY

Ancient Historiography

Greco-Roman era - The older, pre-18th-century outlook has been particularly well studied in the historiography of the ancient Greeks and Romans. But, although two of the most important ancient historians. Herodotus and Thucydides, wrote as early as the 5th century BC, when recorded Greek historiography was only just beginning, they had few successors of comparable quality. It is as symptom of the relative lack of importance attached in antiquity to this type of activity.

Ancient history was a branch of literature. The most appreciated historians were the writers who, like Thucydides, were able to touch on universal human problems or who, like the Roman author Tacit us (died c. AD 120), wrote in a dramatic way about important events or who, at least, attracted readers by their excellent style and skill in composition. Many of the works that lacked some of these literary qualities failed to survive.

About 1,000 ancient Greeks wrote in antiquity on historical subjects, but most of these writers are mere names. Many of the losses appear to have occurred in antiquity itself. Even historians of first rank have fared badly. Only in a few cases have complete texts of all their writings survived. Of the voluminous history of Polybius (covering originally the period 220-144 BC) only about one-third survives. Nearly half of Livy's Roman history (originally covering the period 753-9 BC) is lost. The text that remains is reasonably good only through the efforts of a group of Roman aristocrats who, in about AD 500, were trying to salvage the chief glories of Roman literature. A considerable part of Tacit us is missing, and the surviving portions of his *Annals* and *Histories* (originally AD 14-96) derive from two unique manuscripts.

Herodotus, whom the Roman statesman Cicero called "the father of history", came from the western coast of Asia Minor. The writers who preceded him were mainly lonians from the Greek settlements in the same area. The origin of Greek historiography lies in the lonian thought of the 6th century. The lonian philosophers were dong universe is an intelligible whole and that through rational inquiries men might discover the general principles that govern it. Hecateus of Miletus, the most important Ionian predecessor of Herodotus, was applying the same critical spirit to the largely mythical Greek traditions when he wrote, early in the 5th century, "the stories of the Greeks are numerous and in my opinion ridiculous". Herodotus was more of a traditionalist, but the introduced his work as an "inquiry" (*historia).*

A glance at the older historiography of the Egyptians, the Babylonians, and the other peoples of the ancient Near East will heighten one's appreciation of the novelty of the task undertaken by Herodotus. The kings of Egypt, of Babylonia and Assyna, and of the Hittites and the Persiant all sought to preserve their glonous deeds for posterity in monumental inscriptions. The more important rulers also accumulated large archives, including both ordinary administrative documents and records specially commemorating their achievements. Some 20,000 clay tablets remain from the collections written for Ashurbanipal of Assyria (668-627 BC). Both in Egypt and in Babylonia lists of kings were kept in the temples, and these were sometimes supplemented by brief annals recording the principal events, though the hatred felt by certain rulers for their predecessors led to periodic destructions of older maternal. The exceptional meagreness of the narrative sources for Babylonia history before 474 BC seems due to the obliteration of the older annals by Nabonassar of Babylonia (ruled 747 -734). Apart from changes in literary style, there was surprisingly little development over a period of more than 1,000 years in all these types of commemorative records. The inscriptions and temple records were normally intended to perpetuate the glory of the gods in whose service these rulers had accomplished great deeds. The names and dates of dynasties and of particular rulers can be reconstructed fairly adequately with the and of these sources, but one cannot expect much accurate information about particular events. Nor, with rare exceptions, were those who had access to this material interested in using it to write continuous histories.

Herodotus and his immediate Ionian predecessors shared a very novel outlook. Its distinctive features were a lively curiosity and a capacity to treat sources in a critical spirit. Boundless curiosity about people and their diverse customs is one of the most endearing traits of Herodotus. Like other Greeks from western Asia Minor, he was particularly stimulated by contacts with the great Perian Empire, which offered opportunities for reasonably secure travel. The resultant immense widening of historical perspective is illustrated by a story told by Herodotus about Hecateus.

When the latter assured the Egyptian priests at The best that he could trace his descent through 16 generations, the Egyptians showed him evidence of the descent of their high priests through 345 generations. Herodotus was the first to link his geographic inquiries with true history. His descriptions of the barbarian world that confronted the Greeks provided an introduction to the epic of the successful Greek resistance to the Persians.

The types of history written by the ancient Greeks and Romans influenced profoundly all subsequent historiography down to the 18th century in order to interpret sympathetically this classical historiography it is necessary to bear in mind the literary conventions that governed this branch of literature. The ancient Greeks distinguished between history and biography,. The origin of both forms can be traced back to at least the 5th century BC, and the differences between them were observed throughout antiquity. The writer of history was supposed to aim at giving a true story, but the biographer was entitled to treat historical personages in a manner that resembled legend. There existed, or course, some exceptions. The lives of the early Roman emperors written by Suetonius in the 2nd century AD, while conforming to the traditional, topical arrangement of biographies, constitute an unusually valuable historical source, especially for Augustus, whose correspondence in repeatedly quoted. Yet another distinction was drawn between history and the study of "antiquities", to use a term employed by Varro (116-27 BC). This distinction was already implicit in Aristotle's contemptuous dismissal of history (in his *Poetics)* *as* a branch of literature dealing with the particular rather than with of literature dealing with the particular rather than with things of general significance. The histories he condemned provided chronological narratives of wars and political events. Aristotle and his disciples we re-engaged in several enterprises that they regarded as something quite different from history. For example, they embarked on the study of the constitutions of all the Greek states,. Such work was to be based on systematic inquiries. The student of the "antiquities" tried to use a wider range of evidence than the sources normally consulted by the ancient historians, and he arranged his results systematically by topics.

In antiquity a writer of history was usually preoccupied at least as much with style as with content. A generation before Aristotle, the rules of rhetoric, as they might be applied to history, were fully elaborated by Isocrates, a teacher of rhetoric at Athens. Cicero tried (especially in his *De oratore,* 55 BC) to familiarize the Romans with these Isocratean precepts. History was to be written in a clear but solemn style, akin to fine oratory. The historian was to introduce all manner of literary embellishments but was also to stress the moral lessons of his story. At its worst this type of historiography could lead to serious misrepresentations of the past. Among the Roman historians. Livy (died AD 17) was an important practitioner of this kind of writing, which was particularly well suited to a Rome that owed its magnificent destiny to the unique virtues of its citizens and the perfection of its antique institutions. Some outstanding historians, such as Polybius (2nd century BC) and Caesar (died 44 BC), eschewed these rhetorical precepts, but in all the ancient writers an important element of literary artifice was always present. This is one of the reasons why they offend modern standards, which demand absolute accuracy in the presentation of evidence. One of the most striking contrasts is the reluctance of the ancient historians to quote documents. Tacitus might rely heavily on the archives of the Roman Senate, but he never mentions his documentary sources. An inscription discovered at Lyons. France, preserves a speech delivered by the emperor Claudius to the Senate in Ad 48, and it is clear that Tacitus utilized another version of the same text. His skill in using it is matched by the freedom with which he adapts it so suit his purpose.

The greatest and the most original achievement of the best Greek historians lay in their clear grasp of the need to distinguish truth from fiction and their conscious preoccupation with the methods of achieving this. This is admirably conveyed in a famous passage of Thucydides. And with reference to the narrative one events, far from permitting myself to derive it from the first source that came to hand. I did not even trust my own impressions, but it rests partly on what I saw myself, partly on what other saw for me, the accuracy of the report being always tried by the most severe and detailed rests possible. My conclusions have cost me some labour from the want of coincidence between accounts of the same occurrences by different eye-witnesses, arising sometimes from deficient memory, sometimes from deficient impartiality.

His practice did not fully live up to third ideal, however. The greatest of his Greek successors, Polybius, is reasonably impartial, except in his treatment of some of the events in Greece. Among the Romans, the writing of history was chiefly the preserve of members of the senatorial class, who almost invariably has some personal axes to grind. But the correctness of the rules formulated by Thucydides was accepted, in principle, by most ancient historians.

Thucydides had deliberately restricted himself to the history of his own time, and many of the subsequent ancient historians did likewise. They could depend on their own experience of could question well-informed contemporaries. The surviving fragments of Livy relating to his own lifetime (64/59 BC - AD 17) are much more vivid and convincing than the earlier books of his history (surviving today only down to 167 BC). The tendency to prefer contemporary history was strengthened by the practical bent of many of these writers. Several ancient historians were men of action familiar with warfare and politics. Interested in history as a source of instruction for statement, they could write with authority only about wars and political transactions of their own time. Polybius, the exiled Achaean general and a great traveler, derides unpractical, sedentary historians such as Timaeus, who had been writing about the peoples of the western Mediterranean without stirring for 50 years from Athens.

The historians of antiquity were much less skillful in dealing with no contemporary history, for which they relied on older historians. Where none was to be found, they felt lost, as Livy complains in the early portions of his Roman history. The modern recourse to non-narrative sources was alien to the habits of most ancient historians. They were usually incapable of doing this successfully, just as they were ill equipped to discuss critically the sources used by the older writers.

Herodotus chose for his theme the successful resistance of the Greeks against the Persians at the beginning of the 5th century BC. Thucydides wrote about the Peloponnesian War. In which virtually all the Greek states became involved in the last decades of that century. These were limited subjects of obvious importance for which it was possible to find ample evidence. The strength of the ancient historians lay precisely in imposing an interesting pattern on the events of a selected period, usually contemporary or fairly recent, for which they had manageable sources. The best of them could thereby achieve a sense of dramatic unity and produce literary masterpieces. The speeches that Thucydides invented for some of the main protagonists in his story are artistically the most satisfying parts of his work, and at times they even seem to recapture the spirit of what might have been said on these occasions. In a superb writer like Tacitus, whose political career had included long periods of frustration and insecurity. One does not look for impartiality of for scrupulous truthfulness but, rather, for fascinating insight into what the development of Roman imperial power from Augustus to Domitian (the period Ad 14-96) meant to the proud, sophisticated Roman aristocracy for whom he was writing.

The study of "antiquities", as opposed to narrative history, did not normally produce works of literary merit, and this is probably the main reason why most of them disappeared. One important group of such writing originated with Aristotle and his collaborators, writing in the third quarter of the 4th century BC. They were interested in both literary "antiquities" and in the systematic study of the constitutions of Greek states. They had described 158 different constitutions, though only their account of Athens now survives. A comparison of its two main parts illustrates the contrast between the deficiencies of ancient historiography and the impressive achievement of the antiquarian researchers. In the introductory, historical section.. Aristotle was baffled by the problem of dealing with the fairly remote past. For each particular period he tried of follow some contemporary sources. The resultant juxtaposition of several writers differing widely in their political outlook produced an account full of contradictions. The second part, however, containing a systematic description of the Athenian constitution, is a masterpiece of shrewd analysis, as are the empirical portions of Aristotle's *Politics* (Books IV -VI), which are based on a wealth of concrete examples derived from the different Greek states.

Aristotle inspired in the 3rd and 2nd centuries BC a great mass of phi logical and antiquarian research. The most important scholars were to be found in the new Hellenistic states, especially at Alexandria in Egypt and at Pergamum in Asia Minor. Among the surviving Hellenistic fragments, there are commentaries on Herodotus and Thucydides. The Hellenistic scholars were interested in many subjects connected with history and did pioneering work in chronology, geography, and topography. They were accustomed to using every kind of source and to quoting documents extensively. Their greatest Roman disciple was Varro, who tried to recover all the vestiges of the old Roman society and to make systematic survey of Roman life based on the evidence provided by language, literature, religion, and ancient customs. Most of his writings have been lost, but the supplied the conjectural (though incorrect) date of 753 BC for the foundation of Rome and knowledge of the probable boundaries between some of the groups whose union produced the city of Rome. Unfortunately, antiquarian researches of such penetrating nature were almost never applied in antiquity to the writing of narrative histories.

Early Christian ear - The triumph of Christianity in the Roman Empire during the 4th century assured the predominance of a type of historiography radically different from the works of the pagan Greek and Roman historians.

Its origins were jewie. The Jews were the only people of antiquity who had the supreme religious duty of remembering the past because their traditional histories commemorated the working out of God's plan for his chosen people. By contrast, no Greek ever heard his gods orderings him to remember. It was the duty of every jew to be familiar with the Jewish sacred writings, which were ultimately gathered into what became the Old Testament. The writers of these biblical books only gave an authoritative version of what everybody was supposed to know, and they were only concerned with the selection of such facts as seemed relevant in interpreting God's purpose. In addition, the Jews also cherished unwritten traditions. To quote Josephus, a Jewish historian of the 1st century AD. "What had not been written down, was yet entrusted to the collective memory of the people of Israel and especially of its priests."

The Christians took over the Old Testament and added to it an additional body of sacred history. The writers of the four Gospels included in the New Testament were bearing witness to assured truths that the faithful ought to know, and no convincing reconstruction of historical facts is possible from these books of the New Testament. The only avowedly historical book in it is the Acts of the Apostles. The New Testament as a whole represents merely a selection from the early Christian writings. It includes only what conformed to the doctrine of the church when, later on, that doctrine became fixed in one from. Between the Acts of the Apostles, dating probably from the late 1st century, and the writings of Eusebius of Caewsarea (died c. 340) and his contemporaries in the first quarter of the 4th century, there is a almost complete gap in Christian historiography.

For the Christian writers the story of Jesus, as recorded in the Gospels, represented the fulfilment of the prophecies that could be found in various part of the Old Testament. The Jewish part of the Bible also assured for Christianity the authority of a long antiquity. The history contained in the two parts of the Bible, now indissolubly linked together, became the only authentic record of God's revelation for mankind, dwarfing into insignificance all the records of other peoples and religious groups. The concept of a universal history had been wholly unknown to the pagan world, but the Christians were the first to apply it effectively. Christian history had to be a universal history, though of a very peculiar sort, where only one sequence of privileged events, Hewish and Christian, deserved detailed record. The Christian claims must have seemed more extravagant to the pagans than even the Jewish ones. Thus Eusebius stated that the Christians were, in fact, born with the world, anticipating St. Augustine's vision of the city of God existing since the beginning of time.

In defending their religion against hostile critics, the early Christians were forced to fit some pagan history in their universal scheme. This was achieved by means of universal chronologies from the creation of the world to each writer's own time. The events of Jewish and Christian history were thus synchronized with the main dates of the pagan myth and history. Sextons Julius Africans, who wrote in the early 3rd century, is the first Christian writer known to have attempted this feat. He allotted 6,000 years to the whole span of human history and placed the birth of Christ in the year 5500 from the creation of the world. This work provided the model for the more elaborate *Chronographic (Chronicle)* of Eusebius. It became the foundation for a long succession of Greek choreographies produced by Byzantine writers. A Latin adaptation by St. Jerome (died 419/420) was immensely influential in western Europe for more than 1,000 years. A modern scholar is filled with mingled admiration and despair at the ingenuity of Eusebius and of his more eminent successors and at the absurdity of many of their conclusions. But they did originate and impose on the world a unified scheme of universal chronology. The dating from the birth of Christ was introduced by Dionysius Exiguous, who wrote at Rome in the early 6th century, and it was successfully popularized in the 8th century by the English historian Bade.

The writing of history of their own time was not an essential task for the Christians of the 4th and 5th centuries, when they did so, they wrote mainly in defence of their religion against the pagan world or against rival Christian groups branded as heretical. All these histories belong to religious apologetic. They suffer from inevitable distortions in the choice of what should be mentioned and what must be suppressed, and they are often excessively unfair to outsiders and opponents. These faults were not uncommon among the classical historians, though the Christians were somewhat unusual in their extreme conviction that they alone must be right. A comparison between the Christian historians and an outstanding pagan write, such as Ammianus Marceline's (second half of the 4th century), who was very ready to admire those Christians who merited it, brings out the intolerance and narrowness of outlook of his Christian contemporaries.

Eusebius was the earliest and the most important of the Christian historians of the 4th century. He is quite frank about the practical and apologetic aims of his *Historia ecclestastica* (written 312-324; *Ecclestastical History)* designed to show how, through a long series of acts of Divine Providence, a Christian empire was finally brought into existence by Constantine. He admits that "we shall introduce into this history in general only those events which may be useful first to ourselves and afterward, to posterity." This work, like his other historical writings, is a mixture of devout fiction and invaluable detail. But there is plenty of the latter if *Ecclesiastical History*, Contrary to the usual practice of the ancient historians. Eusebius tries to specify his sources and the quotes from them extensively in order to document as fully as possible the developments that resulted in the triumph of Christianity. He provided in this respect a valuable model for his medieval successors. The most astonishing thing about Eusebius was his capacity of handled his sources critically, in matters where is seemed permissible to do so. In one passage of his *Chronicle* he sets aside the authority of St. Paul in favour of a piece of evidence contained in the Book of Judges. In later patristic literature nothing similar is found.

Biography, as it was Christian purposes. St, Jerome modelled himself on Suetonius in compiling the lives of 135

Christian writers (written in 392) as a way of demonstrating the high level of culture attained by his coreligionists. The ancient biographers had freely mingled fact with fiction for the edification of their readers and could be readily imitated by the writers of the lives of Christian Saints. The life of St. Anthony of Egypt by St. Athanasius (mid 4th century) set the pattern for this most popular type of medieval literature.

St. Augustine, the greatest of the Latin Church Fathers of the 4th and 5th centuries, was certainly not concerned with writing of history in any ordinars, sense of the term. In his *De civitate det (City of Gudy)* he might invoke historical evidence to demonstrate the utter degradation of all the non-Christian societies, and he encouraged his pupil Orosius to develop this theme more fully in the latter's *History Auainst the Pagans,* to 417), Nearly 200 manuscripts of Orosius have survived, testifying to the immense popularity of his work in the Middle Ages. Augustine's greatest influence on historiography lay in his main message. His vision of the divine and the fearthly cities confronting each other dominated the outlook of all the medieval Christian thinkers and profoundly affected their treatment of history. Within that divine plan for the world, purely secular history seemed an insignificant thing.

Early China. The preservation of some records of historical events can be traced in China to at least the early part of the its millenumum BC. Confucius 9551+479 BC) was credited, rightly or wrongly, in the later Chinese tradition with editing the annals of his native state of Lu. But the appearance of the first works fully deserving the name of histories resulted from the unification of China under a single ruler in 221 BC. The first such work to survive, the *Shih Chi* (Historical Records), dates from C. 85 BC. Its author. Ssu-ma Chíen, is quite justifiably called the father of Chinese historiography. His history exhibits many of the main features of the later Chinese official histories as they continued to be written down to the deposition of the its Chinese imperial dynasty in 1911. Within this fairly united tradition. China produced a mass of historical writings unequalled by any other country before modern times Until the late 19th century, Japanese historiography formed an offshoot of this tradition.

Chinese scholars showed an interest in the history of China from the earliest times. According to the Chinese conception, history makes sense only if it can furnish practical directives for action of supply correct information upon which action can wisely be based. All the schools of Chinese thought quoted the lessons of history. Confucius, with his stress on the moral content of these lessons, formed part of this universal belief in the value of history. One of the duties inculcated by him was the scrupulous transmission of authentic records. When, some centuries after his death, the unified imperial state began to recruit its bureaucracy among the Confucian scholars, the recording of all the necessary information and the careful preservation of records became one of the main functions of the Chinese government, both centrally and locally. A long series of official histories and of records connected with them has survived form the time of the T'ang dynasty (618-907) onward. From then on, the great bulk of Chinese history was written by bureaucrats for bureaucrats. For a practical point of view this immense body of historical writings fulfilled a very useful purpose. Such histories were bound to be highly stereotyped and restricted in content to what interested the higher officialdom. It is easy to condemn it by modern Western standards for its excessive preoccupation with concrete detail and inability to produce work of wider synthesis. But this Chinese tradition did gradually evolve in the direction of greater rationality and subtlety. Its scope widened as the sphere of government expanded. Furthermore, within this tradition there appeared from time to time writers of gennius, man of bold critical spirit, genuine historical insight, and overriding integrity. One of eh greatest was Liu Chih-chi (661-721), the writer of the *Shih I'ung*, the first thorough treatise in Chinese, or any other language, on historical method, which also constituted in effect a history of Chinese historiography. He had a successor in Ssu-ma kuang (1019-86), the author of the first fairly comprehensive general history of China (covering the years

403 BC -AD 959). In the 17th century a remarkable group of historical scholars virtually founded a school of critical Chinese philology. Note of these writers succeeded in radically transforming Chinese historiography, but they created an increasingly sophisticated and critical tradition. Their successors in the 20th century assimilated some valuable features of modem Western historiography.

Medieval Historiogrpahy

Europe from the 5th the 11th century. The period stretching from the 5th to the 11th century was a time of very profound cultural decline in regions that had once constituted the western half of the Roman Empire. Almost all the inhabitants of these provinces again became illiterate. There are long periods for which there are virtually no narrative sources, and the bulk of surviving historical writings consists merely of meagre factual annals. Virtually all the writers were ecclesiastics, in marked contrast to the Byzanune lands, where a strong tradition of lay historiography persisted throughout the Middle Ages. The annalists and chronicters of the West were predominantly monks, and their lack of experience of the secular world outside their cloisters made them into blinkered and unpractical historians. This was true even of Bede, an Anglo-Saxon monk, who was by far the greatest historian of the early Middle Ages.

All the historians of this period were seriously affected by the cultural decline around them, They were having to write in part for a more uncultured audience. Suspicious Severs, probably the best Western historian of the early 5th century, still intended his *Chronica* (to 403) for educated Roman Christians, but his life of St. Martin of Tours is a piece of medieval hagiography. This model could inspire lives full of folkiore and miracle, form which the real human personalities of the saints were almost wholly absent. The same duality of purpose is a notable feature of Bede's voluminous writings. He explicitly recognized that he must adapt himself of his audience when he explained that he was writing in a simple Latin style so that he might be more easily understood by his Anglo-Saxon readers. There is a marked contrast of tone between his theological and his historical writings. As a theologian. Bede follows Eusebius and the earlier Church Fathers in not exaggerating the frequency of miracles and in believing that they were most common in the earliest day of Christianity. But Bede's live of the English saints and his *Historia ecclesiastica gents Anglorum (Exdesiastical History of the English Peoples.* Covering chietly the years 597-731, are full of miracles and visions. There is one or other on almost every page. It is possible that some of these incidents were included by Bede because he thought that his readers expected mentions of these familiar traditions stories.

In preparing his historical works, Bede not only took great care to assemble the widest possible collection of sources but also tells the reader what he is using. In dedicating his *Ecclestastical History* to King Ceolwulf of Northumbria, he requests that in order to remove all occasions of doubt about those things. I have written, either in your mind or in the minds of any others who listen to or read this history. I will make it my business to state Bentley from what sources I have gained my information.

An impressive list follows, including mentions of documents copied for him by friends at Rome. Canterbury, and other places. Like Eusebius, on whom Bede modelled himself, he quotes some of the documents integrally. Bede's methods of securing and recording information are so similar to the practices of modern historians and the judicious tone of his writing is so impressive that the reader is almost taken in into treating him as if he were a modern scholar. But Bede's *Ecclesiatical History* was written as a work of edification in order to strengthen the faith of his readers in Divine providence, through which, as he saw it, his Anglo-Saxon countrymen had been converted to Christianity. All matters not connected with his main theme are ignored. Bede's handling of evidence on subjects that her regarded as embarrassing inspires mistrust. But these are small matters in comparison with the enormous mass of information that he alone has preserved and the encouragement that Bede continued to give for many centuries to the writing of history.

The influence of Bede and other Anglo-Saxon scholars was greatly felt during the later 8th and the 9th centuries in the Frankish kingdom, where under Charlemagne and his successor. Louis the Pious,. there was a modest trivial of historical writing. Beside the annals kept at various monasteries, which tended to convey information in a manner that suited the Frankish rulers, there were a few more ambitious ventures. The important *Historia Langobardorum (History of the Lombards)*, written c. 774-785 by Paulus Diaconus, or Paul the Deacon, was the work of one of the best educated men of the time. Nithard, a grandson of Charlemagne, left an invaluable narrative of the disintegration of the Carolingian state during his lifetime. The work that exerted the greatest influence on the medieval writers of biographies was einhard's *Vita Karoli Magni* (written c. 830-833 : *Life of Charlemagney.* The author was a leading official and a close companion of Charles, and his work was naturally intended as a eulogy of the great king. Einhard says that Chariemagne retreated safely from Spain, returning with his army safe and sound, except that on a ridge of the Pyreneses, on the way home, his happened to experience some small effects of Gascon perfidyt. Nobody would gather from this that the Franks had narrowly escaped a major disaster. Einhard was merely echoing the story told in the semiofficial contemporary annals. Another source of distortion was Einhard's use of a classical model, the *Live of the Caesare* by Suetonius. The subject headings under which he described Charies and even the very words used were partly borrowed from the lives of Roman emperors, but his Charlemagne is probably in essentials an authentic and credible portrait.

If bulk alone is to be taken as a centurian, annals were the main product of medieval historiography. The annalist merely sets down the most important events of the current year. In the case of the earliest medieval annals, the events were often noted down in Easter tables, in the blank spaces between the dates calculated for the forthcoming Easters. Such paschal annals would be extremely brief. When, as often happened, annals came to be written down in separate manuscripts, distinct from the Easter tables, there was room of the expansion of individual entries. In either case, the resultant annals cannot be regarded as history since the vents are necessarily recorded in isolation. But they preserve in a right order the essential facts, which could be rearranged into a continuous narrative. Such as of its various annalistic sources, should properly be termed a chronicle.

Medieval historians show little awareness of the process of historical hanger. They were unable to imagine that any earlier change. They were unable to imagine that any earlier age was substantially different from their own. The unawareness of the meaning of anachronism helps to explain the strange wanderings of medieval annals and chronicles. If a religious community wanted a acquire a historical narrative, it copied some work that happened to be most readily accessible. A continuation might then be added at the manuscript's new abode, and later on, this composite version might be copied and further altered by a succession of other writers. Hence there are at least six main versions of the annals known as the *Angio-Saxon Chronicle.* They all derive from the annals kept down to 892 at Winchester, the West Saxon capital. Thereafter, copies were acquired by religious centers in the most diverse parts of England, and one manuscript was being kept up to date at the abbey of Peterborough as late as 1154. An extreme case of wanderings is represented by the snails of the cathedral church of Cracow, the medieval Polish capital. The first section of based on Orosius, the next comprises annals beginning with the death of Bede and containing notices of Frankish and German events, while the Polish section starts with the conversion of Poland to Christianity (965-966) and ends in the 13th century.

Europe from the 12th to the 14th century. Historians are accustomed to regarding the late 11th and 12th centuries as an age of intensified progress in culture and learning; this development, however, did not greatly affect iconography. There was a modest revival of interest in some of the ancient Latin writers, but would-be historians were unsure which ancient models they ought to imitate. A whole series of attempts was made to apply to other race other theme in Virgil's *Aeneid* of a noble group of people guided by the gods towards a splendid destiny. The first essential step was top establish the descent of one's nation from the ancient Trojans and then to trace subsequent history through a series of heroic conquests. The most ambitious of these writing was the *Historia regum Britanniae (History of the Kings of Britain)*, by Geoffrey of Monmouth (died 1155), which attempted to establish off the Celt a historical destiny greater than any other, Although some, even contemporary, readers were not deceived by the work, and William of Newburgh, one of the best English historians of the 12th century, denounced it as a tissue of absurdities, many seriously accepted it is history.

With a few exceptions, the ablest minds of the 12th century were attracted into enterprises that ignored history; they were more concerned with systematization of thought and with philosophical speculations. One of the exceptions was Otto, bishop of Freising, in Bavaria. He was a grandson of the Holy Roman emperor Henry IV. He received the bet education that his age could give, but he was also briefly a Cistercian monk during the most austere period of that order's history. Otto was torn between conflicting impulses to seek the city of God as the only reality and yet to hope for the progress of the German empire. Out of this conflict came his first work. *Chronica (The Two Cines).* A chronicle of world history to 1146, perhaps the most profound medieval attempt at a Christian philosophy of history. As Otto himself confessed, it was composed "in bitterness of spirit ...in the manner of tragedy". The election in 1152 of his nephew and friends Frederick Barbarossa, as emperor, filled Otto with a new elation. The excellence of his second work, *Gesta Friderici I imperatoris (The Deeds of Frederick Barbarossa)*, derives in a considerable measure from a quality rate in medieval historians, a sense of optimistic belief in the value of writing history because it might become a record of human progress. *The Deeds of Frederick Barbarossa* contains a penetrating analysis of the problems encountered by the German rulers in trying to rule the precociously urbanized Italian society.

As in antiquity, the best medieval works were accounts of contemporary history by men who had participated in the events that they were describing. It is, however, very significant that some of the writers that are prized most highly today survive in only very few manuscripts and were presumably no appreciated by most of their contemporaries. One such work was the *Historia pontificalls* ('Pontifical History") covering the period 1148-52, of John of Salisbury, one of the most accomplished scholars of his age, who was writing about the period when he was in the papal service. Another instance of undeserved neglect is furnished by the *Liber de regno Siciliae* ("Book of the Kingdom of Sicily") covering the period 1154-69, written by a anonymous member of the Sicilian court.

Unlike the ancient historians, the medieval writers of contemporary history had no inhibitions about extensively quoting official documents. In England, a succession of writers preserved a large quantity of such texts. Roger of Hoverden was, in the last quarter of the 12th century, treated by the English kings as a king of court historian. He preserved valuable legal and administrative records with which her was familiar through his activities as a royal official and justice. Mathew Pans, the most important English monastic historian of the 13th century, was highly regarded by king Henry III and had excellent sources of information. He left behind a collection of transcripts of royal and ecclesiastical documents that toddy fills a large printed volume. Some writers made their chronicles into an anthology of official records, thinly connected by the authors brief comments. Such is the chronicle of Robert of Avesbuty, consisting mainly of the military dispatches of king Edward III and other interesting documents to 1356. Another vacant of the sand method was for a wholly mediocre chronicle to incorporate exciting pieces of eyewitness narratives by to their writes. A dull English monastic product of the late 14th century, the *Anonumalle chronicle,* includes a narrative of the Peasants's Revolt of 1381, which is one of the most dramatic and interesting eyewitness accounts to be found in medieval historiography.

The most popular histories of the 13th and 14th centuries were encyclopedia compilations giving all the important fact nearly arranged under the dates of popes, emperors, and other rulers. There were even more ambitious ventures aiming at summarizing all the important facts from all the different branches of human actability. The Dominican Order, related at the beginning of the 13th century, was especially concerned with producing such aids for the dissemination of useful knowledge. The best known of these Dominican works is the immense *Speulum historiale* ("Mirror of History"), by Vincent of Beauvais, written under the patronage of king Louis IX of France. It is a compilation made up of excerpts from many authors.

The 13th and 14th centuries were not a period of any fundamental invocations in the techniques and nature of historiography, but there was a growing diversity of types of historical writing. Very detailed, chatty narratives multiplied, often badly organized and inaccurate, but conveying the authentic atmosphere of the times and vividly portraying leading personalities. Such were the St. Albans chronicles of Matthew Paris (to 1259), the reminiscences of Joinville about St. Louis during the Seventh Crusade *1248-54), the Lombard chronicle of Far Salimbene (to 1287), or the vast history of the first part of the Hundred Years' War written in the second half of the 14th century by Froissart. Memories and histories written in vernacular languages, such as those of Joinville and Froissart, came to be quite common. Laymen began to write histories. Some were great men, like Geoffrey de Villehardouin, one of the leaders of the Fourth Crusade (Which captured Constantinople 1202-04), of which he wrote an account. Important urban chronicles began to appear, such as the Florentine chronicle of Giovanni Villam, with its invaluable statistics of Florentine populations and activities around 1338. The extraordinary personality of St,. Francis, who died in 1226, inspired lives of him more convincingly human than any previous medieval biographies of saints.

The Humanist historians of the 15th century tried to make

a deliberate break with the tradition of medieval historiography. By their insistence on a more coherent assuagement of subject matter, by their superior critical outlook., and above all, by their much more accurate awareness of the process of historical change, they had introduced innovations of fundamental importance. In part they owed their grasp of these new possibilities to the influence of Byzantine scholars. In historiography, as in other matters, the new humanistic scholarship was a joint product of Western and Byzantine traditions.

Byzantine Historiography

During the millennium that elapsed between the collapse of the Roman Empire in the West in the 5th century AD and the Italian Renaissance of the 15th century, in no part of Europe did the writers of history consistently maintain as high a standard of achievement as in the Byzantine Empire. Part of the 7th and the 8th centuries from lengthy gaps in the record of Byzantine historiography, but this seems mainly to be the result of subsequent losses of manuscripts. When, in the middle of the 9th century, Photius, future patriarch of Constantinople, compiled a record of some 280 books that he had read, he mentioned works of 33 Greek historians, dating mostly from the late Roman Empire and the Byzantine period, 20 of which are mow lost. But, among the Byzantines of the 7th and 8th centuries, there was certainly no paralleled to the Dark Ages in western Europe.

The Byzantine historians were heirs to the combined traditions of classical Greek writing, of the subsequent Hellenistic historiography, and of the Christian historical writing of the 4th century. Few ancient Latin historians were eve translated into Greek, and their influence on the Byzntine was, therefore, very slight. The older classical Greek historians provided the Byzantines with their cherished models of language and style. Like all educated Byzantines, the historians continued for a millennium to write in a literary language that soon became unintelligible to the vast majority of their compatriot. Hence, from the 6th century onward, there appeared, side by side with the learned historiography, a succession of popular chronicles written in the ordinary language. Most of these popular writing from in their prejudice, ignorance, and crudity- a starting contrast to the work of the more eminent classicizing historians, but they do provide valuable glimpses of the sort of hagiographical history, more religious myth than sober fact, that ordinary Byzantines apparently wanted to read.

Herodotus and Thucydides were frequently invoked by Byzantine historians as models of fine prose. The influence of these two writers on the substance of what was written usually remained slight and superficial, however. The only Byzantine writers who seriously modelled themselves on these two oldest Greek historians wrote during the 15th century. The earlier Byzantine historians owed most to Polybius and to the Greek biographer Plutarch (died c. Ad 119), the two Hellenistic writers who had the greatest influence on Byzantine notions of how history and historical biography should be written.

Like Polybius, the majority of Byzantine historians, including most of the best ones, preferred to write about their own times, and within these limits they produced some real masterpieces. Unlike the majority of the ancient historians, Polybius and included much autobiographical detail, and his influence reinforced the readiness of the Byzantine historians to talk about themselves, thus providing abundant information about several of these authors. Their histories are likely to be one-sided and full of details about what interested them, while remaining silent about a great mass of other contemporary happenings. They are frequently gossipy and patently prejudiced, inspiring much less confidence than the austere, impartial writings of authors such as Thucydides. This in one of the main reasons why the Byzantine historians have often been excessively underestimated by modern redraws. The bulk of the Bytzantine contemporary histories were written by statement, high officials, and prelates-men with access to important information. They have to be used critically and cautiously but can be immensely valuable.

Priscus of Panium (c. 450), a member of a Byzantine embassy to Attila's camp, is the best source of information about that terrible king of the Huns and his followers. A century later, the reconquest of Vandal Africa and of Ostrogothic Italy by the emperor Justinian was the main theme of the *History of the Wars of* Procopius, a leading civilian adviser of Belisarius, the Byzantine commander. Subsequently, Proceopius also wrote a *History arcana (Secrel History)*, containing a horrible indicentment of the activities of Justinian and Belisarius. Many of his details about the corruption at court and the oppressive nature of the government may be substantially correct. In the 11th century Michael Psellus, who wrote a history of his own times, was a leading Byzantine scholar and official, for a time even the chief adviser of emperors. His *Chronographia* is concerned almost entirely with the happenings at the Byzantine court and is one of the most gossipy and amusing narratives ever written on such a subject. His psychological insight and his lively and subtle style delighted the educated Byzantines. Anna Comnena, the daughter and biographer of the emperor alexius I, greatly admired Psellus. Her own *Alextad* is a much less fascinating work. But the recovery of the Byzaantine power under her father provided her with an important theme.

The last, increasingly disastrous, centuries of Byzantine history are recorded by a series of scholarly and interesting historians. Niceties Choniates, a high imperial official, provides a surprisingly balanced eyewitness account of the siege and capture of Constantinople by the forces of the Fourth Crusade (1202-04). George Acropolises, a leading adviser of the Greek emperors of Nicaea, carries the story from 1203 to the recapture of Constantinople by the Byzantines in 1261. The later 13th and 14th centuries are covered by a succession of writers deeply immersed in contemporary theological disputations. Perhaps the most readable of all Btzantine histories is the largely autobiographical work of the leading politician and emperor

John VI (reigned 1347 to 1354), written after his deposition during his years of enforced retirement in a monastery. George Sphrantzes, a close friend of the last emperor, Constantine XI , included in his history an eyewitness account of the siege and capture of Constantinople by Mehmed II in 1453. Two of Sphrantzes' contemporaries chose to write primarily about the Turkes. Their methods place them among Renaissance historians. Laonicos Chalcocondyles wrote (in about 1464) an account of the rise of the Turkish state. He did so in the manner of Herodotus, with long digressions on various neighbouring nations. A little later, Critobulos of Imbros, in his account of the Turkish conquest of Constantinople, made Mehmed II his chief hero and modelled his history on Thucydides.

The study of what might be called "historical antiquities" was not much cultivated by Byzantine scholars. The most notable exception was the emperor Constantine VII, but only some fragments of his voluminous collections have survived (dating from about 940 to 959). They include a very interesting account of the various peoples with whom the Byzantines had to deal. Such ancient Greek literature as still survives, including that of all the historians, was preserved by the Byzantine scholars. When, aground the year 1400, the teaching of Greek was introduced into Italian universities by Bytzantine scholars, they brought also their superior techniques of literary scholarship, transformation thereby the study of Latin authors as well as introducing into western Europe the treasures of Greek literature. One result was the emergence of the new Renaissance historiography.

Muslim Historiography

Muslim historiography appears to have originally developed independently of European influences. Until the 19th century Muslim writers only very seldom consulted Christian sources and almost never noted events in Christian countries. Fortunately, they displayed at times more curiosity about the non-Muslim peoples in the first half of the 13th century was the work of a Persian, Javelin. On a visit to Mongolia in 1252-

53, he was able to consult the recently compiled, earliest Mongol narrative *(Secret History of the Mongols.)*

The origins of Arabic historiography still remain obscure because of the gap between the legendary traditions of pre-Islamic Arabia before the start of the Muslim era (AD 622) and the sophisticated and fairly exact chronicles that began to appear in the later 8th and 9th centuries. But while the detailed stages of this development still await reconstruction, the main influences shaping the early Muslim historiography are clear enough. As in the caws of the ancient Jews, it was created and perpetuated by religion. Muhammad (died 632) regarded himself as a successor to a long series of Jewish and Christian prophets, and he made Islam a religion with a strong sense of history. The Qurán, Islam's holy book, is full of warnings derived from the lessons of history.

Teachings of Muhammad not included in the Qurán came to be regarded after his death as authoritative tradition left behind by him. All his sayings and actions were therefore carefully treasured and ultimately came to from., in combination with the Qurán, the foundation fit the body of Muslim laws (Shariáh), common to all Islamic communities. These traditions (Hadith_) were transmitted orally for several generations, until they were written down in the 8th and 9th centuries. The resultant collections were only partly historical, as myths and inventions crept into them the scholars who were engaged in preserving and verifying these traditions were chiefly preoccupied with organizing them into legal and theological systems, and they were frequently hostile to the historians. The earliest authoritative life of Muhammad, written by Ibn Sihaq (died 768), was attacked by a leading exponent of the legal "traditionalist" learning. This confirms the independence of the historical scholars from the theological and legal interests. But both groups shared some common materials, and the strict rules evolved by the legal "traditions" for recording their sources and tracing a continuous chain of authoritative transmitters of the traditions encouraged similar exact habits in the Muslim historians. The resultant histories were often pedantic, full of unrelated facts, and deficient in reflective comment, though there are some astonishing exceptions, such as the writings of Ibn Khaldun (1332-1406). But the better Muslim historians scrupulously quoted their authorities and tried to be truthful. This was particularly true of the "classical" school of historians, who were writing at the centre of the "Abbasid caliphate in Iraq in the 9th and 10th centuries. At- Tabari (died 923), the most authoritative of them all, wrote his "History of Prophets and Kings" as a supplement to his earlier commentary on the Qurán, and subsequent Muslim historians were content to follow his reconstruction of the early Islamic history. The Syrian and Iraqi historiography of the 12th and early 13th centuries is at lest as valuable as the Western historical writing of this period, and sometimes it is clearly better.

To orthodox Muslims, the development of the Islamic community represented a continuous manifestation of God's purpose. Consequently, the recording of the religious progress of the Islamic society continued to be sacred duty. One of the original features of Muslim historiography is the large amount of attention devoted to the lives of devout men and of scholars. To many Muslim historians these spiritual and intellectual activities were of much greater importance than the doings of princes and warriors. One of the peculiarities of Muslim historiography was the liking for encyclopedic dictionaries of famous men. The earliest of these were devoted to the Companions of Muhammad and to the early transmitters of the Muslim traditions. For a thousand years extremely diverse types of biographical collections have continued to appear in the Muslim world. Those devoted to religious scholars attained a particularly wide diffusion. Saladin (Salah ad- Din), who took Jerusalem from the crusaders in 1187 and later opposed the Third Crusade, offered to the Muslim writers the particularly congenial subject of a ruler dominated by a sense of religious duty. A particularly fine example of medieval Muslim historiography is the biography of satadin by Baha ad-Dn (died 1234), which gives an exceptional insight into Saladin's motives for many of his critical decisions.

But the greatest Arab historian and one of the most penetrating thinkers about historiography in any time or place was undoubtedly Ibn khaldun. The introduction (*al-Muqaddimah)* to his *Kitab al-'ibar,* a universal history (begun in 1375), is in A. J. Toynbee's judgment (1934), "the greatest work of its kind that has ever yet been created by any mind." Ibn Khaldun had absorbed all the learning accessible to a Muslim of his time. He was a master of religious learning, an outstanding judge, a writer on logic. He turned a subtle and most disciplined mind to historiography in order to explain his personal tragedy. He had served a succession of rulers in Islamic Spain and the Maghnb (Northwest Africa) as a general, a politician, and even once as a chief minister, and his activities had always ended in disaster. In order to explain what had gone wrong, he sought to achieve a correct understanding of the forces that governed the societies known to him. He concluded that political stability had become impossible in his native Maghrib, because over centuries economic prosperity had declined excessively and the forces of lawlessness had become too strong.

As a detailed chronicler of events Ibn Khaldun is not always exact, but, like contemporary historians, he knew how to reconstruct correctly the main trends over several centuries. His ability to formulate general laws that govern the fate of societies and to establish rules for the criticism of sources provided him with an intelligent framework for the correct reconstruction of past history.

Ibn Khaldun's *Muqaddimah* has survived in at least a score of manuscripts, but he had no effective influence on Muslim historiography until recently; after his time, as before, the writing of history continued to be a normal feature of Muslim civilization in the more advanced Islamic societies. In several countries, notably in parts of India, the first works that deserve the name of history appeared only after the Muslim conquest or the conversion to Islam. After the 12th century Arabic ceased to be the man language of Muslim historiography. Distinguished histories were written in Persian in the 13th century, and subsequently Turkish and other vernaculars came to be used by historians in different parts of the Islamic world. But, in its isolation from non-Muslim influences and its traditional interests, Islamic historiography underwent no intrinsic hang until the 19th century, when it began to be affected by the impact of modern Western civilization.

Historiogrpahy in the European Renaissance

If there is one thing that united the men of the Renaissance, it was the notion of belonging to a new time Lorenzo valla, one of the ablest of the early Humanists, in a preliminary draft of his history of King Ferdinand I of aragon (written in 1445-46), proudly enumerates the modern technical inventions made in recent centuries, and especially near his own day. The sense of the novelty and excellence of their achievements was particularly felt by the men of the Renaissance in connection with their attempts to imitate the works of the ancient Greek and Roman writers and artists. They were not year claiming that an era of unlimited progress was dawning for mankind such concepts belong to the 18th century- but the belief in the progressiveness of their own age soon spurred the best Renaissance scholars and artists into achievements that, in some important respects, surpassed their ancient models. This happened in historiography as a systematic discipline did not emerge during the Renaissance and, in fact, this development did not occur until the 19th century. The reasons for this delay from one of the main problems in any study of historiography between the years 1400 and 1800.

In the early Renaissance one by-product of the newly won sense of modernity was the tendency to regard the millennium between the collapse of the Roman Empire in the west and the 15th century as an era of prolonged decline. The concept of the middle Ages was thus introduced for this intervening period. Two very important histories written in the first half of the 15th century deliberately concentrate on the medieval century. Their authors were leading Italian Humanists. The first to appear was the *Historiae Florentint*

Populi ("History of Florence") of Leonardo Bruni, the city's chancellor from 1427 to 1444. The second, the *Historiarum ab inclinatione Romanorum imperti decades* ("Decades" mainly devoted to Italy), was written by Flavio Biondo, an important papal official. It covered the period from the sack of Rome by Alance in AD 410 to the writer's own time. The "invention" of the Middle Ages as a separate historical period remains one of the most enduring legacies of Renaissance historiography.

Unlike the medieval historians, the Renaissance Humanists became much more acutely aware of the process of historical change. This was a gradual development. They were trying to understand the ancient writers, whom they were seeking to emulate, and they became increasingly aware of the need to replace these writers in their correct historical setting. When Patriarch (1304-74), the pioneer Italian Humanist, unearthed in 1345 a collection of Cicero's letters, he was shocked to discover that Cicero was not a cloistered scholar of the medieval tradition but a busy politician who wrote his dialogues in moments of banishment from active life. In 1361, in a letter to the Holy Roman emperor Charles IV. Patriarch was able to use his increased familiarity with classical documents to use his increased familiarity with classical documents to expose a medieval forgery of the Austrian archduke masquerading as a charter of Julius Caesar.

Between about 1440 and his death in 1457. Valla was one of the most influential Humanists, His *Elegantiae lingude latinae (1444 : "Elegancies of the Latin Language")* was a treasury of information about correct Latin usages.; For Valla the meaning of words was not natural but conventional and historical, because it was derived from changing custom. Thus a sense of ceaseless historical evolution was planted at the very centre of Humanist preoccupations with the recovery, the correction, and the interpretation of ancient texts.

In 1440 Valla's patron, King Alfonso of Naples, at war with the papacy, asked Valla to write a treatise against Pope Eugenius IV. Valla obliged by decisively disproving, on both linguistic and historical grounds, the genuineness of the "Donation of

Constantine". From the middle of the 8th century, when this document was probably concocted, it had been used by the popes as one of the weightiest justifications for their claims to secular authority in Italy. Its authenticity had been sometimes questioned in the past by some of the acutest minds, such as Bishop Otto of Freising in the 12th century and Marsilius of Padua in the first half of the 14th century, but it required Valla's expert techniques to dispose of the "Donation" forever. The validity of Valla's methods of historical enticism was at once recognized by at least one other leading Humanist. Biondo wrote the relevant portions of his "Decades" of papal and Italian history between 1440 and 1443; while remaining in the service of the very same Eugenius IV who had been the chief object of Valla's attack. Yet Biondo tacitly accepted Valla's conclusion, and he never mentions the "Donation of Constantine". Bondo's critical outlook found still an other expression in his summary dismissal of the fabulous history of Geoffrey of Monmouth. In his copy of Geofrey he entered only a single note: "I have never come across anything so stuffed with lies and frivolities."

Valla's work on the texts of the New Testament proved in the long run to be one of the most influential applications of the new science of historical philology. His aim was to recover, so far as possible, the original Greek version through the use of the oldest extant manuscripts. He defended these researches by pointing out that he was not correcting the Holy Scriptures but merely the Latin Vulgate translation of St. Jerome that had been adopted by the catholic Church. The revolutionary nature of Valla's historical approach comes out most strikingly in his comment that "none of the words of Christ have come to us, for Christ spoke in Hebrew and never wrote down anything". The corrections assembled by Valla became generally known when, in 1505. Erasmus published them as *Annotationes* on the New Testament. They provided a model for Erasmus' edition of a Greek New Testament in 1516, form which stem all the new Protestant versions of the 16th century.

The new historical philology was also soon applied to the

study of philosophical and legal texts. In this, the most striking progress was made in the second half of the 15th century by Politian, who lectured at Florence, and by his friend Ermolao Barbaro, who taught at Padua. They were inaugurating the history of ideas and of intellectual movements. In his studies of Aristotelian texts. Barbaro insisted on using only the commentators of antiquity. In his lectures and writings (1489-94), Politian tried to re-establish from internal evidence the correct sequence of Aristotelian treatises, and he traced the gradual liberation of Aristotle's thought from the influence of Plato. The meaning of the terms used by Aristotle was rigorously investigated in the light of the linguistic usage of his Greek contemporaries. Politian's ventures into the field of legal texts proved particularly influential. He had as his disposal a very good 6th-century version of the Digest- that is, the section of Justinian's Corpus Juris Civilis (Body of Civil Law) based on the rulings of the Roman jurists. Politian's collation of it with the first printed edition of the Digest (in 1490) formed part of an inquiry into the transmission of the texts of the Roman law during the Middle Ages. Politian's researches stimulated a remarkable school of Humanist jurists, mostly Frenchmen, headed by Guillaume Bude, who published the first historical commentary on the Digest in 1508. In the course of the 16th century, these scholars land the foundations of a new branch of scholarship, the history of laws and institutions.

The methods of textual criticism used by Politian and his friends were designed to produce definitive editions of classical texts. Politian was aware of the need to establish the correct descent of manuscripts and to disentangle the best textual tradition. In all this he was for ahead of almost all his contemporaries, and he was anticipating the procedures that were systematically adopted for the first time by Karl Lachmann and other German scholars in the 19th century. The historical phiology of Politian was a program for the future rather than a dawn of a new era in the editing of classical texts. In contrast to his methods, most of the other Humanist editions of the Latin and Greek classics are very unsatisfactory. This is particularly true of the editions produced between about 1400 and 1550. The reckless emendations of Humanist editors, coupled with the subsequent disappearance of some of the manuscripts used by them, created grave problems for later scholars. Ever since the 17th century the task of the more modern editors has consisted largely in reconstructing, so far as possible, the manuscript versions available before 1400.

Modern historiography was created in the 19th century through a successful combination of the use of narrative sources with every other type of evidence. Some 15th century Italian Humanists were already aware of these possibilities. The idea of recovering an entire civilization through a systematic collection of all the relics of the past was not alien to them. Biondo used mainly conventional narrative sources for his "Decades" of Italian history, but his description of the city of Rome in antiquity (*Roma instaurata, 1444-46)* was based on a novel combination of the narratives of other historians with a wide range of miscellaneous sources. These included topographical guides, public and private documents, studies of surviving buildings, inscriptions, and coins. But in practice most histories and biographies continued to be written in a conventional way, while the revived study of "antiquities" was cultivated in separation from narrative historiography.

Imitation of ancient models is the feature most often stressed in the modern descriptions of Humanist histories. This meant that style mattered at least as much as content and that historical truth might be obscured by literary conventions. On the more positive side, there was the renewed insistence on the choice of definite, clearly delimited subjects and on a more coherent arrangement of material. The abler Humanist historians, however, were also making innovations that bring their practice a little nearer to present notions of writing history.

Several Humanist historians were particularly attracted to the study of the origins of the state about which they were writing. In the 15th century Bruni did this for Florence, and

Biondo and Bernardo Giustiniani for Venice, to mention some notable examples. In the 16th and early 17th centuries. French and English scholars inaugurated a critical study of the origins of their national institutions. Humanist historians prided themselves on their critical ability to overthrow the legends in which various countries has concealed their ignorance of their own origins. The incentives to revise the earliest history were often political. Bruni deemed in essential to prove that Florence had not been founded under the tyranny of the Roman emperors but in the time of the free republic. He happened to be right. The Humanist historians were more confident than their ancient predecessors that they could write competent histories of a remote past. In practice they were much less successful in this than they imagined. In dealing with periods before their own time, they usually followed only a restricted number of earlier narratives, though the best of them, such as Bruni and Biondo, displayed in their histories of medieval Italy a novel ingenuity in combining well-chosen sources. Biondo, for example, made effective use of Dante's correspondence.

There was also some modest progress through the better use of documentary sources. This is often far from obvious, because Humanist historians, like their ancient predecessors, do not usually refer to their sources, even when they quote texts verbatim. Hence came Leopold von Ranke's ùtter misjudgment of the historical value of the *Storta d'Italia* ("History of Italy") of Francesco Guicciardini. Before Ranke's time it was universally accepted as the most authoritative contemporary history of Italy in the years 1949 to 1534 Ranke, who became one of the pioneers of "scientific" history in Germany, first established his reputation in 1824 by his attack on the reliability of Guicciardini. Ranke argued that the statements of that great Florentine statesman were contradicted by documentary evidence and that his history must have been based on unreliable secondary authorities. The discovery in the 20th century of Guicciardini's private archive proved that his history was scrupulously based on original documents of the highest value.

Guicciardini, in a work that forms the nearest Renaissance parallel to the history of Thucydides, tries to comprehend the succession of tragedies that befell Italy from the start of the French invasions in 1494. This desire to recapture the rational causes of events in one of the most mature features of the best Renaissance historiography.

Early Modern Historiogrpahy

Italian Humanist historians provided models that could be imitated easily in other countries. Almost everywhere in western and central Europe, local writers were encouraged to produce descriptions and histories of their own lands, intent with patriotic pride. In such countries as Spain and Poland, which had only recently achieved their unity, this was way of commemorating their newly won cohesion. In the 15th century it was the object of a pioneer work on the earliest antiquities of Spain, the *Paralipomena Hispaniae,* by the Catalan Humanist bishop Joan Margarit I Pau, and of the invaluable *Annales seucronicaw incliti regni Poloniae* ("History of Poland"), by Jan Dlugosz, which included an exceptionally precise geographic description of his country. In Germany a sense of national identity could be vindicated by Humanist historians striving to minimize the importance of the continued political division of their land. The *Germania* of Tacitus was printed in Germany as early as 1473 and started the fashion of using this collective name of that country. Gacitus called the Germans "the indigenous inhabitants". This was used by a leading patriotic Humanist, Conradus Celtis, as a proof that Germany should be free from all foreign domination. Celtis and his other Humanist contemporaries deliberately hunted for manuscripts of medieval German writers to prove that their country, despite its disunity, could have a national history. Some important masterpieces were recovered including the histories of Otto of Freising, Celtis' pet project of a description of Germany modelled in Biondo's *Italia illustrate* was carried out in 1530 by Sebastian Munster, and Munster's fuller *Cosmographia* (1544, "Cosmogrpahy"), though purporting to describe the known world, devoted one-half of its 818 pages to "the German nation". There was also a spate of histories of Germany, mostly very laborious and unreflective but incorporating the newly rediscovered medieval narratives and even some documentary sources. Greater originality came only in the wake of the Reformation. The same thing happened in France and in England. In both countries patriotic preoccupations were a leading feature of works written by humanist historians, and the appearance of Protestantism reinforced in a peculiar way the existing nationalist tendencies.

The influence of the Reformation on historiography must first be discussed at a more universal level. As the philosopher Francis Bacon shrewdly observed. Martin Luther had been obliged "to awake all antiquity and to call former times to his succours ....so that the ancient authors ...which had a long time slept in libraries, began generally to be read." This was not because Luther would have regarded himself as a historian. But as early as 1519. In his disputation with Johann Eck. He encountered the assertion that the primacy of the pope was of divine origin. In order to disprove this and to demonstrate that they alone represented the true church, the Protestants had to preface to the *Vitae Romanorum Ponificum* ("Lives of the Pontiffs"), published by Robert Barnes in 1535. Luther himself confessed that, although he himself had not originally attacked the papacy with historical arguments.

Now it is a wonderful delight to me to find that others are doing the same thing .. from history- and it gives me the greatest joy ...to see .. that history and Scripture entirely coincide in this respect.

The starting point for the Protestant rewriting of Christian history could best be found in St. Augustine's teachings. The true church, the city of God, had always existed, even though at times it seemed to be overshadowed by the enemies of the divine order. Those enemies were not only the pagans and the heretics, as St. Augustine had believed. In more recent times they had included also the upholders of the papal authority and the persecutors of such medieval true Christians as John Wycliffe (died 1384) and

John Hus (died 14150. The writings of Eusebius provided the model for chronicling the sufferings of the faithful until the dawn of freedom for the true church in the 16th century. These views about the correct history of Christianity were presented with exceptional cogency in John Calvin's *Christianiae religionls institutio* (fullest edition 1559; *Institutes of the Christian Religion*) and were shared by most Protestant scholars. The only obvious disagreements arose when Protestants tried to pinpoint the moment at which the church took the fatal turn away from God's true purpose. While the radical sectarians considered that the papacy had always been corrupt, less extremist Protestants were prepared to accept the earlier popes and to argue that the rot set in at some date between the time of Eusebius (died c. 340) and the 7th century. The choice of precise date might depend on the national traditions of each country. Thus, Bishop Richard Davies, in his preface to the New Testament in Welsh (1567), treats Pope Gregory the Great (died 604) as a special enemy because Gregory's effort to convert the Anglo-Saxons led ultimately to the subjugation of the autonomous British church.

Historians writing in this spirit were incapable of impartiality. But the historical controversies between the Catholics and the Protestants produced from both sides huge compilations. Their authors were determined to prove their respective cases by a stupendous marshalling of authorities and documentary sources. The habit of giving copious references and long, exact quotations, missing from the Humanist historiography, was reintroduced by the religious controversialists. On the Protestant side, the largest work is the *Ecclesiastica historia*, or the so-called *Centuriae Magdeburgenses* (13 volumes, 1559-74; "Magdeburg Centuries"), retelling the history of the church down to 1200. The Catholic reply, equally huge and graceless, was produced in 12 volumes by Cardinal Baronius. The chief Protestant critic of this work, the great Greek scholar Isaac Casaubon, was astonished by the Cardinal's ignorance of Greek and Hebrew, his gross mistakes, and his boundless credulity.

The narratives of contemporary events written in the 16th and early 17th centuries by the participants in the religious struggles, though equally partisan, include some works of great historical value and high literary merit. The earliest and best German Protestant narrative, that by Johannes Sleidanus, received age grudging tribute from his great opponent, the Holy Roman emperor Charles V, who remarked that "the rogue had certainly known much .., he has either been in our privy council or our Councilors have been traitors", Hohn Foxe's *Book of Martyrs* (1563) contains a great mass of exact information about the persecution of reformed religion in England and Wales during the reign of Mary Tudor, and it had influenced many generations of British Protestants. The achievements of Queen Elizabeth I and the Agnlican Church's settlement of her reign found an outstanding defender in William Camden, who was encouraged to write by Elizabeth's leading ministers. In his *Annales Rerum Anglicarum, et Hibernicarum Regnante Ellicaberha* ("Annals of Elizabeth's Reign") Camden made excellent use of mass of official records at his disposal, though his treatment of confidential matters had to be discreet.

Out of a conflict between Venice and the papacy in the first years of the 17th century was born the *Istoria del concilio tridentino* (1691 : *History of the Council of Trent.* 1676) of Fra Paolo Sarpi. A Catholic friar, but a passionate defender of Venetian autonomy, Sarpi dre a dark picture of worldly papal policies and the unscrupulous machinations of the Jesuits. It is a bitter, prejudiced, but splendidly written and well-informed work, which profoundly influenced the anticlerical historians of the 18th century. All these contemporary narratives, however, have one serious limitation. They deal almost exclusively with political events and with changes in ecclesiastical organization. The Protestant schism is treated as merely a revolt against the abuses of the old church, and the deeper reasons for the alienation of the Protestants from the Catholic faith are never explained. Furthermore, these historians, by attributing the origins of the schism almost exclusively to Luther's sudden conflict with the papacy, obscured the existence in the early 16th century of numerous Catholic reformers, whose sole aim was to transform the Catholic Church from within. This one-side approach to the history of the Reformation was destined to persist for a long time. Two influential histories published in the years 1683-88, one by a great Catholic prelate, Bishop Jacques Benigne Bossuet, and the other by Pierre Jurieeu, a leading Protestant, still agreed on the same superficial account of the causes of the Reformation.

The rewriting by the Protestants of universal church history naturally involved drastic revision of the history of the national churches. In Germany, particularly, the history of the church had become inextricably intermixed with the destinies of the German empire. Their hatred of the papacy made the Lutherans visualize the course of German history with unusual clarity. Nobody before them had attempted to impose on that history a single intelligible pattern of any sort. Theirs was bound to be a prejudiced pattern, a story of gradual national disintegration as the result of the successive defeats of the German emperors by the papacy. Johannes Stumps tragic chronicle of the Holy Roman emperor Henry IV (published in 1556) treated his struggles with Pope Gregory VII as the beginning of the empire's tribulations. The whole course of German history was retraced in this fashion under the influence of Luther's chief humanist collaborator. Phillip Melanchthon, in the so-called *Chronicle of* Canon, written in its final versions (1572-73) by Melanchthon's son-in-law, Caspar Peucer.

One of the most novel features of the English Protestant historiography was the reawakening of scholarly interest in the period before the Norman Conquest of England in the 11th century. Matthew Parker, Queen Elizabeth's first archbishop of Canterbury, though he could discern in the pre-Conquest church elements of true Christianity that were destroyed thereafter and had only been reintroduced by the Protestants. The Agglican Church could be represented as a return to the traditional practices and beliefs of the early English Christians. Thus the replacement of Latin by English in the Protestant church services could be justified by citing the presence in Anglo-Saxon England of Bibles, liturgies, and devotional literature in the Old English language. Parker and his friend Lord Burghley. Elizabeth's most trusted minister, gathered around them a circle of enthusiastic scholars, whose work preserved most of the important Anglo-Saxon texts as well as of some leading post-Conquest chronicles. Parker's own method of editing texts horrifies modern scholars, but some of the antiquarian works published by members of this group were of high quality. Camden's *Britannia* (first edition 1586, later much enlarged) was a pioneer work on the topography of Roman and early medieval Britain. The edition by Sir Henry Spelman of the records of the pre-Conquest church councils was the first serious attempt to apply to an important type of early sources the best methods of continental scholarship.

The growth of a historical outlook can be traced in the 16th century in many diverse fields of learning. For the first time men were realizing that there was a historical side to every branch of knowledge concerned with human affairs. "I have become aware that law books are the products of history", wrote the French legal historian Francois Baudouin in 1561. In each branch of study there developed a special historical technique particularly appropriate to it. The most sophisticated scholarship was to be found in the field of classical studies. A group of scholars active in the second half of the 16th century were achieving results much superior to the work of the earlier Renaissance classicists. They combined philological expertise with a determination to reach a really adequate understanding of the ancient Greek and Roman civilizations. A few were Italians, such as Carlo Sigonio, but most of the important works were written in France and in the Protestant centers of Switzerland and Holland. As textual critics these scholars were reacting sharply to the earlier, more haphazard, methods of emending and editing classical authors. They were trying to bring the text of one writer after another to a state of near perfection. Some leading ancient historians, such as Tacitus, benefited greatly from this treatment (edition of Lipsius in 1575). Though their methods do not quite reach the standards of modern scholarship, they anticipate intelligently many of the procedures more systematically adopted in the 19th century. Isaace Casaubon was the first to point out in his edition of Suetonius (1595) that Einhard's 9th century life of Charlemagne was modelled on the work of that Roman historian. Casaubon's friend Joseph Scaliger renewed the science of classical chronology (1583) and was the first to reconstruct the original Greek *Chronicle* of Eusebius lying behind St, Jerome's Latin translation. Sigonio's pioneer work on the rights and duties of Roman citizens (1560) was alter much used by The Odor Mommsen. One of the founders in the 19th century of the modern study of Roman history.

In the course of the 16th century, non-narrative historical work of the highest originality and complexity was being carried on in the legal faculties of French universities. One important stimulus was provided by the existence in France of different legal system- the unmodified provincial customs in the north and the written law in the south. The latter ultimately derived from the Roman law, and in the southern French universities, there arose an eager demand for the introduction of the new Italian methods of interpreting the Roman legal texts. Andrea Alciato, a pioneer in the historical treatment of the Roman law, taught at Bourges from 1529 to 1533, and his pupils founded the "Romanist" school of French legal historians.

Important advances were made in the study both of the Roman law and of the origins of the French legal customs, laying virtually the foundations of a new branch of scholarship, the history of law and institutions. Francois Baudouin published in 1545 the first historical survey of the development of the Roman legal science. The treatise on the custom of Paris by Charles Dumoulin (published 1539-58) resulted from his advocacy of the codification of the northern French legal customs. It was the first scholarly exposition of a body of customary French laws derived from feudal practices, and it amounted to a first comprehensive history of Europen feudalism. It prompted a series of controversial works by a succession of scholars. The Roman, the Germanic, and the Celetic roots of feudalism all found advocates, and the respective claims of Lombard and Frankish texts to provide the best clues were vigorously canvassed. The complexity of the problems presented by the unravelling of the origins of feudalism dawned on scholars for the first time. The most valuable of these attempts to rediscover the "ancient French constitution" were the researches on "the antiquities of France" of Etienne Pasquier (published 1560-1607), which from a basis for all later study of medieval French institutions.

One of the novel features of European civilization in the later 16th and 17th centuries was a secularization of mental interests. Secular learning could now produce ideas more fascinating to intelligent men than theology. History was one of the most popular types of literature sought by a growing reading public. Several treatises on the proper way of writing history appeared in the third quarter or the 16th century. An anthology consisting of 12 such works, including the famous *Methodus* of the French political philosopher Jean Bodin, was published at Basel in 1576. Nearly 100 years later a "Catalogue of the Most Vendible Books in England"(1657) showed that history books constituted a large proportion of the total works published. It has been estimated that between 1460 and 1700 at least 2,500,000 copies of 17 leading ancient historians were published in Europe.

The late 16th century and the 17th winessed the publication of several great collections of historical materials. The men who undertook these gigantic tasks often were qntiquarians accumulating miscellaneous records rather than historians, but they were supplying materials for generations of future historians. Some if the most important publications of sources appeared in France and the Netherlands. Pierre Pithou was a pioneer in editing materials for the history of the Frankish period. The collections of Andre Duchesne are a vast storehouse of chronicles and other sources for the study of medieval French history. Le Nain de Tillemont edited 20 volumes of records devoted to Roman and church history during the first six centuries of the Christian Era, which a century later furnished one of the principal sources for Edward Gibbon's work *The History of the Decline and Fall of the Roman Empire*. In 1629 a Belgian Jesuit, Jean Bolland, embarked systematically on the editing of records connected with all the saints whose feasts had at any time been celebrated by the church, and this series of publications has been continued to the present day. In the second half of the 17th century, the French Bewnedictine congregation of Saint-Maur started an immense series of publications commemorating the history of the Benedictines and of other monastic orders. The greatest Maurist scholar, Jean Mabillon, was accepted throughout Europe as the most erudite historian of his time.

In spite of its popularity among an expanding reading public and of the large number of learned deditions of materials that it inspired, history was not, for most of the 17th century, one of the sciences that made men proud of living in a modern age. Immense progress was taking place in mathematics, astronomy, and physics. History not only did not seem capable of much further development, but scientifically minded men were beginning to dismiss it as a branch of knowledge that would never be worthy of serious respect. Mabillon's *De Re Diplomatica* (1681) helped to challenge this pessimistic view, but a further century elapsed before history began to be accepted as an authoritative discipline.

One major obstacle to the progress of historiography was the hostility of rulers to publications that did not favour their governments. The growth of an influential reading public made rulers increasingly suspicious of historical writings; for example. The censorship exercised by Cosimo I de' Medici, ruler of Florence from 1537 to 1547, precipitated the decline of Florentine historiography. Comparisons with the past also could be invidious. In 1599 Elizabeth I of England censured as author for describing the deposition of one of her predecessors, Richard II. 200 years earlier. Fear of possible trouble made highly intelligent scholars into one-sided historians. The great jurist Hugo Grotius avoided in his history of the wars of the Dutch against Spain discussions of the religious aspects. Samuel Pufendorf, the historian of the Swedish conquests, carefully left out the internal development in 17th century Sweden.

The scholars who in that century were responsible for the great advances in the mathematical sciences were convinced that their achievements would ultimately give making a novel mastery over its natural environment. This is particularly true of Francis Bacon and of Rene Descartes. Their optimism was laying the foundations for a belief in a possibility of continuous progress without which the purposeful and assured historiography of the 19th century would be inconceivable. But the attitude towards history of most of the leading thinkers and scientists of the 17th century was not helpful to its immediate development. Bacon, who wrote a readable and rationally argued biography of King Henry VII of England, attached no importance to accuracy; for example, he antedated Henry's death by a whole year and could not be bothered to undertake any detailed research. Gottfried Wilhelm Leibniz was a great mathematician, but his attempts to apply science to historiography led to mechanistic constructions form which real human beings were largely missing. Numerous influential thinkers were decidedly hostile to history. Descartes, the most eminent of the anti-historical scientists, was not simply disgusted by the unsystematic and imprecise methods of the historians of his time but also doubted whether, strictly speaking, history could be regarded as a branch of knowledge at all But it is important to remember that mush of the 17th century criticism of history was an attitude of men who simply had other priorities and were concerned to attack doctrines that, for one reason or another, historians seemed to support. In the late 17th century the most successful defenders of history were the members of certain particularly scholarly Catholic orders. Catholicism rested its authority on tradition to a much greater extent than did its Protestant opponents. For Catholic scholars such as

Mabillon, the defence of history became really a defence of their religion. The were trying to show that historians were capable of discovering scientifically demonstrable truths. The decisive publication was Mabillon's *De Re Diplomatica* of 1681., A member of a rival order, the Jesuit Daniel van Papebroch, had challenged (in 1675) the authenticity of the oldest charters of two French Benedictine monasteries. Saint Denis and Corbie. Mabillon applied his powerful critical intelligence not only to vindicating these documents but also to formulating the general rules that must be used to prove the authenticity of medieval records. He illustrated his rules by admirable examples and stated his conclusions with a candor and a common sense that convinced most readers. Mabillon's survey of the test that must be applied by scholars covered the writing materials, the scripts (thus founding the science of medieval Latin paleography), the seals and other devices of authentication, the official formulas, and the vocabulary used at different periods. Above all, he stressed that the authenticity of a document usually rested not just on isolated details but on consistent correctness of all its features.

Mabillon was not just a "historical scientist", He had a passionate interest in the past and a vivid historical imagination. He displayed these qualities abundantly in his last and most important work, the *Annales Ordinis s, Benedicti* ("Annals of the Benedictine Order", to 1066). In the *Traite des etudes monastiques,* (1691 : "Manual of Monastic Studies"), he defended the importance of scholarly work as the principal activity of an elite of benedictine monks. But it would be an anachronism to regard Mabillon and his chief associates as fully comparable to modern historians. They were constrained by the limitations of their time and of their special position as monks. For example, Bernard de Montfaucon. Mabillon's most important successor, is the creator of the science of medieval Greek paleography. But he shares with most of his contemporaneous a complete inability to treat the Old Testament as a historical source.

Historical and antiquarian studies developed in 17th century England in several very distinctive ways. The political struggles and religious controversies of that period made some issues of older English history into matters of immediate practical importance. The other distinctive feature was the delay in the absorption of European continental learning, so that the great progress made in the study of feudal origins in the 16th century began to affect the thinking of English scholars only by about 1625. But there persisted also elements of continuity growing out of earlier Tudor scholarship. The interest in the Anglo-Saxon church and civilization continuity growing out of earlier Tudor scholarship. The interest in the Anglo-Saxon church and civilization continued to stimulate important editions of records throughout the 17th and early 18th centuries, including, especially. Sir Henry Spelman's edition of the records of church councils and Sir William Dugdale's *Monasticon Anglicanum* (1655-73), which is still valuable today. Another element of continuity with the Tudor period was the perennial interest of the English notables in heraldry, genealogy, and the antiquities of their native regions. Dugdale's *Annquities of Warwickshire* (1656) set a pattern and a standard for country histories.

Students of English law and institutions, lacking the stimulus that was provided for French lawyers by the diversity of legal systems and by the notable progress in the study of Roman law in that country, continued to ascribe immemorial origins to the common law of England and to approach the development of English institutions in a completely unhistorical spirit. Among the parliamentary opposition to the Stuarts, these attitudes were part of a belief in the "ancient constitution", which these sovereigns were supposed to be defying. Spelman, who was a devout Anglican and a royalist, though a moderate one, was perhaps the first major scholar to break away from this myth. Under the influence of continental publications and correspondents, he accepted that feudal tenure had been introduced into England after the Norman Conquest and that all the English institutions after 1066 must be redefined in feudal terms. But his discoveries were hidden in a dictionary of antiquarian words *(archaeologus,* vol. 1. 1626; 2 vol. 1664) and made very little impact until some 50 years had elapsed. Spelman had an acute sense of historical development, and the sadly castigated this countrymen for their lack of it in their attitude to parliamentary origins.

When States are departed from their original Constitution and that original by tract of time worn out of memory; the succeeding Ages viewing what is past by the present, conceive the former to have been like to that they live in . *(Of Parliaments,* written in about 1640), published 1698)

His greatest contribution to English history was to grasp that parliaments had enveloped out of feudal assemblies convoked by the Norman kings and that the Commons were introduced into parliaments subsequently, as a result of the growing prosperity of the lesser landholders. These views first became generally accessible in the 1664 edition of Spelman's dictionary. They were adopted by Robert Brady (in 1681) and by other partisans of the Stuarts and expanded into a Royalist statement of the English pat. Violently polemical though this view was, it did at least lay to rest the myth of the immemorial "ancient constitution". The Whig triumph at the Glorious Revolution of 1688. Which established a doctrine that the king ruled by parliamentary consent, led to the neglect of these discoveries for much of the 18th century. This was the common fate of much of the research of 17th century antiquarians, who were very much ahead of their time and were writing for a limited audience. John Aubrey's pioneer description in the 1670s of the prehistoric sites of Avebury and Stonehenge had to wait two centuries for full publication. Even the best to these antiquarians, such as Spelman and Dugdale, were less critical in their handling of the original sources than Mabillon was. Higher standards were reached by a few of their successors in the early 18th century, especially by Thomas Madox, whose *Formulare Anglicanum* (1702) imitated Mabillon by attempting a systematic introduction to English medieval documents. But this did not save Madox from prolonged oblivion. After about 1730 this English tradition of antiquarian scholarship largely ended and remained unfashionable for most of the 18th century.

Historiogrpahy in the Age of the Enlightenment

The impulse given to historiography by the Italian Humanists and the religious controversialists had largely spent itself by about 1715. Men knew again how to write rationally satisfying contemporary histories, though often it needed courage to do so. Much less progress had been achieved in reconstructing the more distant past. Impressive collections of historical materials were being accumulated, but most scholars still lacked the capacity to rethink the thoughts of past generations and thus really to understand them. Mabillon could write with insight about early Benedictine history, as the possessed both sympathy with the subject and adequate technical expertise. But he was exceptional. Spelman had grasped that a particular society would be moulded in a peculiar way by its institutions. He could not reconstruct and explain the gradual changes from one set of institutions to a later one, but he was aware of the problem.

Judged by the quality of its historical output, the 18th century was not, on the whole, an age of successful historians, but some of the defects of earlier historiography were beginning to be overcome. There were also losses, however, for some of the achievements of the preceding period were in danger of being forgotten. In the leading countries of western Europe, religious controversies were becoming less important, and a massive secularization of interests took place, which affected even ecclesiastical scholars. The French Maurists continued until 1790 to publish imposing historical collections, but their choice of subjects was determined much less than in the time of Mabillon by religious priorities. The greatest Italian ecclesiastical disciple of Mabillon was Ludovico Antonio Muratori, a social reformer. In a divided country like Italy, the best way of expressing his patriotism lay in reminding Italians of the former greatness of their country. Muratori spent much of his long life on his editions of Italian medieval sources.

The nationalist motivation shown by Muratori was peculiar to Italy and also to parts of Germany, another divided country. Elsewhere in Europe there was a danger that, as men lost interest in constitutional or religious disputes that might be settled by appeals to the past, they might turn away altogether from history or at least neglect long stretches of it. This did happen to some extent in the 18th century. Some of the radical French reformers, such as Jean Le Rond d'Alembert, one of the main inspirers in the 170s of the French *Encyclopedie,* wanted to jettison completely much of the past. The Marquis de Condorcet, an early prophet of the doctrine of endless progress of mankind and a pioneer historian of European civilization, mission that in 1792-93 deliberately destroyed some of the royal records as comprising relics of past servitude.

During much of the 18th century it was safer and easier to publish controversial works of history than it had been in the past. The point is important, as without their greater freedom, the peculiarly radical "philosophical" historiography, so typical of that century, would have been inconceivable. In Italy such writing was still dangerous. Pietro Giannone, the author of an anticlerical history of Nepalese (1723), was tracked down by the inquisition and spent 12 years in prison, where he died in 1748. Even the great Muraton, who tried to help Giannone, came into danger of having some of his works banned and Benedict XIV. In France, Louts XIV in 1714 imprisoned Nicolas Freret in the Bastille for alleging (correctly) that the Franks were originally a confederacy of German tribes and not descendants of more illustrious ancestors. Under the successors of Louis, noting quite so absurd happened again, but critics of the government of the church were often in trouble. Great Britain. Hoiland, Switzerland, and parts of Germany, on the other hand, provided safe oases where most things could be published. It was no accident that the most independent and historically minded group of German professors should have congregated at the University of Gottingen, founded in 1734, in the Hanoverian territory of the kings of Great Britain.

A real renewal of historiography in the 18th century could only come of fresh reasons were discovered for making in again worthwhile. Nationalism could supply one such motive; but this only became decisively influential in the 19th century. An alternative was a historiography inspired by the progress in the natural sciences and based on formulating the general rules governing the development of human societies. The chief features of this "new" historiography were a sense of the unity of all human history, including an interest in the continents outside Europe; a capacity for bold generalizations about the salient features of particular periods or societies; and a preference for topic connected with the progress of human civilization. Condorcet's historical sketch of the progress of the human mind, written in 1794, subdivided all known history into nine periods, each starting with some great invention or with geographical discoveries.

The shortcomings of this "rationalistic" historiography have been rehearsed often enough. For many of its writers it was primarily a weapon of propaganda against their enemies in church and state. Their redeeming virtue was the fearlessly critical attitude to all existing authorities, however august of sacred. The vast scale of their generalizations often precluded any detailed research. This was particularly true of the attempts to write histories of civilization, as the existing collections of printed materials did not cater for such interests, while systematic research in archives was seldom possible in the 18th century. In preparing his pioneer essay on the history of civilization, covering the millennium from the Carolingians to Louis XIV (*Essal sur les moeurs et I'esprit des nations*, 1745-54), the French author Voitaire had to collect bits and pieces from most diverse sources.

One of the most valuable achievements of the thinkers of the 18th century was their capacity to study particular societies as coherent units and to formulate the theory that the various aspects of each society's life were closely interrelated. This was not an entirely novel idea, but it first became commonly accepted during this period. Nor were all its adherents anticlericals, Giambattista Vico, a Neapolitan

Catholic, was ahead of his contemporaries in his particularly subtle sense of the complex influences by which one phase of society gives place to another. In his reconstruction of these transitions during the early stages of Roman history, he makes no clear line between periods. His countryman Giannone explains in his autobiography that he had studied Roman law not for its own sake but in order to understand the changes in the society of the Roman Empire. The French philosopher Montesquieu, who owed much to Giannone, was not really a historian, but he displays an acute sense of historical realities. His *De l'esprit des lois* (1748; The Spirit of Laws), more than any other book, accustomed his contemporaries to ponder the complex factors that shaped each society. It inspired Gibbon's definition of the kind of history he wanted to write. It was to be a "history related to and explained by the social institutions in which it is contained."

This ideal was realized in Gibbon's *History of the Decline and Fall of the Roman Empire* (1776-88), one of the masterpieces of "philosophical" historiography. Gibbon was preoccupied above all with the problem of human progress. The belief that continuous progress was possible for mankind had been publicly formulated in the mid 18th century by Anne-Robert-Jacques Turgot in France and by Adam Smith in Scotland, independently, it seems, of each other, Gibbon had read works and known scholars influenced by both these thinkers. A belief in continuous progress would confer a new purposefulness on the study of the entire course of human history and could justify a lengthy account of what otherwise might have seemed very obscure stretches of the past. Such a justification was to inspire most of the historiography of the 19th century. But the problem of progress had a special urgency for Gibbon's generation, which worried at the thought that their own enlightened civilization might also subsequently collapse. By unravelling the causes of the decline of the Roman Empire. Gibbon was determined to show that the degree of development and was immune from the fate of the ancient world.

In the 18th century, historiography was still only very rarely connected with the universities; and thus, except in such isolated places as Gottingen in Germany, no continuous schools of history could develop. Some of the most important achievements of the 18th century historians meant much less to their contemporaries than to their successors in the 19th century. Gibbon was a pioneer in utilizing in a "rationalist" history the vast materials accumulated by generations of erudite antiquarians, but he had no immediate followers. The German archaeologist Johann Joachim Winckelmann tried to revive the true understanding of Greek sculpture and to make the history of art into something more than just the biographies of artists, but his work bore little fruit until the next century. The saddest fate was that of Vico's work. He was hardly ever read before the 19th century, when he at last influenced Barthold Georg. Niebuhr and the rest of the German historical school, while Jules Michelet's rediscovery of Vico in 1824 started a new era in French writing on the Middle Ages.

Historiogrpahy in the 19th and 20th century

From the early 19th century, historiography began to develop in a radically different way. The decisive changes occurred among the German historians, largely through a reaction to the French Revolution and a temporary subjugation of their country by Napoleon, Organized teaching of history in schools and universities became a matter of national importance, first in Prussia and then in other parts of Germany. As universal education spread to most European countries in the course of the 19th century, history was accepted everywhere as a necessary subject in schools. For the first time the bulk of historical writing came to be done by professional historians, for whom it became a condition of securing academic appointments or of consolidating their standings as university teachers. Historiography eventually became a continuously cooperative venture, where the achievements of past historians could be used systematically by their successors. But the growth of specialization and the bewildering number of types of works that came to be published constituted a new danger. In the past, important discoveries were frequently lost through lack of interest. But, by the second half of the 20th century, discoveries were in danger of being simply overlooked amid the flood of publications.

Another great change lay in the growth of intellectual freedom. Free expression of independent or unorthodox ideas had become dangerous during the French Revolution and under Napoleon, both in the territories controlled by the French and, by way of frightened reaction, in the lands of their unconquered opponents. After 1815 conditions for freer historiography improved gradually in much of Europe. Charles darwin's *Origin of Species* (1859), which put forth a theory of evolution at first unacceptable to church authorities, probably could not have been published with the same impunity any earlier.

One feature of the growing tolerance of governments towards historiography was the gradual creation of public archives, such as the British Public Record Office in London, created in 1838, and the freer opening of the collections already in existence. Even the papacy accepted these changes, and Pope Leo XIII opened up the papal archive in 1883 as part of a deliberate new policy of encouraging historical study of Catholicism. For the first time historiography came to be based largely on unpublished records, and scholars were tempted into excessive reliance on original documents while unduly neglecting the older types of narrative sources.

In the 20th century some envious threats to the persistence of free scholarship recurred, and historiography suffered with other branches of human studies. The establishment of a Communist regime in Russia led, at first, to the rejection of most pre-1917 history as a fit subject for schools and universities, This decision was reversed in the 1930's and from 1945 Communist countries were encouraging a from of historiography especially concerned with economic history and the class struggles of the past. There was also an enthusiastic interest in the material remains of past ages, leading to an impressive development of archaeology, particularly in Poland. The rise of dictatorships in Italy and Germany had disastrous effects on historiography in those countries, and recovery after World War II was only gradual.

Judged merely by the number of "practicing" historians and of their publications, historiography seemed in a very flourishing state in the 1970s. Its European traditions had spread to all the other continents and were largely accepted in all non-Communist countries.

The *Introduction aux etudes historiques (Introduction to the Study of History)* of Charles V. Langlois and Charles Seignobos (1898), supplemented by critical comments of another outstanding French historian, Ferdinand Lot (in *Le. Moyen Age,* 1898), - provides an excellent starting point for the discussion of modern historical methods. History in an autonomous branch of learning, and some of its methods may be unique. Historians should not try to formulate general laws; their branch of learning, merely "aims at explaining reality". Langlois and Seignobos particularly stress that history is not a science of observation but a science of reasoning how to extract from imperfect documentary or narrative records some glimpses of what actually happened.

A historian has to subject his sources to a whole series of preliminary investigations. First comes "external criticism", aimed at determining whether the sources are appropriate and adequate for the particular task in hand. The provenance, date, and authenticity of each source must be established by using the techniques of diplomatic, the detailed study and assessment of documents, and of paleography, the study of ancient handwriting and of other auxiliary sciences that were elaborated after the 17th century. In France a special institution for teaching some of these techniques, the Ecole des Chatres, was created in 1821. The first specialized seminar for instruction in these subjects was established in 1854 at Vienna by Theodor von Sickel, one of the greatest medievalists of the 19th century, and it was gradually imitated by leading German universities. One of the most important critical refinements introduced in the course of the

19th century was the improved handling of narrative sources that lay behind them. Leopoled von Ranke, one of the foremost German historians, who began his career as a teacher of classics, was gradually attracted to history through a desire to understand better the sources of the Greek and Latin authors whom he was expounding. In the later decades of the 19th century, such a quest became a normal feature of historical scholarship.

Once a historian has decided, through the application of "external criticism", on the sources that are relevant to his purpose, he must next, by "internal criticism", make sure that he fully understands what he has selected. German classical philologists were the first to bring these latter investigations to a high degree of perfection. Karl Lachmann, an editor of the Latin poets, is justly regarded as the creator of modern textual criticism in its most rigorous forms, and historians gradually adopted similar methods. The language of the sources must be understood, corruptions in the text must be eliminated, and the historian must, as accurately as possible, penetrate the minds of the author with whom he is dealing.

All these critical operations on the sources are merely preliminaries, and the work of the historian proper only starts when he attempts a synthesis of his materials, F. Lot come into play. There must be sympathy with the subjects under study, for without it there can be no imaginative insight into the past. Ideally, a historian must display capacities akin to those of a poet or an artist.

Such a quality was, by and large, lacking in the work of the historians of the Enlightenment, who had been unable to achieve imaginative insight into civilizations very different from their own. The greatest shortcoming a Gibbon was his temperamental inability to appreciate religion. The new historiography of the 19th century was created chiefly by Germans. Who, through a reaction to the ungodly and cosmopolitan Enlightenment, were endowed to excess with a passion for extoiling the unique nature of their fatherland and for tracing the roots of this uniqueness through the whole course of German history. These developments in German historiography can be traced back to some strands of German thought in the 18th century, especially to some features of the writings of Johann Gottfried von Herder. He denied that the purpose of history was to provide a birds's-eye view of the progress of the human mind. It was, rather, to reconstruct history as it had been, which means that all countries and periods are equally deserving of study. This view anticipated Rank's oft-quoted aim to describe what has actually happened and his conviction that the description of all human history displays the workings of God's providence. The disasters inflicted upon Germany by Napoleon brought forth a patriotic school of historians whose urgent task it became to propagate these views as a means of restoring German independence. The centre of this movement was in Prussia. At the newly founded University of Berlin (1809). Wilhelm von Humboldt, its effective founder, be lived that the task of the historian lay in discovering the ideas behind the facts. The concepts that had special validity for him were ideas of religion and of a national state. The German historical school ended itself on the scientific precision of its methods, on its determination to get all the details right, and on the scrupulous quotation of sources. This display of exact scholarship represented a great gain for historical sciences, but its chief purpose was to convince the reader. Yet these German historians were fundamentally inspired by a prejudiced, arbitrary set of assumptions. It is particularly difficult to detect Ranke's hidden bias, as he made a parade of refusing to pass judgments on the past. His preference for the study of foreign relations between states and his treatment of states as natural entities with a right to fulfil their individual destinies justified the successes of Prussia. The defeat in 1848 of the German aspirations to national unity inspired his pupil wilhelm von Giesebrecht to write the history of the medieval German empire to remained his countrymen of their past glories. When German unification was achieved in 1871. Giesebrecht doubted whether there was any need to bring out any further volumes of his great work. But many German historians, having contributed mightily to the unification of Germany, continued to describe complacently the triumphs of the Bismarckian state. This was one of the purposes of the school of historical economists led by Gustav von Schmoller. There were some dissenting vices., Theodor Mommsen, the greatest historian of antiquity produced by the 19th century, deplored the tendency of his countrymen to worship state power. Friedrich Meinecke, a leading German historian of political ideas, who until 1914 accepted the ordinary nationalistic assumptions of his countrymen, gradually entirely changed his views and, after the defeat of Germany in two world wars, pleaded in his *Deutsche Katastrophe* (1946; *the German Catastrophe)* for a historiography concerned with the higher values of general civilization. Among the German historians, particularly striking progress was achieved in medieval studies. Meanwhile, attempts at imaginative reconstructions of the past were being made in other countries of western Europe. Jules Michelet wrote in 1833-43 the first history of medieval France based on the French national archives, of which he was at that time keeper, Macaulay's *History of England* (1848-61), covering chiefly the years 1785-1702, represented again a remarkable though prejudiced attempt to relive the past.

German scholarly techniques and the methods of German historical teaching spread to other countries in the course of the later 19th century, though it is important to note that until 1914 a significant proportion of leading historians from states outside Germany spent some time in that country. This is particularly true of some of the greatest Russian scholars, such as M. I. Rostovizeff, one of the most important modern historians of antiquity. In England, William Stubbs, though self-taught, applied the results of German scholarship to the reconstruction of English medieval history. Gabriei Monod, who had studied in Germany, was prominent in introducing more scientific techniques into medieval French historiography, and he founded in 1876 the Revue Historique as the main organ of French historical scholarship. A succession of American students went to Germany, and some, on their return home, reorganized historical studies.

Measured by the sheer bulk of publications, the amount of American history written since the 18th century is probably greater than that of any other modern nation. But apart from editions of sources, very few works on American history published before about 1900 are of much practical use today. The most influential pioneer in organizing scientific historiography was Herbert Baxter Adams, who between 1876 and his death in 1901 made the Johns Hopking University at Baltimore into the foremost American centre of historical studies. He was also one of the founders of the American Historical Association in 1884 and played a large part in successfully launching the *American Historical Review* in 1895 as the main organ of historical scholarship. Some of Adams publish became great scholars in various fields of general history. Charles Homer Haskins' works on Norman institution and on science and culture in the 12th and 13th centuries made him one of the foremost medievalists of the 20th century. But a movement for creating a purely American history was launched in 1893 by another of Adams' pupils. Frederick Jackson Turner, who inaugurated a "progressive" school of historians through his conviction that the fundamental fact of American history down to 1890 was the settlement of a continent. In Turner's eyes the main theme of American history in the 19th century was the conflict between the patrician and capitalist groups of the Eastern Seaboard and the needs of the new settlers in the Middle West. Charles A. Beard inaugurated by his *Economic Interpretation of the American Constitution* (1913) an attempt to rewrite the entire history of the U.S. in terms of conflicts between different groups of economic interests. The weakness of this type of historiography was that it encouraged an excessive parochialism. After 1945 the "progressive" historians came under fire both from more conservative scholars who preferred to stress elements of common tradition and purpose in American development and from the historians of the "new left. In the 1960 and 1970s the close connection between writings on American history and the active political life was infusing great variety and vitality into its historiography, though making it perhaps too susceptible to rapidly changing external pressures.

Methodology of Historiogrpahy

The methodology of history does not differ in broadest outline from that of other disciplines in its regard for existing knowledge, its search for new and relevant data, and its creation of hypotheses. It is the same for all historical writing, success depending on skill and experience; and division of the past on temporal or topical lines merely reflects the human limitations of historians. Although historical methodology has four facets, the more skilled the historian the less he gives them conscious consideration; and any historian in likely to be concerned with two or more concurrently. The four facets are heuristic, knowledge of current interpretation, research, and writing.

The first two may be firefly considered. Heuristic has been adopted as a convenient term for the technique of investigation that can be acquired solely by practice and experience. In the caws of the historian in embraces such things as knowledge of manuscript collections, methods of card indexing and classifying material, and knowledge of bibliography. It underlies other aspects of methodology as in knowledge of the capabilities of historians working in the same and similar fields or in the power of dealing expeditiously with documentary material. The necessity for knowledge of current interpretation its based on the working principle that inquiry proceeds from the known to the unknown; and the historian has to be well acquainted with existing work in his own field, in contiguous historical fields and in allied disciplines. The work in each case consists of both "fact" and interpretation, and the amount the historian accepts will vary. In his own field he will normally not accept facts, and certainly not current interpretation, on trust; in contiguous historical fields he will accept facts and current interpretation by experts in those fields, but qualified by heuristic and his general historical knowledge; in allied disciplines, such as anthropology, economics, geography, natural science, philology, psychology, sociology, he must unless there is strong evidence to the contrary presume the technical skill and intellectual honesty of scholars in those fields. There is, of course, no reason why a historian cannot be reasonably versed in one or more of these and other disciplines, and should the nature of his enquiry demand in the must be.

Historical research is the term applied to the work necessary for the establishing of occurrences, happenings, or events in the field with which the historian in concerned. Knowledge of these is entirely dependent on the transmission of information from those living at the time, and this information forms what is known as the source material for the particular period or topic. The occurrences themselves can never be experienced by the historian, and what he has at his disposal are either account of occurrences as seen by contemporaries or something, be it verbal, written, or material, that is the end product of an occurrence. These accounts or end products have been variously termed relics, tracks, or traces of the occurrences that gave rise to them; and from them the historian can, with varying degrees of certainty, deduce the occurrences. The traces are thus the "facts" of history, the actual occurrences deductions from the facts; and historical research is concerned with the discovery of relevant traces and with deduction from those traces insofar as this will aid the search for further relevant traces.

Source Material

Source material falls into three groups which can be differentiated as written, material, and traditional. Written source material has two subdivisions, literary, sometimes called subjective, and official. The first consists of events as seen through the eyes of an individual and therefore as interpreted by him, normally entailing selection of occurrences or attribution of motive. The second subdivision, the official, consists of records produced in transacting business at any level from individual to international. The information given is basically in statement from, impersonal, and containing only the most superficial suggestions of causation and motivation. In practice the boundary between literary and official sources is blurred and a document may contain elements of both. The second main division, material source material, consists of objects that have resulted from activities of human beings in the past. The third group, traditional source material, covers what is handed on verbally or as practices, although later generations may commit such things to writing. Obvious examples are archaic forms, traditional practices, nursery rhymes, folklore, and place names. Comparison with parallel source material and knowledge of current interpretation will normally show the historian whether his particular source can be presumed true, partially true, or faked. If true or partially true allowance has to be made for the subjective element in literary and some traditional sources and for the difficulty of reconstructing the events themselves from the traces surviving in official, material, or other traditional sources.

The classification of source material is essentially pragmatic, based on the differing techniques required in handling sources of the different groups; an inscribed tombstone, for example, can be either a written or a material source depending on whether the historian's concern is with the content of the inscription or with the stone. Specializes training in what are sometimes known as ancillary disciplines may, depending on the nature of his investigation, be necessary for the historian. The most important of these are archaeology, bibliography, chronology, diplomatic, epigraphy, generalogy, paleography, sigillogrpahy, and textual criticism. It need hardly be said that the historian must have competence in the languages used in his source material. Many historians give part of their time to the editing of source material. This is not historical writing but is of use to other historians in the same field. The collection of facts as an end in itself is, however, antiquarianism not history, and the essential end product of historical investigation is the historian's own writing.

Using Source Material

The question of what history is belongs to the philosophy rather than the methodology of history. The word history itself is used ambiguously to describe both the past and what is written about the past; but it is this second meaning that is relevant to the working definition that history is the past experience of society. For what reasons society may wish to utilize its past experience is not the concern of the historian, whose task is to make available to society that past experience and to records it for future reference. An individual utilizing his own past experience has to recall the significant elements of that experience with accuracy and establish their causal and chronological relationships. The historian behaves similarly concerning the past experiences of society; but the reconstruction of events from traces, the selection of those relevant to his task, and the establishing of relationships allow a varying freedom of choice by the historian. Which thus introduces the subjective element of the historian's personality. This cannot be eliminated from historical writing, and the historian's aim is to make the margin of intellectual error as small as possible. The handling of source material demands only care and technical competence, and it is mainly in the construction of hypotheses and in the establishing of relationship that this intellectual error can enter. A check is provided by the opinions of other historians working in the same field. His work will, if accepted, become part of current interpretation, sometimes described as accepted history but, as with all current interpretation, subject to revision by himself or others.

Historical methodology became more clearly formulated during the 19th and 20th centuries, but there have been historians at times long past whose work can be judged by present-day standards. There are, however, certain important differences between present methodology and the general run of past methodology. Much medieval writing, for example, bows to precedent in literary sources and in current interpretation, and uncritical acceptance of an earlier writer's work can occur century after century. The comparative neglect of official sources by the majority of European historians before the 19th century gave no corrective to literary sources. The greatest impediment to the development of modern methodology lay, however, in the varying concepts of history, some of which survive today. The concept of history as a from of literature made it a type of imaginative art on which judgment was passed on grounds of elegance rather than accuracy. Closely allied with this is the "ethical" concept of history whereby historical writing became a series of clue judgment on individuals and actions. The converse of this was the impossible "objective" or "scientific" history of the later 19th century, though it did popularize the concept of research and developed the ancillary disciplines. The use of history for propaganda purposes is in its crudest from virtually a branch of fiction and thus independent of research; in its more subtle forms it can encourage accuracy in research, but it will encourage also the suppression of inconvenient traces and intellectual dishonesty in the elucidation of relationships. In this it indicates one of the main impediments to methodological and historical development; the holding by the historian of *a priori* theories or laws to which all events and relationships must conform, whether it be the theory of divine intervention in human affairs favoured in medieval times or the Marxist theory current over much of the modern world.

ANCILLARY FIELDS

Archaeology

The word archaeology comes from the Greek *archaia* ("ancient things"), and *logos* ("theory" or "science"). It has been used in varying ways, but from the late 18th century onward has come to mean that branch of learning that studies the material remains of man's past. This includes man's artifacts, from the very earliest stone tools, of perhaps 2,00,000 years ago, to the men-made objects that are buried or thrown away at the present day; everything made by human beings from simple tools to complex machines, from the earliest houses and temples and tombs to palaces, cathedrals, and pyramids.

The archaeologist is first a descriptive worker, he has to describe, classify, and analyze the artifacts he studies. An adequate and objective taxonomy is the basis of all archaeology, and many good archaeologists spend their lives in this activity of description and classification. But the main aim of the archeologist is to place the material remains in historical contexts, to supplement what may be known from written sources, and, thus, to increase understanding of the past. Ultimately, then, the archaeologist is a historian; his aim is the interpretive description of the past of man.

Increasingly, man scientific techniques are used by the archeologist, and he uses the scientific expertise of many persons who are not archaeologists in his work. The artifacts he studies must often be studied in their environmental contexts; and botanists, zoologists, soil scientists, and geologists may be brought in to identify and describe plants, animals, soils, and rocks, Radioactive carbon dating, which has revolutionized much of archaeological chronology, is a by-product of research in atomic physics. But although archaeology, uses extensively the methods, techniques, and results of the physical and biological sciences, it is not a natural science; some consider it a discipline that is half science and half humanity. Perhaps it is more accurate to say that the archaeologist is first a craftsman, practicing many specialized crafts (of which excavation is the most familiar to the general public), and then a historian.

The justification for this work is the justification of all historical scholarship, namely, to enrich the present by our knowledge of the experiences and achievements of our predecessors. Because it concerns itself with things people have made, the most direct findings of archaeology bear on the history of art and technology; but, by inference it also yields information about the society, religion, and economy of the people who created the artifacts. Also, it may bring to light and interpret previously unknown written documents, providing an even more certain from of evidence about the past.

But no one archaeologist can cover the whole range of man's history, and there are many branches of archaeology divided by geographical areas (such as classical archaeology, the archaeology of ancient Greece and Rome; or Egyptology, the archaeology of ancient Egypt) or by periods (such as medieval archaeology and industrial archaeology). Writing began 5,000 years ago in Mesopotamia and Egypt; its beginnings were somewhat later in India and China, and later still in Europe. The aspect of archaeology that deals with the past of man before he learned to write has, since the middle of the 19th century, been referred to as prehistoric archaeology, or prehistory. In prehistory the archaeologist is paramount, for here the only sources are material and environmental.

The scope of this article is to describe briefly how archaeology came into existence as a learned discipline; how the archaeologist works in the field, museum, laboratory, and study; and how he assesses and interprets his evidence and transmutes it into history.

History of archaeology. No doubt there have always been people who were interested in the material remains of the past, but archaeology as a discipline has its earliest origins in 15th and 16th century Europe, when the Renaissance Humanists looked back upon the glories of Greece and Rome. Popes, cardinals, and noblemen in Italy in the 16th century began to collect antiquities and to sponsor excavations of find more works in ancient art. These collectors were imitated by others in northern Europe who were similarly interested in antique culture. All this activity, however, was still not archaeology in the strict sense. It was more like what would be called art collecting today.

The Mediterranean and the Middle East. Archaeology proper began with a interest in the Greeks and Romans and first developed in 18th century Italy with the excavations of the Roman cities of Pompeii and Herculaneum. Classical archaeology was established on a more scientific basis by the work of Heinnch Schliemann, who investigated the origins of Greek civilization at Troy and Mycenae in the 1870s; of

M. A. Biliotti at Rhodes in this same period; of the German Archaeological Institute under Ernst Curtius at Olympia from 1875 to 1881; and of Alexander Conze at Samothrace in 1873 and 1875. Conze was the first person to include photographs in the publication of his report. Schliemann had intended to dig in Crete but did not do so, and it was left to Arthur Evans to begin work at Knossos in 1900 and to discover the Minoan civilization, ancestor of classical Greece.

Egyptian archaeology began with Napoleon's invasion of Egypt in 1789. He brought with him scholars who set to work recording the archaeological remains of the country. The results of their work were published in the *Description de I'Egypte* (1808-25). As a result of discoveries made by this expedition. Jean-Francois Champollion was able to decipher ancient Egyptian writing for the first time in 1822. This decipherment, which enabled scholars to read the numerous writings left by the Egyptians, was the first great step forward in Egyptian archaeology. The demands for Egyptian antiquities led to organized tomb robbing by men such as Giovanni Battista Belzoni. A new era in systematic and controlled archaeological research began with the Frenchman Auguste Mariette, who also founded the Egyptian Museum at Cairo. The British archaeologist Flinders Petrie, who began work in Egypt in 1880, made great discoveries there and in Palestine during his long lifetime. Petrie developed a systematic method of excavation, the principles of which he summarized in *Methods and Aims in Archaeology* (1904). It was left to Howard Carter and Lord Carnarvon to make the most spectacular discovery in Egyptian archaeology, that of the tomb of Tutankhamen in 1922.

Mesopotamian archaeology also began with hectic digging into mounds in the hopes of finding treasure and works of art, but gradually these gave way in the 1840s to planned digs such as those of the Frenchman Paul-Emile Botta at Nineveh and Khorsabad, and the Gnglishman Austen Henry Layard at Nimrud. Kuyunjik. Nabi Yunus, and other sites, Layard's popular account of his excavations, *Nineveh and Its RemainsI* (1849), became the earliest and one of the most successful archaeological best sellers. In 1846 Henry Creswicke Rawlinson became the first man to decipher the Mesopotamian confirm writing. Towards the end of the 19th century, systematic excavation revealed a previously unknown people, the Sumerians, who had lived in Mesopotamia before the Babylonians and Assyrians. The most impressive Sumerians excavation was that of the Royal Tombs at Ur by Leonard Woolley in 1926.

First steps to archaeology. The development of scientific archaeology in 19th century Europe from the antiquarianism and treasure collecting of the previous three centuries was due to three things; a geological revolution an antiquarian revolution, and the propagation of the doctrine of evolution. Geology was revolutionized in the early 19th century with the discovery and demonstration of the principles of uniformitarian stratigraphy (which determines the age of fossil remains by the stratum they occupy below the earth) by men like William Smith, Georges Cuvier, and Charles Lyell, Lyell, in his *Principles of Geology* (1830-33), popularized this new system and paved the way for the acceptance of the great antiquity of man. Charles Darwin regarded Lyell's *Principles* as one of the two germinal works in the formation of his own ideas on evolution. Early stone tools had first been discovered and identified in the late 18th century. The location of these genuine artifacts in certain strata demonstrated, on the principle of uniformitatianism, that man had been in existence long before 4004 BC, the date calculated according to the chronology of the Bible. The discoveries of Jacques Boucher de Perthes in the Somme Valley in France, and of William Pengelly in the some Valley in France, and of William Pengelly in the caves of South Devon in England, were used to demonstrate the antiquity of man in 1859, the same year that saw the publication of Darwin's revolutionary *Origin of Spectes.* Approximate dates for the Paleolithic Period (Old Stone Age) of the pression "Palaeolithic" was not used until John Lubbock coined it in his book *Pre-historic Times* (1865).

Half a century before this, Scandinavian archaeologists

had created a revolution in antiquarian thought by postulating, on archaeological grounds, successive technological stages in man's past. C.J. Thomsen classified the material in the Copenhagen Museum, opened to the public in 1819, On the basis of three successive ages of Stone. Bronze, and Iron. His pupil and successor,. J. J. A. Worsaae, whowed the correctness of this museum arrangement by observed stratigraphy in the Danish peat bogs and barrows (funerary mounds). Low lake levels in Switzerland in the mid 1950s permitted the excavation of the prehistoric Swiss lake dwellings, and here again the theory of a succession of technological states was confirmed.

Darwin's *Origin of Species* implied a long past for man, and the acceptance of the idea of human evolution in the last four decades of the 19th century created a climate of thought in which archaeology flourished and that led to great advances in the unfolding of the full story of man's development.

In his *Pre-historic Times.* Lubbock expanded the three age system of Thomsen and Worsaae to a four-age system, dividing the Stone Age into Old and New periods (Paleolithic and Neolithic). In the last quarter of the 19th century remarkable Paleolithic discoveries were made in France and Spain: these included the discovery and authentication of actual works of sculpture and cave paintings from the Upper (late) Paleolithic Period (c. 30,000-c, 10,000 BC). When Marcellino de Sautuola discovered the cave paintings at Altamira, Spain (1875-80), most experts refused to believe they were Paleolithic; but after similar discoveries at Les Eyzies in France around 1900, they were accepted as such and were recognized as one of the most surprising and exciting archaeological discoveries. A succession of similar finds has continued in the 20th century. The most famous of these was at Lascaux, France, in 1940.

During the last quarter of the 19th century, Gen. A. H. Pitt-Rivers excavations of prehistoric and Roman sites at Cranborne Chase, Dorset, laid the foundations of modern scientific archaeological field technique, which was later developed and improved in England and Wales by men such as Sir Mortimer Wheeler and Sir Cyril Fox.

20th-century developments. The 20th century has seen the extension of archaeology outside the areas of the Near East, the Mediterranean, and Europe to other parts of the world. In the early 20s, excavations at Mohenjo-Daro and Harappa, in present Pakistan, revealed the existence of the prehistoric Indus civilization. In the late 20s, excavations at An-yang in eastern China established the existence of a prehistoric Chinese culture that could be identified with the Shang dynasty of early Chinese records.

The Stone Age has been described and studied through out the world; among the most sensational discoveries are those of L. S. B. Leakey, who found stone tools and skeletal remains of early man dating back 2,000,000 years in importance has brought to light early Neolithic site at Jericho in Palestine; Hassuna, Iraq; Catalhuyuk, Turkey; and elsewhere in the Near East. Establishing the origins of agriculture in that region.

Serious archaeological work bean later in American than Europe, but as early at 1784 Thomas Jefferson has excavated mounds in Virginia and made careful stratifraphical observations. The 20th century has seen a great increase in archaeological knowledge about prehistoric America; two startling advances were the discovery of the origin of domesticated crops (including maize) in Central America and of the Olmec civilization of Mexico (100-300 BC) the oldest of the New World civilization and probably the parent of all the others.

The enormous growth of archaeological work has meant the establishment of archaeology as an academic discipline; few important universities anywhere in the world are now without professors and departments of archaeology. There are now a very large number of scholarly journals in the field, as well as a considerable body of popularized books and journals that attempt to bridge the gap between professional and layman.

Fieldwork. *Preliminarly work.* Some archaeologists call everything they do out-of-doors fieldwork, but other distinguish between fieldwork, in a narrower sense, and excavation. Fieldwork, in the narrow sense, consists of the discovery and recording of archaeological sites and their examination by methods other than the use of the spade and the trowel. Sites hitherto unknown are discovered ate reconnaissance is an essential part of archaeological fieldwork.

In Europe, a study of old records and place-names may lead to the discovery of long-forgotten sites. The mapping of new and old sites is an essential part of archaeological survey. This process has been brought to a very high standard of perfection, both in the marking of archaeological sites on ordinary topographical maps and in the production of special period maps. The distribution map of artifacts, especially when studied against the background of the natural environment, is a key method of archaeological study.

The formerly earthbound archaeologist has been greatly helped by the development of aerial photography. The application of aerial photography to archaeological investigation began in a small way during World War I, as a side effect of military reconnaissance, and was given further impetus by World War II: the photographic intelligence departments of all the combatant nations were extensively staffed by archaeologists, who then carried their expertise and enthusiasm into the postwar years. The University of Cambridge now has its own department of air photography under J. K.S. St Joseph: using its own pilot and aircraft, it flies photographic missions over Ireland., Great Britain. Denmark, and The Netherlands. The number of new sites discovered each year by aerial photography is very large. Some of these are surface sites, especially partly destroyed sites that show up well in special conditions of light, as in early morning or late evening. But many are sites that could not be found on the ground and that show up in aerial photographs as variations in soil color or in the density of crop.

Archaeological reconnaissance may be advanced from

ordinary surface or aerial methods in a wide variety of ways. A very simple method is tapping the ground to sound for substructures and inequalities in the subsoil. Deep probes have made it possible to trace walls and ditches. The Lerici Foundations of Milan and Rome has had great success with this methods since its development of he Nistri periscope, first used in 1957 in an Etruscan tomb in the cemetery of Monte Abbatone. The periscope is inserted into the burial chamber and can photograph the walls and contents of the whole tomb.

Other modern techniques that have been applied to archaeological prospecting employ electricity and magnetic fields (geophysical prospecting). A method of electrical prospecting had been developed in large-scale oil prospecting: this technique, based on the degree of electrical conductivity present in the soil, began to be used by archaeologists in the late 1940s and has since proved very useful. Magnetic methods of prospecting detect buried features by locating the magnetic disturbances they cause: these were introduced in 1957-58 and use such machines at the proton magnetometer, the proton gradiometer, and the fluxgate gradiometer,. An American expedition discovered the site of Sybris in Sicily by magnetic prospecting. Electromagnetic methods have been in use only since 1962; they employ developments of the concepts used in mine detectors. Instruments such as the pulsed induction meter and the soil-conductivity meter detect magnetic soil anomalies, but only if the features are fairly shallow.

Excavation. Excavation is the surgical aspect of archaeology: it is surgery of the buried landscape and is carried out with all the skilled craftsmanship that has been built up in the last hundred years since Schliemann and Flinders view of their purpose, as planned, rescue; or accidental. Most important excavations are the result of a prepared plan-that is to say, their purpose is to locate buried evidence about an archaeological site. Many are project oriented: as, for example, when a scholar studying the life of the pre-Roman, Celtic-speaking Gauls of France may deliberately select a group of hassle forts and excavate them, at s=Sir Mortimer Wheeler did in northwestern France in the years before the outbreak of World War II. But many excavations, particularly in the heavily populated areas of central and northern Europe, are done not from choice but from necessity. Gravel digging, clearing the ground for airports, quarrying, road widening and building, the construction of houses, factories, and public buildings frequently threaten the destruction of sites known to contain archaeological remains. Emergency excavations then have to be mounted to rescue whatever knowledge of the past can be obtained before these remains are obliterated forever. Partial destruction of cities in western Europe by bombing during World War II allowed rescue excavations to take place before rebuilding. A temple of Mithras in the City of London. Viking settlements in Dublin and at Arhus, Denmark, and the original 6th century BC Greek settlement of Massalia (Marseille) were discovered in this way. An extension of the runways at London Airport led to the discovery of a pre-Roman Celtic temple there.

The role of chance in the discovery of archaeological sites and portable finds is considerable. Farmers have often unearthed archaeological finds while ploughing their fields. The famous painted and engraved Upper Paleolithic cave of Lascaux in southern France was discovered by chance in 1940 when four French schoolboys decided to investigate a hole left by an uprooted tree. They widened a smaller shaft at the base of the hole and jumped through to find themselves in the middle of this remarkable pagan sanctuary. Similarly, the first cache of the Dead Sea Scrolls was discovered in 1947 by a Bedouin looking for a stray animal. These accidental finds often lead to important excavations. At Barnenes, in north Brittany, a contractor building a road got his stone from a neighbouring prehistoric cairn (burial mound) and, in so doing, discovered and partially destroyed a number of prehistoric burial chambers. The French archaeologist P. R. Giot was able to halt these depredations and carry out scientific excavations that revealed Barnenes to be one of the most remarkable and interesting prehistoric burial mounds in western Europe.

All forms of archaeological excavation require great skill and careful preparation. Years of training in the field, first as an ordinary digger, then as a site supervisor, with spells of work as recorder, surveyor, and photographer, are required before anyone can organize and direct an excavation himself. Most museums, universities, and government archaeological departments organize training excavations. The very words dig and digging may give the impression to many that excavation is merely a matter of shifting away the soil and subsoil with a spade or shovel; the titles of such admirable and widely read books as Leonard Woolley's *Spadework* (1953) and *Digging Up the Pst (1930)* and Geoffrey Bibby's *Testimony of the Spade* (1956) might appear to give credence to that view. Actually, much of the work of excavation is careful work with trowel., penknife, and brush. It is often the recovery of features that are almost indistinguishable from no archaeological aspects of the buried landscape; one example of this is the recovery of mud-brick walls in Mesopotamia: another is the tracing of collapsed walls of dry stone slabs in a cairn in stony country in the southwest Midlands of England. Sometimes it is the recovery of features of which only ghost traces remain, like the burnt-out bodies from the buried city of Pompeii, or the strings of a harp that were found among the furnishings of Mesopotamian tombs at Ur.

Because of the damage he may cause by inexperience and haste, the untrained amateur archaeologist often hinders the work of the professional. Amateur archaeology is forbidden in many countries by stringent antiquity laws. At the same time, it is certainly true that nonprofessionals have made important contributions in many areas of archaeology. Occasionally, an amateur does make an important discovery the further excavation of which can then be taken over by trained professionals. Such was the case at Sutton Hoo in Suffolk in 1939, when work begun by a competent amateur was taken over by a team of experts who were able to uncover a great Angio-Saxon burial boat and its treasure, without doubt the most remarkable archaeological find ever made in Britain.

There are, of course, many different types of archaeological sites, and there is no one set of precepts and rules that will apply to excavation as a whole. Some sites, such as temples, forts, roads, villages, ancient cities, palaces, and industrial remains, are easily visible on the surface of and industrial remains, are easily visible on the surface of the ground. Among the most obvious archaeological sites that have yielded spectacular results by excavation are the huge men-made mounds (tells) in the Near East, called in Arabic *lital,* and in Turkish *tepes or huyliks.* They result from the accumulation of remains caused by centuries of human habitation on one spot. The site of the ancient cities of Troy and Ur are examples. Another type concities of closed sites such as pyramids, chambered tombs, barrows (burial mounds), sealed caves, and rock sheiters. In other cases there are no surface traces, and the outline of suspected structures is revealed only by aerial or geophysical reconnaissance as described above. Finally, there are sites in cliffs and gravel beds, where many Paleolithic finds have been made.

The wide range of techniques employed by the archaeologist vary in their application to different kinds of sites. The opening of the tomb chmber in an Egyptian pyramid is, for example. A very different operation from the excavation of a tell in Mesopotamia or a barrow grave in western Europe. Some sites are explored provisionally by sampling custs known as sondages. Large sites are not usually dug out entirely, although a moderate-sized round barrow may be completely moved by excavation. Whatever the site and the extent of the excavation, one element of the technique is common to all digs, namely, the use of the greatest care in the actual surgery and in the recording of what is found by word, diagram, survey, and photography,. To a certain extent all excavation is destruction, and the total excavation of a site subsequently engulfed by a housing estate or gravel digging is total destruction. This is why the archaeologist's field notes and his published report become primary archaeological documents. They are not themselves, strictly speaking, archaeological facts: they are the excavator's interpretation of what he saw, or thought he saw, but this is the nearest the discipline can ever get to archaeological facts as established by excavation. The really great excavators leave such a fine records of their digs that subsequent archaeologists can re-create and reinterpret what they saw and found. Tod delay publishing the results of an excavation within a reasonable time is a serious fault from the point of view of archaeological method. An excavation is not complete until the printed report is available to the world. Often the publication of the report takes as long as, or much longer than, the actual work in the field.

When a site like the Palace of Minos at Knossos or the city of Harappa in Pakistan has been excavated and the excavations are over, the excavator and the antiquities service of the country concerned have to face the problem of what to do with the excavated structures. Should they be covered in again, or should they be preserved for posterity, and if preserved, what degree of conservation and restoration is permissible ? This is the same kind of problem that arises in connection with the removal of antiquities from their homeland to foreign museums, and there is no generally accepted answer to it. These problems remain to beset archaeology: should Sir Arthur Evans have reconstructed the Palace of Minos at Knossos ? Should the art treasures of ancient Greece and Egypt, now in western European museums, be returned ? There is no simple, straightforward, overall answer to these difficult questions.

Underwater archaeology. Underwater archaeology is a branch of reconnaissance and excavation that has been developed only during the 20th century. It involves the same techniques of observation, discovery, and recording that are the basis of archaeology on land, but adapted to the special conditions of working underwater. It is obvious that no archaeologist working on submarine sites can get far unless he is trained as a diver. Helmeted sponge divers have made most of the important archaeological discoveries in the Mediterranean. The French scientist Jacques Yves Cousteau developed the self-contained breathing apparatus known as the scuba, of which the most commonly used type is the aqualung. Couteau's work at Le Grand Congloue near Marseille was a pioneer underwater excavation, as was the work of the Americans Peter Throckmortion and George Bass off the coast of southern Turkey. In 1958 Throckmorton found a graveyard of ancient ships at Yassi Ada then discovered the oldest shipwreck ever recorded, at Cape Gelidonya- a Bronze Age shipwreck of the 14th century BC. George Bass of the University of Pennsylvania worked on a Byzantine wreck at Yassi Ada from 1961 onwards, developing the mapping of wrecks photogram metrically with stereophotogrpahs and using a two-man submarine, the "Asherah". Launched in 1964. The "Asherah" was the first submarine ever built for archaeological investigation.

Interpretation. Excavation often seems to the general public the main and certainly the most glamorous aspect of archaeology; but fieldwork and excavation represent only a part of the archaeologist's work. The other part is the interpretation in cultural and historical contexts of the facts established by chance, by fieldwork, and by digging- about the material remains of man's past. This task of interpretation has five main aspects.

Calssification and analysis. The first concern is the accurate and exact description of all the artifacts concerned. Classification and description are essential to all archaeological work, and as in botany and zoology, the first requirement is a good and objective taxonomy. Second, there is a need for interpretive analysis of the material from which artifacts were made. This is something that the archaeologist himself is rarely equipped to do; he has to rely on colleagues specializing in geology, petrology (analysis of rocks), and metallurgy. In the early 1920s, H. H. Thomas of the Geological Survey of Great Britain was able to show that stones used in the construction of Stonehenge (a prehistoric construction on Salisbury Plain in southern England) had come from the Prescelly Mountains of north Pembroke shire: and he established as a fact of prehistory that over 4,000 years ago these large stones had been transported 200 miles from west Wales to Salisbury Plain. Detailed metrological analysis of the material of Neolithic polished stone axes have enabled archaeologists to establish the location of prehistoric ax factories and trade toutes. It is also now possible, entirely on a metrological basis, to study the prehistoric distribution of obsidian (a voleanic glass used to make prirmitive tools).

In the third place, the archaeologist, having dealt with the material of his artifacts by classification and taxonomy, and with its physical nature by petrology and metallurgy., turns to the remaining information he can get from his colleagues in the natural sciences. These tell him the environmental conditions in which the people he is studying lived; he now sees his material remains not as isolated artifacts but in the context of their original environments.

Dating. Having analyzed his discoveries according to their from, material, and biological association, the archaeologist then comes to the all-important problem of dating. Many material remains of man's past have no dating problem: they may be, like coins, or most coins., self-dating, or they may be dated by man-made dates in written records. But the great and difficult part of the archaeologists work is dating material remains that are not themselves dated. This can be done in one of there ways. Sometimes an object from another culture, the date of which is known (e.g., in the case of pottery, by its style_, is found at a previously undated site. Then, using the relative dating principle (see below) the archaeologist reasons that the material found with the imported object is contemporary with it. Conversely, an object from an undated culture may be found at a site whose date is known. Thus nonliterate communities can be dated by their contact with literate ones. This technique is known as cross dating; it was first developed by Sir Flinders Petrie when he dated Palestinian and early Greek (Aegean) sites by reference to Egyptian ones. Much of the prehistoric chronology of Europe in the Neolithic, Bronze, and Early Iron ages is based on cross dating with the ancient Near East.

Aside from cross dating, the archaeologist faced with material in a site having no literate chronological evidence of its own has two other ways of dating his material. The first is relative, the second absolute. Relative dating merely means the relation of the date of anything found to the date of other things found in its immediate neighbourhood. As has already been described, this method also plays a part in cross dating. Stratigraphy is the essence of relative dating. The archaeologist observes the accumulation of deposits in a gravel pit, a peat bog, in the construction of a barrow, or in accumulated settlements in a tell, and, like the geologists who introduced the principles of stratigraphy in the late 18th and early 19th centuries, he can see the succession of layers in the site and can then establish the chronology of different levels of layers relative to each other. In the excavation of a great tell like Ur or Troy the relative chronology of the various levels of occupation is the first thing to be established. Some archaeologists, even until quite recent times, have mistakenly supposed that depth below ground level is itself an indication of antiquary.

But even in properly observed and recorded stratigraphic levels there is often doubt, and the questions arises: are all the artifacts and human remains found in the same level contemporary ? Is it possible that there could have been later intrusions that have been difficult to distinguish in the field ? The analysis of the fluorine content of bones has been very helpful here. Recognized as a valuable technique by French scientists in the 19th century, it was developed in England by K. P. Oakley in the 1950s. If bones in apparently the same geological of archaeological level have markedly different fluorine content, then it is clear that there must be interference- for example, by a later burial, or by deliberate planting of faked remains, as happened in the case of the Piltdown "Man" hoax in England.

Absolute man-made chronology based on king lists and records in Egypt and Mesopotamia goes back only 5,000 years. For a long time archaeologists searched for an absolute chronology that went beyond this and could turn their relative chronologies into absolute dates. Clay-varve counting seemed to provide the first answer to this need for a nonhuman absolute chronology. Called geochronology by Baron GerardDe Geer, its Swedish inventor, this method was based on counting the thin layers of clay left behind by the melting glaciers when the European Ice Age came to an end. This gave a chronology of about 18,000 years- three times as on as the man-made chronology based on Egyptian and Mesopotamian king lists. Thus, absolute dates could be established for artifacts from the Late Paleolithic Period, the whole of the Mesolithic Period, or Middle Stone Age, and much of the Early Neolithic Period.

Dendrochronology, the dating of trees by counting their growth rings, was first developed for archaeological purposes by A. E. Douglass in the United States. The application of this methods to archaeology depends, obviously, on the use in antiquity of old datable trees in the construction of houses and buildings. It has been possible by dendrochronology to date prehistoric American sites as far back as the 3rd and 4th centuries BC.

The greatest revolution in prehistoric archaeology occurred in 1948, when Willard F. Libby, at the University of Chicago, developed the process of radioactive carbon dating. In this method, the activity of radioactive carbon (carbon-14) present in bones, wood, or ash found in archaeological sites in measured. Because the rate at which this activity decreases in time is known, the approximate age of the material can be determined by comparing it to carbon-14 activity in presently living organic matter. There have been problems and uncertainties about the application of the radioactive carbon method, abut, although it is less than perfect, it has given archaeology a new and absolute chronology that goes back 40,000 years.

Following the revolutionary discovery of radioactive carbon dating, other physical techniques of absolute dating were developed, among them potassium argon dating and dating by thermo luminescence. Potassium-argon dating had made it possible to establish that the earliest tremains of man and his artifacts in East Africa to back at least 2,000,000 years, and probably further.

Historical judgements. The last and most important task of the archaeologist is to transmute his interpretation of the material remains he studies into historical judgments. When he is dealing with medieval and modern history he is often doing no more than adding to knowledge already available from documentary sources: but even so his contribution is often of great importance: for example, in relation to the growth and development of towns and the study of deserted medieval villages. When has is dealing with ancient history and prehistory, he is making a contribution of the greatest importance and often one that is more important than that of purely literary and epigraphically sources. For the prehistoric period, which now appears to stretch from 2,000,000 years ago to about 2000 BC, archaeological evidence is the only source of knowledge about human activities. But prehistoric remains have always been the most difficult to interpret, precipsely because there are no written records to aid in the task now, with exact dating techniques at his disposal, the prehistory is becoming more like the historical archaeologist and is concerned with the periodization and the historical contexts of his finds.

Bibliography

Bibliography, the art of science of the description of books, has acquired special importance in the 20th century because of the need for effective organization of the records of human communication in the face of the enormous growth of publishing activity and the need, especially in undeveloped countries, for informed access to the world's scientific and technical information. It has been said that without bibliography, the records of civilization would be an uncharted chaos of miscellaneous contributions to knowledge, unorganized and inapplicable to human needs.

The word bibliography, in its literal sense, derived from the Greek *bibliographic* (2nd century AD), means the writing of books, and it was so defined in the 17th century; since the 18th century, it has been used to denote the systematic description and history of books. It is now commonly used in two widely divergent, though basically connected senses: (1) the listing of books, arranged according to some system (in this sense it is called enumerative, systematic, or descriptive bibliography); and (2) the study of books as material objects; *i.e.* the study of the material of which books are made and the manner in which they are put together (in this sense commonly called critical bibliography). It is the function of bibliography to provide useful information for the student, in the one case supplying him with information about material for study, in the other helping him to establish the place of a book (or a piece of writing) in an author's production and its quality and authenticity as a text for study.

Descriptive bibliography. The tasks of the compiler of a bibliography are (1) to find out what books on a particular subject exist; (2) to describe them item by item; and (3) to assemble the resulting entries into useful arrangements for reference and study. The need for lists of this king arises as soon as the number of books in any subject is too great to be easily remembered. Among the earliest lists of books are those compiled by certain writers as guides to their own books- *e.g.* the celebrated physician Galen compiled, in the 2nd century AD, a description in subject order of his own writings *(De properties libris liber,* "A Book about My Own Books"); the Venerable Bede attached at the end of his *Ecclesiastical History of the English People,* in 731, an autobiographical note with a list of his writings; Erasmus also published a catalog of his own writings in narrative from in 1423. Early bibliographies, however, the last decade of the 4th century AD. The idea of attaching lists of works to lives of ecclesiastical writers was adopted by St, Jerome in his *De viris illustribus* ("Concerning Famous Men").

The invention of printing in the 1440s made possible the rapid multiplication of books, thereby increasing the need for guides to the resultant literature and also bringing about changes in the manner of compilation. The earliest substantial bibliography after the invention of printing was that Johannes Tritheim, abbot of Sponheim in the diocese of Mainz, who in *Liber de scriptaribus ecclestasticis* ("Book About Ecclesiastical Writers", 1494) included in chronological order, with a alphabetical index, about 1,000 ecclesiastical writers and their books. In 1545 a German-Swiss writer and naturalist. Conrade Gesner, who has been known as the father of bibliography, published his *Bibliotheca Universalis (Universal Bibliography)* of all Latin, Greek, and Hebrew writers, living and dead: this was followed three years later by a second volume, *Pandectarum sive Partitionum universalium libri XXI* ("Twenty-one Book of Encyclopedia or Universal Divisions (of Knowledge)", in which the entries, arranged alphabetically in the earlier volume, are rearranged under 21 subject headings. Although gesner was not the earliest descriptive bibliographer, his attempts at universality and classification earn him his fame. Gesner's idea of universality remained an ideal until recent times; in the face of the formidable problems of size, cost, and complexity, however, it has receded into the background of human aspirations. The Institute International de Bibliographies, founded in 1895 in Brussels by Henry Lafontaine and Paul Otlet with the object in periodicals, arranged according to a specially designed system of classification, the Universal Decimal Classification (UDC), has assembled a card catalog of many millions of entries; but because of the immense bulk of the material and the growing cost of compilation, it is unlikely that it will ever reach the goal set by its founders. The hopes for universal bibliographies have been largely replaced by the published catalogs of such great comprehensive libraries as the British Museum (1961-67), the Bibliotheque Nationale (beginning in 1897), the Library of Congress, and most promising of all, the United States National Union Catalogue, maintained in the Library of Congress and, in the early 1970s, in the course of being printed in an estimated 625 volumes. Investigations were (early 1970's) being made into the problems involved in programming and computerizing such catalogs, and if the complexities of programming Multilanguage material can be solved, if the necessary financing can be found, and if world operation in the production and standardization of catalog entries can be assured, it seems possible that the ideals of the Brussels Institute may yet to some extent be realized.

Gesner's achievement was remarkable; besides writing many other books, including a number of bibliographical works, his universal bibliography with its appendix (1555) describes and classifies some 15,000 works by about 3,000 writers and provides alphabetical and subject indexes. His contemporaries turned their attention to detailed bibliographies of writings on particular subjects or in particular languages or relating to particular countries or places. Thus, John Bale, bishop of Ossory, published the earliest national bibliography, *illustrium maioris britanntae scriptorum ...summarium* ("Summary of the Writings of the Most Eminent Britons", 1548), which lists British writers chronologically and sets out their writings in detail. The vastly improved extended second edition of this work, *Scriptorum illustrium majoris Brytanniae ...catalogus* (1557), acknowledges Bale's indebtedness to John Leland. Henry VIII's library keeper and antiquary, who had made an antiquarian tour through England in 1534-42 and had made a survey of the writings of British authors. Other national bibliographies followed, such as those of the Italian Antonio Francesco Doni, *La Libratiadel Doni Fiorentino Nella quale sono scritu tultl gl'autori vulgart* ('Library of ...All Secular Authors", 1550; 2nd theologian cornelius Loos. *Illustrum Germaniae scriptorum catalogus* (1582); the French bibliographer Francois Grude de la Croix due Maine. *Premier Volume de la bibliotheque dud Sieur de la Croix du Maine* ("The First Volume of the Library of ..."1584). The catalogs of the German book fairs held in Frankfurt and Leipzig each spring and autumn, beginning in 1564 and continuing until 1749, while not bibliographies in the strict sense, were nevertheless widely used as foundation material by early German bibliographers.

I'ypes of descriptive bibliographies. Most countries now have national bibliographies, in a majority of cases published officially by the national library and based on copies of national publication deposited in accordance with provisions of copyright acts. Notable exceptions are the United States and The Netherlands, whose national bibliographies are published commercially: East Germany, whose *Deutsche Nationalbibliogrpahie* is published by the Deutsche Bucherei at Leipzig, an organization maintained since 1913 by German publishers; and the United Kingdom, whose *British National Bibliography* is polished by a council representing libraries, publishers, and book sellers. These national bibliographies aim at, and attain , a high degree of completeness and promptitude. The *British National Bibliography* (beginning in 1950), for example, is published weekly and cumulated quarterly and annually: it is arranged in a classified order according to the decimal classification of the U. S. librarian Melvil Dewey, with a alphabetical index of authors, titles, and subjects. The *Bibliographies de la France* (beginning in 1931) is published in to parts: (1) commercial publications, published weekly and (2) publications of societies and institutions, published semi-monthly. The West German *Deutsche Bibliographies* (beginning in 1947) is published weekly, with author and catchword index: this work has been published by computer since the beginning of 1968 the first such work to be so produced.

Bibliographies of books published in particular countries are of great value to students. Outstanding examples of such bibliographies are Charles Evans, *American Bibliography* (1903-34), covering the period 1639-1799 *A Short Title Catalogue of Books Printed in England. Scotland and Ireland, and of English Books Printed Abroad, 1475-1640)* complied by A. W. Pollard and G. R. Redgra e (1926 : revised and enlarged 2nd ed., 3 vol. 1972-82). While not strictly bibliographies, the British Museum catalogs of its holdings of pre-1600 books from several European countries are similarly valuable because of the richness of the museum's collections.

Personal bibliographies my consist of no more than a simple list of an author's works: e.g. those attached to articles in the *Dictionary of National Biography*. But they may be more elaborate - e.g. Ebisch and L. L. Schucking. *A Shakespeare*

Bibliography (1931 : supplement 1937); Michael Sadleir. *Trollope; A Bibliography* (1928); Bertha Collidge State. *Maria Edgeworth* (1937). Personal bibliographies are sometimes based on private collections- e.g. *A Stevenson Library* (1951-64) based on the collection of Edwin J. Beinecke: T. J. Wise's bibliographies, based on his own collections, of tennyson. Swinburne, and others. A variant of personal bibliography consists of a narrative setting out an author's works with a comprehensive account of the circumstances surrounding the composition and publication of each work. An example is J. E. Norton. *A Bibliography of the works of edward Gibbon* (1940).

Subject bibliographies vary in size, scope, and method, according to the purpose they are designed to serve. The following are examples of bibliographies that aim at offering comprehensive guidance: A and a, de Backer and A. Carayon, *Bibliotheque de la Compagnie de Jesus.* ("Library of the Society of Jesus, "9 vol: new ed. 1890-1909); F. W. Bateson. *The Cambridge Bibliography of English Literature* (4 vol. 1940; New ed. 1970 ff.); *Bibliography of British History;* C. Read, *Tudor Period, 1485-1603* (1933). G. Davies, *Stuart Period, 1603-1714* (1928). S. Pargellis and D. J. Medley, *The Eighteenth Century, 1714-1789* (1951); P. Caron. *Manuel pratique pour l'etude de la Revolution Francaise* ("Practical Manual for the Study of the French Revolution" : latest ed. 1947); F. C. Dahlmann and G. Waitz, *Quellenkunde der deutschen geschichte,* ("Published Sources of German History ": 9th ed. 1931-32): W. W. Greg. *A Bibliography of the English Printed Drama to the Restoration* (4 vol. 1939-59); G. Lanson. *Manuel bibliographique de la litterature francaise moderne* ("bibliographic Manual of Modern French Literature": latest ed. 1947): F. Madan, *The Early Oxford press* (3 vol. 1895-1931): L. N. Malcles. *Les sources du travail bibliographique* ("Sources of Bibliographic Work," 3 vol. 1950-52). Bibliographies of publications on particular subjects, frequently including articles on periodicals, are numerous and cover many branches of human knowledge and interests.

The proliferation of bibliographies has led to the publication of bibliographical guides- bibliographies of bibliographies. Among these should be mentioned *Bibliotheca*

Bibliographical (1866), compiled by Julius Petzholdt, librarian of the Royal Library at dresden. Germany and *World Bibliography of Bibliographies* (5 vol.; 1965-66) by Theodore besterman. Guidesto current publications in a number of subject fields are published annually sometimes in narrative from - *e.g. The Year's Work in English Studies (1921 ff.)* and *The Year's Work in Libraianship* (1929 ff. : later title *Five Year's Work in Librarianship,* 1959 ff.)- and sometimes in list from- *e. g. International Bibliographies des Buch und Bibliothekswesens* ("International Bibliogrpahy of Book and Library System". 1926-41).

Methods of compilation. The method of compiling a bibliography and the amount of detail included vary according to the author's purpose, his view of the importance of the subject, and his knowledge of it. The task of compiling a bibliography of any subject is a matter for a specialist in that subject. Having determined his objective and what material exists, the author must proceed to describe and arrange it as usefully for his purpose as he can. To ensure that the descriptions are accurate and consistent, they should be made from the works themselves. If, for any reason, this is impossible, the source of the information given should be stated.

For most bibliographies it is usually necessary to given only the author, short title, place of imprint, and date; but these should be transcribed accurately from the book or article. Notes may be added on the scope and quality of the text and the location of a copy. In an author bibliography a chronological arrangement is often adopted, enabling the user to follow the development of the author's work. In such cases, later editions are listed with the earliest edition but additional mention is made at the appropriate chronological point. Subject bibliographies may be arranged in a systematic order to bring out the features important for the author's purpose, or a recognized classification system, such as the Dewey Decimal Classification of Universal Decimal Classification, may be used.

Full description are often given for early or rare books

and for detailed author bibliographies. Elaborate rules have been evolved for compiling such descriptions, which made it possible for a skilled bibliographer to reconstruct from the text before him the makeup and appearance of a book. Such description include information about the details of publication, number of copies printed, price, and binding. Semi-facsimile transcriptions are sometimes given, illustrating the various types of font used and the spacing of the title page. Modern methods of reproduction, however, make it possible to reproduce title pages photographically and thus obviate the use of such expedients. Which in any case are not entirely satisfactory. The use of reproductions, however, has certain disadvantages, such as high cost and difficulty of layout, and more important, reproductions themselves may be misleading, especially when the quality of the printing and paper of the original are poor. In 17th-century printing, for example, it is sometimes difficult to distinguish a mark of punctuation from a flaw in the paper, and a reproduction may give a wrong impression. If facsimiles are used, they should be as carefully edited as the text and the source of the reproduction should be stated.

The advent of computers and the application of data-processing techniques to library procedures such as cataloging have great potential value in bibliography. If a catalog is maintained in machine-readable from, it can be printed out in a number of different arrangements, or a variety of sublistings can be produced, with a relatively small increase in costs over the cost of printing the original arrangement. This method depends on the planning of requirements in advance and on the work of the programmer. It is thus possible for specialized lists, taken from the contents of a particular library, to be made available to a wide range of users. The best known and most highly sophisticated retrieval project of this kind is the Medlars project (Medical Literature Analysis and Retrieval System), which has as its main objective the publication of the *Index Medicus* (a monthly) listing of current articles form about 2,300 biomedical journals throughout the world) but which also supplies printed listings on particular subjects in the field or medicine.

The full benefit of these methods will accrue when it is economically and administratively possible to contemplate the storage of the enormous amounts of information available in the large comprehensive libraries.

In 1968 the Library of congress began the production and distribution of cataloging data in machine-readable from. The scope of this enterprise was limited initially to monographic works in the English language, but with the intention of expanding the coverage to include other languages. The creation of the machine record of material already in the library before 1968, which is necessary if a full system of machine-readable records is to be created, was being investigated both in the Library of Congress and elsewhere in other large comprehensive libraries. The problems likely to cause most difficulty are the magnitude of the data storage. Clearly such costly and complex operations have to be related to a realistic assessment of the benefits to be derived there from. Such assessments are in keeping with an interest, current in the early 1970s, in research library management. The rapid rise in library costs has emphasized the need for libraries, particularly large research libraries, to study whether and how they can apply accepted management techniques to the fuller exploitation of the bibliographical riches of their own institutions.

Critical bibliography. A valuable approach to the study of English literature, particularly, though not exclusively, of the 27th and 18th centuries, was developed about the turn of the 20th century out of a concern with Shakespearean texts in general and in particular with the nature and authority of the so-called quarto texts and their relation to the text printed in the First Folio, Editors had previously tended to assume that all the early texts of Shakespeare had equal authority and that it was perfectly proper to select readings which, in their view, improved the text of the author. The earlier editors were handicapped, in addition, by their ignorance of printing and book production in Shakespeare's time and by a lack of understanding of the nature of the texts they were dealing with. The change that took place stemmed from a variety with. The change that took place stemmed from a variety of causes, of which the most important were probably two: (1) the close association in studies of English literature, especially drama, of three eminent scholars. A. W. Pollard. R. B. McKerrow, and W. W. Greg, all of them interested in bibliography: and (2) the remarkable progress made by Robert Proctor, a colleague of Pollard's in the British Museum, in the study of inclinable, the name given to books printed in the first 50 years after the invention of printing (*i.e.* before 1501). The earliest printed books display the very individual characteristics of their printers in the type used, the typesetting, and the layout of the page, and it was found that, by studying these characteristics, useful deduction could be made about the place of individual books in a printer's total production and hence their approximate dates: in cases in which books contained no indication of the printer, it was often possible, using the same means, to assign a book to a particular printer. Important stages in the study of these earliest printed books, which has always been prized for their early date, their great aesthetic quality, and their rarity, were marked by a study of William caxton. England's earliest printer, by william Blades, *The Life and Typography of William Caxton* (1861-63), in which typographical details were used to arrange Caxton's publications in chronological order; and by the work of a great antiquarian scholar and librarian. Henry Bradshaw, who made a special study of 15th century books printed in the Netherlands. Bradshaw laid down an important principle: let the book speak for itself. This new method was still more widely applied by Robert Proctor, who succeeded in allotting the large collections of incunabula in the British Museum and the Bodleian Library at Oxford to places of origin, by countries and towns, and to printers. Proctor's work firmly established this method of study, and the definitive catalog of the incunabula in the British Museum, which he began, demonstrated the valuable results that can be obtained by the meticulous examination of all the features of a book - paper, type, makeup, ornamentation, sewing, binding, manuscript notes, and marks of ownership.

It was against this background and, applying these methods to the literary and dramatic work of English authors of the 16th and 17th centuries, that Greg. Mckerrow, and Polilard developed what is now called critical, or analytical, bibliography, which has been succinctly described as the study of books as tangible objects. By using the evidence of the physical features of books, it was often found possible to arrive at conclusions about the place of a book in an author's production that are beyond the scope of literary judgment.

One of the earliest and most illuminating examples of the application of this method concerns the question of the priority between the two 1609 issues of Shakespeare's play *Troilus and Cressida*. These differ in the preliminary matter: the title of one describes the play as having been acted at the Globe Theatre: in the other, the title page makes no mention of a production of the play, and an epistle to the reader stresses this fact by stating that the piece had never been "clapper-clawed with the plames of the vulger." Literary considerations would suggest that the latter issue was the earlier. An examination of the books themselves. However, shows that the title page of the former is in its original state, while the latter's original title page had been cut away and two leaves substituted, containing the new title page and the address to the reader, thus demonstrating, without question, the order of the two.

In his edition of Beaumont and Fletcher's *Elder Brother* (1905), Greg similarly provided an irrefutable demonstration of the correct chronological order of the two quarto editions of 1637. In Ql an improperly adjusted quad or space lead had produced a mark above the line before the word "young" in Act 1, scene 2, line 72, which was mistaken by the compositor printing Q2 for an apostophe and printed as such. Hence, Q2 was shown to have been printed from Q1 and not from the author's manuscript.

The success of such demonstrations led to a much more detailed study of the physical features of books and the bibliographical deductions that can be made from them. The methods of critical bibliography have been substantially developed and have been widely applied to books of later periods, and it has been shown that, even in the sophisticated machine age, careful bibliographical examination has a significant role to play in determining the reliability of an author's text and the place of a book in an author's production.

The method was spectacularly displayed in the exposure or a number of alleged first editions of poems, essays, and other minor productions of well-know 19th century authors, such as the "Reading" sonnets of Elizabeth Barrett Browning-*i.e.* an edition of these sonnets, dated 1847, with Reading as the place of imprint. These books, more than 50 in number, were shown, in *An Enquiry into the Nature of Certain Nineteenth Century Pamphlets* (1934), by John Carter and Graham Pollard, to have been printed on kinds of paper, made from esparto grass or wood pulp, known not to have been in use at the dates shown on the title pages, and using printing types that were first cut much later.

It has been clearly demonstrated that machine-printed books of the 19th and 20th centuries produce textual problems rivalling those found in hand-printed books. While additional procedures and the principles governing the interpretation of bibliographical evidence remain the same, new printing methods force bibliographers to devise new procedures to deal with the new problems presented to them.

A widely used guide for the bibliographical study of English book up to the end of the 17th century is provided by R.B. McKerrow's *Introduction to Bibliography for Literary Students* (1927). The publications of the Bibliographical Society of London, especially its journal. *The Library* (1889 ff.), contain valuable information about bibliographical methods and their application. A useful account of the work of the society and a study by F. P. Wilson of that application of bibliographical techniques to the works of William Shakespeare "Shakespeare and the New Bibliography," is contained in *The Bibliographical Society, 1892-1942. Studies in Retrospect,* (1945). Other bibliographical journals that may be usefully consulted are :

The Papers of the Bibliographical Society of America (1904 ff.), the *Publications* of the *Oxford Bibliographical Society* (1922 ff.), and the *Transactions of the Cambridge Bibliographical society* (1949 ff.), *Studies in Bibliography* (1948 ff.), published by the Bibliographical Society of the University of Virginia, is especially valuable.

Chronology

Chronology, in the broadest, is a time scale, a method of ordering time. This article, however, deals mainly with systems of chronology used by different peoples in recording their history.

Scientific chronology, which seeks to place all happenings in the order in which they occurred and at correctly proportioned intervals on a fixed scale, is used in many disciplines and can be utilized to cover vast epochs. Astronomy, for example, measures the sequence of cosmic phenomena in thousands of millions of years: geology and palaeontology, when tracing the evolution of the earth and of life, us similar epochs of hundreds or thousands of millions of years. Geochronology reckons the more distant periods with which it deals on a similar scale: but it descends as far as human prehistoric and even historic times, and its shorter subdivisions consist only of thousands of years. Shortest of all are the chronological scales used in the recording of human events in a more or less systematic and permanent manner. These vary in scope, accuracy, and method according to the purpose, degree of sophistication, and skill of the peoples using them, as do the calendrical systems with which they are inextricably bound up. For further details see the article CALENDAR.

It is difficult to fix ancient historical chronologies in relation to scientific chronology. The terms of reference of ancient peoples were vague and inconsistent when judged by modern standards, and many of their inscriptions and writings have inevitably disappeared. The gaps in their records are increasingly filled in and their inconsistencies removed by the results of archaeological excavation. Guided by these findings, scholars can confirm, refute, or amend chronological calculation and dating by radioactive carbon content are also helpful in the work or fixing ancient chronologies.

Chinese. Chinese legendary history can be traced back to 1697 BC, the first year of Huang Ti (Chinese : Yellow Emperor), who was followed by many successors and by the three dynasties, the hsia, the Shang, and the Chou, Recent archaeological findings, however, have established an authentic chronology beginning with the Shang dynasty, though the exact date of its end remains a controversial topic among experts. The so-alled oracle-bone inscriptions of the last nine Shang kings (1324-1122 BC) record the number of months up to the 12th, with periodical additions of a 13th month, and regular religious services on the summer and winter solstice days, all of which indicates the adjustment of the length of the lunar year by means of calculations based on the solar year. Individual days in the inscriptions are named according to the designations in the sexagenary cycle formed by the combination of the 10 celestial stems and 12 terrestrial branches. Every set of 60 days is divided into six 10-day "weeks". Also recorded are numerous eclipses that can be used to verify the accuracy of the Shang chronology. In the oracular sentences of the last Shang King, Chou Hsin, the year of his reign is referred to as "the King's nth annual sacrifice."

From the beginning of the following (Chou) dynasty, the word year was etymological identical with "harvest". Thus, "King X's *n*th harvest" meant the *n*th year of his reign. The lunar month was then divided into four quarters- Ch'u-chi. Tsai-sheng pa, Chi-sheng pa and Chi-szu pa- and the practice of using the 60 cyclical names for the days was continued. Thus, in the inscription on a chou bronze vessel, a typical date would read; "In the King's nth harvest, in the *n*th quarter of *n*th month, on the day X-y. etc."

The tradition of recording events by referring to the king's regional year continued until 163 BC, when a new system, *nien-hao* ("regin-period title"), was introduced by Emperor Han Wen Ti of the Former Han dynasty (206 BC - AD 8).

Thereafter, every emperor proclaimed a new *nien-hao*for his reign at the beginning of the year following his accession (sometimes as emperor redesignated his *nien-hao* on special occasions during his reign). A typical date in the *nien-hao* system might read, "the third year of the Wan-li reign period" (Wan-li san nien). In order to date any event in Chinese history, it is necessary to convert the year in the period of the designated *nien-hao* into the Western calendar.

During the Chou dynasty the civil year began with the new moon, which occurred before or on the day of the winter solstice. This "first month" of the Chou year (Chou *cheng)* was equivalent to the 11th month of the Hsia year (Hsia *cheng)* or to the 12th month of the Shang year. The first emperor. Shih Huang-ti, of the short-lived Ch'in dynasty (221-206 BC) made the year begin one month earlier- *i.e.* with the lunation (the period of time between one new moon and the next) before the one in which the winter solstice occurred. The Ch'in year was continuously used until 104 BC, when Emperor Han Wu Ti promulgated the T'ai-chçu calendar by reverting to the Hsia *cheng-i.e.* by taking the third month of the Chou year, or the second lunation after the winter solstice, as the first month of the civil year. This lunar year (or Hsia *cheng)* was used till the last day of the Ch'ing, or Manchu, dynasty (1644-1911/12). when in 1911 the first republic was founded, the solar year was officially adopted, but successive governments kept the *nien-hao* tradition by referring any date to the number of years since the establishment of the republic-*e.g.* 1948 was chronicled "the 37th year of the republic". In 1949, when the People's Republic of China was proclaimed, the old system was replaced by the Gregorian calendar.

Japanese. The principal chronicles describing the origins of Japanese history are the *Nihon shoki* ("Chronicle of Japan") and the *Koji-ki* ("Record or Ancient Matters"). The *Nihon shoki* (compiled in AD 720) assembled information in a chronological order of days, months, and years starting several years before 660 BC. which was the years of the enthronement of the first Japanese emperor, who was posthumously named Jimmu. the *Koji-ki* (compiled in AD 712) related events under the reign of each emperor without a strict chronological order. Sometimes the *Koji-ki* gave the years of emperors' deaths and their ages at death. This information is different from that recorded in the *Nihon shoki.*

Native Japanese scholars since Fujiwara Teikan in the 18th century have realized that the *Nihon shoki* was historically inadequate and different from the *Koji-ki,* at least insofar as the chronological information is concerned. They have suggested that the foundation year of Japan was 600 years later than stated in the *Nihon shoki.* Naka Michiyo (late 19th century) argued with minute detail about the question of Japanese chronology. His ideas were supplemented by those of other Japanese scholars, who pointed out that: (1) the reigns of the earlier Japanese emperors as stated in the *Nihon shoki* are unnaturally long: (2) the date of the enthronement of the emperor Jimmu should be reconsidered: (3) a chronological gap exists between the *Nihon shoki* and contemporary Chinese and Korean chronicles. In comparision with Korean chronicles, they argued, the *Nihon shokiI* has created an intentional expansion of chronology- *i.e.* the entries about the empress Jingo and the emperor Ojin can be identified with historical facts relating to the Korea of the 4th and 5th centuries and therefore must be placed 120 years later than mentioned in the *Nihon shoki.* when comparing the *Nihon shoki* with Chinese chronicles, one finds the chronological gap somewhat reduced. The Chinese chronicles provide information about the tributes sent individually by five Japanese "kings" to Liu-Sung and Southern Chí during the 5th century. There are still question about the identification of these kings, but it is generally accepted that the "king" written in Chinese character as Wu must be the Japanese emperor yuryaku. By the late 5th century the gap between Japanese and Korean records, on the one hand, and Japanese and Chinese, on the other hand, disappears.

The intentional expansion of the chronology of the *Nihon shoki* was adopted by its compilets, who identified Queen Himiko (Pimihu) of Yamatai of the chronicle of Wei China with the Empress Jingo of Japanese legend.

The method of designating a year by the *Ian-shi* (sexagenary cycle) appears to have begun about the reign of emperor yuryaku, when, as mentioned above, the gap between the continental and Japanse chronologies was bridged. The inscription on remarkable copper images of Buddha cast just after the period of Prince Shotoku's regency (AD 593-621) bears a *nengo (nien-hao,* or reign year title), although not a strictly authorized one. It was at this time that the Chinese luni-solar calendar system was adopted by the imperial court in 645. Since 701, when the second title. Taiho, was adopted, the reign-year system has been continuously used in relation to the emperors' reigns up to the present day. In medieval times Japanese chronology underwent a remarkable evolution; (1) when the Imperial dynasty split into two courts (1336-92), two series of *nengo* began to be used; (2) during the Ashikaga period some private *nengo* again appeared; (3) some dates of the authorized "central" calendars did not correspond with those of locally compiled calendars. Moreover, military leaders would not accept some of the new *nengo.* Minamoto Yoritomo, for example, did not use the *nengo* that was adopted by the emperor Antoku and the Taira regime, and Ashikaga Mochiuji and Ashikaga Shigeuji did not use the official, respectively Eikyo and Kosho, *nengo.*

In the Tokugawa period (1603-1867), gaps between central and provincial calendars disappeared, especially after the establishment of the jokyo calendar, the first native calendar compiled in Japan, instead of the Chinese-based one that was in use until this period. On January 1, 1873, Emperor Meiji adopted the Gregorian calendar in use in the West and at the same time adopted the "Japanese Era," with Emperor Jimmu as its founder, in addition to the *nengo* system.

Indian. Two kinds of chronological systems have been used in India by the Hindus from antiquity. The first requires the years to be reckoned from some historical event. The second starts the reckoning from the position of some heavenly body. The historical system, the more common in modern times, exists side-by-side with Muslim and international systems successively introduced.

Reckonings dated from a historical event. The inscriptions of the Buddhist king Asoka (*c.* 265-238 BC) give the first epigraphically evidence of the mode of reckoning from a signs' consecration (*abhiseka).* In these inscriptions (Middle Indian language in India or Greek and Aramaean) in what is now Qandahar. Afghanistan) the dates are indicated by the number of complete years elapsed since the kings's consecration. But the earlier existence of a reckoning of duration of reigns and dynasties is evidenced by the testimony of the Greek historian Metatheses, who in 302 BC was the ambassador of Seleucus I Nicator, founder of the Seleucide Empire, to the court of Candragupta Maurya, Ashoka's grandfather. According to Metatheses, the people of the Magadha kingdom, with its capital Pataliputra (Patna), kept very long dynastic lists, preserved in the later Sanskrit Puranas (legends of the gods and heroes) and later Buddhist and Jain chronicles. They generally indicate, in years or parts of years, the duration of each reign.

Similar records of other periods and regions exits, and a relative chronology may be established. Unfortunately, it is not always possible to connect them with any absolute chronology, the precise dates of the reigns given being still unsettled. For example, in the Scythian period of the history of northern India, several inscriptions are dated from the beginning of the reign of Kaniska, the greatest king of the Asian (Kushan) invaders, but his dates are still uncertain (Ad 78, 128-129, 144 etc., have been suggested for the beginning of a Kaniska era).

Other records give regional years than can be linked with absolute chronology through other date- *e.g.* those of several rulers of the Rastrakuta of the Deccan.

The dynastic eras, founded by several rulers and kept up or adopted by others, are also numerous. The most important were the Licchavi era (AD 110), used in ancient Nepal; the kalacuri era (AD 248), founded by the Abhuri king Isvarasena and first used in Gujarat and Maharashtra and later (until the 13th century) in Madhya Pradesh and as far north as

Uttar Pradesh; the Valabhi era (AD 318, employed in Saurastra and the Gupta era (AD 320), used throughout the Gupta Empire and preserved in Nepal until the 13th century. Later came the era of the Thakur dynasty of Nepal (AD 395), founded by Amsuvarman; the Harsa era (AD 606), founded by Harsa (Harsavardhana), long preserved also in Nepal; the western Calukya ear (AD 1075), founded by Vikramaditya VI and fallen into disuse after 1162; the Laksmana era (AD 1119), wrongly said to have been founded by the king Laksmanasena of Bengal and still used throughout Bengal in the 16th century and preserved until modern times in Mithila; the Rajyabhisekasaka or Maratha era (1674), founded by sivaji but ephemeral.

Later, instead of the beginning of a reign or of a dynasty, the death of a religious founder was adopted as the starting point of an era. Among Buddhists the death of the Buddha and among the Jains the death of the Jina were taken as the beginning of eras. The Jain era (*virasamyat)* began in 528 BC. Several Buddhist sects (no longer existing in India) adopted different dates for the death (Nirvana) of the Buddha. The Buddhist era prevailing in Ceylon and Buddhist Southeast Asia begins in 544 BC.

Historical events, now obscure, were the basis of the two most popular Indian eras: the Vikrama and the Saka.

The Vikrama era (58 BC) is said in the Jain book *Kalakacaryakatha* to have been founded after a victory of King Vikramaditya over the Saka. But some scholars credit the Scytho-Parthian ruler Azes with the foundation of this era. It is sometimes called the Malava era because Vikramaditya ruled over the Malava country, but it was no confined to this region, being widespread throughout India. The years reckoned in this era are generally indicated with the word *vikramasamyat*, or simply *samyat*. They are elapsed years. In the north the custom is to begin each year with Caitra (March-April) and each month with the full moon. But in the south and in Gujarat the months with the new moon; in part of Gujarat, the new moon of Asadha (June-July) is taken as the beginning of the year. To reduce Vikrama dates to dates

AD, 57 must be sutracted from the former for dates before January 1 and 56 for dates after.

The Saka, or Salivahana, era (AD 78), now used throughout India., is in the most important of all. It has been used not only in many Indian inscriptions but also in ancient Sanskrit in inscriptions in Indo-China and Indonesia. The reformed calendar promulgated by the Indian government from 1957 is reckoned by this era. It is variously alleged to have been founded by King Kaniska or by the Hindu King Salivahana or by the satrap Nahapana. According to different practices, the reckoning used to refer to elapsed years in the north or current years in the south and was either solar or luni-solar. The luni-solar months begin with full moon in the north and with new moon in the south. To reduce Saka dates (elapsed years) to dates AD, 78 must be added for a date within the period ending with the day equivalent to December 31 and 79 for a later date. For Saka current years the numbers to be added are 77 and 78. The official Saka year is the elapsed year, starting from the day following that of the vernal equinox. A normal year consists of 365 days, while the leap year has 366. The first month is Chaitra, with 30 days in a normal year and 31 in a leap year; the five following months have 31 days, the others 30.

A Nepalese era (AD 878) of obscure origin was commonly used in Nepal until modern times. The years were elapsed, starting from Karttika, with months beginning at new moon. Another era, the use of which is limited to the Malabar Coast (Malayalam-speaking area) and to the Tirunelveli district of the Tamil-speaking area, is connected with the legend of the hero Parasurama, an avatar (incarnation) of the god Vishnu. It is called the Kollam era (AD 825). Its years are current and solar: they start when the Sun enters into the zodiacal sign of Virgo in north Malabar and when in enters into Leo in south Malabar. It from (176 BC. Thus, Ad 825 would have been the first year of the era's third millennium.

Eras based on astronomical speculation. During the period of elaboration of the classical Hindu astronomy, which was definitively expounded in the treatises called *stddhantas* and by authors such as Aryabhata I (born AD 476), Varahamihira, Brahmagupta (7th century AD), etc. were developed the ancient Vedic notions on the cycle of years, embracing round numbers of solar and lunar years together. On the one hand, greater cycles were calculated in order to include the revolutions of planets, and the theory was elaborated of a general conjunction of heavenly bodies at O longitude after the completion of each cycle. On the other hand, cosmologists speculated as to the existence of several successive cycles constituting successive periods of evolution and involution of the universe. The period calculated as the basis of the chronology of the universe was the *mahayuga,* consisting of 4,320,000 sidereal years. It was divided into four *yugas,* or stages, on the hypothesis of an original "order" (*dharma)* established in the first stage, the Krta *yuga,* gradually decaying in the three others, the Treta, Dvapara, and Kali *yugas.* The respective durations of these four *yuga* were 1,728,000, 1,296,000, 864,000, and 432,000 years. According to the astronomer Aryabhata, however, the duration of each of the four *yugas*was the same *i.e.* 1,080,000 years. The basic figures in thee calculations were derived from the Brahmanical reckoning of a years of 10,800 *muhurta* (see CALENDAR: *The Hindu calendar),* together with combinations of other basic numbers, such as four phases, 27 *naksutrus,* etc. The movement of the equinoxes was at the same time interpreted not as a circular precession but as a liberation (periodic oscillation) at the rate of 54 seconds of are per year. It is in accordance with these principles that the calculation of the beginning of the Kali *yuga* was done in order to fix for this chronology a point starting at the beginning of the agreed world cycle. Such a beginning could not be observed, since it was purely theoretical, consisting of a general conjunction of alanets at longitude O, the last point of the *naksatra* Revati (Pisces). It has been calculated as corresponding to February 18,3102 BC (old style), O hour, and taken as the beginning of the Kali era. In this era, the years mostly reckoned as elapsed and solar or luni-solar.

In Hindu tradition the beginning of the era was connected

with (1) events of the Mahabharata war: (2) King yudhisthira's accession to the throne; (3) 36 years later, King Pariksit's consecration; (4) Lord Krishna's death. Its years are still regularly given in Hindu almanacs.

An era resting upon a fictitious assumption of a complete 100-year revolution of the Ursa Major, the Great Bear (*saptarsi)*, around the northern pole was the Saptarsi, or Laukika, era (3076 BC), formerly used in Kashmir and the Punjab. The alleged movement of this constellation has been used in Purana compilations and even by astronomer for indicating the centuries.

Two chronological cycles were worked out on a basis or the planet Jupiter's revolutions, one corresponding to a single yea of Jupiter consisting of 12 solar years and the other to five of Jupiter's years. The second, the *brhaspaticakra,* starts, according to different traditions, from AD 427 or from 3116 BC. Before Ad 907 one year was periodically omitted in order to keep the cycle in concordance with the solar years. Since 907 the special names by which every year of the cycle is designated are simply given to present years of the almanac.

Side-by-side with Hindu and foreign eras adopted in India, several eras were created in the country under foreign influence, chiefly of the Mughal emperor Akbar: Bengali San (AD 593), Amli of Orissa and Vilayati (AD 592). Fasli (AD 590, 592 or 593 according to the district), and Sursan of Maharashtra (599).

Egyptian. At the end of the 4th millennium BC, when King Menes, the first king of a united Egypt, started his reign, the ancient Egyptians began to name each year by its main events, presumably to facilitate the dating of documents. These names were entered into an official register together with the height of the Nile during its annual inundation. Short notes at first, the year names developed into lengthy records of historical and religious events, especially of royal grants to the gods. These lists grew into annals, which were kept during the entire history of Egypt so that later kings could, after important events, consult the annals and ascertain whether a comparable occurrence had happened before.

Unfortunately, thee annals are lost. Only fragments from the 1st to the 5th dynasty (c. 3100-c. 23345 BC) are preserved, copied on stone. These fragments, however, are in such poor condition that they raise more chronological problems than they solve.

The Egyptian priests of the Ramessid period (c. 1300 BC: see below) copied the names and reigns of the kings from Menes down to their time from the annals, omitting all references to events. Even this king list would have given a safe foundation of an Egyptian chronology, but the only extant copy, on a papyrus now kept at the Museo Egizio in Turin, has survived only in shreds, entire sections having been lost. Extracts from this king list, which name only the more important kings, are preserved in the temples of the kings Seti I and Ramses II at Abydos and on the wall of a private tomb at Saqqarah (now in the Egyptian Museum), but they give little help in chronological matters.

When the Greeks began to rule Egypt after the conquest of Alexander the Great, King Ptolemy II Philadelphus, hoping to acquaint the new ruling class with the history of the conquered country, commissioned Manetho, an Egyptian priest from Sebennytus, to write a history of Egypt in the Greek language. As Manetho had access to the ancient and reigns, especially during the first dynasties. The more he progressed in time, the more he added semihistorical traditions and stories as they were composed by the Egyptian priests to discuss moral problems in the disguise of a historical "novel". There had been, undoubtedly, fewer historical facts in Manetho's history than one might expect. But Manetho's work, too, is lost except for some excerpts used by Sextus Julius Africans and Eusebius in material used in part by George Syncellus in the 8th century AD. During copying and recopying, Manetho's text clearly suffered many change, unintentionally or by dynastes, for instrance, were enlarged when ome of the early Christian historians tried to equate King Menes with Adam. In addition, the excerpts were done carelessly. Therefore, Manetho's work, as handed down to us, is short of useless, Nevertheless, together with the fragments of the annals and of the king list of Turin, they create a framework of Egyptian chronology; so the division into dynasties was taken over from Manetho. But to achieve a continuous history of Egypt and to bridge the gaps left by the fragmentary state of the extant chronological material, scholars must turn to other means, particularly astronomical references found in dated texts. These are related principally to the rising of Sothis and to the new moon.

Theoretically, the Egyptian civil year began when the Dog Star, Sirius (Egyptian Sothis), could first be seen on the eastern horizon just before the rising of the Sun (*i.e.* 19/20of July). As the civil calendar of the ancient Egyptians consisted of 12 months (each of 30 days) and five odd days (called epagomenal days), the civil year was a quarter of a day too long in relation to the rising of Sothis, so that the new year advanced by one day every four years. New year's Day and the rising of Sothis coincided again only after approximately 1,460 years, the so-called Sothic cycle. Dated documents mentioning the rising of Sothis can be translated into the present calendar by multiplying the number of days elapsed since the first day of the year by four and subtracting this sum form the date of the beginning of the particular Sothic cycle. The dates for the start of each Sothic cycle are fortunately known because the Roman historian Censorinus fixed the coincidence of New Year's Day and helical rising of sothis in AD 139. Taking into account a slight difference between a Sothic year and a year of the fixed starts, the years, 1322, 2782, and 4242 BC are taken as starting points of a Sothic cycle.

There are six ancient Egyptian documents extant giving Sothis dates, but only three of these are of value. The oldest is a letter from the town of Kahun warning a priest that the heliacal rising of Sothis will take place on the 16th day of the 8th month of year 7 of a king who, according to internal evidence, is Sesostris III of the 12th dynasty. This date corresponds to 1866 BC, according to the corrected Sothic cycle. The next date is given by a medical papyrus writtèn at the beginning of the 18th dynasty. This date corresponds to 1866 BC, according to the corrected Sothic cycle. The next date is given by a medical papyrus written at the beginning of the 18th dynasty, to which a calendar is added, possibly to ensure a correct conversion of dates used in the receipts to the actual timetable. Here it is said that the 9th day of the 11th month of year 9 of King Amenhotep I was the day of the heliacal rising of Sothis- *i.e.* 1538 BC. This date, however, is only accurated provided that the astronomical observations were taken at the old residence of Memphis; if observed at Thebes in Upper Egypt, the residence of the 18th dynasty, the date must be lowered by 20 years- *i.e.* 1518 BC. The third Sothis date shows that Sirius rose heliacally sometime during the reign of Thutmose III, which lasted for 54 years, on the 28th day of the 11th month; so year 1'458 BC (point of observation at Memphis) or 1438 BC (point of observation at Thebes) must have belonged to the reign of this king. From these dates it is possible to calculate the absolute dates for the reigns of the 12th dynasty, as the durations of most of the reigns of the kings belonging to this dynasty are preserved on the king list of the Turin Papyrus. On the other hand, chronologists are able to compute the reigns of the kings of the 18th dynasty by utilizing the highest dates of their documents helped by the fact that the Egyptians sometimes identified a certain day as "exactly new moon", they reckoned new moon from the morning after the last crescent of the waning moon had become invisible in the east just before sunrise. As there is a 25 year lunar cycle, such ancient Egyptian moon dates could be calculated with a fair amount of certainty but of course only if the ancient Egyptians themselves observed this celestial phenomenon accurately. There is some doubt, however, as it is shown by the attempts of very competent scholars to convert these moon dates. Sometimes even moon dates given by the same papyrus contradict themselves; in another case, the date given by a document has to be amended to achieve a reasonable result. These and other examples show that ancient Egyptian statements on celestial phenomena, especially on new moons, tend to be inaccurate because of faulty or inexact observations. Therefore, every date given for a fixed reign should be used with caution as the astronomical observation on which it is based may be inexact. Sometimes they are controlled by synchronism with Babyionian. Assyrian, or Hittite king lists or, later on, by the close interconnections between Greek and Egyptian history. Sometimes even biographical data re helpful. The statements found on small steal inside the burial ground of the holy bulls of Memphis (Apis) register the dates of birth, enthronement, and death of these animals accurately. But the more time recedes, the more the chronology of the Egyptian history becomes uncertain, even when astronomical data are available. Up till now even carbon-14 data are of no great help, as uncertainties are mostly not greater than the standard deviations to be expected in a carbon-14 calculation.

Nevertheless, Egyptologists believe themselves to be on fairly firm ground when dating the beginning of the Ancient Kingdom (1st and 2nd dynasty) about 3090 BC, the beginning of the 11th dynasty at 2133 BC, and of the Middle Kingdom (12th dynasty) at 1991 BC. The New Kingdom started at 1567 or 1552 BC, depending on a choice for the first year of Ramses II of either 1290 BC or 1304 BC- one lunar cycle earlier. The following centuries still pose many chronological questions down to 664 BC, when Greek historiography took over.

Babylonia and Assyrian. *Mesopotamian chronology, 747 to 539 BC.* The source from which the exploration of Mesopotamian chronology started is a text called Ptolemy's Canon. This king list covers a period of about 1,000 years, beginning with the kings of Babylon after the accession of Nabonassar in 747 BC. The text itself belongs to the period of the Roman Empire and was written by a Greek astronomer resident in Egypt. Proof of the fundamental correctness of Ptolemy's Canon has come from the ancient cuneiform tablets excavated in Mesopotamia, including some that refer to astronomical events, chiefly eclipses of the Moon. Thus, by the time excavations beban, a fairly detailed picture of Babylonian chronology was already available for the period after 474 BC. Ptolemy's Canon covers the Persian and Seleucid periods of Mesopotamian history, but this section will deal only with the period up to the Persian conquest (539 BC).

The chief problem in the early years of Assyriology was to reconstruct a sequence for Assyria for the period after 747 BC. This was done chiefly by means of *limmu* or eponym, lists, several of which were found by early excavators. These texts are lists of officials who held the office of *limmu* for one year only and whom historians also call by the Greek name of eponym. Annals of the Assyrian kings were being found at the same time as eponym lists, and a number of these annals, or the campaigns mentioned in them, were dated by eponyms who figured in the eponym lists. Moreover, some of the Assyrian kings in the annals were also kings of Babylonia and as such were included in Ptolemy's Canon.

Good progress was therefore being made when, soon after 1880, two chronological texts of outstanding importance were discovered. One of these, now known as King List A, is damaged in parts, but the end of it, which is well preserved, coincides with the first part of Ptolemy's Canon down to 626 BC. The other text, *The Babylonian Chronicle,* also coincides with the beginning of the cannon, though it breaks of earlier than King List A. With the publication of these texts, the first phase in the reconstruction of Mesopotamian chronology was over. For the period after 747 BC, there remained only one serious lacuna- *i.e.* the lack of the eponym sequence for the last 40 years or so of Assyrian history. This had not been established by the early 1970s.

Assyrian chronology before 747 BC. German excavations at Ashur, ancient capital of Assyria, yielded further eponym lists. By World War I the full sequence of eponyms was known from about 900 to 650 BC. A further fragmentary list carried the record back to about 1100 BC, and on this basis Assyrian chronology was reconstructed with little error, back to the first full regional year to Tiglathpileser I in 1115 BC. Without another pony list, a king list was needed for substantial further progress. King lists found at Ashur proved disappointing. Those fairly well preserved did not include figures for the reigns, and those with figures were very badly damaged.

In 1933, however, an expedition from the University of Chicago discovered at Khorsabad, site of ancient Dur Sharrukin, an Assyrian king list going back to about 1700 BC. But for the period before 1700 BC the list is damaged and otherwise deficient, and Assyrian chronology prior to this date is still far from clear.

Before 747 BC it was the custom of the Assyrian kings to hold eponym office in their first or second regional year. Thus, in an eponym list, the number of names between the names of two successive kings usually equals the number of years in the reign of the first of the two kings. It would have been easy to compile a king list from an eponym list, and there is evidence that this Assyrian king list was compiled from an eponym list probably in the middle of the 11th century BC. As an eponym list is a reliable chronological source, since omission of a name entails an error of only one year, the king list, if based on one, will have preserved much of the structure of older eponym lists now lost. (Except for one fragment, no known cponym list goes back further than the beginning of the 11th century BC.)

Babylonian chronology before 747 BC. In the long interval between the fall of the last Sumerian dynasty C. 2000 BC and 747 BC there are two substantial gaps in chronology, each about two centuries long. The earlier gap is in the 2nd millennium, from approximately 1600-1400 BC, the later gap in the 1st millennium, from c, 943-747 BC. During these gaps the names of most of the king are known, as well as the order, but usually not the length of their reigns.

A means of checking the reliability of the Babylonian king list is provided by the chronicles, annals, and other historical texts that show that a given Assyrian King was contemporaneous with a given Babylonian king. There are no fewer than 15 such synchronisms between 1350 and 1050 BC, and, when the Babylonian and Assyrian king lists are compared, they all fit in easily. Only one of them, however, provides a close approximate date in Babylonian chronology.

This synchronism shows that the two-year reign of the Assyrian King Ashared-zeri. The Assyrian's dates are probably correct to within one year. Thus, if Marduk-shapik-zeri id dated so that equal proportions of his reign fall before and after that of Ashared-apil-Ekur a date is obtained for the former that should not be in error more than six year. This synchronism constitutes a key to the structure of Babylonian chronology by providing the base date for all the reigns in the interval c. 1400-943 BC for which the Babylonian king list gives figures. All the dates thus obtained a subject to the six-year margin of error.

These synchronism between Assyrian and Babylonian kings continue throughout the period that corresponds to the second gap in the Babylonian king list- from *c.* 943-747 BC. Since the Assyrian chronology in that period is firmly established, these synchronisms provide a useful framework of the structure of Babylonian chronology in that period.

The gap in the 2nd millennium BC, however, is not as easy to fill. The fact that the magnitude of the gap is uncertain constitutes the man problem in the chronology of the 2nd millennium BC and also affects the chronology of the preceding Sumerian period. The problem is not yet solved. Observations of the planet Venus made during the reign of King Ammisaduqa, less than 50 years before the end of the 1st dynasty of Babylon, permit only certain possible dates for his reign. Translated into dates for the end of the dynasty, the three most likely possibilities are 1651, 1595 and 1587 BC. The evidence is not yet conclusive and leaves uncertain what choice should be made among and leaves uncertain what choice should be made among the three. The chronology adopted here is based on the second of these dates for the end of the 1st Babylonian dynasty- *i.e.*, 1595 BC.

Prior to this gap in the 2nd millennium BC, there is period of five centuries with a well-established chronological structure. All the kings in the major city-state are known, as well as their sequence and the length of their reigns. Which sets of dates should be assigned to these reigns, however, depends on the date adopted for the 1st dynasty of Babylon.

This period of five centuries extends from the beginning of the 3rd dynasty of Ur to the end of the 1st dynasty of Babylon- *i.e.* on the chronology adopted here. 2113-1595 BC. During this period the Babylonians dated their history not by regional years but by the names of the years Each year had an individual name, usually from an important event that had taken place in the preceding year. The lists of these names, called year lists or date lists, constitute as reliable a source in Babylonian chronology as the eponym lists do in Assyrian chronology. One of the events which almost invariably gave a name to the following year was the accession of a new king. Hence, the first full regional year of a king was called "the year (after) NN became king". In Assyria the number of personal names in an eponym list between the names of two successive kings normally equalled the number of years in the reign of the first king, and, similarly, in Babylonia the number of year names between two year names of the above king nearly always equalled the number of years in the reign of the first king. Just as in Assyria, the eponym lists are almost certainly the source of the king lists, so in Babylonia the king lists are based on the year lists. Several of these king lists, compiled at a time when the year lists were still in use, survive. One gives the 3rd dynasty of Ur and the dynasty of Isin another gives the dynasty of Larsa. Both may be school texts.

The 3rd dynasty of Ur and dynasty of Isin also figure in the Sumerian king list, which reaches far back into the Sumerian period. The original version probably ended before the 3rd dynasty of Ur, but later scribes brought it up to date by adding that dynasty as well as the dynasty of Isin.

Jewish. The era at present in vogue among the Jews, counted from the creation of the world *(anno mundi:* abbreviated to AM), came into popular use about the 9th century Ad. Traceable indates recorded much earlier, this era has five styles conventionally indicated by Hebrew letters used as numerals and combined into mnemonics, which state the times of occurrence of the epochal mean conjunctions of *moladim* (seem CALENDAR : *Middle Eastern calendar systems :*

The Jewish calendar) or the orders of intercalation in the 19 years cycle or both. The respective epochs of these styles fall in the years 3762-3758 BC, inclusive, By about the 12th century AD the second of the mentioned styles, that which is in use at present, superseded the other styles of the era *anno mundi.*

The styles of this era arise from variations in the conventional rabbinical computation of the era of the creation. This computation, like hundreds of other calculations even more variable and no less arbitrary, is founded on synchronisms of chronological elements expressed in the terms of biblical and early postbiblical Jewish eras.

The biblical era *anno mundi* underlies the dating of events (mainly in the book of Genesis) prior to the Exodus from Egypt. This period of biblical chronology abounds in intractable problems caused by discrepancies between the Jewish and Samaritan Hebrew texts and the Greek version known as the Septuagint, by apparent inconsistencies in some of the synchronisms, and by uncertainties about the method of reckoning.

During the period from the Exodus to the founding of Solomon's Temple, the only continuous biblical era (chiefly in the remaining books of the Pentateuch) is the era of the Exodus. With regard to a crucial date expressed in this era- "In the four hundred and eightieth year after the people of Israel came out of the land of Egypt, in the fourth year of Solomon's reign over Israei, in the month of Ziv, which is the second month, he began to build the house of the Lord" (1 Kings 6M1)- there is again a discrepancy between the Hebrew text and the Septuagint. Other problems to be met with during this period are due to the obscurity of chronological data in the book of Judges and in I and II Samuel.

During the following period, the Bible uses the eras of the regional years of monarchs (the kings of Judah, Israel, and Babylon) and of the Babylonian Exile. These period of biblical chronology likewise poses numerous problems, also the result of apparent inconsistencies of the synchronisms- *e.g.* in the period from the accession of Rehoboam of Judah and of Jeroboam of Israel to the fall of Samaria "in the sixth year of Hezekiah (of Judah), which was the ninth year of Hoshea king of Israel" (II Kings 18M10) the reigns of the southern kingdom exceed those of the northern kingdom by 25 years.

The biblical data might be easier to harmonize if the occurrence of coregencies were assumed. Yet, as an ever variable factor, these evidently would not lead to the determination of the true chronology of this period. Scholars therefore seek additional information from sources outside the Bible- *e.g.* inscriptions on Assyrian monuments, which are dated by the so-called eponym lists. Substantial use also has been made of the data in the king list known as Ptolemy's Canon (compiled in the 2nd Christian century) commencing in 747 BC with the reigns of the Babylonian kings (see above *Babylonian and Assyrian)*. Scholars differ widely, however, in their interpretation of details, and numerous chronological problems remain unsolved. Only a few dates in this period can be fixed with any degree of confidence.

After the Babylonian Exile, as evidenced by the data in the Bible and the Aswan papyri, the Jews reckoned by the years of the Persian kings. The chronological problems of this period are caused by the apparent disorder in the sequence of events related in the biblical books of Ezra and Nehemiah and by the difficulty of identifying some of the Persian kings in question. For example, the King Artaxerxes of these books may stand for Artaxerxes I Longimanus (465-425 BC), for Artaxerxes II Mnemon (404-359/358 BC), or in the case of Ezra at any rate, for Artaxerxes III Ochus (359/358-338/337 BC.).

From the Grecian period onward, Jews used the Seleucid era (especially in dating deeds: hence its name Minyan Shetarot, or "Era of Contracts"). In vogue in the East until the 16th century, this as the only popular Jewish era of antiquity to survive. The others soon became extinct. These included, among others, national eras dating (1) from the accession of the Hasmonean princes (*e.g.* Simon the Hasmonean in 143/142 BC) and (2) from the anti-Roman risings ("era of the Redemption of Zion") in the years 66 and

131 of the Common (Christian) Era. Dates have also been reckoned from the destruction of the Second Temple (*le-hurban ha-Bavit*). The various styles of the latter, as also of the Seleucide era and of the era *anno mundi*, have often led to erroneous coversions of dates. The respective general styles of these eras correlate as follows: 3830 AM = year 381 of the Seleucid era = year 1 of the Era of the Destruction = year 69/70 of the Common (Christian) Era.

The earliest Jewish chronologies have not survived. Of the work of the Alexandrian Jew Demetrius (3rd century BC), which deduced Jewish historical dates from the Scriptures, only a few fragments are extant. In the *Book of Jubilees*, events from the creation to the Exodus are dated in jubilee and sabbatical cycles of 49 and 7 years, respectively. Scholars differ as to the date and origin of this book. The era of the creation therein is unlikely to have been other than hypothetical.

The earliest and most important of all Jewish chronologies extant is the *Seder 'olam rabba"* ("Order of the World"), transmitted, according to Talmudic tradition, by rabbi Yosi ben Halafta in the 2nd century AD. The author was possibly the first to use the rabbinic Era of the Creation. His chronology extends from the creation to Bar Kokhba in the days of the Roman emperor Hadrian (2nd century AD); but the period from Nehemiah to Bar Kokhba (*i.e.* from Artaxerxes I or II to Hadrian) is compressed into one single chapter. The persian phase shrinks to a mere 54 years. The smaller work *Seder'Olam cuta"* completes the *Rtabba"*. It aims to show the Babylonian exilarchs as lineal descendants of David.

Megillat ta'anit ("Scroll of Fasting"), although recording only the days and months of the year without the dates of the years, is nevertheless an important source for Jewish chronology. It lists events on 35 days of the year that have been identified with events in five chronological periods: (1) pre-Hasmonean, (2) Hasmonean, (3) Roman (up to AD 65), (5) the war against Rome (65-66), and (5) miscellaneous. The authors, or rather the last revisers, are identified with Zealots guided by Hananiah ben Hezekiah ben Gurion and his son Eliezer.

Greek. As the cities of ancient Greece progressed to their classical maturity, the need arose among them for a chronological system on a universally understood basis. In the archaic period, genealogies of local monarchs or aristocrats sufficed for the historical tradition of a given area, and events were associated with the lifetimes of well-known ancestors or "heroes". The *synoikismos* (founding of the united city) of Athens took place "in the time of These us", the Spartan ephorate (chief magistracy) was established "in the reign of King Theopomus", When the city-states adopted annual magistracies, the years were designated by the eponymousofficials "in the archonship of Glaucippus" or "when Pleistolas was ephor". This was the local usage throughout classical and Hellenistic Greece, the title of the magistrate varying in different cities. Sometimes tenure of a priesthood provided the chronological basis, as at Argos, where years were dated as the *n*th of the (named) priestess of Hera. The correctness of the series was a matter first of memory and later of careful record. The list of annual archons at Athens was known back to 683 BC (in modern terms). List of annual archons at Athens was known back to 683 BC (in modern terms). Lists of dynasties also amounted to recorded folk memory, and in all genealogical reckoning there is a point, for modern critics, at which acceptable tradition shades into myth. Corruption of the records was introduced through error or political design, and traditions often conflicted.

Chronology became subject to systematization when cities felt a national need for accurate clarification of their past. In literature the growth of historiography initiated a search for a method of dating that could be universally applied and acknowledged. In the 5th and 4th centuries, local historians used local magistracies as their framework: research was devoted to rationalization of conflicting traditions and production of definitive lists. Charon of Lampas us, perhaps in the early 5th century, compiled a record of Spartan magistrates; Hellanicus of Lesbos, author of the earliest history of Athens, wrote on the priestesses of argos. Lists of victors in the great Olympic games were valid for all Greece, pointing the way to the widely accepted reckoning by Olympiads (see below). The Athenran Philochorus was the latest (early 3rd century BC) of compilers of Olympionikai.

The 5th century historian Herodotus relied for his chronology principally upon the reckoning by generations used by his informants, conventionally accepted as showing three generations to a century. In some cases a 40 year, or other reckoning was used, and varying traditions sometimes produced difficulty of synchronism. Thucydides, writing "contemporary" history, recognized the chronological problems involved. He dated the beginning of the Peloponnesian War by the Athenian, Spartan, and Argive systems and thenceforward marked the passage of time by seasonal indications. Synchronization was not helped by the fact that the official year began at different times in different cities. In later historical writing the impossibility of accurately coordinating the Athenian and Roman years resulted in serious chronological difficulties.

The system of dating by Athenian archons came to be recognized outside Attica as of wider value, but, in the Hellenistic period, Alexandrian scholarship, represented especially by Eratosthenes of Cyrene, the "father of chronology", was instrumental in promoting the use of the Olympiads as an acceptable system, reckoning a four year period from each celebration of the Olympic Games. Timaeus of tauromenium (c. 356-260 BC) was the first historian to employ it, but it was little used outside historical writing. Aristotle had been concerned to identify the generation of the first Olympiad, accepted as 776 BC on modern reckoning. For convenience, the beginning of the Olympic year was equated with the summer solstice, when the Athenian year also began. This makes it generally necessary for a Greek year to receive a double date in modern terms (*e.g.* the death of the philosopher Epicurus in 271/270 BC). Eratosthenes' system produced table of dates, from which, for example, the fall to Troy could be dated to 1184/83 BC. The "Parian Marble" of 264/263 BC is an inscribed record of events from the time of Cecrops, first king of Athens, reckoning years between the date of the inscription, fixed by the Athenian archon, and each event concerned. Some cities inscribed lists of their eponymous magistrates: the Althenians were the first to do so c. 425 BC. A list from Sicilian Tauromenium originally spanned some 300 years. The regional years of the Hellenistic monarchs or the count from a fixed event (a city foundation or recondition) also provided acceptable chronological reckoning often useful for more than contemporary of local purposes.

The use of these chronological possibilities is best seen in historians using the annalistic method, of whom Diodorus Siculus is most notable. In the Christian period. Eusebius, followed by St. Jerome, began the work of reconciling all these indications to the Judaic tradition and produced the foundation of chronology in terms of the Julian calendar upon which modern historians have constructed their framework.

For modern scholarship the problem, in E. J. Beckerman's words is "how we know Caesar was assassinated on March 15, 44 BC". Before 480 BC, no date can be precise in terms of the Julian calendar unless confirmed by astronomical phenomena. Archaic chronology relies upon the typology of Corinthian potter in relation to the foundation dates for Greek colonies in Sicily implicit in Thucydides, book vi, Julian dates given for this period (*e.g.* for the tyranny of Peisistratus in Athens) stem from a complex combination of ancient chronographic tradition with modern archaeology, acceptable only with appropriate reserve. Literary tradition gives the succession of Athenian archons from 480 to 294 BC. The regional, era, and Olympiad years also provide dates within a 12 month period. Closer dating is seldom possible unless the sources give precise information in calendric terms, as occasionally in literature and regularly in Athenian and Egyptian public documents. Even these are not translatable into Julian months and days unless coordinated with knowledge of contemporary solar or lunar phenomena and of possible official interference with calendar.

Roman. The establishment of a sound chronology for Roman history, as for Greek, depends on the assessment of the evidence agailable, which falls into two categories literary and archaeological.

Literary evidence. Although by the late 3rd century BC the Greek mathematician Eratosthenes was working on the systematization of chronograph and a series of learned historians had used the documentary method- *e.g.* for Roman history. Timaeus of Tauromenium, to whom are probably due many of the synchronizations of Roman history with the Greek Olympiads unfortunately this tradition of documentation and concern for chronology did not immediately pass over into Roman historiography. According to Cicero in *De oratore,* the earliest roman historians did no more than "compile yearbooks- for example. Fabius picture in the late 3rd century BC. Luctus Calpurnius Piso in the 2nd, and the so-called Sullan annalists in the 1st. Of these authors it is possible to judge only at second hand, and only those of the 1st century were much used directly by the historians whose work survives in any quantity, notably Livy, dionysius, of Halicarnassus, and Diodorus Siculus. In these authors, as in other 1st century historians such as Sallust, there is little concept of documentation or research other than comparison of literary sources; for none was chronology a direct concern, and in many cases dramatic effectiveness took priority over fidelity to truth. Apart from the Greek Polybius, who treated the rise of Roman power in the Mediterranean from 264 to 146 BC. It was not until Cicero's time that the conception of historical scholarship developed in Rome. Cicero's friends Attics not only was concerned to draw up a chronological table in his *Liber annalis* but has undertaken research to that end, and the great scholar Marcus Terentius Varro and a little later the learned Marcus Verrius Flaccus produced a vast body of erudite work, nearly all lost. To this source must probably be ascribed the *fast Capitolini,* a list of magistrates from the earliest republic to the contemporary period, set up near the *regta* (the office and archive of the *pontifices,* or high priests), perhaps on the adjacent Arch of Augustus, at the end of the 1st century BC. This work, since it is based on inscriptions, is sometimes given precedence over literary evidence, but, since it is a compilation, it is still subject to serious error.

Sources used by Roman historians. The traditionally early extant bodies of law, such as the Twelve Tables from the early republic, were of little chronological value, and juristic *commentarti* were liable to mislead through their zeal for precedent, while Cicero, in spite of Polybius clam to have inspected early treaties preserved in the Capitol definitely states that there were no public records of early laws. S source frequently referred to is the *Annales maximi,* a collection made about 130 BC of the annual notices displayed on a white board by the *ponufices* and containing notes of food prices, eclipses, etc. Dionysius of Halicranassus implied that they gave a date for the foundation of the city but was reluctant to accept their authority; and one of the eclipses is referred to by Cicero as being mentioned also by Ennius, but unfortunately the number of the year "from the foundation of the city" is corrupt in the text. Although it is possible to calculate the dates of eclipses astronomically in terms of the modern era, it is difficult to link these to Roman chronology because of the uncertainly of the figures and because of the confused state of the Roman calendar before the Julian reform (see CALENDAR : *early calendar systems: The early Roman calendar).* Another difficulty is that the early records may have been burned in 390 BC when Celtic tribes sacked the city: also they would probably have been largely unintelligible unauthentic.

Livy quoted the 1st century annalist Gaius Licinius Macer as having found in the temple of Juno Moneta "linen rolls" giving lists of magistrates: but he also said that Macer and Quintus Aelius Tubero both cited the rolls for the consuls of 434 but gave different names. In any case, it is unlikely that the list could have been older than the temple, which dates from 344 BC. It is clear that the chief sources for the lists were the pedigrees of prominent Roman families, such as the

Claudii Marcelli. Fabii, and Aemilii, drawn up by Atticus; but Cicero and Livy agree that tendentious falsifications had in many cases corrupted the records, and other suspicious facts are the appearance of obviously later or invented *cognomina,* or third names, and of plebeian gentile names for the earliest period, when only patricians bore them. Many scholars, however, accept the general authenticity of the lists- one reason being the appearance in them of extinct patrician families- but prefer Livy's version to that of the Capitoline lists, which show signs of late revision, often give names in incorrect order, and contain other anomalies.

The question, therefore, remains whether Roman chronograph was dependent on the lists of magistrates or whether these wee adapted to fit other know dating. The apparent advantages of the existence of a terminal dates, the "foundation of the city", is issusory for Roman chronology, since it depended on back reckoning and was not agreed even in antiquity. Various ancient scholars each assumed a different date. Each computed his date by adding a different number of years of kingly rule from the foundation of the city to his estimate of the date of the foundation of the republic. This, is turn, was presumably computed by counting back over the yearly lists of magistrates. There may have been traditions about the intervals between certain events in early Roman history, but the frequently accepted reckoning of 244 years of kingly rule seems to be a calculation based only on the conventional 35 year generation for the rule of the seven legendary kings. Polybius claimed that the dating of the first republican consulship to 508/750, reckoned inclusively, and 752-751, exclusively (Cato's date). The chronological scheme worked the foundation of Rome was put in 754/753 and the beginning of the republic in 510/509. Varro's dates became standard for later Romans and are sometimes also used by modern scholars in a purely conventional sense. But it remains uncertain whether these wee "doctored" to synchronize with given dates or intervals, whether these were traditional or calculated in some other way. Anomalies such as Livy's five year anarchy 15 years after the Gallic invasion. Diodoruss repetition of magistrates names, and the "dictator years" in the lists are perhaps attempts to synchronize the various pedigrees.

Contribution of archaeology. Archaeology can provide many dates useful to the detailed study of Roman history, especially from coins and inscriptions, but, for the general scheme of early chronology, its value is largely negative. It shows, for example, that Rome evolved over a lengthy period and was not really "founded", though a "foundation" date might perhaps refer to the first common celebration of the septimontium, or festival of the seven hills: again, if that dating is dependent on the seven kings, archaeology shows that the tradition about them, though it may preserve genuine names and events, is largely legendary.

Dating after the 1st century BC. In this better documented period, dating to consul years, or later to the years of tribunician power of the emperors, are normally intelligible, despite a few notorious cruxes, although up to the Julian reform the state of the calendar has always to be taken into account. In parts of the empire, however, be taken into account. In parts of the empire, however, different eras were used- *e.g.* that of the Seleucids and from the 4th century AD dates were often calculated in terms of the years of the induction, a 15 year cycle connected with the levying of taxes, a method that continued in use for many centuries in spite of difficulties, such as lack of synchronization among the vinous provinces.

Christian. The Christian Eara is the ear now in general use throughout the world. Its epoch, or commencement, is January 1, 754 AUC (*ab urbe condita-* "from the foundation of the city [of Rome]"- *or anno urbis conditae-* "in the year of the foundation of the city"). Christ's birth was at first believed to have occurred on the December 25 immediately preceding. Years are reckoned as before or after the Nativity, those before being denoted BC (before Christ) and those after by AD (*anno domini,* "in the year of the Lord"). Chronologers admit no year zero between 1 BC and AD 1. The precise date of commencing the annual cycle was widely disputed almost until modern times. December 25, January 1, March 25, and Easter day each being favoured in different parts of Europe at different periods.

The Christian Era was invented by Dionysius Exiguus (*c.* AD 500- after 525), a monk of Scythian birth resident in Italy; it was a by-product of the dispute that had long vexed the churches as to the correct method of calculating Easter. Many churches, including those in close contact with Rome, followed 95 year tables evolved by Theophilus, bishop of Alexandria, and by his successor, St, Cyril; but some Western churches followed other systems, notably a 532-year cycle prepared for Pope Hilarius (561-468) by Victorius of Aquitaine. In 525, at the request of Pope St. John 1, Dionysius Exiguus prepared a modified Alexandrian computation based on Victorius' cycle. He discarded the Alexandrian era of Diocletian, rekoned from AD 384, on the ground that he "did not wish to perpetuate the name of the Great Persecutor, but rather to number the years from the Incarnation of Our Lord Jesus Christ."

Somehow Dionysius reckoned the birth of Christ to have occurred in 753 AUC, but the gospels state that Christ was born under Herod the Great- *i.e.* at the latest in 750 AUC. Dionysius' dating was questioned by the English saint Bede in the 8th century and rejected outright by the German monk' Region of Prum at the end of the 9th, Nevertheless, it has continued in use to the present day, and, as a result, the Nativity is reckoned to have taken place in or shortly before the year 5 BC, when Herod died.

The new chronology was not regarded as a major discovery by its author; Dionysius' own letters are all dated by the induction (see below). The use of the Christian Era spread through the employment of his new Easter tables. In England the era was adopted with the table at the Synod of Whit by in 664, But it was the use, above all by Bede, of the margins of the tables for preserving annalistic notices and the consequent juxtaposition of historical writing with calendrical computations that popularized the new era. Outside Italy it is first found in England (in a charter of 676) and shortly after in Spain and Gaul. It was not quickly adopted in royal diplomas and other solemn documents, however, and in the papal chancery it did not replace the induction until the time of John XIII (965-972). The era did not become general in Europe until the 11th century; in most of Spain it was not adopted until the 14th and in the Greek world not until the 15th.

Of the alternative chronologies used by Christians, the most important were : (1) the induction. (20 the Era of Spain, and (3) the Era of the Passion. The induction was a cycle of 15 years originally based on the interval between imperial tax assessments but during the Middle Ages always reckoned from the accession of Constantine, in 312 Years were given according to their place in the cycle of 15, the number of the indiction itself being ignored. This chronology was the most widespread in the early Middle Ages, but its use diminished rapidly in the 13th century, although public notaries continued to use it until the 16th. The Era of Spain was based on a Waster cycle that began on January 1, 716 AUC (38 BC), marking he completion of the Roman conquest of Spain. First recorded in the 5th century, it was in general use in Visigothic Spain of the 6th and 7th centuries and, after the Arab invasions, in the unconquered Christian kingdoms in the north of the Iberian Peninsula. It was abolished, in favour of the Era of the Incarnation, in Catalonia in 1180, in Aragon in 1350, in Castile in 1383, and in Portugal in 1422. The Era of the Passion, commencing 44 years after that of the incarnation, enjoyed a short vogue, mainly in 11th century France.

Muslim. Unlike earlier chronological systems in use before Islam. Islamic chronology was instituted so soon after the event that was to be the beginning of the Muslim era that no serious problems were encountered in its application. According to the most reliable authorities, it was "Umar I, the second caliph (reigned 634-644), who introduced the era used by the Muslim world. When his attention was drawn by Abu Musa al-Ash'ari to the fact that his letters were not dated, "Umar consulted with men at Medina and then ordered that the year of the *hijrah* (hegira), the Prophet's flight from Mecca to Medina, be taken as the beginning of an era for the Muslim state and community. According to the Muslim calendar, the *hijrach* took place on 8 Rabi' I, which corresponds to September 20, 622 (AD), in the Julian calendar. But, as Muharram had been already accepted as the first month of the lunar year, 'Umar ordered that (Friday) 1 Muharram (July 16, 622) be the beginning of the reckoning. It is generally accepted that this was done in AH 17 *(anno Hegirae.* "in the year of the hegira").

There are a few points in connection with this that deserve mention: first, there is no real agreement on the exact date of the *hijrah*- other dates given include 2 and 12 Rabi' I; second, the year in which 'Umar issued the orer in a point of contention- the years 16 and 17 are sometimes given; third, some people have ascribed the use of the chronology to the Prophet himself. According to some sources, the *hijrah* date was first used by ya'la ibn Umayyah, Abu Bakr's governor in Yemen. This sounds somewhat plausible because yemenis were probably used to affixing daes to their documents. There is, however, a consensus among workers in the field that 8 Rabi' I was the day of the *hijrah.* that 'Umar instituted the use of the date for the new era, and that this was done in AH 17. The choice of the *hijrah* as the beginning of the epoch has two reasons. On the one hand, its date had been fixe; on the other, 'Umar and his advisers must have recognized the importance of the migration- Islam had become, as a result, a religion and a state.

Before the introduction of the new epoch, the Arabs had been acquainted with chronologies used by their neighbours, the Seleucids and the Persians. In Yemen the practice of dating had been perfected to the extent that inscriptions who the day, the month, and the year. In Mecca the "year of the Elephant", supposedly coinciding with the birth of the Prophet, had been in use. For the period between the migration and the institution of the period between the Muslims of Medina resorted to aiming the year after local events- "the year of the order of fighting" and "they year of the earthquake", etc.

The lunar year was adopted by the Muslims for the new chronology. In this there was hardly any innovation insofar as Arabia was concerned.

The chronology introduced by 'Umar was adopted throughout the Muslim world, although earlier epochs continued in use in outlying provinces. Muslim historians annalists, and chroniclers met with difficulties when writing their book on pre-Islamic history. No practice had as yet developed for pre-*hijrah* dating: therefore, when writing about the history of various landlaws in pre-Islamic times. Authors resorted to the use of chronologies previously in existence there (*e.g.* Persian. Indian. Seleucid, Alexandrian). For the histories of the area under Islam, writers used only Muslim chronology, while non-Muslim authors (*e.g.* Bar Hebraeus) used the Seleucid and the *hijrah* dates when discussing events pertaining to provinces that had been Byzantine and therefore still had fairly large groups of Christians.

The ear of the *hijrah* is in official use in Saudi Arabia, the two Yemens, and in the Persian Gulf area. Egypt, Syria, Jordan, Morocco, Algeria. Libya, and Tunisia use both the Muslim and the Christian eras. Many Muslim countries, such as Turkey. Nigeria, and Pakistan, use the Christian Era.

Within the general uniformity of applying the *hijrah* era proper, there existed differences, some of which were the result of earlier pre-Islamic practices; others were the result of continuous contacts of Muslim countries with their European neighbours, with whom they had economic as well as political relations. An example of the former was the work of the "abbasid caliph all-Mu'tadid, who brought the Nowruz (Persian New Year's Day) back to date in keeping with the agricultural activities of the community. Mahmud Ghazan introduced the Khanian era in Persia in AH 701, which was a reversion to the regional chronologies of antiquity. It continued in use for some generations, then the ordinary *hijrah* era was reintroduced. A similar step was taken by Akbar when he established the Ilahi era, which began on Rabi II 963 (February 13, 1556), the date of his accession; the years were solar.

Two Muslim countries, Turkey and Iran, introduced more drastic changes into their chronology because of European influences.

In Turkey the Julian calendar was adopted in AH 1088 (AD 1676-77) and used solar months with *hijrah* dating. The year was officially called the Ottoman fiscal year but was popularly known as the marti year, after mart (Turkish for March), which was the beginning of the year. Under Mustafa Kemal Atarurk, the Gregorian calendar and the Christian Era were officialy adopted in Turkey (1929), Iran also adopted a solar year, the norms of the months in its calendar are Persian, and the era is still that of the *hijrah.*

Pre-Columbian American. *Mava and Mexioan.* The lowland Maya had a 365 day year formed of 18, months",. Each month consisted of 20 days, plus five "nameless" days, which the Maya considered an extremely dangerous and unlucky period and during which activities were kept to a minimum.. Leap days were not intercalated.

Reckoning was not by those years, but by *iuns* (360 days) and their multiples of 20: *katuns (20 tuns), baktuns* (400 *tuns). pictuns* (8,000 *tuns), calabtions* (160,000 *tuns).* and *kinchiltuns* (3,200,000).In *tun* comprised 18 *ulnals,* each of 20 *kins* (days), but these did not coincide with the equivalent divisions of the 365-day year. The Maya normally carved or wrote these in descending order; students transcribe them in Arabic numerals- *e.g.* 9,10,6,5.9 represents nine *baktuns,* ten *katuns,* six *uinals,* nine ikins.

With this system, current dates were related to the start of the Maya era, which, because of the Maya system of re-entering cycles marked both the end of 13 *baktions* (written 13,0.0.0.0) and the start of another cycle of *baktuns,* and perhaps commemorated a recreation of the world, the *baktun* about to enter being numbered 1 not 14, Because of the construction of the calendar, this start of the era happened to be day 4 Ahau falling on the eighth day of the month Cumku.

Such reckonings are called Initial Series, or Long Counts, the former because they usually stand at the start of an inscription (see CALENDAR). For example, the combination day 8 Muluc, falling on second of Zip (third month), recurs every 52 years, but the initial Series (here 9, 10, 6, 5, 9, 8 Muluc 2 Zip) pinpoints its position. The next occurrence, 52 years later, would be 9, 12, 19, 0, 9, 8 Muluc 2 Zip. Each until had its own glyph (or symbolic character), with appropriate number (normally a dot for 1 and bar for 5) attached.

A shorter dating system was by "Period Endings"- that is, by recording the ending of the current *baktun, katun,* or *tun.* Thus, day 13 Ahau and month position 13 Muan with 13 *tuns* added is an abbreviation of 9.17.13.0.0 13 Ahau 13 Muan, a combination that will not repeat for over 900 years (949 *tuns).* A still shorter but less precise method was to give the day and its number ending the current *katun.*

Several Maya dates were commonly linked to Initial Series or Period Endings by series of additions or subtractions- a glyph signifying count indicated forward or backward by secondary attachments.

Dates were normally reckoned from the 4 Ahau 8 Cumku base, nearly 1,000 years before most inscriptions, but some calculations ranged far into the past and a few into the distant future. One reaches backwards nearly 1,350,000 years, but the deepest probings of eternity are embodied in texts that seemingly record positions respectively 90 and 400 million years ago. Although the interpretation of these last computations is disputable, the Maya certainly thought in millions of years a millennium before Europe discarded the view that the world was only some 6,000 years old.

The Maya conceived of time as a journey through eternity in which each deified number- all time periods and their numbers were gods- carried his period on his back supported by a dump line. Each evening the procession rested. Next morning, carriers whose period was completed were replaced. For instance, if the *uinal* and *kin* numbers were 15 and 19 respectively, the new carriers would be the deified 16 and 0 (the latter because *kin* unumbers go no higher than 19). Other period numbers would journey on until it came time to change the *tun* carrier. Much ritual and imagery grew out of the concept of the march of time: sculpture illustrates bearers lowering their burdens at journey's end.

Correlation of the Maya calendar with ours depends on several factors. First, the 260 day almanac still functions in some Maya villages in the Guatemalan highlands. As there is excellent evidence it has neither gained nor lost a day since the Spanish conquest, despite strong Spanish efforts to suppress it, one may reasonably assume no break under the more favourable pre-Columbian conditions. Lunar and other data support such a view, Second, month position in Yucatan and southern Peten at the Spanish conquest also are reliably correlated to the day with the present Western calendar. Third, the combined day and month parts of the Maya calendar are in day-for-day agreement with the present Western calendar within a 52 year span (after that given day and month positions repeat). The *katun* ('spherically, 13 Ahau) current at the Spanish conquest is, however, known, thereby fixing any day and month position in a longer range of 260 years because a named *katun* repeats only after 260 *tuns*. Those conditions produce a correlation of the two calendars that is either correct to the day or is 260 or even 520 years wrong, since historical evidence does not specify which particular *katun* 13 Ahau coincided with the Spaniards' arrival. Fourth, such factors as stronomy (Maya records of heliacal risings of Venus and of many dates with moon age stated)., pottery sequences, architectural changes (less reliable), and data from neighbouring areas govern choice of the applicable *katun* 13 Ahau, Weight of evidence led to wide acceptance of the Goodman- Martinez Thompson correlation that equates 13.0.0.0.0. 4 Ahau 8 Cumku, start of the Maya era, with August 10,3113 BC, the carbon-14 dating technique was first applied to the problem, various difficulties attendant on the use of new techniques and failure to take into account that a tree dies year by year from its centre outward (so that a sample from the core might give a date well over a century before felling) distorted readings, producing results favourable to the correlation making Maya dates 260 years earlier. Now, with better technique and averaging of many "runs" of samples of latest growth from beams at Tikal with secure Maya dates, carbon-14 readings overwhelmingly support the Goodman-Martinez- Thompson correlation/

The only other Middle American calendar with a known era is that of the Cakchiquel of highland Guatemala. The system was vigesimal : *kih.* day; *uinak,* 20 days; a. 4000 days: and *may.* 8,000 days. The 400-day "year" ran concurrently with the 260 day almanac, which, in turn, synchronized with all other Maya almanacs. Like the 360 day *tun* of the lowlands, the 400 day a was the counting unit, for reckoning was laways in multiples of the *a.* never by days, as in our Julian calendar, *May* signifies twenty, and is so named because it comprised 20*a.* At the arrival of the Spaniards, reckoning was from a revolt in AD 1493. Earlier eras may be postulated, but inscribed calendrical texts are lacking in cacique territory.

Aziec. The Aztec and related peoples of central Mexico employed the cycle of 52 years, constructed, like its Maya equivalent, of concurrent 365 day years and 260 day cycles, any position of the former coinciding with a given position of the latter only at 52 year intervals. Again leap day were not used. At completion of the 52 years, known as "binding of the years", elaborate ceremonies were held to avert destruction of the world expected on that occasion. The last occurrence before the Spanish conquest was in AD 1507. Although the last creation of the world was designated by a day name, neither that nor any other was in general use in central Mexico as the start of an era. Aztec reckoning is normally form their arrival in the Valley of Mexico, supposedly the year I Flint (AD 1168).

There is much confusion in placing events in Mexican history because no system of distinguishing one 52 year cycle from another was employed except by writing every year glyph throughout the period covered, a clumsly arrangement. Each year was named for either its last day (omitting the five-day munlucky period) or for the last day of the fifth month (both choices have distinguished supporters). In either case, only four day names (House, Rabbit, Cane, and Flint), each with its accompanying numeral, could designate a year. The

Spanish conqueror Hernan Cortes seized the aztec capital in 1521, year 2 House, but some past event, also assigned to a year 3 House but unlocated in a full sequence of year, might refer to AD 1261, 1313 or 1365 etc. Month positions were rarely given in chronological statements.

Peoples of Oaxaca and the Isthmus of Tehuantepec. Pictorial books of the Mixtec of Oaxaca record events in the lives of ruling families covering seven centuries, but, again, happenings are fixed only by the day on which each occurred and the year in which the day fell. Sequence is usually clear, but at times there is doubt as to which 52 year period is meant when parenthetical material, such as life histories of secondary characters, is inserted.

No era is recognizable. A clouded entry concerning the descent of Earth of the Sun and Venus, perhaps assignable to AD 749. Is a logical starting point, but other entries are earlier.

Little is known of the calendar of the Zaporec, neighbours of the Mixtec. Years began on a different set of days, and glyphs differ from those of Mixtec and Aztec. Months are not recorded on monuments, which are numerous, and no chronological system has survived. Most Zapotec texts are early.

Rare inscriptions in western Chiapas, southern Veracruz, and the Guatemalan Pacific coast resemble the abbreviated lowland Maya Initial Series used in script and on a single sculpture in that numerical bars and dots are in a vertical column with period glyphs and month signs suppressed, clearly place numeration, that is, the value of each unit was shown by its position in the column. The linguistic affiliation of other sculptors is unknown.

All texts are either fragmentary of damaged; the two complete ones, unlike Maya Initial Series. Open with days signs (and different ones at that), If, as one may reasonably assume, the series of bars and dots departed from those day signs, a fixed era is questionable. Nevertheless, some scholars postulate use of the Maya era (13.0.0.0.0. 4 Ahau 8 Cumku). This little understood system may have been ancestral to the

Maya Initial series, the Maya perhaps developing a fixed era, for they alone seem to have been interested in an exact chronological system.

Diplomatics

Diplomatics, broadly speaking, is the study of documents. The term is derived from the Greek word *diploma,* meaning "doubled" or "folded". Besides the documents of legal and administrative import with which it is properly concerned, diplomatic also includes the study of other records such as bills, reports, cartularies, registers, and rolls. Diplomatics is therefore a basic and not simply and auxiliary historical science. This article deals with its development and practice in the Roman Empire and in Europe. During Roman antiquity certain documents containing different sorts of authorizations were engraved on a bronze diptych and then folded and sealesd, in order to keep the contents secret- hence the term diploma. Rarely found during the Middle Ages, the word was used by the Renaissance Humanists to denote formal documents of ancient rulers. The interest in and description of such documents came to be called *res diplomatica* after the famous 17th century work *De Re Diplomatica Libri VI,* by Jean Mabillon, a member of the scholarly Benedictine congregation of saint-Maur. Mabillon's work first made the study of ole documents a reputable science. The major task of diplomatics is to distinguish between genuine and false documents, and this involves detailed examination of their external and internal features. Diplomatic studies have been applied mainly to Western documents, usually medieval ones, because it requires less specialist training to analyze more recent documents.

History of the study of documents. *Medieval and Renalssance work.* The forging of documents took place on a vast scale during the earlier Middle Ages, partly because wars and disturbances so frequently upset possession and also because the increasing use of written records made it necessary for those whose title was, in fact, perfectly good in old unwritten "customary" law to give it written substantiation. Thus forgeries, partly intentionally honest, partly dishonest, occurred frequently, despite the fact that the Germanic tribes that settled in western Europe inherited, with other aspects of Roman law, the concept of forgery as a felony, which was soon also reinforced by the church's canon law. This legal concept of forgery was however, mainly applied to case concerning property or inheritance; and literary forgeries, such as the famous Donation of Constantine, which purported to be the gift by the Roman emperor Constantine 1 the Great (died 337) to Pope Sylvester 1 of spiritual primacy throughout the church and of temporal power in Italy, were not concerned. Serious critical efforts to detect forgery did not begin in the Middle Ages, although obvious forgeries might be challenged in the course of a dispute. As early as the 6th century, the Merovingian king childebert II declared a charter recording the gift of land from himself to the Bishop of Reims a forgery on the simple ground that the royal official denied the signature on to it be his. Pope Innocent III (1198-1216) tried to establish infallible criteria for the detection of fraudulent papal documents, but knowledge of earlier documentary forms was totally inadequate. In the Renaissance the Humanists began to use philological and technical criteria: on these grounds Lorenzo Valla authoritatively pronounced the Donation of Constantine to be a forgery, though authenticity had already been questioned.

Post- Renaissance scholarship. There events in the 17th century forced the development of more sophisticated standards of evaluation. The Thirty Year's War in Germany led to endless legal conflicts, and in France the nobility engaged in a concerted action known as the *bella diplomatica* ("diplomatic wars") to assert their ancient privileges against royal absolutism. The decisive impetus, however, came from a much more particularist dispute. Daniel van Papenbroeck, a member of the Jesuit commission known as the Bollandists (from another member, JeanBolland), which was charged with the publication of the *Acta Sanctorum* ("acts of the Saints"), finding that some monastic documents he inspected were forgeries, assumed (1675) that this was true of almost all early medieval documents. Since most of the monasteries with which the documents had been concerned were of the Benedictine Order, the Benedictines resented the suggestion, and Mabillon undertook to refute it. In his *De Re Diplomatica* (1681), Mabillon set out the fundamental principles of the science of verifying documents; Papenbroeck soon afterwards acknowledged the correctness of his tenets. Nearly a century later, Rene-Prosper Tassin and Charles Francois Toustain published their six-volume *Nouveau traite de diplomatique* (1750-65; "New Treatise on Diplomatic"), a work that surpassed Mabillon's only in its greater wealth of material. Another important event in the history of the science of diplomatics was the founding of the Ecole des Chartes (an institute for the training of French archivists) in Paris in 1821. During the next decades important collections of early medieval French documents were printed in the *Recueil des actes* by a variety of eminent editors. But the greatest advances were made by German and Austrian scholars, among whom Julius von Ficker investigated the differentiation between *actum* and *datum* (that is, between verbal legal procedure and its formal documentation), and Theodor von Sickel defined a basic technique of studying and comparing the script of charters and thus of identifying the individual notaries or scribes. The diplomas of the Carolingian and the German kings and emperors were edited in the series of the *Monumenta Germaniae Historical.* by members of the Institute fur osterreichische Geschichtsforschung (Institute of Austrian History Research), established by Sickel in 1854, Meanwhile, the *Regesta,* comprising short, synoptically condensations of the contents of papal documents down to 1198, published by Philipp Jaffe in 1851, gave a decisive momentum to the study of the papal chancery, while August Potthast covered the period from 1198 to 1304. Prominent scholars in the research of papal records in Germany at the beginning of the 20th century were Michael Tangl. Fudolf von Heckel, and, particularly, Paul Fridolin Kehr. In comparison with the amount of work done in France and Germany, historical scholarship in England long paid relatively little attention to legal, as opposed to literary, records. Although John Mitchell Kemble published his collection of Anglo-Saxon documents, the *Codex Dilomaticus Aevi Saxonici* (1839-48), an extensive study of Anglo-Saxon and Normal legal and administrative documents was delayed until the 20th century. Since then notable contributions have been made by scholars such as Helen Cam. H. W. c. Davis, Vivian Hunter Galbraith, Frank M. Stention. Dorothy While lock, David Charles Douglas, and many others, Christopher Roberts Cheney has made important contributions to the research of papal documents. In Italy Luigi Schiaparelli made vital contributions to the study of Lombard documents. From the 19th century, some study of documents has formed part of the medieval history curriculum in most European universities.

Diplomatic method. *Types of documents.* Documents that have been preserved are either originals, drafts, or copies, Originals, of which many survive, are formal documents drawn up on the order of the sender or donor, and they were designated to serve the recipient or beneficiary as evidence of the transaction recorded. Handwritten copies of documents, made either before or after the deed was actually executed (sealed), are not classified as originals. If made before an "original", they were in fact rough drafts of it; if made afterward, they were copies. The particularly Anglo-Saxon method of chirography, however, gave the possibility of producing several "originals". By this process two or more specimens of a documents were written on the same pase of the vallum sheet, and the free space between the texts was filled in with the word *chyrographum* ("handwriting") or other words and symbols. Then the sheet was cut irregularly right through these words or symbols; the originals thus separated could later be reassembled, provide documents having the force of "originals", copies of the original were usually made and formally certified as such, by public notaries, or by high ecclesiastical or secular dignitaries. Copies certified in this way were accorded the same legal value as the originals. In practice, lack of critical judgment on the part of the certifiers often led to the certification of forged records. In documents known as transmutes, which recited earlier documents or charters as part of their text, it often happened that the earlier document was forged, but, being included in the new, it received validation. The original documents and copies considered above were issued at the request of the recipient or beneficiary or of his legal heir. It also happened quite often that the sender ordonorwished for various reasons to retain a record of the documents issued by him. The chanceries (record offices) of secular rulers or great ecclesiastics therefore kept copies of outgoing documents in registers, and often of incoming documents, too. The popes were among the first to adopt the old Roman practice of keeping registers; although nearly all the earlier ones have been lost, an almost uninterrupted series of papal registers is extant from the pontificate of Innocent III onward. An important group of registers are the rolls kept by the medieval kings of England: the earliest extant rolls date from the 12th century. The keeping of registers in the chanceries of the French kings began about the year 1200, in Aragon about 1215, in Sicily under the Hohenstaufen emperor Frederick II (died 1250), and in the German imperial chancery from the early 14th century. Another manner of studying documents is in the formula books of the various chanceries. Notaries drawing up the various forms of medieval documents did not usually compose each new text afresh but, rather, copied from books in which such text formulas had been collected, a practice that can be traced back to Roman procedure. These model texts frequently contained only the legally relevant passages, while the individually applicable parts, such as names, figures, and dates, were either abridged or totally omitted. During the time or the Frankish kings, important collections were made, such as the *Formulae MarcufiI* (early 8th century) and the *Formulae imperiales* (828-832). Significant collections of formulas serving as models forpapal documents have been preserved from the 13th century.

Classification of documents. The documents of the Middle Ages are usually classified under two groups: public documents, which are those of emperors, kings, and popes, and private documents, which comprise all others. Another way of classifying documents is according to whether they are evidentiary or dispositive. The former merely record a valid legal act already executed orally, while the actual issuing of the latter forms in itself the legal act. This distinction, found among Roman documents from the 3rd century AD onward, gardually ceased to exist after the early Middle Ages. After the collapse of the Carolingian empire in the 9th century, private documents lost much of their function and were replaced by simple memorandums about legal acts and the witnesses to them. It was not until the late 11th and early 12th centuries that sealed charters of high secular or ecclesiastical dignitaries were again gradually considered as dispositive. Papal documents can be classified mainly as either letters or privileges, and royal documents can be classified as diplomas or mandates. Privileges and diplomas give evidence of legal transactions designed to be of long duration of even of permanent effect, while mandates and many papal letters contain commands.

Physical appearance of documents. Documents were written on a variety of material. In antiquity there were documents of stone, metal, wax, papyrus, and, occasionally, of parchment, but only papyrus and parchment (and very occasionally, wax) were used during the Middle Ages. From the 12th to the 13th centuries, paper also was sometimes available. Papyrus, made from the stem of the papyrus plant, was produced mainly in Egypt; after the Arab conquest of Egypt in the 7th century, the import of papyrus to Europe became difficult. The Merovingian kings wrote their documents on papyrus until the second half of the 7th century, and the popes did so until far into the 11th century. North of the Alps papyrus had finally disappeared by the 8th century, when it was replaced by parchment. Parchment was made from animal hides and was thus easier to obtain. In southern Europe it was made mainly from sheep and goat hides; the insides of the skin were thoroughly smoothed and calcined, while the hairy sides were left rougher. In central and northern Europe, parchment was usually made from calves skins, and both sides of the hides were thoroughly smoothed and calcined. Paper came originally from China. During the 8th century Ad, it spread to the Arab world and from thence to Byzantium, where it was manufactured from linen and was used from the 11th to the 13th centuries for imperial documents. After that time ordinary paper was used in the Byzantine Empire. In the West the use of paper, most common at first in southern Italy and Spain. Germany and southern France began to import paper from Spain and Italy in the 13th century, and soon afterward it had reached England by way of Bordeaux. But paper did not altogether replace parchment, which long remained in use, especially for solemn documents. The medium for writing was ink, generally a mixture of oak gall and copper vitriol. Originally black, ink made north of the Alps sometimes shows a reddish-brown hue, while that made in Italy may contain tinges of brown and yellow. Over the centuries most of these of these colours have lightened as a result of atmospheric conditions. The Byzantine emperors used purple ink for their signatures. This custom was occasionally taken over by the Lombard rulers of Italy and, later, by the Norman kings of Sicily. Another custom of Byzantine origin is the use of gold lettering.

Throughout the entire Roman Empire, the language used in documents was primarily Latin. Greek was also used, and during the latter part of the 6th century AD, it slowly superseded Latin in the East. From then onward, Greek was the language of Byzantine documents until the end of the Byzantine Empire (1453). In the West, the collapse of the empire and the establishment of barbarian kingdoms led to a vulgarization of Latin, written as well as spoken.

Latin has always been used for papal documents and for most public and private charters, and it was used for international documents well into post-Renaissance times, until it was superseded by French as the language of diplomacy. In public and private documents, use of the vernacular alongside Latin gradually developed. Apart from its early and unique appearance in the documents of the Anglo-Saxons in England, no vernacular was used in charters before the 12th century. At the Norman Conquet (1066), use of Anglo-Saxon in English documents soon stopped, and no more vernacular was used there until some Norman French was introduced in the 13th century. And Middle English in the 15th century. There was an increasing use of the vernacular in Italian and French documents from the 12th century and in Germany from the 13th; but in medieval times Latin was never outstripped by the vernacular.

A correct assessment of the hand in which it was written is vital to ascertaining the provenance and authenticity of a document. Thus, the knowledge of paleography, different styles of ancient writing, is a skill essential to diplomatics. The broad basis of such knowledge begins with acquaintance with the general styles of writing current at particular times and places. This varied with the way the pen was held; whether the writing was cursive or had the letters formed separately; whether it was majuscule, all the letters being contained between a single pair of horizontal lines, or minuscule, with parts of the letters extending above and below the lines. There is a further distinction between what is called book hand and the business, or court, hand at one time used for documents.

In Europe the Roman capital letters, distinguished as rustic or square, uncial, and Roman majuscule and minuscule cursive, influenced all subsequent writing in the West. The Roman curial style (from the Curia, or papal court), used in the papal chancery until the 12th century, was a derivation of late Roman minuscule cursive. After the disintegration of the Western Empire, the Merovingian Franks used a Roman provincial script for the documents. Distinctive forms developed elsewhere, in Visigothic Spain and in Ireland. The Irish script, a half uncial (uncials are rounded lteeters) and a minuscule script, spread to Anglo Saxon England and thence to the European continent. Under the Carolingian rulers, a particularly clear and attractive kminuscule book hand (Caroline minuscule) was developed, modifications of this gradually became used in documents and eventually spread also to Italy. England, and Spain. A "Gothic", more pointed from the script developed since the 11th century in northern France and soon spread all over Europe, so that writing beame more spidery in appearance. In the early years of the Renaissance, Italian scholars such as Poggio (poggio Bracciolini) and Niccolo Niccoli developed a minuscule based on the Carolingian, and variants of this style were used by the Venetian Aldus Manutius and other pioneers of printing.

Abbreviations were used in both documents and books Again, their particular characteristics would contribute to a correct assessment of the probable date and provenance of a document. Roughly two types were used: the suspension, involving the writing of only the first letter of syllable of a word: and the contraction, used first for Hebrew and Christian sacred names, the writing of only the first and last letter of letters of a words or syllable. The Carolingians sometimes used Tironian notes, a form of shorthand devised by Tiro, a freedman of the Roman orator Cicero.

From Toman times the two most important methods of validating documents were by appending the signature or the seal of the sender of promulgator. The practice of using seals for this purpose (and not merely to close a document) was carried over from imperial usage and, by the 8th century, was current among the Lombards and other Germanic tribes in western Europe. Until about the 8th century, the signature of the Merovingian ruler or his delegate was also required for the validation of public documents, but thereafter the seal alone, together with the recognition by a high chancery official, was held sufficient, the King's signature dwindling into a monogram or mere stroke (the "stoke of execution"). This change was probably accelerated because many medieval kings could not write. Thus, in England, King John sealed, and did not sign, the Magna Carta.

Seals were made of wax or of metal; if the latter, they were called buils (hence, the use of this term for a certain group of papal documents). The Byzantine officials and ecclesiastics used lead and silver for their bulls. Papal seals were of lead or gold. Wax seals were increasingly used from about the 11th and 12th centuries, and wax was also used for the impression when, later, less formal documents were validated by use of the signet or privy seal Seals could be two-sided, suspended from the document, or impressed upon it.

From and content of documents. Normally, each document was divided into three distinct parts; the introduction (protocol), the main text (context), and the concluding formulas or final protocol. There were various subdivisions, and not all the parts here mentioned are necessarily found in every document. The introduction comprises, first, the invocation *(invocatio)* of god, either by name or through a symbol such as the cross; second, the superscription *(intitulatio)*, giving the name and title of the sender; and thired, and address *(inscriptio)*. The actual text of the document can be divided into a number of parts. The first, known as the *arenga*, expresses in general terms the motive for the issue of the document. The notification *(promulgatio)*, briefly explaining the legal purpose of the document, is followed, by the *narratio*. or exposition of the particular circumstances involved. In the *dispositio* the donor or promulgator firmly declares his purpose ("I hereby decree" or "I hereby give"); this clause is the vital core of the document, its legal decree of enactment. There usually followed the *sanction*. a threat of punishment should the *corroboration*, a statement of the means to be used for validation of the document. The final protocol consisted of subscriptions of lists of names of all those, such as the scribe, who took part in the issue of the document and of witnesses to the enactment. The date and place of issue are given, and the final sentence, the *appreciation*, is a short prayer for the realization of the contents of the charter. At the bottom of the document, the sings of validation (the recognition, monogram, seal) were then added.

The date give on a document might be either that of legal enactment *(action)* or that of the issue of the document recording the (already performed) legal enactment (*datum*). The form in which dates are given in a document is of particular import in determining its provenance and authenticity. A wide variety of practices were followed at different places and times. For instance, days of the month could be given according to the old Roman system of calends, ides, and nones; by continuous counting throughout the month; or by reference to a saint's day. Years might be computed from the presumed time of the creation of the world; by the Roman indication, a 15 year cycle; by the name of officiating Roman consuls; by regional years of emperor, king, or pope; or from the birth of Christ. Moreover, there were also a variety of ways to determine when the year began.

Development and characteristics of chanceries. *The Roman and Byzantine empire.* Rulers, all of whom needed to issue directive and edicts, developed writing offices, of chanceries, in which formal documents were drawn up. The Roman imperial chancery, called the office of Letters (*ab rpistulis*), was subdivided into a Greek and a Latin department. In the 5th century four letter offices existed, all under the ultimate control of the *magister oficiorum* ("master of offices"); the *scrinium epistolarum* ("laetter office") handled mainly foreign, legal, and administrative affairs; the *scrinium libeilorum* ("petitions office") handled petitions and investigations; the *scrinium memoriae* ("memorandum office") composed shorter imperial decrees; and the *scrinium dispositionum* dealt with administration. From the 4th century, a group (*schola*) of notaries had come into being, some of whom served the emperor as personal secretaries. Two centuries later a special confidential (*a secretis*) secretary existed. In the Byzantine Empire in the 8th to 9th centuries, the *scrinium eplstolarum* and the *scrinium* libellorum merged to from a new department under the *koiaistor* (a high palace official); while the secretaries had all come under the office of the *protoasekretis* (head of the secretaries). an official called the *mystikos* handled the emperor's secret correspondence. In preparing edicts or other laws, the *kolaistor*, after consulting the emperor, made a first draft of the bill, had the official copy drawn up by notaries, and then verified its accuracy before it was validated. From the 9th century onward other high court officials participated in the validation of Byzantine charters.

The important governmental documents of the late Roman and early Byzantine empires include laws, edicts, decress (imperial decrsiong concerning civil and penal law), and rescripts (the emperor's replies to inquiries from corporate and administrative bodies or private persons). In the Byzantine era documents concerning more day to day affairs can be grouped dundr the haadings of foreign letters, privileges, and administration. Foreign letters include correspondence with other rulers, treaties (regarded not as in agreements between equals but as an act of grace or privilege granted by the emperor, and made out as such), and letters accrediting imperial ambassadors. The most solemn and splendid from of privilege was the *chrysobuilos logos,* so named because the word *logos,* meaning the emperors's solemn word, appeared in it three times, picked out in red ink. Written in the carefully embellished chancery script reserved for the emperor's personal documents, the text consists of the usual parts that is, the *invocatio, intitulatio, inscriptio, arenga, narratio, dispositio, sanctto,* date, and the *subscriptio.* It was sealed with the golden bull.

From about 12th to the mid-14th century, a simplified from, the *chrysobullon stgillion,* was used fro privileges of lesser importance. It was not signed by the emperor himself but was held to be validated by the insertion, buy the emperor, in red ink of the *menologema,* a statement of month and indication. It, too, was sealed with a golden bull. The administrative documents of the Byzantine imperial chancery include the *prostagma,* or *horismos,* a plain and short document known since the beginning of the 13th century. If directed to a single person, the document starts out with a short address, but, in all other cases, it begins immediately with the *narratio,* followed by the *dispositio.* The emperor replaced his signature with the *menologema.* Unlike the privileges, this document was not rolled up but, instead, was folded, and then closed by means of a wax seal stamped with the imprint of the imperial signet ring.

In addition to those emanating from the imperial offices, there were other types of documents issued in the Byzantine Empire. These include those issued by despots and imperial officials and, in the ecclesiastical sphere, by patriarchs and bishops. There were also private documents. The documents sealsed with the gold seal and that of documents drawn up by imperial officials and sealed with lead bulls. Documents issued by imperial officials were simpler. They lacked the protocol, and the personal signature of the issuing official was written in black ink. The detailed date comprises the *menologema*. The documents of the Byzantine patriarchs are in many respects analogous to the imperial documents and symbolize the high status of the patriarch of Constantinople. They were, however, sealed with lead bulls. Byzantine private documents are almost exclusively notarial instruments. They are immediately recognizable by the crosses marked at the top of the documents. Used in lieu of the signature, the cross was the mark of the sender and contrained his name and official function in one of its angles. The document was either signed by witnesses, or at least the cross preceding their names is autograph. Following that is the signature of the notary. These documents were not usually sealed.

The papal chancery. Knowledge about early papal documents is scant because no originals surivive from before the 9th century, and extant copies of earlier documents are often much abridged. But it is clear that the poepe at first imitated the form of the letters of the Roman emperors. The papal protocol consisted only of the superscription and address and the final protocol of the pope's personal "signature" not a mention of the 8th century, it became customary in certain documents to mention in the final clauses the name of the scribe responsible for the drawing up of the document; this was given with the date of issue, indicated by month and indication, immediately following the subject matter of the document. There followed another clause, the great dating formula, *datum per manus* ("given by the hand of ..."), naming a high chancery of ficial and giving the date by reference to the regional years of both emperor and pope. Both were used in documents containing decress of permanent legal force, which came to be called privileges. Under Pople Leo IX (1049-54), the benediction written by the pope was changed into a monogram not written by him, but his signature was now introduced, placed in a round symbol, the *tota.* By the early 13th century, papal documents had evolved into two distinetive groups: solemn privileges and letters. Solemn privileges can be distinguished by there enlarged letters *(elongata)* of the first line, by the phrase *in perpetuun* ("in perpetuity") at the end of the address, by a threefold *amen* at the end of the text, by use of the *rota.* the pope's signature, the monogram, signatures of the cardinals, and by the *datum per manus.* Among letters, those whose bull was fastened on silken cords (*litterae cum serico)* brought some benefit to the recipient, while those with bulls fastened on a bempen cord *(Litterae cum filo canapis)* contained either orders or the papal delegation in a dispute.

The number of solemn privileges began to decline from the mid-13th century, and eventually they were completely discontinued, their function being partly taken over by the *litterae cum serico,* which became increasingly elaborate in from. A new type of document also developed, the papal buil, distinguishable primarily but its use of formulas such as *ad perpetuam rei memoriam* ("that the matter may be perpetually known") in the superscription. Yet another new papal document appeared at the end of the 14th century, the brief *(breve),* used for the popes' private or even secret correspondence. Written not in the chancery but, instead, by papal secretaries (an office dating from about 1338), the briefs were sealed on wax with the imprint of the papal signet ring.

The papal chancery of the 4th to the 8th centuries was similar to the late Roman imperial chancery. Its notaries *(notari, scriniarit),* organized in a guid *(scholary),* were headed by the *primicerius notariorum* and the *secundicerius notariorum* (first and second of notaries) and included the especially important notaries of Rome's seven ecclesiastical regions. But, during the 9th century, the *bibliothecarius,* the papal librarian, became the most important chancery official; a little later, various important bishops and dignitaries seem to have acted occasionally as *datartus* (the official named in the *datum per manus* formula). During the mid-11th century, a phase of German influence led to the temporary employment of notaries from the court of the emperor Henry III, who drew up papal privileges according to imperial formulas. A more important and permanent outcome of German influence was the gradual replacement of the *bibliothecarius* by a chancellor as the highest chancery official. The chancellor was invariably a cardinal, and in his absence another cardinal acted in his place as vie chancellor. Lesser chancery personnel still included the seven regional notaries; increasing business involved the use of lesser paid scribes in addition to the established notaries. From the late 11th century, a papal chapel, modelled on those of contemporary emperors and kings, developed, and its staff was often employed in chancery tasks.

From the early 13th century, the vice chancellor became the permanent head of the chancery, the office of chancellor remaining vacant. During that century the vice chancellors were ordinary clerics, who renounced the office if elevated to the cardinalate; thus, the chancery became directly subordinate to the pope himself. Both the numbers and the official standing of the notaries in the chancery, which then functioned entirely separately from the chapel, gradually increased. Higher chancery officials were often distinguished canonists (legal experts), such as Sinibaldo Fleschi (later Pope Innocent IV). Godfrey of Trani, and Richard of Siena. From the beginning of the 14th century, bishops or cardinals filled the office of vice chancellor. During the Great Schism (1378-1417) there were two papal chanceries and two vice chancellors, one in Rome and one in Avignon.

Under Innocent III the procedure of the papal chancery had changed. Letters concerning matters of import to the papal Curia (*de Curia)* were drafted by the pope himself or else by a cardinal, the vice chancellor, or a notary. But the majority of the papal documents were elicited by their recipients, who had first to present to a notary the substance of their petition in a form the text of which largely anticipated the wording of the desired document. Professional proctors attached to the Curia assisted in the drafting and were also responsible for the documents during later stages of the procedure. Once a pertition was approved, the notaries or the *abbreviatores* drafted a suitable document, drawing on a selection of formula books. After a final copy (engrossment) had been made and checked, it was read, if necessary to the pope or in a special department of the chancery, the *Audientia litteraum contradictarun.* It was then passed to the Cistercian lay brothers who had charge of the papal bull, sealed, and given to the peritoner, who had had to pay a fee at almost every stage of the proceedings.

Insufficient research has so far been done on the papal chancery during the 14th and 15th centuries. Whereas formerly, when the vice chancellor was absent, one of the notaries had deputized for him, a new official, the *regens cancellariam,* was now created to fulfill this function. The number of notaries increased steadily, and, from the 13th century onward, an increasing number of public notaries worked in the papal administration. In order to distinguish between them and the papal notaries proper, the latter became unofficially known as protonotanes. The notaries were now in charge of the letters of justice, while she letters of grace were handled by the *abbrevlatores.* The scribes remained in charge of the engrossments. A *compotator,* aided by several assistants, was responsible for collecting fees.

The royal chanceries of medieval western Europe. Of the nations that held power in western Europe after the collapse of the Roman Empire there, the Ostrogoths, who occupied Italy from the late 5th to the mid- 6th century, too over the ancient Roman imperial chancery system in its entirery. Very little is known about the royal documents of the Lombards, their successors in Northern Italy, since not one of them has been preserved in its original form. But Lombard officials in charge of drawing up the documents were still trained in the Roman tradition. As well as *referendarii,* there were notaries who also acted as senbes. It is very likely that all of them were laymen.

Until the 12th century two main types of documents, diplomas and mandates, were produced north of the Alps, in the Merovingian. Carolingian, German, and French royal chanceries. Very little is known about the Merovingran royal chancery and its organizations. The names of the scribes are never mentioned in the documents, but they were signed by high chancery officials, the *reterendaru.*

When the Merovingian dynasty was supplanted by the Carolingians, chancery procedure changed drastically. In contrast to the merovingian kings, the first Carolingian king. Pepin the Short, was unable either to read or write. He therefore entrusted the responsibility for the correctness of the royal documents to an official of the court. At about the same time, the task of drawing up documents was taken over by those clerics whose original duty had been to look after the most important relic of the royal court, the coat *(cappa)* of St. Martin of Tours. Collectively named the *capeila* (chapei), these clerks were individually called *capeilant,* chaplains. This close connection between the court chapel and the chancery existed under the late Carolingians and at the German and French and other royal courts, including that of England. Until well into the 12th century. European chanceries were not bureaucratic offices in the Modern sense but, rather, in most cases an assemblage of chaplains suited for the task of issuing documents and usually working under a cleric who was not the head of the chapel. Not all chaplains wrote documents, however, and the chapel and chancery thus remained separate institutions. From the reign of the emperor Louis 1 the Pious (814-840), the heads of the chancery were not personally involved in writing the documents, a task performed by unnamed and unknown scribes. At first the scribes were indiscriminately designated as either *notaril or cancellarii* (higher. Roman provincial officials of the 5th and 6th century, who stood at the harriers, *cancelli,* of the council rooms), but, by the 9th century, the title of *cancellarius* was gaining ground and was increasingly applied to the head of the chancery. The 9th century was a period of transition, during which, for a while, the archchaplain, the head of the chapel, became also the head of the clerks who wrote the charters.

Under the Ottonian dynasty, which came to power in the eastern division of the original Carolingian empire early in the 10th century, the German royal chancery developed the organization that was to characterize it throughout the remainder of the Middle Ages. The heads of the chancery were the arch chancellors, but the office was entirely honorary and soom came to be automatically held, as for as Germany was concerned, by whoever was archbishop of Mainz. When the German kings or emperors established administrations in Italy, Italian bishops were at first made archehancellors for Italy, but in 1031 the office was attached to the archbishopric of Cologne. From the 11th century. Burgundian bishops were arch chancellors for Burgundy, but, in the second half of the 13th century, the archbishop of Trier took over the office.

The actual heads of the chancery were the chancellors. At first there was a chancellor, as well as an archehancellor, for each separate part of the empire- Germany. Italy cellor for all three kingdoms. But even the chancellors, all of whom were clerics, were rerely involved in the actual composition and engraossing of documents, being usually engaged, as important advisers to the king or emperor, in much weightier matters. They do seem to have been especially concerned, however, with decision about the granting of charters, and they supervised the work of the scribes or notaries. From among the ranks of these notaries, a group of promontories gradually developed after the mid-12th century, as a result of influence from the chancery of the Norman rulers of Sicily. Often called upon to deputize for the chancellor, the promontories, from the late 13th century onward, frequently titled themselves vice chancellors.

From the 12th century onward, the documents issued by the German royal chancery were divided into various classifications. The diploma, by then usually called a privilege, existed in two categories, the solemn and the simple privilege. A slolemn privilege included the *invocatiio*, the signup and recognition line, and a detailed dating or at least one of these there elements, which were entirely lacking in simple privileges, Gradually, simple privileges merged into documents called mandates, it is not always easy to distinguish between them, but, in general, privileges were concerned with right in perpetuity, while the mandates dealt mainly with matters of only temporary importance. From the early 14th century mandates were superseded by the use of letters patent and letters close (open or closed letters). Privileges continued to be sealed with a hanging seal, the seal on letters patent was impressed on the document and was used to seal up letters close.

As the power of the German kings declined during the later Middle Ages, so that of the arch chancellors increased, and in the 14th century they attempted to win control of the chancery. But, despite fluctuations in the power struggle, the king retained control of the chancellor, who, by the end of the 15th century, held the title of imperial vice chancellor.

Under the Carolingians and the first Capertians in France, various bishops and archbishops, especially the archbishops of Reims, held the office of royal chancellor. But at that time the office was merely titular, and, by the end of the 11th century, it disappeared entirely. From the 12th century onward, the title of chancellor beame reserved to the head of the chancery. These new chancellors became so powerful that in 1185 King Philip 11 Augustus left the office vacant, and during almost the whole of the 13th century the chancery was administered by subordinate office vacant, and, during almost the whole of the 13th century, the chancery was administered by subordinate in the14th century, however, and the office remained important until 1789.As in other parts of Europe, the French chancellor merely directed the work of the notaries, and it was they who were responsible for drawing up the documents. From 1350 onward, the notaries were called secretaries, and both their numbers and their importance steadily increased. From the 15th century, the tremendous expansion of business occupying the Grande Chanceilerie led to the establishment of several subsidiary *petites chancelleries*, all issuing royal documents sealed with the kings signet. Until the reign of Henry 1 (1031-60), the old Frankish type of diplomas, and, during the 13the century, the *lettres patentes* became the common type of document. These lacked the *invocatio*, the common type of document. These lacked the *invocatio*, the monogram, and the signature of the high dignitaries, and they gave the simple from the dating. From the 14th century, two forms of *lettres patentes* existed; the *charte*, which was sealed with a green wax seal hanging on red and green silk cords; and the *lettre patente*, used mainly for administrative mandates, which was sealed with a yellow wax seal on double and single cord. Besides, *lettres closes* were used from the 13th century onward.

The English royal documents of the Anglo-Saxon period (before 1066) can be divided into two large groups; the charters, mostly written in Latin: and the writs, written in Old English. The charters, for the most part concerning grants of land, began with either a verbal or a symbolic *invocatio* (a cross or the monogram XP for Christ). *There was an* arenga but no *intitulatio*. Charters were not sealed, the validation comprising the no autographed signatures of the king and of ecclesiastic and secular dignitaries. Many of the extant charters of this era are forged or interpolated; the series of those apparently genuine starts shortly after the arrival in Canterbury (669) of the archbishop Theodore, and these show similarities with late-Roman private documents. It therefore seems probable that the Angio-Saxon charters derive from Italian models brought to England by the Roman missionaries. Most of the charters were apparently written by the recipients. From the 11thc century, the charters were gradually superseded by sealed writs, which became the most important type of document in medieval England. At first written in Anglo-Saxon, they were produced in Latin soon after the Norman Conquest. No continental document was anything like them. Written on a narrow strip of parchment, their entire text occupied only a few lines. A symbolic *invocatio* in the from of a cross was followed by the king's name and the address, which contained a salutation clause. There was no *arenga,* and the address was followed by a short description of the bequest, if the writ concerried a grant, or a directive, if the write was a mandate. The Anglo-Saxon writs had no signatures of witnesses and no date, but after 1066 these elements were added. The dating consisted at first only of a mention of the place of issue, days and month being usually given only toward the end of the 12th century. From the very beginning the writs wee supplied with a pendant seal as a means of validation. From the ring of Henry 11 (1154-89), it is possible to distinguish mandate-like writs of the old type and charter writs, which mainly concerned questions of feudal enfeoffments and confirmations of privileges and were usually more carefully executed than the mandate writs. By the early 13th century, the charter write had developed into a new from of charter. It contained the *intitulatio,* including all the titles of the king; the general address; the dispositive text, which in most instances was introduced with the expression *sciatis* ("know that"); and the final clauses, consisting of the names of several witnesses and of the *datum per manus* clause mentioning the chancellor and giving the date and place of issue. During the final stage of its development, the great seal of green wax, pendant on silk cords, served as the means of validation. The ordinary writs further evolved into the common law writs (containing orders to persons mentioned by name), the writs of summons, and, particularly, the letters patent (the latter eventually assuming the function of the charter writs , when disappeared at the end of the 13th century) and a general address. Often introduced with the *sciatis,* the text concerns either limited grants or commissions to royal officials, introduced by the word *precipio* ("I order") or a similar expression.

The dating begains with a series of witnesses and contains the place of issue, day, month, and year of the king's reign. Occasionally the dating is followed by the words "per N'" which are assumed to designate the household official transmitting to the scribe the royal order to Issue the writ.

The means of validation was the great seal in white wax, pendant on a single strip of parchment *(simple queue)* or on a double strip of parchment of silk *(doublequeue).* The letters close obtained their name from the contained either commands or information directed to a single individual or to several persons. Characteristic of these letters are the words *leste me ipso* ("witnessed my self") introducing the regular dating clause. These types of royal documents remained essentially unchanged throughout the Middle Ages and were imitated by both secular and ecclesiastic English magnates and dignitaries.

The English royal chancery grew out of the royal house hold. As on the Continent, it was at first merely a group of royal chaplains, and, until the Norman Conquest, there was no chancellor at their head. The chancellor was the keeper of the seal but usually took no part in the issuing of documents. During the 12th century the number of scribes was still low, between two and eight. At first this "chancery" travelled about with the King, only in the course of the 13th century establishing a permanent location at Westminster. At first English royal documents ere not dispositive but merely evidentiary, confirming a previously arranged, orally discharged legal act, and the king's order for issuing the coumdnet was given orally. But, from the late 13thc century, a royal secretariat came into existence, which was in charge of relaying to the chancellor, by warrant sealed with the parivy seal, the royal order for issuing a write under the great seal. In many ways the secretariat thus became a competitor of the chancery. In addition, during the first half of the 14th century, the Signet Office was established, so called after the small seal (signet). The king's secretary was also the head of this office. All these shifts made the issuing of royal documents increasingly complicated. from the end of the 14th century, the common procedure involved, first, the petitioner submitting a petition to the king. If the king approved of it, his secretary forwarded a warrant carrying the signet to the keeper of the privy seal with the request to send, in his turn, a warrant carrying the privy seal to the chancellor. The chancellor then ordered the issue of the document, which would bear the great seal. So far as the issuing of royal documents is concerned, the fact that the secretariat development into the secretariat of state is of great significance. The king's secretary (later on, there were two of them) became the centre of the royal administration. It was in his office that the state papers originated, which already under Henry VIII (died 1547) far surpassed in importance the old chancery records. Among the state papers there are in-letters, out-letters, drafts, reports, and schedules. The decline of the rolls (document registers) during the 16th century gabe rise tȯ yet another new office, the State Paper Office, headed since 1578 by the clerk of the papers. The second holder of this office. Sir Thomas Wilson, established the division of the state papers into foreign and domestic. As departments of state proliferated during the 18th and 19th centuries, they developed their own archives. In 1838 all the public archives became subject to an official called the master of the rolls.

Smaller European nations usually modelled their documents on those of the papacy, the empire. France,. or England. The influence of papal letters and privileges can England. The influence of papal letters and privileges can be observed particularly in Aragon. Castile, and Portugal, while German royal diplomas served as models in bohemia (which was part of the empire),, Hungry, and Poland. Because of the close political ties between the two kingdoms. Anglo-Saxon influence can be traced in the seal of the royal Danish documents during the 11th century, but, in the course of the 12thc century, royal and princely German documents became the models for Danish as well as Swedish royal documents. Norwegian royal documents were modelled on Anglo-Saxon writs, probably as a result of the influence of English missionaries working in Norway from the early 11th century. The Norwegian writs were drawn up in the vernacular. The chancery of the Norman rulers of southern Italy and Sicily was highly developed. Influenced by the from of papal documents, the Norman documents comprise mainly privileges, either formal (with *rota*, or wax seal), and mandates. They all have a detailed dateline that includes the name of the chancellor or other high court officials, the number of years since the birth of Christ, the regnal year of the king, and the *appreciation*. The mandates are more simply executed. they lack the *invocatio* and start out with a simple *intitulatio* and *inscriptio* that ends with a salutation clause. There is neither *arenga* nor *corroboration*, but there is a command clause in the text. The dating consists only of the place of issue, the day of the month, and the *induction*. There is no *rota* or signature. The seal is of red wax. The head of the royal chancery of the Norman kingdom of Sicily was the chancellor, a layman who was an influential court official. The notaries who drafted and wrote the documents were also laymen. Because the German Hohenstaufen emperors also ruled in Sicily from 1194 to 1250. Norman chancery practice influenced subsequent German documents.

Epigraphy

Epigraphy (from the classical Greek *epigraphein*, "to write upon, incise", and *epigraphe*, "inscription") denotes a branch of scholarship deveoted to the study of written matter recorded on hard or durable material. Because such media were exclusibve or predominant in many of mankind's carliest civilizations, epigraphy is a prime tool in recovering much of the firsthand record of antiquity. It is thus an essential adjunct of the study of ancient man; is secures and delivers the primary data on which historical and philological disciplines alike depend for their understanding of the recorded past. In a narrower sense, epigraphy is the study of such documents as remains of the written self-expression of early cultures and as communication media in their own right, attesting to the development of visible sign systems and the art of writing as such. Finally, in later periods including our own, where perishable writing media predominate, epigraphy affords insights into the styles and purposes of monumental or otherwise exceptional techniques of written recording.

Materials and techniques. The delimitation of epigraphy

vis-à-vis contiguous and related areas of antiquarian scholarship meets with some ambiguity. In a wide sense, epigrpahy concerns itself with the total firsthand transmission of the written remains of ancient civilization (as opposed to *post-factum* copying) and the nature of the material (*e.g.* stone, marble, metal, clay, terra-cotta, pottery, wood, wax tablets, papyrus, parchment) and the rechnique of recording (cutting, carving, engraving, casting, embossing, scratching, painting, drawing, etc.) have mere secondary relevance. Under this maximum definition certain sub disciplines may be included under the overall canopy of epigraphy; notably numismatics, which concerns itself with legends on coins and medals, and papyrology, the study of a especial type of perishable record that is normally preserved only in the dry climate of Egypt and in adjacent desert regions. In the case of Egypt, papyrology tends to impinge upon wood and elay media as well, thus leaving mainly stone and metal objects as the concern of epigraphy proper.

In general, however, unless so subdivided, epigraphy encompasses inscriptions at large, be they on primary writing surfaces or on such assorted objects as vases, potshereds, gems, seals, stamps, weights, rigs, lamps, and mirrors. A further related discipline is paleography, which concerns itself with the study of scribal hands and styles of writing and has significance for the dating of epigraphic as well as other written documents.

The nature of the materials and techniques used for inscriptions is closely tied to the external purpose of monumental, archival, and inclidental. Monumental inscriptions were intended for enduring display and were therefore, as a rule, executed in lasting material, such as stone or metal. Maximal exposure to mortal eyes need not have been the prime purpose of their origninators- *e.g.* the tomb chambers of Egyptian pharaohs, intended to be sealed forever, had their inner surfaces covered with monumental hieroglyphs; the great Bisitun inscription of King Darius I of Persia is on a high rock surface and legible only after precarious rock-climbing or from airborne conveyances.

Under this classification may be included also micromonumeental inscriptions found on such objects as coins, seals, and rings, meant to endure in their own right.

Archival inscriptions were essentially a feature of those early societies that kept records and that used such materials as have been preserved thanks to their intrinsic, accidental, or incidental durability. Many ancient Near Eastern cultures employed class tables for writing, which they fired to insure their soundness. Minoan and Mycenaean archivists in ancient Crete and Greece used perishable temporary elay records that were preserved by unintentional baking in the conflagrations that destroyed their storerooms, Papyrus records from Egypt have survived as a result of climatologically chace- mainly low humidity. The official purposes of public display and of archival preservation were sometimes complementary, and therefore coincidental or overlapping matter has been preserved. In some cultures the techniques employed in monumental and archival writing tended to differ (notably in Egypt, where increasingly cursive hieratic or demotic script contrasted sharply with monumental hieroglyphic), and occasionally the language itself would be different (for example, in the Hittite Empire, where the clay tablets in cuneiform employed mainly straight Hittite or Akkadian, whereas the monumental "hieroglyphic" rock inscriptions and seals used a distinect language.).

Incidental inscriptions may be defined as those not seriously meant for preservation. They include, for example, will scrawlings of the graffits type and casual records that wee kept on cheap writing matter such as potsherds (*as-lrac a)* and scraps of papyrus. Many a city dump of ancient Egypt has ytelded a rich harvest fro the study of daily life.

Inscriptions as historical source material. In studying the political, administrative, legislative, and dynastic records of extinct civilizations, the modern historian must bring to bear all the evidence at his disposal; and such evidence may vary sharply from once locality and period to another. Historiography in the modern sense- the analytical ordering and interpretation of past institutions and events- is a invention of ancient Greece, and even there it only gradually eschewed the fabulous. In many early societies (*e.g. I Mesopotamia, Egypt*), chronographic records were either annalistic or legendary in kind and sometimes apologetic or propagandistic in purport; and in others (*e.g.* India) a cyclical world view prevailed and a lack of feeling for linear time depth precluded an ordered appreciation of the past, leaving only legendry- in such cases only synchronisms with time anchored events elsewhere allow a precise dating.

Thus, the amount of predigested ancient information bearing on antecedent events may vary from sophisticated literary to scrupulous epigraphic, or may be wholly lacking of largely valueless. In the latter instances the historian is almost exclusively dependent for native information on primary documents, and such documents are in most cases inscriptional.

Ancient Mesopotamia. Surviving epigraphic matter from the 3rd and early 2nd millennia BC includes both historical and quest-historical material. The Sumerian king list is a compilation of names, places, and wholly fabulous dates and exploits, apparently edited to show and promote time hallowed oneness of kingship in the face of the splintered city-states of the period. The Sargon Chronicle is a piece of literary legendry concentrating on spectacular figures and feats of the past, whereas contemporary royal inscriptions, notably by Sargon I of Akkad and Gudea of Lagash, are historical documents in the proper sense.

Both kinds of texts are preserved also from the Babylonian and Assyrian periods, from the reign of Hammurabi (1792-1750 BC) to the 6th century BC. There are lists of date formulas and year names from Hammurabi's reign and from that of his son Samsuiluna; lists of Assyrian eponymous year names, based on those of dignisaries; the Babylonian king lists, running from Hammurabi through the Kassite era and the Assyrian domination of Babylon to the last flicker of Babylonian self-assertion in the early 6h century BC: the Assyrian king list from Khorsabad which made good use of earlier compilations; and notably the so-called Synchronistic

Chronicie, which Juxtaposed the kings of Assyria and Babylonia in the same millennial sequence. Historical documents comprise above all the stately sequence of annals by the kings of Assyria, recorded on stone slabs, stelae, foundation markers of buildings, bronze gates, statues, and obelisks and in clay archives (prisms, cylinders, tablets). Starting in the Old Assyrian period, they were especially extensive in the reigns of Tiglath pileser I (1115-1077 BC). shurnasirpal II (883-859 BC), Shalmaneser III (858-824 BC). Adadniran III (810-783 BC). Tiglath pileser III (744-727 BC). Shaimaneser V (726-722 BC). Esarhaddon (e. 680-669 BC), and Ashurbanipal (668-627 BC).

For all their swaggering bombast and flaunting of deliberate cruelty, the annals provide prime historical source material. The detail of the Assyrian conquest of Syria. Palestine, parts of Asia Minor, cyprus, Arbia, and Egypt would be spotty indeed without recourse to these annals, for they show the centre of political power, unlike such provincial records as those from contemporary Egypt or the Old Testament.

Legal compilations and law codes also have pride of place in the epigraphic record of ancient Mesopotamia. These from a unique succession, starting in the 3rd millennium BC with that of King Ur-Nammu of the Sumerian 3rd dynasty of Ur (c. 2100 BC), continuing with those of the Sumero-Akkadian king Lipit-Ishtar (in Sumerian) and King Bilalama of Eshnunna (in Akkadian) during the interval of the 3rd dynasty of Ur, and the rise of the amorite dynasty of Hammurabi (c. 2000 BC), culminating in the great dionrite stela of Hammurabi (c. 1750 BC), showing retardation and recrudescence in the Middle Assyrian laws that are found on elay tablets at Ashur (at the time of Tiglath-pileser 1), and petering out in the fragmentary Neo-Babylonian laws dating from the 7th century BC.

The stela of Hammurabi must have been originally set up in some Babylonian population centre for the literate to read and know their rights. Some Elamite invader must have carried it off to Susa (perhaps c. 1200 BC), where it was found in 1901 and removed to the Louvre in Paris. The bulk of the stela contains the text of the code, partly erased on the obverse but restorable in some measure from clay-tablet versions of the same laws. The top depicts the king in a worshipful pose, receiving the laws from the sun god. shamash. In reality Hammurabi- the sixth of 11 king of the Old Babylonian or Amorite dynasty was a practical codifier rather than a revelatiory mediator of law. His code was an effort to fuse into a workable whole the ancient inheritance of Sumerian based jurisprudence and the Semitic talion law (punishment according to the "eye-for-an-eye and tooth-for-a-tooth" principle) of the Akkadian super stratum. The result is not a model of economy of arrangement of logical organization, but the code of Hammurabi constitutes nevertheless the first great legal monument in the history of making. the later Assyrian laws show traces of further removal from the cradle of Sienna civilization since they are both harsher and noticeably more primitive.

Incient Egypt. Egypt attracted the special curiosity of the Greeks, and Herodotus (5th century BC) devoted an entire book to on- the spot observation and fanciful tales about the land of the Nile. The lost *Aigyptiaka (or Aegyptiaca)* of Manetho (3rd century BC) contained the roster of 30 dynasties, which still underlies the chronology of ancient Egypt. Such classical writers as Strabo, Plutarch, and Pliny the Elder all dealt with various aspects of Egyptian antiquities.

Yet the fund of knowledge would be woefully skeletal and inaccurate without the explicit testimony of contemporary records from Egypt itself. The decipherment of the Egyptian writings gave the impetus to Egyptian epigraphy. The progress of excavations multiplied the corpora of texts, especially adding the papyrological dimension. In addition, cuneiform Akkadian on clay tablets was the international diplomatic medium of writing during the most brilliant phases of Egyptian history and is hence an internal part of the Egyptian epigraphic record.

The historically significant Egyptian epigraphic texts, apart from their external peculiarities, have likewise special traits relating to genres. There is little attempt at historiography and great fluctuation in bulk in the course of dynastic vicissitudes. They are mainly annalistic and thus firsthand accounts of pharaonic or other high-leval deeds; but the pecullar features of stylization, stereotyping, and usurpation must frequently give the careful historian pause and sometimes debase the face value of the record. Written monuments became somewhat numerous during the 4th dynasty (c. 261-2494 BC), that of the pyramid builders Khufu, Khafre, and Menkaure. Notable are the fragmentary annals of Snefru, which already alluded to dealings with Asian, aht chronic goal of Egyptian territorial ambitions. Historic records persisted under the following two dynasties, with particular articulateness in the rign of Pepi I, third king of the 6th dynasty (c. 2345- c. 2181 BC), then subsided until a modest reemergence in the (Theban) Middle Kingdom of the 12th dynasty (1991-1786 BC). Another silence shrouded the period of the Hyksos king (c. 1720-1570 BC), broken only subsequently by such retrospective revulsion at the memory of barbarian domination as that in Queen Hatshepsut's temple inscription (c. 1475 BC) at Istable Antar in Middle Egypt. The golden age of historical recording began in the 15th century BC with the central rulers of the 18th dynasty, notably Thutmose III and Amenhotep II and III. Thutmose's annals on the walls of the temple of Karnak describe 20 years of ceaseless military activity in Asia, some 16 campaigns in all, and are supplemented by stelae from Armant in Upper Egypt and Gebei Barkal near the Fourth Cataract, s well as by lists of conquered lands at Karnak. Similar material continued in the reigns of Amenhotep II and III, in the latter's case importantly supplemented by the cuneiform correspondence with foreign powers (Mitanni, Arzawa etc.), which was subsequently stockpiled and archived by Ikhnation in his transitory new capital, where it lay buned to await the modern excavators of Tell el-Amarna. Ikhnation's religious preoccupations (he changed the official religion to the worship of the sun god Aton), and political apathy led to the loss of many of Egypt's Asian possessions. Records of Ikhnaton's short-lived son-in-law. Tutankhamen, at Thebes (c. 1350 BC), make recantation and restoration for the heresy. Tutankhamen's successor, the warlord pharaoh Horemheb, left boastful accounts of foreign conquest that sound suspiciously grandiose in relation to plausible reality.

In the 19th dynasty (1320-1200 BC) Sen. I went to war against the Syrians. Hittites, and Libyans, letting the world know about it on the walls of Karnak. But in this respect hew was no match for this long-lived son. Rames II, who usurped the monuments of other and covered unprecedented amounts of wall spcacewith his own real or inflated exploits. (The Battle of Kadesh against the Hittites in 1299 BC, which ended in a stalemate, was given Lavish coverage as a triumph on temple wails at Karnak. Abydos, and Abu Simbel.) In the 20th dynasty (1200-1085 BC) occurred incursion of the "sea peoples", and the records of Ramese III detailed both the crisis and the increasing accumulation of wealth and power in the religious establishment. subsequently, Egyptian history receded from the world scene, with "Libyan" and "Ethiopic" dynasties and a brief Saite renaissance of the 26th dynasty (664-525 BC), already under the Assyrian and Babylonian shadow, soon to be replaced by the Persian. The firsthand political records declined accordingly, although they remain of significance for local history down to the Ptolemaic era, a dynasty that ruled Egypt beginning in 305 BC, founded by Ptolemy I Soter, a general under Alexander the Great.

No Law codes have been found in Egypt, presumably because codification was not practied. there are, however, toyal administrative and legal decrees granting privileges and immunities and also records of legal proceeding, especially of the Theban tomb-robbery trials during the 20th dynasty.

Other ancient Middle Eastern regions. Regions adjacent to the power centre of Mesopotamia. Egypt, and Iran were frequently mere political and administrative adjuncts, often obscure vassaldoms of adverseness with out notable or attested written traditions. The Mitanni kingdom in northern Mesopotamia had some ephemeral big-power dealing with Egypt in the days of Amenhotep III, but its capital city is still lost in the sands, and thus its presently known epigraphic tradition in merely part of the correspondence in the Tell el-Amarna archives. The records of the Elamite kingdom with its capital at Susa were mostly ancilary to Mesopotamia in the 2nd millennium BC, and to Iran later on. The region of Syria and what later cameto be called Palestine was in the 2nd millennium the object of an extended tug-of-war between Egypt and the Hittite kingdom.

The Hittites were, in fact, the third great international power in the Near East during part of the 2nd millennium BC, and the epigraphic yield of their royal archives at Bogazkoy in central Asia Minor matches or even surpasses in richness that of Mesopotamia and Egypt for the few centuries in question. The cuneiform records of the Hittites contain a tradition of unique royal political self expression. These documents begin with the oldest known Hittite text. The inscription of the early ruler Anittas, detailing dynastic struggles of an obscure and possibly apocryphal past. From the founder of the Old Kingdom, the firmly historical Haittusilis I (Labarnas II), came an annalistic autobiography (excavated in 1957) and a "fare well address" or political testament, in Hittite as well as Akkadian versions. Subsequent events, including the capture of Babylon by Hattusilis son. Mursilis I (c. 1590 BC), and the succeeding era of regicidal upheavals, are known from an edict of King Telipinus, who detailed them as he set about regulating the rights of royal succession. The subsequent founder of the Hittite Empire. Suppiluliumas I (c. 1350 BC), and his son Mursilis II left annals detaling their military and political deeds. Mursilis was a particularly prolific annalist and edited his father's annals as well. The great encounter with Ramese II at kadesh in 1299 BC occurred in the reign of Mursilis son, Muwatallis and left an echo in the autobiography of his brother and successor. hattusilis III. Hattusilis autobiography is a tract of self-justification for a breach of the edict of telipinus in deposing his nephew and predecessorurhi-Teshub (Mursilis III).

Other Hittite documents inveigh against treasonable

behavior ("Indictment of Modulates') or contain detailed instructions for military, civil, and court officialdom. Hittite queens had prerogatives of independent high-level initiative, and examples of their correspondence with foreign potentates supplement the archives of their husbands. The most remarkable external political documents are numerous state treaties, sometimes between equals but more often covenants specifying protectorate of vassaldom status for subordinate states on the fringes of the kingdom. Equally notable is the Hittite Law Code, relatively enlightened and mild in the face of its contemporary counterparts in Mesopotamia. Altogether, the inscriptional documents are practically the exclusive source material for knowledge often Hittites; not even the existence of location of their empire was surmised prior to the discovery of their archives.

After the collapse of the Hittite Empire (c. 1190 BC), significant records from Asia Minor ceased for many centuries, whereas local history in the Syro-Palestinian area was recorded in the inscriptions of petty dynasts increasingly under the shadow of Assyrian domination. The brek with the past in evident in the writing systems (Hittite Hieroglyphs or West Semitic alphabet rather than cuneiform) and in the languages (Indo-European Anatolian, Canaanite, Aramaic). Into this category fall the stela of King Mesha of Moab (c. 830 BC) now in the Louvre, the Phoenician Hieroglyphic Luvian bilingual inscription of azitawadda of adana (late 8th century BC), and those of the kings of Ya'diya-Samál. Contemporary cuneiform documents from the Urartyu kingdom around Lake Van in eastern Anatolia are historically and culturally an offshoot of the history of 8th century Assyria.

Ancient Iran. Epigraphically recorded history in ancient Persia began dramatically with the rise of the Achaemenid dynasty in the 6th century BC. Cyrus II the great's conquest of Media, Lydia, and Babylonia, Cambyses' occupation of Egypt, and the incursions into Greece of the succeeding side branch of the family, beginning with Darius I, created in short order a world power destined for centre stage on the international scene for the following rwo centuries. The international character of the empire is reflected in the frequently trailingual royal inscriptions with Akkadian and Elamite versions in traditional syllabic cuneiform, and the Old Persian text in its own simplified quasi-alphabetic system of Wedge-Shaped writing. The Achaemenids'time span ranges from Darius great grandfather. Ariaramnes, to their less glorious progeny, who were ultimately extinguished by Alexander the Great. The empire was centred in Persia; but a granite stela of Darius, found near the Suez Canal, recorded in Old Persian, Elamite, Akkadian, and hieroglyphic Egyptian the opening of a canal from the Red Sea to the Nile. The epigraphic material included rock surfaces, building walls, columns, doorways, cornices, statues, and doorknobs; bricks, plaques, plates, and tabletes ofclay, stone, gold, and silver; vases, weights, and seals. Almost all the longer texts were by Darius and Xerxes I; an important one of Xerxes was found on a stone tablet at Persepolis in 1967. The great Bisitun rock inscription of Darius runs to several hundred long lines in Old Persian alone, besides the Elamite and Akkadian versions. It is accompanied by 11minor inscriptions, serving as keys to the sculpted scene of the panel, which dhows Darius triumphant over the usurping impostor Gaumata and hine other rebels. The text is a self statement of how Darius gained and consolidated his rule. It apparently had currency in the realm, apart from being tucked away on a sheer cliff wall, for a partial duplicate of the Akkadian version has been found on a dolerite (basait) block from Babylon, and papyrus fragments from Elephantine have yieided scraps of an Aramatic edition. One peculiar documentary value of the text is that the same period in Persian history is extensively covered in the Greek literary tradition by Herodotus. Ctesias, and others, and scholars can thus juxtapose Darius own accounts with those of almost contemporary foreign historians. As an example, Darius stressed his role as saviour of the fatherland from the elutches of an upstart who pretended to be Smerdis, the brother ofDarius predecessor Campbyses. The latter had murdered Smerdis and was carrying on various outrages in Egypt when word came of the impostor's takeover back home. Darius stated that it was a fatal matter without human interference, and that thus Darius hands were clean in taking action against the impostor. According to Herodotus. Cambyese legendary death involved a freak occurrence as he prepared to leave for home an accidentally self-inflickted wound leading to gangrene. Both the meaning and intent of Darius description are thus confirmed/

From later Arsacid (Parthian) and Sasanid period of Iranian history, there are likewise royal inscriptions that shed light on their respective eras down to the Islamic conquest in the 8th century AD, and new specimens re still being discovered.

Ancient India. India's past became anchored in historical times and separable from legend only with the establishment of firm synchronisms with outside data. One such link is the Seleucid embassy of Megasthenes to the Maurya king Candragupta (Greek Sandrokottos) at Pataliputra (Greek Palimbothra) in Magadha (modern day Bihar). The Maurya dynasty was continued in the early 3rd century BC by Candragupt's son Bindusara (Amitrochates in the Greek sources) and had extended its power over much of the subcontinent. But then the Greek sources fall silent, and Indic literary tradition supplies only the usual web of Bindusara's son and successor Asoka. As a matter of epigraphic fact. Asoka ruled all of northern India and a large portion of the south, from Taxila an beyond to Mysore and Kalinga (coast of Orissa and Andhra Pradesh). His 14 rock edicts and seven pillar edicts of Bindusara's son and successor asoka. As a matter of epigrpahic fact. asoka ruled all of northern India and a large portion of the south, from taxila and beyond to Mysore and Kalinga (coast of Orissa and Andhra Pradesh). His 14 rock edicts and seven pillar edicts in numerous versions and copies, plus separate minor texts, are scattered over this expanse in the Prakrit language of his time and in the Brahmi script, except fro some northwestern examples of the Aramaic-inspired kharosthi writing. Even a Greek

Aramaic bilingual version was found in 1958 ner Kandahar in Afghanistan. Ashoka's edicts re proclamations and ordinances in a Buddhistic spirit designed to impart good order, morality, and moderation by the Emperor's personal enjoining and example. Particularly notable in the 13th rock edict, which bares the ruler's pangs of conscience over the conquest of Kalinga eight years after his coronation, his continuing sorrow over the cruelties committed, and his pledge to substitute the victory of Buddhist religious law *(dhamma)* for all earthly conquest.

Asoka's edicts would rate am mere historiography footnote for their inconsequential transitoriness, were it not that in the same breath Asoka supplied the very synchronisms that are the main key to ancient Indian chronology. Among his western neighbours he mentioned Amtiyoge (Antiochus II Theos of Syria), tulamaye (Ptolemy II Philadelphus of Egypt). Antekine (Antigonus II Gonatas of Macedonia). Maka (Magas of Cyrene), and Alikasudaro (Alexander of Epirus or Alexander of Corinth). The dates of these contemporaries circumscribe the time of Asok's reign; combined with the earlier Greek synchronisms, they afford a firm foundation for the correlation of Indic and Mediterranean events. The edicts of Asoka are thus a prime example of the value of inscriptions for historiography dating and constitute a fixed record unparalleled in ancient Indian tradition. Later periods of Indian history, such as those of the Indo-Seythian and Gupta rulers, are also represented in epigraphic documents of some historical value.

Ancint China. In China also, inscriptions ae a means of separating chronological fact from historiography legend. Nonepigraphic book composition on wood or bamboo strips had an early history in China, beginning in the later 2nd millennium BC; its scope was such that the Chín emperor Shih Huang-ti went down in history as a book burner in 213 BC. The Sn Tai, or three periods of early chinese history (Hsia, c. 2205-1766 BC, shang, c. 1766-1122 BC; Chou and Chín, c. 1122-206 BC), were long considered by Western scholars purely legendary down to the early Chou period, and the literary documents (such as the *Shu Ching* or "Classic of History") were dismissed s compilations consisting mostly of successive overlays of little historical value. But the historicity of written records from the later Shang era (c. 1400-1122 BC) is now apparent from the mass of inscribed archeological material found especially in northern Honan Province. These include, in particular, the so-called oracle bones (mostly tortoise shells and scapulae of animals), bearing incised records of royal divination. At the site of the Shang capital. Yin, were discovered inscribed vessels of bronze, bone, pottery, jade, and stone, probably ceremonial in nature and related to official ritual uses such as ancestor worship. The script is a mixture of pictograms, word signs, and phonograms. From the ensuing Chou era, bronze inscriptions of official provenance have likewise been found, especially records of royal largesse. Inscriptions from later periods from a steady but subsidiary source of information beside the larger, no epigraphic written record.

Ancient Greece. The historically significant epigraphic record of classical Greece differs in many ways from most of those discussed above. Much of it is parallelled by a mature and independent tradition of professional literary historiography. except fro the preclassical Helladic (Mycenaean) period of the 3rd millennium BC (see below), there was no archival tradition, although the bulk of "monumental" records sometimes approximates the same purpose of massive preservation. There was no allimportant power centre and no dominant rulership before Hellenistic and Roman times; thus the geographical scattering of records was extereme, although naturally with some focuses of emphasis such as Athens. Above all, there was continuity from the inception of literacy, with gradual but steady increase in bulk.

Epigraphically transmitted historiography in Greece is extremely scarce because the probing of past events has passed beyond the stage of dynastically centred and sheltered annalism; an example is the "Marmor Parium" (from the island of Paros and now at Oxford), which contains a chronographic rundown of traditional dates and events of Greek history. Rather than monolithic records of autocracy, there is history in the making by a plethora of tyrannical, oligarchic, or democratic microentities. Treaties of alliance and various other agreements between the multiple city states recorded on metal or stone and publicly displayed, or consecrated at such pan Hellenic sanctuaries as Delphi or Olympia from an important part of the epigraphic yield. Joint citizenship covenants, decrees concerning the return of exiles, monetary agreements on coinage and debts, and tribute lists are typical examples. They are supplemented by the records of arbitration of interstate disputes, most often boundary matters, by third party commissions. Thus, when around 240 BC a territorial disagreement arose between Epidaurus and Corinth, the Achaean League appointed a group of 151 Megarians as mediators, and their report survives. Further extensions of such "international" documentation are the *proxenia* decrees, which amount to letters of patent and resolutions of appreciation issued by one state to a citizen of another for service as *proxenos,* a kind of honorary consul looking after the interests of the other state's citizens. The extensive colonization efforts by the Greeks around the Mediterranean produced a further kind of political document- regulations governing conditions for emigration and retun, citizenship rights of the colonists, and relations between the colony and the mother community. Not all historically meaningful international records are of the monumental type. Greek mercenaries, of Pharaoh psamtik I (ruled 594-589 BC_ left their scrawlings on the legs of a colossal statue at Abu Simbel on the upper Nile, proving by their names and dialect that they ame from Rhodes and Ionia and were far abroad on foreign adventure.

Internal documents of the various Greek states include numerous records of decrees and ordinances, both administrative and legislative. Stereotyped Athenian ones are complemented by variant forms in other localities; most contain a preamble setting forth the date and the officialdom in charge, the circumstances occasioning the action, the decision itself, means and sanctions for its enforcemet, and sometimes instructions for providing and affixing the very physical record that has been preserved. Sometimes they amount to formal laws, such as those directed against extravagances in funeral practices.

Financial data of the states were minutely and permanently inscribed on stone, and the accounts thus displayed recorded in detail the receipts, expenditures, and balances of public funds. Very specific reports cover projects of public construction, including both technical and budgetal details, allowing sometimes the integral modern reconstruction of the buildings from the reports alone. The records of the Erechtheum and the Parthenon at Athens are well preserved, as are inventories of military expenditures, especially those of the Athenian navy. Knowledge of the ephebic system at Athens, a paramilitary youth organization, is in the main based on epigraphic material.

The only law code in the Greek epigraphic tradition is the laws of Gortyn in central Crete., inscribed on the slabs of a circular wall which, if completely preserved, would have been nearly 100 yet (30 meters) in diameter. The 12t columns of text, each on four layers of stone and some five feet (1.5 meters) high, are about 30 fet (nine metres) in sideways length and contain more than 600 lines of text, gbeing the longest Greek epigraphic monument; parts of some columns of further text survive, the so-called Second Code. The probable date of this inscription is the first half of the 5th century BC. The code deals with such matters as disputed ownership of slaves, rape and adultery, rights of a wife upon divotce or death of husband, disposition of children born after divorce, inheritance, sale and mortgaging of property, ransom, children of mixed marriages, and adoption. While self-contained, it evidently does not represent the entirety of laws; curiously, it stresses those areas of civil law (inheritance, adoption) that are notably lacking in the Hittite Law Code. The uniqueness of this code in the Greek world points up the relative isolation and marginality of the Cretan tradition, with tendencies to codification more reminiscent of Anatolia and the Near East generally.

Ancient Rome. While partly overlapping Greek inscriptions in time and type, those of Rome nevertheless present distinct peculiarities. There is a high measure of standardization in kind and style, despite lingering local traditions in more remote areas. Extensive and excessive use was made of initials and abbreviations, to the point of serious impediments to comprehension' lists of such abbreviations are standard adjuncts to modern handbooks on Latin epigraphy. Stone and bronze were standard material, but there was more use made of bricks, tiles, and terra-cotta, and practices of stamping and signing such matter are of help in identification and dating.

Literary and epigraphic records of early republican Rome are scant and fragmentary. Latin was at the time still largely confined to Rome proper, with Oscan, Etruscan, and colonial Greek spoken and written in much of Italy. With the arrival of extended political power there was little early literacy to fall back on, and historiography attempts at retrospection ended in epicized myth and legendry (*e.g.* in Livy_. The Greeks on the southern coastal fringe had little truck with the hinterlands of early times. The Etruscan impact on Rome is evident, but shortcomings in discovering epigraphic records of Etruscan city sites (as opposed to necropolises_ and in understanding the Etruscan language. Limit the historical data derivable from Etruscology. The potential for, such illumination is seen from the discovery of gold tablets at Pyrgi in 1964 that contain a dedication in Etruscan and Phoenician by the Etruscan king of Caere, Thefarie Velianas, to the syncretized goddess Uni (Juno) Astartc. Datable to around 500 BC, the text shows Etruscans ruling in the outskirts of Rome, with enough Phoenician or Punic (Carthaginian) martitime presence to warrant symbiotic and syncrestic bilingualism. The vital historical import of such attestations, pieced together with later Greek and Roman historiography data, is patently manifest.

No historically important epigraphic Latin text from republican Rome antedates the 2nd century Bc. The marble

Columna Rostrata- found in Rome in 1565 and now at the Palazzo der Conseryatori on the Capitoline Hillrecords a naval victory of Duilius (consul in 260 BC) over the Carthaginians; but the inscription, replete with fake archaism, dates from a restoration effort in early imperial days. The *fasti consulares* and similar lists afford a summary sequence of consulates, magistratures, and triumphs. The one truly significant epigraphic historical text is the "Res gestae divi Augusti." an autobiogrpahical record of Augustus' rule, which was exhibited in many places but is bestknown as the Monumental ancyranum, from the bilingual (Latin and Greek) version carved on the walls of the Temple of Rome and Augustus at Ankara (Turkey).

By the time the epigraphic record became abundant. Rome's domination was secure and the political documentation was one of imperial outflow and of local sycophancy. Treaties of republican Rome with foreign powers survive merely in the works of literary historians. Among "internal" documents from republican days are several epigraphic texts of "significance: the Senatusconsultum de Bacchanalibus, on a bronze table found in 1640 in Bruttium (the "toe" of Italy) and now in Vienna, is a consular edict on Senate authority, regulating Dionysiac outbursts in Italy in 186 BC; pieces of the laws Lex Acilia Repetundarum (123 BC) and Lex agraria (111 BC) were found in the 16th century on opposite sides of what was once a large bronze tablet; the local laws of the town of Bantia (on the borderlands of Lucania and Apulia in southern Italy) are inscribed on a fragmentary bronze tablet found in 1790 (now in Naples), with a Latin-language texton one side and the longest known Oscan inscription on the other, both datable to the late 2nd century BC; parts of the Lex Cornelia de Viginti Quaestoribus (81 BC) are preserved on a large bronze tablet found at Rome; Julius Caesare's Lex Julia Municipalis of 45 BC was found near Heraclea in Lucania. On the whole, however, the transmission of Roman law, from the earliest fragments to the mature codifications, is no epigraphic. In later times the flood of administrative decrees increases with the growth of centralized autocracy. Typically Roman epigraphic material of imperial date comprise further building inscriptions, military records, and honorific texts.

The Turkic peoples. The oldest monuments of turkic languages- inscribed on stones, and datable to the early 8th century AD- were discovered in the late 19th century in southern Siberia around the Yenisey River and in northern Mongolia near the capital of Urga 9modern Ulaanbaatar), Deciphered in 1893 by the Danish scholar Vilhelm thomsen, they provide valuagle insights into the history of central Asia around the 7th century AD. These records of the rurk dynasty (Chinese T'u-chueh)comprise especially texts found at Kosh-Tsaidam on the Orhon (Orkhon) Gol (rive), including also Chinese text. These texts throw light on the nomadic culture of the tribal empire controlled by the Turk dynasty, including shamanism, calendar, customs, and social structure, with strong Chinese influence detectable in the latter. After the decline of the Turk people (c. 745), their successor, the Uighurs, perpetuated for a time the same kind of monumental dynastic epigraphy, the writing system of which is an offshoot of the Aramaic alphabet, presumably mediated by the Iranian-scripts took over (especially the so-called Uighur alphabet, of Syriac origin, which was further transmitted to the Mongols and the Manchus) and inscriptional monuments gave way to manuscript records such as those found in Chinese Turkistan (Turfan) in the lat 19th century (along with texts in Sanskrit, Sogdian, Tocharain, and other Indo-European idioms), attesting to a coexistence of Buddhist. Manichaean, and Nestorian Christian religious communities. The later Turkish peoples, including the Anatolian Seljuqs and Ottomans, has an Islamic book-tradition, to which the inscriptional record is merely incidental.

Northern Europe. The advent of writing was slow north of the Alps; it came either from direct expansionary exportation by Greek coastal colonies and the Roman Empire, as in Gaul and the Iberain Peninsula, or indirect inspiration from the same quarter, as in writing in the Irish and British ogham alphabet and the Germanic runes.

Celt-Iberian inscriptions from Spain and Celtic ones from Gaul and Ireland are scarce, mostly brie, and notably devold of usable historical information, apart from their mere monumental existence and linguistic and onomastic (pertaining to names) content. Occasional items such as the fragmentary Gaulish Calendar of Coligny afford insights into local cultural practices apart from an overwhelming trend to romanization.

The runic alphabet- a Germanic alphabet, originally of 124 letters, also called futhark- and its offshoots (the scandinavian, especially Danish, 16-letter veriety from the 9th century AD, and Anglo-Saxon versions, from the 3td to the 10th centuries AD, also called futhorc) are probably of "North Etuscan" or "Sub-Alpine"Italic inspiration, datable to around 200BC. The "North Italic" letters of the Germanic text *harixasti teiva.* "to the god Harigast", on a helmet from Negau (southern Austria) are probably from that time of transmission. Runic inscriptions from the era of migrations, raining from eastern France through Germany up to Denmark and eastward via Poland to Romania, are supplemented by the later, richer yield from England and Scandinavia. Native Anglo-Saxon runic epigraphy, mostly in Northumbria, Mercta, and Kent, petered out around the 10th century, whereas the Scandinavian tradition (including its enclaves on British soil) endured for several more centuries. Sweden has some 3,000 runic monuments; Norway and Denmark, perhaps 400 each: while Iceland has remarkably few, apparently in inverse proportion to the literary flowering in that colonial outpost. The Vikings left their runic calling cards in far-flung place, including those in the Greek port of Piraeus, on the Black Sea coast, in varangian Russia, in Scotland. Ireland, and the Isle of Man, and the Orkneys. Hebrides, and Shetland islands; Greenland has its share, but alleged specimens from North America, notably the Kensington Stone from Minnesota, telling of the westward trek of an exploration party from Vinland, ard invanably crude latter day forgeries.

The purposes of runic inscriptions were usually either

dedicatory or commemorative, sometimes magic, and frequently sepulchral. The longest, that from Rok in Sweden (725 runes), seems to contain a catalog of cpic deeds possibly those of the Ostrogoth king Theoderic. The prime historical value of runic epigraphs is usually what and where they are, rather than what they depict of record.

Inscriptions as social and cultural records. In the preceding section, inscriptions were evaluated as sources for the presence and migrations of peoples, the existence and chronology of political states, their dynastic histories, foreign relations, internal governance, legal institutions, and official acts. In this section, epigraphy is surveyed for information about how past civilizations lived; their religious beliefs and practices; their business, financial, legal, and social relations; and what shape their aspirations assumed in terms of verbal creativity. The subdivision of civilizations surveyed differs somewhat arbitrarily from the earlier section by the omission of certain areas and the inclusion of Crete and Mycenaean Greece. In fact, Indic and Chinese epigraphic matter discussed above could just as well have fitted the "religious" slot, but its royal character and chronological importance for official history dictated otherwise, Conversely, the Cretan and Mycenaean tablets are purely economic inventories, but they might possibly have been included with history above for the very important historical fact that they prove the ruling presence of Greeks at Knossos during the 2nd millennium BC. The varying degree of importance of epigraphic material in various cultures persists; in Mesopotamia and the ancient Near East its dominance was nearly total; in Egypt in combined with the papyrological dimension; in Crete it was merely a flash in a prehistoric darkness, while in ancient Greece and Rome, it was a supplementary concomitant of the no epigraphic literary tradition.

Ancient Mesopotamia. Apmle specimens of Akkadian language clay-tablet epistolography have been found at severl sties, notably Tell el-Amarna in Egypt and Tell al-Hariri on the middle Euphrates (the ancient Mari of c. 1700 BC). The Amarna letters, about 400 of them, were composed in corrupt

Akkadian by Canaanite scribes in Syria and Palestine and were largely official in character. The Mari letters, some 5,000 in number, are more illustrative of normal day-to-day written communication in a Mesopotamian milieu proper.

Another aspect of everyday life in ancient Mesopotamia is amply illustrated by thousands of ealy tablets of a practical legal nature, as distinct from the formal laws. These archivally preserved records from various periods use Sumerian. Old Akkadian, Babylonian, and Assyrian alike. They detail law suis, court decision, marriage contracts, divorce procedings and settlements, sale adoptions (fictitious acts circumventing prohibitions against land sales outside the family), loan agreements, tax receipts, and much else. Commercial inventories, such as those of the Old Assyrian merchant colony at *Karum Kanes* in central Asia Minor (20th century BC), complete the picture.

Due to the religious sanction of law, legal records were often stockpiled in temple archives. These latter are also the source of more directly cultic texts, such as descriptions of rituals, which come under such headings as "Temple Program for the New Year's Festivals at Babylon", "Ritual to be Followed by the Kalu (priest) when Covering the Temple Kettle-Drum", "Ritual for the Repair of a Temple", and "Program of the Pageant of the Statue of the God Anu at Uruk". Prayers, lamentations, and hymns in both Sumerian and Akkadian are extant, addressed to deities such as the goddess Ishtar, the moon god Sin, the sun god Shamash, the great triad Anu, Enlil, and Ea, and the Babylonian patron god Marduk. The Sumerian "Lament for the Destruction of Ur" bemoans the city's fall to Elamites and Subarians. Often the king himself is the spokesman in the text. Wisdom literature, such as proverbs and fables (*e.g.* "Dispute between the date Palm and the Tamarisk"), poetic meditations, oracles, divination records, omens, and prophecies are further examples of Mesopotamian genres that only epigraphy has preserved.

Sumerian and Akkadian narrative literature is likewise of wholly inscriptional transmission. It contains man's earliest preserved literary creations in the Sumerian sequence, especially the texts from tablets found at Nippur. These include the "Paradise myth" of th god Enki and the goddess Ninhursag in the pure, clean, and bright land of Dilmun; the story of Dumuzi and Enkimdu (the petulant shepherd god versus the peace-loving farmer god, inversely reminiscent of the Cain-Abel antagonism in Genesis but not culminating in murder); "The Deluge" with its, Noah-hero Ziusudra; "Inanna's Descent to the Nether World", which prefigures the later Akkadian "Ishtar's Descent", and the lays of Gilgamesh, which show the Sumerian traditions there were later partly organized and transformed into the Akkadian epic. The latter include "Gilgamesh and Agga of Kish", a story of confrontation between early sumerian city-states; "Gilgamesh and the Land of the Living"; and "The Death of Gilgamesh", with its haunting parallelistic refrain "he lies, he rises not". The Akkadian *Epic of Gilgamesh* is divided into 12 tablets, the longest of which is more than 300 lines; this "Flood Tablet" (the 11th) is virtually intact and comes, like almost all Assyrian language Gilgamesh texts, from the library of Ashurbanipal at Ninveh (7th century BC). from the 2nd millennium there are fragments of a Hittite version from Bogazkoy, as well as minor traces of a Hurrian translation. Old Babylonian correspondences to tablets 1-3 and 10 are found on a tablet from Sippar (c. 1800 BC). The 12th tablet is a literal translation from Sumerian, whereas the rest amounts to a self-contained Akkadian epic original, based on Sumerian motifs but with a thrust of its own. The most complete reconstruction involves a combination of Assyrian. Old Babylonian, and Hittite versions.

The other famous Mesopotamian epic. *Enuma elish.* "When on high, details the story of cosmic creation and of how Marduk became the breat god of Babylon: it had more immediate cultic attachments because its recitation formed part of the New Year festival.

Further Akkadian literary creation is attested in the epic of Atrahasis, a tale of mankind's punishment through lonian and Assyrian versions. The story of Adapa, found in parts in the Tell el-Amarna archives and the library of Ashurbanipal, is similar to Gilgamesh's quest for immortality. The myth of Zu deals with the theft of the tables of fate and the usurpation of almightiness by the bird god Zu. The legend of Etana, a nemesake of the shepherd king who ascened to heaven in the mythical postdiluvian Sumerian dynasty of Kish, recounts in its Old Babylonan and Assyrian recensions the heavenly flightof etana on the wings of a eagle in order to acquire the magic birth plant that would cure his childlessness. Death-oriented themes apper in the tale of Ishtar's descent, in the story of Nergal and Ereshkigal, and in various netherworld texts associated with th Tammuz myth and liturgy.

Ancient Egypt. The multitude of incidental day-to-day written matter on potsherds and papayrus, preserved by climatological quirks in Egypt, affords insights into the normal living patterns of ordinary people during the pharaonic, the Hellenistic (Ptolemaic0, and the Roman periods. More formal records of similar provenance may be described as legal in the wides sense, comprising such objects as land deeds, cadastrial inventories (tax surveys), wills, adoption decrees, and trial transcripts. Thus may technicalities or landholding in the Nile Delta during certain ancient periods survive, unwarranted by any normal expectancies of epigraphic preservation elsewhere; only the happenstance of the Creto-Mycenaean records (see below *Crete and Mycenaean Greece)* has accidentally transmitted something analogous.

Ritualistic texts are equally abundant, in both monumental and papyrological transmission. Notable among offertory liturgy was the mortuary service to the dead, acted out as a kind of tritual make-delieve in which the offering was referred to as the eye of Horus (the sacrifice) being given up on behalf of his father. Osiris (the departed). Ritual drama in general is amply attested in Egyptian religious practice; day-to-day ceremonial in the cult of gods or god-kings (pharaohs) was recorded in the minutest detail. Magic texts include incantations and charms against such dangerous creatures as snakes, scorpions, crocodiles, and lions. Even the buried dead were deemed in need of such protection, and hence the preserved samples are largely of mortuary provenance. An important category of epigraphs is constituted by curses, imprecations, and threats of divine vengeance against enemies, evildoers, and tomb violators in particular. Dream interpretation and oracular inquiry are represented on both monuments and papyri.

Of a more secular nature and on th verge of true literature are moral and didactic writings, particularly during the early Middle Kingdom (began c. 2133 BC), when a profound social and spiritual crisis seems to have gripped Egypt. Of such kind are "The Admonitions of Power" (a denunciation of current sin and evil in Hebrew "prophetic" manner_, the "colloquy of a prospective Suicide with His Own Soul", and especially copious compendia of conventional wisdom, frequently formulated as instructions from a royal or noble father to his son. Some part offer remarkable parallels to the Hebrew book of Proverbs.

On the same borderline to real literature stand mythical tales, including in particular the myths of creation by the god Atum of Heliopolis and the Memphite patron deity Ptah, whose eminence is reminiscent of the cultic fortunes of Marduk. The Memphite cosmogony, of 1st dynasty provenance, is an abstract one, with Ptah's creation conceived with his "heart" (mind) and "tongue"(word) rather than the usual physical detail. Other mythic tales concern the perils from the netherworld demon Apepi faced by the sun god re during his nightly journey in his solar boat; the rivalries between Horus and Seth for the succession of Osiris (a patent allegory of the tensions between Lower and Upper Egypt): mortuary texts particularly concerned with the Osiris myth and th prospect of judgment (*e.g.* the "Protestation of Innocence"), attested both monumentally and on papyri (the Book of the Dead); and pieces designed to bolster the supremacy of specified sites and deities, particularly Among-Re at Thebes.

Out of the latter tendency emerged hymnic poetry during the 18th and 19th dynasties, triggerd by an imperial trend toward unicentrism in government and universal syncretism in religion. The great hymns to Amon-Rewere matched during Ikhnaton's "Amarna revolution" by his great Ation-hymn, uncannily reminiscent of the 104th Psalm of the Old Testament. Victory hymns and prayers are further examples of poetic genre, as are purely secular pieces, including several collections of love songs from c. 1300 to 1100 BC, songs of farm workers and herdsmen, and feast songs for entertainment.

In nonreligious literary prose there is preserved the story of sinuhe, an account of the life of a Middle Kingdom official, his prosperous peregrination in Asia but continued yearning for the homeland, relieved at last by a chance to join the pharaonic court. Papyri and ostrich tell this story in a long succession of attestations through most of the 2nd millennium BC. Of later date (c. 1100 BC) is the "picaresque" narrative of the hieratic-script "Moscow papyrus", detailing the ill-financed mission of a certain Wen-Among from Karnak to Byblos to buy timber for a ceremonial barge of Among.

the Hittite Empire. The Bogazkoy archives are the unique central storehouse of Hittite records for the duration of that empire (only minor additions have been found elsewhere, such as letters at Tell el-Amarnaand Alalakh). The past of other cultures was know from external and nonepigraphic sources before the explorational and excavational discoveries of inscriptions; with the Hittites, however, the record is in one place and in toto.

Much may be learned of everyday life and social relations from legal texts, including, property rights, land tenure, and commodity prices are dealt with ain great and sometimes pedantic or amusing detail. More can be learned from gift deeds of land, cadastral lists, and trial records, the latter containing largely depositions of respondents and witnesses in civil suits. Unique in their kind are treatises on the training of racehorses. Astrological omen texts, divination records (hepatoscopy, auspicy, lottery oracles), and dream interpretations abound, largely patterned on Mesopotamian models; rituals of all kinds take up a disproportionate amount of space. Temple foundations and preocedures, festival ceremonies, epidemics, impotence, family quarrels, countermagic, royal welfare, birth, insomnia, and the manipulation of deities are among the topics of Hittite ritual; in a class by itself is a funeral ritual for royalty, reminiscent of Homeric practices. Not only the Hittite language but Hattic. Hurrian, Luwian, and Palaic are used in rituals. another large category is made up of hymns and prayers, most notably those of King Mursilis II. in particular his "plague prayers", in which he confesses sins and begs the storm god for mercy. Other notable examples are the prayer of Muwatallis to the sun god, the vows of Queen Puduhepa to the sun goddess, and the prayer of Kantuzilis with its intimations of mortality. Native Anatolian myuthical texts, such as those of the slaying of the dragon illuyankas and of the disappearance of the god Telipinus, were part of ritual recitation. Other mythical matter points up the crossroads character of Hittite civilization, being made up of Akkadian. Hurrian, and Canaanite themes. Most of the Hittite epigraphic corpus has some connection with religion.

Other countries of the ancient Middle East. Away from the big power centers some quite important site remain to be identified, such as the Mitannian capital of Wassukkani. Others (*e.g.* the fortress-town of Carchemish on the upper Euphrates, for some time a Hittite dependency) have yielded notable data, especially royal inscriptions in Hittite hieroglyphs. in particular the French excavations at Ras Shamra on the Syrian coast since 1929 have uncovered the inscriptional and other remains of the small but strategic city-state of Ugarit, which flourished in the 15th-13th centuries BC. Its own vowelless cuneiform alphabet, a radical departure from the Mesopotamian syllabary prototype, denotes an archaic Semitic dialect closely akin to Canaanite. The written documentation of this crossroads community, in a avariety of scripts and languages, provides information on the history of the area where Hittite and Egyptian power politics collided. But its most significant epigraphic products have been poetic epics of mythical and heroic scope, which go far to elucidate religious traditions otherwise known mainly from Old Testament bias. The great cycle of Baal and Anath brings to life the pantheon to which belonged also El. Asherah (the Astarte of the Phoenicians)., Kothar ("Deft", the craftsman god), and Yamm (the sea god). The tale of Aqhat is also on the borderline of myth, while that of King Keret (or Kret) takes place in a saga world somewhat reminiscent of the Greek Homeric tradition.

Scattered dedicatory inscriptions and papyrus texts shed some light on the lives and practices of the Aramaean speaking populations during the 1st millennium BC. From Palestine there are the Hebrew ostraca of Samaria, datable to the reign of Jeroboam II of Israel (8th century BC), which record names, families, and administrative and religious practices. Of equal significance are the ostraca of Lachish in southern Palestine, which probably immediately preceded the Chaldean onslaught of 589 BC. Phoenician texts are scattered around the Mediterranean, and bear witness to an extensive and protracted maritime supremacy.

The Old Person Achaemenid inscriptions (see above, *Ancient Iran)* are of some value in assessing the state religion of the time, which seems to have been a rather anemic from of official Zoroastrianism. Later monuments from the woder Iranian area help map its complicated religious history, such as the great inscription of the Kusana king Kaniska, found at Surkh-Kota in Afghanistan in 1957 and attesting to the Iranian language and Mithraic cults of ancient Bactria in the 2nd century AD. The Sasanian religious tradition of the 3rd-7th centuries, with its rigidified formal Zoroastrianism, is mainly of nonepigraphic attestation.

Crete and Mycendean Greece. The decipherment of the latest and most copiously attested of the Minoan linear scripts, the so-called Linear B. by British cryptologist Michael Ventris in 1953, is a major example of the dramatic impact epigraphic discovery can have on the most varied antiquarian disciplines. It supplied incontrovertible proof that the Mycenaean's on the Greek mainland during the 2nd millennium BC were Greek in language and likewise that Knossos in Crete was a

Greek speaking stronghold at the time of its final destruction (c. 1400 BC). The records from Knossos, Pylos in Messenia, and Mycenae in the Argolid are exclusively perishable inventories on clay tablets, kept in royal palaces or emporia and apparently meant to be discarded or teused anriually, thus they record data from the very last year of any goven establishment, just before its final destruction in the fire that also accidentally ensured their preservation by baking the clay.

The contents are brief, concise, practical, and quantifying in character. Nevertheless, they reveal an important amount of detail about a civilization that is otherwise accessible only via the testimony of archaeology, iconography, and the poetic memory of early classical Greece across severl "dark" centuries. Apart from the philologically invaluable recording of preclassical linguistic forms and proper nanmes, there is the cryptologic evidence of the syllabic writing system, which may yet help bring about a cogent decipherment and lingustic identification o the earlier forms of Cretan writing.

Something of bureaucratic accounting method can be learned from the system of the tablets. contents yield lists of personnel; of livestock and agricultural produce; of textiles, vessels, and furniture; of metals and military material (swords, corselets, chariots, etc.); as well as records of landholding and of temporal and cultic tribute. The cadastral inventories are significant for the light they shed on the system of land distribution as compared with classical Greece and especially with contemporary practices in adjacent culture areas, such as those recorded in the Hittite Law Code. The religious tributes are revelatory in proving what bold scholarship had merely surmised- that the bulk of the classical Greek deities existed in name and kind already in Mycenaean days. Something of the social order and the system of government can also be incidentally learned.

Classical Greece. Inscriptions in their variety and profusion are an important means of gauging everyday life in classical Greece, especially such more formal aspects as were deserving of recording. This qualification, however, does not prevent some obscene pederasty rock-carvings on the island of There from being the earliest epigraphic texts from the classical period (c. 8th century BC), in a from of the alphabet still strongly marked by its Phoenician source.

In a formal vein there's ample documentation of a business, financial, and legal type, such as regulations for building projects, contracts form dicalservices (*e.g.* the Cypriot bronze tablet of Idalium, in a peculiar syllabaric script reminiscent of the Cretan and Cypro-Minoan types, used to write both Greek and the uninterpreted Eteocypriot language), collection agreements for defaulted notes, manumission decrees, records of bank deposits (frequently in a temple), and reports of land commission (especially the Heraclean Tables from southern Italy).

Even in these formal documents it is impossible to keep out reference to religious establishments. religon was, in fact, big business in classical Greece, and overlap in the records is frequent. Tmeples were often of the order of corporations, with extensive holdings of real estate and banking operations. The epigraphs of their transactions are coupled with minute records of dedicatory offerings, priest lists, administrative regulations, and ritualistic and liturgical instructions. So much of social life was centred around institutionalized religion that most of its documentation my be included under the latter heading. dedicatory texts in eat widest sense are common, often in verse, such as that by Nikandre of Naxos on a 7th-century-BC statue of Artemis at Delos, a kind of propitiatory offering to the maiden goddess on the occasion of marriage. similar hexametric or elegiac texts are found as epitaphs, especially for those who perished in war or at sea.

Tomb inscriptions generally are the most numerous of all but tend to be laconic in style and lacking even in purely statistical data. those from ancillary areas of the Greek speaking world, such as the non-Greek ones from Lycia, Lydia, and Phrygia in Asia Minor, are sometimes more revealing to the extent that they are interpreted. thus the Lyctan stela of X anthus, a tomb monument from the 5th century BC, runs to many hundreds of words, including a dozen lines of Greek. the peculiar Lycian system of matrilineal descent is clearly evident in the texts. The Lydian ones include a marble stela from the necropolis of Sardis with a Lydian-Arnmaic bilingual epitaph that typically calls down the curse of Artemis of Ephesus on potential violators. Such imprecations are also standard in Phrygian sepulchral epigraphs. Some kind of death curses that consigned the object to the infernal avengers. Another type is seen in the Orphic tablets-texts on thin gold found interred with the remains of devotees of the Orphic salvation religion near Sybaris in southern Italy, near Rome, and at Eleutherna in Crete. They are apparently meant as instructions to the deceased- exhortations to the soul on its progress in the beyond, enjoining the shunning of the spring of Lethe ("Oblivion") and the drinking from that of Mnemosyne ("Memory"), thus securing the end of transmigration of the soul and the attainment of perpetual higher consciousness.

The Orphic texts provide the popular parallel to the Platonic myth of Er in the 10th book of *The Republic,* where Plato somewhat recast Lethe and Mnemosyne into Ameles ("Unmindful ness") and Anamneis ("recollection"). thus, epigraphy not merely supplements the literary record of Greek civilization but also complements it in important aspects. If papyrology is included, important additions to the preserved portion of classical greek literature have come from Egypt, especially in the papyri from Oxyrhynchus; these include such otherwise lost treatises as Aristotle's *Constitution of Athens* and entire dramatic works *(e.g.* the *Dyscolus* of Menander).

Ancient Rome. The frequency of Roman inscriptions increased dramatically in direct proportion to the rise of Romean power, but that same rise brought centralization, stereotyping, and a certain sterlity of the more formal parts of the epigraphic record. Much of the bulk is official, unidirectional, and from th top outward. The Greek speaking parts of the empire continued in many of their ancient ways, and other annexed regions (such as Spain or Gaul) developed their own locally colored practices. The spread of a variety of exotic religious cults all over the empire, among them Mithraism and Christianity, added a kind of epigraphic underground initially devoid of official sanctions an largely unmatched by alternative avenues of preserved written transmission. Popular epigraphy, including such matter as graffiti at Pompeii and other Vulgar Latin inscriptions, provides further counterpoise to the official stereotypes.

From early republican days the Roman written record is very spotty. The earliest text of any length, the Forum inscription from the early 5th century BC, seems to refer to an augural rite (referred to by Cicero and Festus as the *Juge auspicium*) which enjoins the immediate unyoking of beasts of burden that produce excrement. A 4th-century vase (the "Quirinal Vase") is apparently a wedding present with an inscribed guarantee by the bride's guardian to use his good offices to further marital concord. Later texts of religious import include the "Song of the Arval Brethren" on a marble tablet found in the Vatican in 1778 (a chant largely reduced to gibberish by age-old ritualistic repetition), records of various other cultic "colleges" (*augures; fettales,* or priestly diplomatic representatives; *salii,* or priests of Mars and Quirinus et al.), and outside of the Latin-speech area especially the seven Umbrian-language bronze tables found at Iguvium (modern Gubbio) in 1444, recording in more than 4,000 words the ritualistic details of a brotherhood (the Fratres, Atiedii) that flourished in republican days. Official religion is further seen in many dedications, such as one found of Caelian Hill in Rome in the 18th century, which records the offering of a temple and statue to Hercules by Lucius Mummius in 146 BC in fulfillment of a vow he had made during his conquest of Greece and sack of Corinth. "Unofficial" cults, especially those of Mithra and Jupiter Dolichenus, can be traced and mapped throughout the empire chiefly with the help of dedicatory epigraphs. Sepulchral inscriptions are recorded in overwhelming numbers, not only in Latin but notably also in Etruscan; among the latter is the mummy wrap, a lengthy funeral liturgy inscribed in Egypt (now in Zagregb). The earliest notable Roman examples are the epitaphs in Saturnian verse on the sarcophagi of the Scipios from the 3rd century BC.

There are many texts of deep sentiment and poetic feeling. Yet the bulk itself is the main source of information because it affords what may be called demographic statistics, including population distribution, occupations, public health, and longevity. the requent inclusion of the *cursus honorum,* or career summary of the departed, has similar informational value. Tombs were usually placed under the divine tutelage of the powers of the beyond. Imprecations against violation were common, as were buried curse tablets in Latin and in Oscan (the *defixiones).* Many of the unofficial inscriptions exhibit substandard degrees of literacy and colloquial features, being thus an important adjunct to the study of the totality of classical Latin and its subsequent developments.

The use of inscription. *The dating of historical events.* Inscriptions are important specimens for chronology because they are often physical objects contemporary in execution with their contents. The dating of the inscription itself frequently yields a trustworthy chronology of its message; a victory stela records something treshly deserving of celebration; an epitaph implies a recent death. Exceptions do exist, which record more or less remote events at a conscious historical remove; archival specimens, for example, and secondhand copies generally lack the contemporaneity of other inscriptions. On the whole, however, external dating is crucial and may be achieved in several ways. excavated monuments can be chronologies by their archeological context, including stratigraphic analysis and radiocarbon dating of any adjacent remains of organic matter. The shape of the monument may permit stylistic and iconographic determination. the type and variety of script used, and especially the style of writing, often allow paleographic dating. thus, the relative age of Hittite texts can be determined by spotting the typical "Old Hittite ductus" of the more ancient period, and the various "scribal hands" of the Linear B tables have been differentiated with extreme subtlety. sometimes a radical reform, such as the official adoption by Athens of the ionic alphabet in 402BC (replacing the local Attic variety), provides a chronological watershed. Internal evidence of the inscription may yield its own kind of dating, either by synchronism with otherwise known facts of events or in true calendared fashion. The year is frequently indicated by a kin's reign or the tenure of a magistrate. Such stable counting of time as, for example. from Rome's legendary founding in 753 BC, or from creation (5509 BC, according to Christian dating) is rare in inscriptions; it became more of a historian's device during the classical and postclassical periods. In smaller communities, however, especially in Asia Minor, analogous local departures were used (legendary or historical foundation dates or other epoch-making events), with confusing results for latter-day chronologists.

The use of inscriptions for the dating of historical events is most pervasive when the historical tradition itself is "timeless", as in ancient India; the entire Indian chronology comes to be anchored around the Asokan inscriptions. Inscriptions also permit a check on the veracity of ancient historians such as Herodotus (dubbed both "father of history" and "father of lies"), as in the case of the Bisitun inscription of Darius. Equally dramatically, the Linear B tablets prove atone stroke that the Greeks were ensconced at Knossos in the 2nd millennium BC and that the builk of the "Olympian" religion was already theirs at the time. Most significant of all, nothing would be known of the great Hittite Empire during the 2nd millennium BC, were it not for the discovery of its inscriptional archives.

The decipherment of ancient languages. Inscriptions as written records are usable only in proportion to their intelligibility. Important epigraphic corpora remain virtually undeciphered: *e.g.* the "Indus script" from Mohenjo-daro and Harappa (3trd millennium BC), the Carian texts from Asia Minor and by Carian mercenaries in Egypt (1st millennium BC), and the pictographic Mayan "hieroglyphs" from Central America (c. AD 500-1500). Sometimes the writing system is intelligible, as in the case of Etruscan, but understanding remains deficient because the language is otherwise unknown and bilingual keys are lacking or inadequate. Chances fro success are best if there are sufficiently extensive bilingual or multilingual copies, of which at least one language is previously understood. Such presence made possible the decipherment of ancient Egyptian (the Rosetta Stone of 196 BC, with hieroglyphic, demotic, and Greek versions). Once the affinity of an underlying language to known idioms is established (*e.g.* Old Egyptian to Coptic. Old Persian to Avestan and Sanskrit. Akkadian to Hebrew), interpretation can procced apace. The recovery of Hittite was not a true decipherment because the script was a relatively common variety of syllabic cuneiforms. The interpretation was helped by the nature of the writing on the one had (including intelligible ideograms, while an alphabet yields no such clues).and by the presence of Akkadian Hittite bilinguals on the other; the soon-recognized Indo-=European affinities of the Hittite language afforded further help. The Hittite hieroglyphs were partly deciphered by painstaking internal analysis based on the correct assumption of an underlying dialect akin to Hittite; a bilingual with Phoenician text brought much welcome confirmation. The decipherment of Linear B was a sheer triumph of methodical cryptology, again based on the correct hunch that the hidden language was Greek.

In sum, the decipherment of ancient scripts and the recovery of lost languages are practically identical with the interpretation of previously unintelligible ancient inscriptions, because texts involved are almost exclusively epigraphic. Even when the language is otherwise preserved (as with classical Greek and Latin), inscriptions yield essential additional data for its history, dialects, and social diversification.

History of epigraphy. *Greek and Latin inscriptions.* Inscriptions have commonly elicited the curiosity of posterity, and such ancient Greek historians as Thucydides and Polybius already made scholarly use of them. Sporadic systematic interest in Greek and Latin inscriptions it attested in later ages: *e.g.* Cola di Rienzo in the 14th century made a collection, and Cyriacus of Ancona (ciriaco de Pizzicolli) in the 15th century was a renowned recorder of ancient written monuments on his mercantile travels to Greece. Anatolia, and Egypt, Cyriacus material formed the nucleus of various compilation in the succeeding centuries, normally on a geographic basis. A rival typological method of publication was launched by Martin Smetus in Leiden in the ladt 16the century and was followed in the early 17th by a monumental collection of Janus Gruter and Joseph Justus Scaliger. After copious additions of martial during the 18th and early 19th centuries, the *Corpus Inscription Graecarum* was launched by August Bockh in 1815 under the aegis of the Berlin Academy and was completed in four volumes with index (1828-77). The material had by then again outrun the publication, and it was resolved in 1868 to re-edit completely all Attic inscriptions. Ulrich von Wilamowitz- Moeilendorff in 1902 took charge of the *Inscriptioes Graecate* (1873-), which continued where the *Corpus Inscriptionum Gratecarum* left off and included the *Corpus Inscriptionum Atticaru,* as well as all Greek inscriptions from European Greece (including Magna Graecia in Italy) and Cyprus. Those of Anatolia were left to the *Tituli Asiae Minorts* of the Viennea Academy, which began with the Lycian-language inscriptions from Lycia in 1901 and continued with the Greek and Latin ones from Lycia in 1920-44. The rest of Greek Anatolia was combed some what by the multivolume American series. *Moniumenta Astae Minoris Antiqua* (since 1928). *Inscriptiones Graecae,* framed in 14 volumes, has turned partly into a kind of overall umbrella for diverse coverage: volumes 6, 8, 10, much of 11, parts of 12, and 13 were never completed, being preempted by such other large publication as *Inschritten von Olympia. Fouilles de Delphes,* V. Latyshev's *Inscriptiones Antiquae Orae Septentrionalls Ponti Euxint Graccac of Latinae* and G. Mikhaylov's *Inscrintines Graecue in Bulgurria Repertae. Inscriptions de Deim,* amd M. Guarducci's *Inscriptiones Creticate* The continous influx of new materialis inventoried and presented in such annual outlets as *Supplemention Epigraphicron Giaccum* (since 1923) and "Bulletin ptgraphique" in the *Reviae desetudey gracques.* Large recent undertakings either supplement or complement the *Inscriptione Graecae,* such as *The Athenian Tribute* Lists (from the American excavations in the Agora) and *Inscriptions grecques et latines de la Syurie* (six volumes,. 1929-67). There are in addition, numbers more localized or specialized collections.

The *Corpus Inscriptionum Latinarum,* founded by Theodore Mommsen in Berlin in 1862, comprises 16 volumes fortified with copious supplements; it covers the classical Latin world and is notable for its homogeneity and systematization. Current finds and studies are presented in *L'unnee 4epigraphique* (since 1888). Etruscan inscriptions are less perfectly published in the antiquate *Corpus Inscriptionum Etruscarum:* many important later finds are included in transcription in Mm Fowler and R. G. Wife, *Materials for the Study of the Etruscan Language* (1955 : a computerized corpus). Of further relevance to the Roman world are collection of the type of E. Diehl. *Inscriptiones Latinae Christianae Veteres:* M. J. Vermaseren. *Corpus Inscriptionu et Monumentorum Religionts Mithriacae* : and *Inscriptiones Italiae.*

Other inscriptions. R. A. S. Macalister's *Corpus Inscriptionum Insularum Celticarum* (1945-49) gathers the oghamic and other early texts from Ireland and elsewhere. the runic inscriptions are inventoried in a varitey of compilations. The *Corups Inscriptionum Semittcarum,* in Parts (since 1881), covers in separate volumes Phoenician. aramaic, and other speech areas. Urartean lexts were collected by C. F. Lehmann-Haupt in *Corpus Inscriptionum chaldicarum* (1928-35); the earlier found Hittite hieroglyphic texts by L. Messeschmidt in the antiquated *Corpus Inscriptionum Hettiticarion.* The *Corpus Inscriptionum Iranicarum,* intended to gather the epigraphs of Persia proper (Achaemenid, Seleucid, Parthian, Sasanid) and of eastern Iran and Central asia, began in London in 1955. The *Corpus Inscriptionum Indicarum* has published four volumes since the 1870s, comprising the Asoka. Indo-Scythian, Gupta, and Kalacuri-Cedi periods, supplemented by the series *Epigraphia Indica and South Indian Inscriptions.*

No equally closed corpora exist for cuniform and

Egyptian documents. the Hittite texts come closest to such organization, issued mainly into great ongoing series. *Keilschritttexte aus bogha-koi* (German Oriental Society). But mostly the publication is haphazard- as part of excavation records *(Keilschrifttexte aus Assure)* depending on storage sites *(Cuneiform Texts* in the British Museum), or on the basis of genres (F. Thureau-Dangin, *Rituels accadiens).* The same pattern holds true of the Egyptain records.

Much epigraphic material is published in excavation reports and in many archeological and antiquarian periodicals; *e.g. Hesperia, Journal of Hellenic Studies, Bulletin de correspondence hellenique. Archeologia classiea, Studi Etruschi,* and *Svria.* Specifically epigraphic serial publications include *Epigraphica* (Milan, since 1939), *Kadmos* (Berlin, since 1962), *Zettschrift fur Papyrologie und Epigraphik* (Bonn, since 1967), and *Chiron* (Munich, since 1971).

GENEALOGY

The word genealogy comes from two Greek words- one meaning "race" or "family" and the other "theory" or "science". Thus is derived "to trace ancestry", the science of studying family history. The term pedigree, used to describe a genealogy as set forth in chart or other written from, comes from the Latin *pes* ("foot") and *grus* ("crane") and is derived from a sign resembling a crane's foot, used to indicate lines of descent in early west European genealogies. Chart pedigrees, familiar to most people from school history books, include arrow shapes, parallel lines, a crinkled line denoting illegitimacy, and the sign= denoting marriage. Genealogy is a universal phenomenon and in forms varying from the rudimentary to the comparatively complex, is found in all nations and periods. In this section the history of genealogy will be outlined, followed by an account of the work of modern genealogists, professional and amateur, and as organized in associations.

History of genealogical study. The history of genealogy can be divided most easily into three stages. The first is that of oral tradition: the second, that in which certain pedigrees were committed to writing. The third stage comprises the period from approximately 1500 in western Europe and later in the English-speaking world, during which the whole basis of genealogy widened touch an extent that it is now possible for the majority of people in western Europe to trace their ancestry.

Oral tradition and biblical sources. In the early says of civilization, before written records were made, oral traditions were necessarily important. Without the art of writing, reliance must be placed on memory, aided possibly by mnemonic systems like that of knot arrangements used by the pre-Hispanic Peruvians,, or beads employed by the Maori of New Zealand. The ancient Scottish sennachy, or royal bard, could recite the pedigree of the old Scots kings at the latter's inauguration, and the nobles of Peru, who boasted a common descent with the soverign, were able to preserve their pedigrees despite the complexity resulting from the practice of polygamy. Oral transmission of genealogical information is almost always as a list of names- the lineages of the ancient Irish kings, for example. Events of outstanding importance are occasionally incorporated in such lists.

Numerous Oriental genealogies appear in the Old Testament. A cursory examination of these will reveal that they belong to the first and second stages in the history of genealogy, as described above. The systematic keeping of genealogical records, as in Europe since 1500, did not occur until very recently in Asia and Africa.

In southern India the ruling house of the maharajas of Travancore claimed to trace its descent, direct and unbroken, from the old Cera kings of southern India (referred to as independent sovereigns in one of the edicts of Asoka, the great Mauryan emperor of the 3rd century BC). A claim that inscriptions of the rulers of Travancore have been found from the 9th century AD comes from a statement issued by the secretariat of the maharaja of Travancore, Its reliability may be judged along with the genealogies of princes in northern India shown in Lt. Col. James Tod's monumental work. *Annals and Antiquities of Rajasthan* (1829, republished 1950). Referring to the lineages of Indian princes as being known since the early centuries BC, Tod wrote, "If, after all, these are fabricated genealogies of the ancient families of India, the fabrication is of ancient date, and they are all they know themselves upon the subject. "The very long Oriental genealogies begin as oral pedigrees and were later written down, but they concern only princes or great persons.

In Africa the one instance of a claim to very long descent, that of the Emperor of Ethiopia, bears a similarity to Tod's Rajput genealogies. The Emperor is said to descend from the marriage of King Solomon with the Queen of Sheba. The tradition was written down more than 15 centuries ago it is therefore older than the history of most European monarchies, but it cannot, of course, be substantiated by documentary proof.

under European influence the greater Oriental countries have adopted the practice of keeping systematic records for all citizens. In China, with its ancient system of ancestor worship. Long, drawn-out pedigrees, including claims to descent from Confucius, are not unknown. The establishment of the Chinese Republic in 1911 brought with it registration of vital statistics.

In modern Japan, as might be expected from its thoroughgoing Westernization, the registration of vital statistics is regulated by law. The Family Registration Law of 1947, and later enactments, require a comprehensive registration of a Japanese national from his birth to his death. Such information, however, is kept in local registration offices, and there is no system in Japan for gathering together, recording, and preserving the information in one central place (although of course the results of statistics, such as the number of births, is known to the central authority). Such an exact system of registration covers only the era of modern Japan. The present-day pedigree of the Japanese emperors has a divine origin: it is mainly s sting of names, easily recited and memorized, mixed with semi fabulous legends and first written down in the early centuries of the Christian Era. It is concerned only with exalted persons, royal or noble.

In the Old Testament there are many genealogies, the object of which is to show descent from Adam, Noah, and Abraha. By the time these genealogies had become part of th jewish scriptures, the concept of racial purity had reinforced the keeping of family records. Genealogies of Jesus Christ in the New Testament aim at showing his descent from David, the one in St. Luke's Gospel going as far back as Adam, "who was the son of God". The idea of diving origin was reflected everywhere in a wildly polytheistic from among the Gentiles. Almost without exception, the heroes whose genealogies were recited by the bards had their paternity ascribed to the gods, or to persons such as Romulus who were regarded as having become divine, Greek fables abound in stories of great men begotten by gods and mortals.

In Roman genealogies heroes were always descended from gods. Julius Caesar, for example, was supposed to have sprung from the line of Aeneas, and thus from that of Venus. Among the Romans, traditions of descent remained vague even when written. Caesar's murderer. Brutus, was popularly supposed to be of the same family as an ancient Brutus, who had expelled the Tarquins, but no pedigre appears to have existed to substantiate the belief.

Among the northern nations that overwhelmed the western Roman Empire, belief in divine sonship was general. For Saxon rulers of the English kingdoms it was ncecessary to be descended from the god Woden.

Early written records. With the invention of writing, the oral became the written tradition. This occurred in Greece and Rome, where genealogies were recorded in poems and in histories. But genealogy did not at this stage become a science, because when writers dealt with it, they did so either incidentally in their narrative or because they were concerned with the family relationships of their gods.

The historian Edward Gibbon's observation that "the proudest families are content to lose in the darkness of the middle ages, the tree of their pedigree" may be challenged in the light of recorded genealogies. The male line of Charlemagne has been traced to St. Arnulf, bishop of Metz, who died about 635. Several royal line descents ae traceable to the 6th century, as, in England, is the tree of Louis Mountbatten. 1st Earl Mountbatten. The ancestry of Queen Elizabeth (I goes to Egbert of Wessex (about 825), beyond him to Cerdic (c. 500), and, if another series of names is accepted, to Woden (an actual man later divinized by the Germans), in the 3rd century AD.

With the convention of the barbarians to Christianity the recording of their regal traditions began. Examples occur in Ireland. Wales, and England. It was natural for the first chroniclers, who were mostly monks, to write down the oral pedigrees of the kings in whose realms they lived. Students of the Irish regal pedigree are prepared to accept two or three generations before the time of St. Patrick (flourished 5th century AD0 as genuine, and it is quite probable that name lists of the Irish kings are valid back to the 3rd century AD. Similarly, in Wales, the ancestry of the greatest Welsh families can be traced for a millennium. Among the Anglo-Saxons there were similar bardic pedigrees recorded by monastic scribes. and many of these might have survived but for the destruction of the Old English ruling class during the Norman Conques. A regular feature of such old pedigrees recorded by monks was an attempt to link them with the genealoies of the Scriptures. In an Anglo-Saxon pedigree of great length that of the king so fessex (the ancestores of Elizabeth II)- the line is thus traced to Sceaf. "a son of Noah born in the Ark". In the process of working out the connection between scriptural and regal genealogies. the monks adopted a reverse technique to that of the 4th century BC Greek mythographer Euhemerus; *i.e.* they downgraded the old gods to human status.

From roughly 1100 to 1500, the emphasis of genealogists was on pedigrees of royal and noble lines. Claims to a throne, as with the dozen or so claimants to the Scottish crown after the death of Alexander III in 1286 and his direct heir. Margaret the Maid of Norway in 1290, frequently involved genealogical trees. The truth was sometimes bent tosuit some political end, but, on the whole, medieval European records are genealogically valid. This is because they were not primarily intended to supply genealogical information but to record land transactions, taxation, and lawsuits. The facts of family history are incidental and are therefore generally reliable. Exact eddies of birth, marriage, and death are rarely given. A man is said to be of age "by Michaelmas 1330."

This period also saw the emergence of pedigrees of lesser folk. Land transactions involved claims in the local courts of the lords. Serfdom gave way to villenage; the latter of the lords. Serfdom gave way to villenage; the latter involved so many days of labour on the lord's demesne and also the inability to move from the estate without the lord's consent. There was strong inducement for a man to prove that he was not a villein and for the bailiff to show that he was. In several parts of England, pedigrees of villeins or persons claimed as such have been worked out over periods of 100-150 years.

It was during the third period in European genealogical history that records that came to include everyone began. This period extends from 1500 to the present. As feudalism gradually gave way, new classes of citizens arose. In England the appearance of a powerful mercantile and business community was reflected in the growth of the middle classes, from which was continually recruited a new nobility and gentry. In turn, owing to the English rule of inheritance by primogeniture and the fact that unlike the continental nobility English nobility has never extended beyond the reigning peer and his wife, the middle classes themselves continually received the younger children of peers and gentry. Two other factors leading to the proliferation of records were the enormous changes caused by the Reformation and the great reemphasis on individual religion and the desire of Renaissance monarchs to have more exact information about all their subjects.

Modern genealogy. Amateures in the subject of genealogy are almost always actuated by the desire to trace their own family history. In the course of so doint they discover and work with general principles which apply to pedigrees other than their own, though records other than those applicable to their own case do not interest them. The professional genealogist is concerned not with one family but with may, and with the principles of genealogical research with arise from a wide study. As there are no university courses in the subject and therefore no degrees or other certificates of professional proficiency, the professional must be largely self-taught.

The disciplines required of a professional genealogist include a deep knowledge of the history of the country with which he is concerned the from of national genealogy, and genealogy can illuminate many aspects of national history that might otherwise remain obscure. The Wars of the Roses, fro example, are hard to grasp unless genealogical trees showing relationships of the contestants are studied, and th course of the American Revolution is easier to understand when the links between George Washington and his compeers with the old English landed families who overthrew the Stuarts are comprehended. An understanding of the principle of law, especially of land law, the ability to decipher court hand or medieval script, an understanding of heraldry, and an intimate knowledge of the study of surnames and place names are also essential to the genealogist. Variations in surname spelling can be bewildering. The key is in the sound of the name, for a medieval scribe could not ask the illiterate prison before him to spell his name.

The main task undertaken by professional genealogists is the tracing of pedigrees for clients, this being the staple of their work. Clients often consult fenealogists when they wish to establish their family background, or when having trided to trace it they have come to a stop.

The writing of private family histories by professionals is very common. The material has usually been worked out by others who wish it to be checked and written by a professional.

Amateure genealogists, as already mentioned, are usually concerned only with their own families. The standard of amateur work varies with the individual, from the truly had to the excellent.

Amateure genealogical work has increased greatly since 1945. In the United States there has been a long interest in the subject. The New England Historic Genealogical Society, the Augustan Society (based in California) and many state societies are of note. The Mormons (the Church of Jesus Christ of Latter-day Saints) have built up in Salf Lake City. Utah, a microfilm library of genealogical records from Britain and continental Europe, which is probably unequalled. In Canada, Austrila, New Zealand, and South Africa the study of genealogy by private persons and by associations is growing rapidly. In England there is a Society of Genealogists, and there are corresponding bodies for Ireland and Scotland. In Denmark there is an International Confederation of Genealogy and Heraldry, which since 1954 has organized international congresses held in many European capital at intervals of two years. In Czechoslovakia, by way of contrast, the national Genealogical society has been dissolved, and in general it has not been feasible to obtain genealogical details from Communist countries, though it is probable that changes are now occurring in this respect. Jewish records are in a separate class. With the establishment of the state of israel in 1948, a very great effort has been made to centralize information about the Jews of continental Europe under the care and direction of The Central Archives for the Study of the Jewish Peoples, in Jerusalem.

In tracing family history, the worker follows certain tules. He works backward from the present. This is an elementary caution constantly put on one side by amateurs, who tend to trace forward from a prisons of the same name who may well be unrelated. As there cannot in the nature of things be a gap in a pedigree, no assumptions as to relationship can be allowed without very strong reason to accept them. Good and bad features in the ancestry have to be accepted: bastardy has to be allowed for, as well as regal ancestry by legitinmate lines. An ancestor's wrongdoing must also be allowed for, though with passage of time this is usually taken in a romantic sense. Registration of birth, marriage, and death first became compulsory in England in 1837. Public records in most other Western countries began at varying dates in the 19th century. Census records are of great importance. They began in the United States as early as 1791; in Britain in 1801 (papers kept only from 1841); and even earlier in French Canada, in 1055 -66. Parish registers began in England in 1838, though they are rearely preserved from that date. In most countries they begin later, but in Spain the oldest extant is dated 1394, and there are 1,636 parishes having records prior to 1570. In England, Nonconformist records have been kept by various bodies, and many are now held officially at Somerset House. London, or the Public Record Office. In America the settlers were generally trying to get away from established church and controlling state. The were vigorous individualists who kept careful records of their lives and of the organization of their new communities. Examples of detail in New England records can be seen in many of the 1,600 pedigrees contained in *American Families with british Ancestry* (500 page supply, to Burke's *Landed Gentry,* 1939), in A. M. Burke's *Prominent Families of the United States of America,* and in the many volumes of family history produced in the United States.

Wills are of the utmost importance as a source of genealogical information. Ships lists of passengers are useful in supplying dates for immigrant ancestors departure for the New World, but since they do not indicate place of origin, but only the port of departure, the original habiltat must be sought elsewhere, without knowledge of the ancestor's place of origin in the homeland it is useless in almost all cases to attempt a search.

With the aid of the type of record mentioned above, and with help from family Bibles, tombstones, and plaques and brasses in churches, it is as a rule possible for a person of English antecedents to trace some 250-300 years of ancestry. Before the 17th century, everything depends on the social position of the ancestors. Tax records, lawsuits, and purchaswes and sales of land are the chief sources for tracing a family before 1600. The Pipe Rolls extend from the reign of Henry II (1154-89) to that of Queen victoria (1837-1901), with an interrupted beginning also in the time of Henry I (1100-35). Monastic records are of great importance as whowing grants or ownership of land. The please of the crown deal with suits at law and contain much detail about families. There are many Rolls besides those of the Pipe that give a great his age and other details. as the centuries are passed, the numbers of those who can prove a descent by the male line dwindle, until by the time of the Norman Conquesto scarcely half adozen pedigrees can be traced in the male line for either Saxon or deal of incidental genealogical information. *Inquistitiones post mortem* show the position of an heir. *i.e.* Norman.

Regarding deposition of public records, two principles have been followed by archivists; that of ecentralization and that of diffused local holdings. The former has many obvious advantages and was adopted in Scotland and in Ireland. It has one disadvantage- destruction of the records at one stroke. This happened in Dublin on April 13, 1922, when Irish factions fighting with each other burned most of the Irish records. The second system, by which records are stored in a number of depositories, prevails to a considerable extent in England. Although the Public Record Office. Somerset House, and the British Museum library are places of centralized record, the parish registers remain outside them, scattered in numerous parishes of country offices. Country records contain masses of material not to be found in London.

From the 16th century there has been an increasing accumulation of written material, which deals either exclusively or incidentally with genealogy. William Camden (1551-1623) , a learned English antiquary and historian, did much to raise the standards of genealogical research. He was the first English writer on surnames, and his work wasnot resumed for nearly 200 years. Sir William dugdale, a younger contemporary of Camden, made a beginning with his *Antiquities of Warwickshre* to the great output of country histories written between the 17th and 19th centuries. The revolution in moderngenearlogy was the application toits study of canons of historical and literary criticism formulated in Europe from 1800. Their application to genealogy was fairly late, asit illustrated by the fact that the 18th century English historian Thomas Macaulay, critically perceptive in most other spheres, accepted what amounted to family myths as true genealogy. Later writers, including J. H. Round, W. Farrer, C. Lewis Loyd, C. T. Clay, and the editors of the *Complete Peerage*, are of the greatest importance.

PALEOGRAPHY

Paleography (from Greek *palaios*, "old", and *graphein*, "to write") is the study of ancient and medieval handwriting. Precise boundaries for the study are hard to define. For example, epigraphy, the study of inscriptions cutonimmovable objects for permanent public inspection, is related to paleogrpahy. Casual graffiti, sale or election notices as foundon the walls of Pompeii, and Christian inscriptions in the Roman catacombs are likewise part of paleographical knowledge. In general, however, paleography embraces writing found principally on papyrus, parchment (veilum), and paper. Today, paleogrpahy is regarded as relaing to Greek and Latin scripts with their derivatives, thus, as a rule, excluding egyptian. Hebrew, and Middle and Far Eastern scripts. It is closely linked with diplomatic (see above), the study of forms in which official and private documents are drawn up.

The scientific study of Latin paleogrpahy (and diplomatic) dates from 1681, when the French monk Jean Mabillon published *De Re Diplomatica*, the first textbook on the subject, while his compatriot Betnard de Montfaucon performed a parallel service for Greek paleography in his *Palaeographia Graeca* in 1708.

The primary tas of the paleogrpaher is to read the writings of the past correctly and to assign a date and place of origin. Close acquaintance with the language of the text is a prerequisite. Help in dating is offered by changes in styles of handwriting and variations from area to area. Abbfeviations in texts likewise help in dating and localization.

Types of writing materials. a paleogrpaher must be familiar with writing materials. Any smooth surface able to accept writing has served in the past, notably, pottery fragments, animals' shouldr blades, slabs of wood, bark, cloth, and metal.

The great writing material of the ancient world was papyrus, in use by 3500 BC. In preparing the surface, strips taken from the papyrus reed *(byblos)* growing in the Nile delta were ladi side by side, while other strips were laid across at right angles, and the whole impregnated with paste. After treatment a fine smooth surface was obtained. Couch of the administration of the Roman Empire depended upon papyrus, in the same way that modern bureaucracies depend upon paper. Warfare and a damp climate resulted in an almost total disappearance of papyrus from Europe, though the dry (if war-scarred0 sands of Egypt have preserved vast numbers of documents, Papyrus was imported into Europe from Egypt even after the fall of Rome. Chance survivals include charters of Merovingian kings in France *7th century) and business documents (5th-10th centuries) at Ravenna, the old administrative capital of the late Roman Empire.

The other great ancient writing material, still in occasional use today, is parchment, or vellum, the terms being often used interchangeably. Vellum is a term usually applied to skin from a calf *(cf,* vel, *veau*), while parchment is an expression often applied to sheepskin or goatskin. The word parchment is dervied from Pergamum in Asia Minor, the ancient centre of its manufacture.

Both papyrus and parchment were expensive and were replaced for everyday use by wax tablets corresponding to today's notebook. Tablets made of wooden blocks were hollowed out and filled with melted, often black wax. Notes were made in the hardened surface. Even documents of permanent significance, such as property conveyances, were made on wax tablets.

Because ancient writing materials were expensive, they were often reused. Papyrus presented difficulties, for ink soon bonded itself firmly into the surface. Parchment could be more readily reused, b3ecause it is tougher and can be washed or scraped clean. Many medieval monks, when short of writing materials, took ancient books topieces, cleaned off the leaves and used them again. The original script can often be brought out under ultraviolet light. Parchments thus cleaned and freshly inscribed are called palimpsests (Greek *paiin,* "again", *psestos,* "scriped").

Paper is the third great writing material. In use in china at a remorte period, it was employed extensively in the Arab world by the 9th century. Not in common use in Europe until the 14th century, it took over the name of the half-gorgotten papyrus.

In the early classical world the standard form of book was the papyrus roll, commonly called *biblion,* taking its name from the material of which it was made. It consisted of papyrus sheets pasted edge to edge with a slight overlap. The text was set out in columns, drawn up at right angles to the edge of the rolls, and started at the left. The reader unrolled as he went along and at the conclusion was boliged to reroll the book. The roll was an probably accounts for the inaccurate quotations found in early literature, caused by an author relying on his memory rather than troubling to unwind a long roll. By the time of Christ, a new from of book was coming into fashion, the codex, or book in the shape in which it is known today. The codex is almost always of parchment, since papyrus creacks when folded. The codex seems first to have been used for notebooks or account books, the conservatism of booksellers and readers ensuring the survival of the roll for centuries. The Christians popularized the codex, using it for the Gospels.

Various instruments have been used for writing. The early Egyptians used a slender rush. From about 300 BC the thicker reed pen was used. The reeed was in general use in the Greco-Roman world. Metal pens, copied from the reed, were also employed. For wax tablets a stylus was used, made of wood, bone, ivory, iron, or bronze. In many northern European areas, where reeds suitable for writing purposes are not indigenous, the feather *(Penna)* became the main writing instrument. It was usually stripped of its vanes and the quill alone used.

Lead, used in classical times for ruling guidelines in manuscripts, was used extensively in the Middle Ages for rough notes and annotations in the margins of books.

Ink has been prepared in a variety of ways. In classical times the black discharge of cuttlefish was used, as well as concoctions of soot and gum. In the Middle Ages oak apples were steeped in water it "vitriol" (ferrous sulphate) to produce ink.

Analysis of texts. The essential skill of a paleogrpaher is the ability to recognize the numerous styles of handwriting prevalent in different ages and places. Most European scripts descend from Greek and Roman capital letters, but variations are enormous. It is a European convention that writing starts on the left at the eop and works line by line down the page. An eccentricity known as boustrophedon (from Greek *boustrophedon.* "following the ox furrow".) whereby alternate lines are written backward in mirror writing, occurs chiefly in very ancient inscriptions.

The Greek and Latin alphabets existed originally as capital, or majuscule, letters. The ancient Greek alphabet, as developed in chiselled inscriptions on stone or marble, saved without much modification as the alphabet used in literary work written on papyrus rolls. This script in literary worst written on papyrus rolls. This script, found in the oldest surviving Greek literary papyri of c. 300 BC or earlier, gave way to more rounded and elegant forms, probably developed in the Greek literary circles of Alexandria. Cursive scripts that were easier to write were developed for everyday use, for business, and to record the acts of the great bureaucracy of Egypt, where the Greeks settled enlarge numbers. The Greek cursive script and the formal book script greatly influenced each other, as can be seen from a vast series of cursive documents dating from the 4th century BC for about 1,000 years. Because so much material survived, early Greek cursive can be better studied than its Latin counterpart. In Greek cursive manuscripts the everyday life of ordinary people becomes a reality; they pay of fail to pay taxes, buy or sell houses, and harass civil servants with awkward demands.

A very rough division in Greek paleogrpahy may be made at around AD 300. The earlier age is called the papyrus period; and the later, the parchment or Byzantine (or Christian) period. The division, however, is imprecise, for parchment was used well before and papyrus long after this, date. The change from papyrus to parchment is signalized by three great monuments of paleogrpahical studies, the Vatican. Alexandrine, and Sinai Bibles, all on parchment and in codex form.

An alphabet of small, or minuscule, letters developed gradually and was in use by the 8th century. Numerous abbreviations exist in Greek manuscripts,. though never so many as in Latin. Accents, an additional complexity, were not systematically applied before the 7th century AD.

The ancient Latin alphabet of capital *(quadrata)* is found in numberless inscriptions in stone and marble all over the Roman world. How far this alphabet was used over the Roman world. How far this alphagt was used for writing books is uncertain, because, though excellently adapted for incision, it is difficult to write. Some speciment of handwring in *quadrata* do exist, such as 4th or 5th century copies of Virgil, but scholarly opinion largely regards these as abnormal productions. By the 1st century a handsome Latin alphabet existed, called rustic, based on the use of a broad pen or brush. Rustic was used for public inscriptions on walls, an in the sale and election notices found at Pompeii. Although specimens are scarce, it is likely that books were extensively written in this hand in classical times. By the 4th century another Latin alphabet existed, the script known as uncial, in the nature of a rounded from of *quadrata.* Uncial survived the fall of Rome and from it developed half-uncial, the ancestor of the small leters in use today.

The stately Roman scripts, *quadratea* rustic, or uncial, were not used for everyday purposes; and as in the case of Greek, a cursive rapidly written hand arose in which letters and business documents were inscribed. This hand is found in graffiti on Pompeian walls and in was tagblets. After the disintegration of the empire. Roman cursive became the ancestor of regional hands in what are now Spain, France, and Italy.

During most successful of Christianity and art in Ireland (c. 500-c. 1000) a beautiful "insular" script developed, which found its way into England. There, two streams of influence commingled, for from 597 Christian missionaries arrived from Rome and brought in books in uncial script. Both scripts prosperedin England, though insular gradually superseded uncial.

The most successful of all scripts proved to be Caroline minuscule, which takes its name from the emperor Charlemagne (died 814), patron of scholars and scripbes, under whom the script was developed. Despite its inherent superiority and clarity, it did not predominate over regional scripts until the mid-12th century, and the local hand of southern Italy (Beneventan) maintained itself for much longer.

In the 12th century, Caroline minuscule, which had undergone moderate developments, strateed to display more obvious changes. It compressed laterally, while its rounded strokes became stiffer and straighter as it was converted into the so-called Gothic hands- very angular in northern Europe and more rounded in Italy. A revulsion against Gothic took place in scholarly circles in Italy in the 14th and 15th centuries, and a return to models based on Caroline minuscule took place. this revived hand, called humanistic because humanist scholars used it, was adopted by 15th century Italian printers, whose type face ultimaterly triumphed over the Gothic. (This encyclopedia is printed in a type scarcely modified from Caroline minuscule.) Meanwhile, Caroline and Gothic scripts had produced cursive hands for quick everyday use, a in the case of the ancient Greek and Latin alphabets. These cursivescripts were used for the vast mass of business documents written in the Middle Ages.

Abbreviation are the principal problem confronting paleographers. They were extensively used in Roman times by lawyers to avoid repetition of technical terms and formulas. Abbreviations fall into two classes, suspension and contraction. Suspension, omission of the end of a word and indication by a point or sign, was used in Roman public inscriptions- *e.g.* IMP, (ERATOR), CAES, (AR), Contraction, the omission of letters from the middle of a word and replacement by a sign or some other device, was common among Greek-speaking Jews, who contracted certain sacred or revered names, such as God, Lord, Isreal, or david, as a mark of veneration. The Christians followed the practicve by contracting their sacred names. such as Jesus and Christos. The great increase in use of abbreviation as a mark of veneration. The Christians followed the practice by contracting their sacred names, such as Jesus and Christos. The great increase in use of abbreviation as a means of saving time and material dates from the 12th century, but some contraction signs are of high antiquity, such as the sign 7 for et (Latin, "and"). Some are quickly written versions of letter groups, such as " "for *est* (Latin, "is"), the top dot standing for e. the bottom dot for t, and the stroke being a logn or f-shaped s., fallen on its side. The letter r is often omitted, the adjacent vowel being written above the line, as c'ta for *carata* ("charter"). In works for semilearned readers such as romances, abbreviations are often few, but books produced for the learned, such as university textbooks, are heavily loaded with abbreviations. The number of signs and devices in use by the end of the Middle Ages was enormous. More than 13,000 are listed in the standard work. Adriano Cappelli's *lexicon Abbreviaturatum* (1912).

Dating of books and documents also offers problems. Even when a precise date is given, the dating system of a given time and a given area must be checked because the year began at different times in different territories, and there were even variations in the same country. Calendar reforms initiated in 1582 by Pope Gregory XIII, for example, were not adopted in Protestant England until 1752. If a year of a monarch's reign is given as a date, it is necessary to determine whether the reign is counted from his accession of coronation. Moreover, few books were dated, the dated title page being nonexistent in medieval works, though sometimes a final paragraph, the colophon, supplies a date with the scribe's name and place of work. Important documents, such as English 12th-century royal characters, are undated.

In the absence of dates, inferences are drawn from handwriting, use of abbreviations, and internal evidence. Caution must be used, however; for an elderly scribe may be using a hand learned over half a century before, and work in the same scriptorium or office as a young clerk anxious to show off all the latest tricks and flourished. Some styles lasted a long time; Caroline minuscule lasted for more than three centuries. Certain kinds of books, such as liturgical volumes, were produced in a highly stylized form for generations, and thus it is often difficult to provide a close date for a late medieval missal (with standard illustrations and marginal decorations) in a mechanical Gothic hand.

Internal evidence must be weighed carefully. A given historical event noted in a chronicle will provide an earliest possible date, unless the entry is an interpolation. evidence for some legal practice or liturgical usage is no safe guide, for legislation on the subject by a king or a pope may merely be ratification of a long standing practice.

A paleographer must get to know his scribes, for their mannerisms can be highly informative. Nearly 50 different scribes have been distinguished in the English royal chancery in the period 1100-89. First-rate scribes, such as notaries public, provide much information about them sleves, giving their names, notarial signs, and information on their authority to act. Even anonymous clerk, who drew up innumerable property conveyances can be identified by their script over a period of years, and their career can be traced through developing mature, and deteriorating handwriting, thereby offering dating evidence.

The provenance (origin) of many manuscripts can be immediately recognized because certain centers developed individual styles. Papal and royal chanceries issued documents of easily identifiable origin, while may monastic scriptoria- for example, that of Canterbury Cathedral in the earlier 12th century- had a virtually private handwriting.

Textual corruptions are another obstacle to correct elucidation. A legal document is certain to have been checked at the time of writing, but one cannot be sure in the case of a literary, philosophical, or theological text. Scribes were fallible, and, if there are no signs of any corrections in a text, then it probably embodies inaccuracies. A popular book, such as Chaucer's works, exists in large numbers of manuscripts, and many manuscripts produce variant readings. If a scribe made a mistake in copying, future scribes using his version are likely to reproduce the error and add others. Sometimes the same muddled passage in a group of manuscripts of a given author can be traced back to damage in a earlier copy say a section eaten by rodents of impenetrably stained. Whenever copyists worked from different and faulty originals, various copies tend to fall into families. A paleogrpaher must bring together various feadings in families and decide which is the best reading.

Sometime a scribe, set to work because he could write a fine hand, did not necessarily possess much knowledge of the language. Such a cribe faced with a text heavily loaded with abbreviations would usually make nonsense of it, Occasionally , a particularly stupid copyist, faced with a master copy in two columns of writing, would copy straight across the top line, then across the second. When the used a different number of words per line, the text was reduced to unintelligibility. In Greek and Roman times there was the difficulty that texts were written continuously, without space between the words. Copyists misread passages. For instance the historian Tacitus reported that some tribesmen went off to guard their own property; ADSVATVTANDA *(ad sua tutanda)*. Some copyist thought "Suatutanda" was a place and this ghost name was perpetuated in geographical works. Later medieval Gothic hands presented a forest of vertical strokes called minims. The letter v rendered as u made two strokes, while I was often left without a dot or at best with a faint hairline, often misplaced. The group of letters *ium* could be rade, as *uim, uiui, niui, mui, miu,* with many other variations. Accordingly, minim corruption, confustion of vertical strokes, is a term constantly heard in paleographical circles.

Latin and Greek are inflected languages in which the same case and tense endings constantly occur, offering scope for error. Moreover, in biblical, theological, or philosophical texts, the same words abound. For example, in one place in the Gospel According to John there occurs the passage :

Verba quae ego loquor
vobis a me ipso non loquor
pater autem in me manens ...

("The words that I speak ..."). The eye of a sleepy scribe might slip from the first *loquor* to the second, whereupon he would go on copying at *pater autem,* leaving out the second line altogether, a common type of error known as *homototeleuton* ("like ending").

Because of the lack of surviving specimens, it is difficult to assess book decoration in classical times, but apparently it was very limited. In the later centuries of the Roman Empire, however, book illustrations were not infrequent. The narrative material in the Bible encouraged illustration. The Irish were foremost in applying decoration to the text in the form if elaboration of capital letters., producing such masterpieces as the Book of Kells (late 7th century), in which Celtic imagination and artistic sense ran riot in elevating the book to an object of outstanding beauty. Some of the greatest creative talent of the Middle Ages was lavished upon books, especially upon those used in worship, such as Bibles, Psalters, and missals. When a book cannot be assigned either a date or provenance upon the appearance of the text alone, its style of illumination will often direct the paleographer to a certain monastery in which the carving on capitals or wall paintings may contain the same motifs.

Because of the immensely high prices of manuscripts, the question of forgery naturally arises, but it is safe to say that no modern forgery could survicve for a moment. A convincing imitation of ancient script is virtually impossible, while the papyrus, parchment, or paper on which it would be written could not stand up to modern scientific inspection. Anything of recent vegetable or animal origin fluoresces brightly under ultraviolet light, to name but one test. William Henry Ireland (died 1835), the Shakespeare forer, used flyleaves from 16th century books, but his handwriting and non-Shakespearean language have him away. A modern would be forger must either copy an existing work, which, in the present state of art history and paleographical study, would be immediately recognized, or be prepared to invent medieval subject matter.

There was fabrication of documents in medieval times on a considerable scale. A monastery might find itself in possession of estates held since remote antiquity but without any title deeds. When some powerful monarch made difficulties, there was a strong inducement to produce the required ancient-looking documents. The borderline between justifying legitimate possession and culpable attempts to gain extra territory or privileges, however, is ill-defined. Monks occasionally descended to falsifications of title deeds and charters of exemption. About 1125 a monk of Soissons on his deathbed confessed to a career of professional forgery for gain and admitted fabricating charters for various monasteries, including Westminster Abbey, Early forgeries, however, give themselves away through such inconsistencies as mentioning bishops of nonexistent sees or embodying legal phrases that came into use generations later or gearing seals when seals were not yet appended to documents.

The modern paleographer has great technical aids; photography since the 19th century and color photography in the 20th . Ultraviolet light brings out faded handwriting. Microfilms makes the contents of a volume in a far-distant repository available quickly cheaply.

SIGILLOGRAPHY

Sigillogrpahy is the study of seals. A sealing is the impression made by the impact of hard engraved surface on a softer material, such as clay or wax, once used to authenticate documents in the manner of a signature to-day; the word seal (Latin *sigillun:* old French *scel*) refers either to the matrix (or die) or to the impression. Seals are usually round or a pointed oval in shape or occasionally triangular, square, diamond, or shield-shaped.

Medieval matrices were usually made of Latten- a kind of bronze- or of silver, Ivory and lead were occasionally used, gold very rarely. Steel was used from the 27th century. Matrices could included intaglio gems. The usual material for the impression was sealing wax, made of beeswax and frsin, often colored red or green. In southern Europe, notably in the papal Curia, lead and occasionally gold were used. Shellac, the wax used today, was introduced in the 16th century.

Seals wee used to establish the authenticity of such documents as charters and legal agreements and for the verification of administrative warrants. In southern Europe, early medieval documents were drawn up by notaries and authenticated with their written *signa,* but this never replaced seals in northern Europe. Forgeries were manufactured as early as the 12thc century, indicating how important seals had become. From that time, also, seals were used to close folded documents and thus to guarantee their secfrecy. Seals were also used to affirm assent; for example, by a jury Under the Statute of Cambridge (1388), sealed letters were used in England for the identification of people and their places of origin.

Sigillography is used to assist other historical studies. Many impressions have survived from the medieval period. Those attached to documents are most avluable, because the documents may datetheiruse precisely and the seal may confirm the documents authenticity. Unattached seals may still provide useful evidence from their inscription ordesign. Fragmentary seal impressions are often difficult to interpret. Fewer matrices have survived and often without related impressions. Seals often reflect the taste of the owner. they provide evidence for changes in fashion in both secular and ecclesiastical costume and for the development of armour. Seals indicate heraldry before the earliestrollsofarms and are an original source for armorial bearings, which thereby enables the historian to trace the distinctions or alliances between various families and so contributes to genealogy. Craftsmen's seals often display tools connected with trade. Depictions of towns, churches, castles, and monasteries, although conventional, can often aid the architectural historian. Sealscan also be used profitably for studying ancient ships, particularly their shape and details of masts and rigging. Themain difficulty in studying seal designs in that they were often conservative, especially since seals were often replaced than exactly similar design.

Seals in antiquary. Seals with designs carved in intaglio were used throughout antiquity. They were of two main types- the cviinder and the stamp. The cylinder first appeared in Mesopotamia in the late 4th millennium BC and continued to be used there until the 4 th century BC. It was also widespread in Elam, Syria, and Egypt (3rd millenium BC) and in Cyprus and the Aegean (2nd millennium BC). Stamp seals preceded cylinders, first appearing in Mesopotamua in the 4th millenniu BC and developing over a period of about 1,500 years until largely replaced by the cylinder in the 3rd millennia. Early stamp seals were also used in Iran, northern Syria, and southeastern Anatolia during the 4th and 3rd millennia; in Anatolia their use was continued in the 2nd milennia by the Hittites. In Mesopotamia the stamp seal gradually came into use again in the 8th -6th centuries, effectively replacing the cylinder by the 3trd century BC. In the Aegean, various types of stamp seals were used throughout the 2nd and much of the 1st millennium BC, until in Hellenistic and Roman times the signet ring became dominant.

The uses of ancient seals are known from textual references and ancient sealings, both on lumps of elay and on documents found in excavations. In historical times most prominent cilizens, including women, carried their own scales. That the rank of office of the owner was often ... in the inscription indicates that many of these may have been official seals. Kings had their own seals, and high officials could hold the king's seal as a mark of delegated authority.

Seals came into use before the invention of writing for

the securing of jars, bales, bags, baskets, boxes, doors, etc., and this use continued throughout ancient times. The method was either to shape clay over the stopper or lid or to make a fastening with cord and place clay around the knot and then impress it with this seal.

The sealing of written documents, of which the two major ancient classes were clay tablets and papyrus scrolls, became regularly established in the latter part of the 3rd millennium BC. The clay talent was the main vehicle or writing in Mesopotamia, where cuneiform was used into th4 Christian Era, and this method spread to Elam. anatolia, syria, and Egypt; clay talets were also used in the Aegean Bronze Age. The tablet was inscribed while the clay was soft, and seal impressions were applied at the same time.

The man kinds of sealed cuneiform documents were contracts, accounts, and letters. Contracts were sealed by the contracting parties and by witnesses and commonly encasedin clay "envelopes", on which the text was either repeated or summarized and the seals again impressed. Two special kinds of contract were the royal grant to a subject, impressed with the royal seal of the grantor, and the treaty between nations, a number of examples of which have been recovered, some of them bearing impressions of the seals of the royal contracting parties. Account talets were sealed to authenticate the transfer of goods. A letter was often encased in an "envelope" and th sender's seal impressed on the outside to identify him to the recipient and, in the case of official letters, to authenticate any commands contained in the letter.

In Egypt, papyrus documents may be assumed from soon after 3000 BC, but surviving evidence dates mostly from the latter part of the 3rd millennium onward. The method of sealing a papyrus document was to roll it into a tube, tie a strand or cord around the centre, and seal a clay lump over the knot. This method continued into the Christian Era, from which time a great number of Greek papyri have survived in Egypt. It was not until the 1st millennium BC that this kind of document, including by then leather and parchment, came into wide use outside Egypt. The spread of this kind of document, on which the space for a seal was small, probably played some part in the gradual replacement of the cylinder by the stamp seal.

No documents or sealings have been discovered from ancient India, but the still undeciphered inscriptions on the seals may include personal names, perhaps of merchants, who could have used the seals in much the same ways as their Near Eastern contemporaries, with whom they are known to have had commercial contacts.

Since seals were used throughout ancient times and are sufficiently durable to have survived in very large numbers, they form one of the few classes of ancient objects in which a continuous development canbe traced. The great majority bear artistic representations, so their chief value is for art history, but, since these include details of environment (plants, animals), equipment (plows, chariots, musical instruments), or dress, they also contribute to cultural history.

Further information is provided by the inscription on seals. The existence of rulers known only from king lists may sometimes be confirmed by the discovery of their seals, and in some cases rulers are known only from their seals, which, because they often mention the names of their fathers, the cities that they ruled, and the chief gods that they served, form a valuable historical source. The assembling of tablets and sealings bearing the impressions of private seals can contribute to the reconstruction of business archives and the destinations of traded goods, thus providing valuable material for economic analysis, and far-flung trade contacts canbe deduced from foreign seals in excavation (*e.g.* Indus Valley seals in Babyloni). Personal names are an important source for ethnic analysis, and inscribed seals, because they often name the owner's father and even grandfather, provide material for this as well as for genealogical reconstruction.

Medieval European seals. The connection between Roman and medieval scales lies in the use of seals in the chanceries of the Merovingian and Carolingian kings. Many Ottonian seals had busts of the emperors. Royal seals of medieval type, with the ruler enthroned and bearing his insignia, appear from the 11th century. The use of seals by boshops and nobles became usual at this time and was widespread by the 13th century. By the 13th century, seal were used by all classes, including small landowners; and, by the 14th century, simple seal matrices could be bought ready-made.

The quality of engraving varied greatly. Some delicately designed seals date from the 12th century, such as the silver seal of Isabella of Hainaut, queen of France in 1180 notable example of the 13th century, the period of the finest seal engraving.

The names of several engravers of medieval seals are known; for example. Luke, who engraved the seal of Exeter, and Walter de Ripa, who engrabed the first great seal of Henry III of England.

Forms of medieval seals. Seal matrices may be single or double, thus producing an impression on either one or both sides of the wax. Single matrices, the older type, often have a ridge along the back and end in a loop. Double matrices, known from the 11th century onward, are flat, with two to four projecting lugs pierced with holes in which vertical pins keep the halves aligned.

Sealing both sides of the wad makes detaching the seal more difficult, and so in medieval times the reverse was often sealed by a counterseal for greater security. The official seal of an institution was often countersealed by the seal of an official, such as a town by its mayor. Single seals were often fitted with a handle; the most common type was a six-sided cone ending in a trefoil. In some matrices the centre screwed outward, enabling the device to be used without a legend. On many seals the back was marked with a cross to indicate the top.

Seals could be either applied to the surface of a document or appended from it by a strip of material. Application was the earlier system, although papal bulls were always appended. Appended seals appeared in England in the 11th century and in France in the 12th seals were appended either on a tongue of parchment cut across from the bottom of the document or on a tag of parchment, leather, or silk inserted through a cut in the document. Some documents had many seals. Seals were often protected by woven bags or by boxes of wood, metal, or ivory known as skippers.

The legend, often abbreviated, usually declared the name of the owner or institution; it often began with a cross and the word *sigillum*, gollowed by the name in the genitive case. Latin remained in fashion for inscriptions, though English and French are occasionally found from the 13th century, more frequently on personal seals. On English seals roman capitals were used in the 11th and 12th centuries and Lombardic ones in the 13th and early 14th centuries and Lombardic onesin the 13th and early 14th centuries. Black letter (Gothic script) was first used in England in the 14th century and was quite popular in the 15th century, although Lombardic often continued for capitals. Roman capitals reappeared in the 16th century.

Royal and official seals. The great seal, or seal of majesty (a round seal showing the seated ruler with the royal insignia), first appeared in Europe on the seal of the emperor Henry II of Germany (ruled 1002-24), in France on the seal of Henry I (ruled 1031-60), and in England on the double seal of Edward the Confessor (ruled 1042-66). The seal of William I of England (ruled 1066-87) had the King on one side and an equestrian figure on the other. The kings of France adopted double seals under Louts VII (ruled 1137-80).

The development of lesser royal seals can be illustrated by the growth of English government. Deputed great seals were used for the major legal courts and for France. Ireland, and Wales. The expansion of the kings affairs caused the additions of smaller, more personal seals, such as the signet. The Chancery did not control these seals, and this freedom led to the evolution of autonomous offices. The privy seal appeared early in the 13th century in the custody of the clerks of the king's chamber. It was soon transferred to the wardrobe clerks, and gradually its importance increased until by the early 14th century the keeper of the privy seal was the third minister of state. The keepership gained further prestige in midcentury, when the great seal was entrusted to the keepers who went aboard with Edward III. As the privy seal grew in importance, the king preferred another small seal for authenticating correspondence and warrants. Under Edward II (ruled 1307-27) there was a secret seal distinct from the privy seal. By 1400 the signet, as the secret seal was then called, was in the charge of the kings' secretary. The signet rather than the privy seal became the originating force in administration, and from 1540 there were two secretaries, each with two signets. The privy seal and signet seal were both single armorial seals.

Royal officials had their own seals. Circular admirals' seals, dating from the late 14th century to the 17th century, include a fine group of 15th century bronze matrices. The seals who ships in great detail, with the sails displaying the arms of the admiral.

Religious seals. The principal episcopal seal was the seal of dignity, always a pointed oval. From the 11th to the 14th century is usually depicted the standing figure of the bishop, from the 13th century with a canopy above him. In the mid-14th century the standing figure was often replaced by a saint or a religiou scene, with the bishop praying beneath a from that had been used earlier on episcopal counterseals. The seal of Thomas Arundel, archbishop of Canterbury (1396), depicts the martyrdom of Becket in the centre of an elaborate series of niches, with the archbishop below.

Monastic seals, usually double-sided and of high quality, normally show the buildings of the monastery, religious scenes, or the patron saint. They were distrinct from abbots' and priors' seals, which were similar to those of bishops. Notable was the celaborate four-part matrix of Box grove Priory (mid-13th century). The seal of Merton Priory (1241), considered the finest English medieval seal, had the Virgin and child on one side with st. Augustine of Hippo on the other.

Papal bulls were doubled sided led seals appended to the document on strings. The earliest known is that of Deusdedit (reigned 615-618). The usual design, with the head of the

Apostles Peter and Paul on one side and the pope's name on the other, first appeared under Paschal II (reigned 1099-1118). Although this style of portrayal of the heads was changed in the Renaissance, the design has not been altered.

Town seals. The possession of a common seal was in important part of a town's independence. Town seals were almost always round and often double. Many towns still possess their original matrices. The earliest in England date from around 1200, when many towns received their charters. The seal of Exeter has been dated to c. 1180. Maritime towns often depicted a ship with a furled sail; inland towns often showed the guildhall or the town itself. The seal of Rochestr depicted the Norman castle within a wall.

Counterseals often bore the figures of saints. Later medieval town seals were less common and beginning with the 124th century were often single seals.

Commercial seals. Commercial seals in England were considerably increased during the reign of Edward I, when double-sided bronze dies occurred for various customs, subsidies, and the delivery of wool and hides. Their obverse displayed the arms of England, and the reverse had the same device without the shield. The sealsofmerchants and craftsmen often displayed either merchant's marks or tools connected with their trade.

Personal seals. The earliest class of personal seals was that of greater barons of the 12th century, who used the device of a fully armed equestrian knight. Their shields often provide the earliest evidence for the use of heraldic charges. Some greater barons used a double seal with an equestrian obverse and an armorial reverse. The most usual type of personal seal was a single seal with the arms of the owner. Women's seals were usually pointed ovals and showed the lady standing, sometimes between shields. Nonheraldic personal seals displayed a variety of devices, such as stars, fleurs-de-lis, armorials, and religious subjects. The inscription sometimes indicated the owner, although it may simply have related to the device, as on those that bore the device of a squirrel and the inscription "I krack nuts".

Modern use of seals. The use of seals declined as the use of signatures grew. Personal fob seals were in fashion from the 17th to the early 19th century; often they were gems in gold settings that were carried in the fob or breeches pocket and were used to seal fold private correspondence before the envelope was introduced. States and institutions continued to sued seals for the formal ratification of their acts, but few of these seals maintained the medieval vigour of design.

Chinese and Japanese seals. The private seals used in China *(I u-chang)* and Japan *(ingyo).* commonly square served as a confirmation of signature or a sign to be verified but have not the legal status of a signature. They are made of ivory, wood, or jade. Used by artists and colllectors to mark their paintings and books, there is hardly a limit to their fanciful designs and phraseology. A man might own scores of seals, using his many sobriquets, especially those suggesting unworldly and rustic tasters. A seal is impressed in red ink- made of cinnabar in water and honey or suspended in sesame oil, hempseed oil, etc. held ready on a pad of cotton or moss. The characters most often appear in line, but they are sometimes reserved against the inked ground.

The first records of a seal in China is from 544 BC. Actual bronze seals survive from the 5th century BC, and the practice of sealing must be some centuries older. The emblematic characters cast on Shang dynasty bronze vessels (13th -11th century BC) imply the use of something like a seal for impressing on the mold. The royal seal and other seals of high office termed *his:* other seals of rank and appointment were *chang*. The imperial *his* (called *pao* beginning in the "I"ang period. Ad 618-907) was traditionally large and square, made of jade or ivory. The most famous one belonged to Shih Huang-ri (ruled 221-209/210 BC); it had as its knob a one-horned dragon and is fabled to have been handed down to the present day.

The official and, no doubt, the personal use of seals began in Japan with the copying the Chinese institutions in the 7th century AD. Both in China and in Japan modern seals generally employ the "small seal" character (chuanshu), the "great seal" character being reserved in the past for the ruler and high officers. To the historian the importance of the Far Eastern seals is greater in the earlier periods, and in China they yield more information that in Japan. Thus, seals recovered archaeologically throw light on government appointments made in the Han period, particularly in the reign of Han Wu Ti (140-87 BC), when they were tokens of rank given to internal officials and some external client rulers. Gold seals of the "king of the Han wei-nu country", found near Fukuoka in 1784, and that of the "King of Tien" excavated near K'unming in 1956 have implications of this kind. But in post Han times the seals have served little if at all as primary historical documents, and in writings on East Asia it is chiefly the art historian who appeals to their testimony in authenticating paintings and calligraphies.

TEXTUAL CRITICISM

The technique of restoring texts as nearly as possible to their original form is called textual criticism. Texts in this connection are defined as writings other than formal documents, inscribed or printed on paper, parchment, papyrus, or similar materials. The study of formal documents such as deeds and charters belongs to the science known as "diplomatic"; the study of writings on stone is part of epigraphy; while inscriptions on coins and seals are the prifvince of numismatics and sigillography. Textual criticisnm, properly speaking, is an ancillary academic discipline designed to lav the foundations fro the so-called higher criticism whkh deals with questions of authenticity and attribution of interpretation and of literary and historical evaluation. This distinction between the lower and the higher branches of criticism was first made explicitly by the German biblical scholar J. G. Eichhorn the first use of the term "testual eriticsm" in English datos from the middle of the 19th century. In practive the operations of textual and "higher" criticism cannot be rigidly differentiated; at the very outset of his work a critic, faced with variant forms of a text, inevitably employs stylistic and other criteria belonging to the "higher" branch. The methods of textual criticism, insofar as they are not codified common sense, are the methods of historical inquiry. Texts have been transmitted in an almost limitless variety of ways, and the criteria employed by the textual critic technical, philological, literary, or aeshetic are valie only if applied in awareness of the particular set of historical circumstances governing each case.

An acquaintance with the history of texts and the principles of textual criticism is indispensable for the student of history, literature, or philosophy. Written texts supply the main foundation for these disciplines, and some knowledge of the processes of their transmission is necessary for understanding and control of the scholar's basic materials. For the advanced student the criticism and editing of texts offers an unrivalled philological training and a uniquely instructive avenue to the history of scholarship; it is broadly trued that all advances in philology have been made in connection with the problems of editing texts. To say this is to recognize that the equipment needed by the critic for his task includes a mastery of the whole field of study within which has text lies; for the editing of Homer (to take an ex4terme case), a period of some 3,000 years. For the general reader the benefits of textual criticism are less apparent but are nevertheless real. Most men are apt to take texts on trust, even to prefer a familiar version, however debased or unauthentic, to the true one. The reader who resists all change is exemplified by Erasmus' story of the priest who preferred his nonsensical *mumpstmus* to the correct *sumpsimus*. Such people are saved from themselves by the activities of the textual critic.

The law of diminishing returns operators in the textual field as in others; improvements in the texts of the great writers cannot be made indefinitely. Yet a surprisingly large number of texts have not yet been edited satisfactorily. This is particularly true of medieval literature, but also of many modern novels. Indeed the basic materials of most textual investigation, the manuscripts themselves, have as yet not all been identified and catalogued, much less systematically exploited. The first edition of the works of Dickens to be founded on critical study of the textual evidence did not begin to appear until 1966, when K. Tillotson's edition of *Oliver Twist* was published. Reliable principles of Shakespearean editing have begun to emerge only with modern developments in the techniques of analytical bibliography. The Revised Standard Version of the Bible (1952) and the New English Bible (1970) both incorporate readings of the Old Testament unknown before 1947, the year in which early biblical manuscripts the so-called Dead Sea Scrolls were discovered in the caves of Qumran.

The materials of the investigation. The premise of the textual critic's work is that whenever a text is transmitted, variation occurs. This is because human beings are careless fallible, and occasionally perverse. Variation can occur in several ways; through mechanical damage or accidental omission; through misunderstanding due to change is fashions of writing; through inattention or stupidity; and through deliberate efforts at correction. The task of the textual critic is to detect and, so far as possible, undo these effects. His concern is with the reconstruction of what no longer exists. A text is not a concrete artifact, like a pot or a statue, but an abstract concept or idea. The original text of Aeschylu' *Agamemnon* or Horace's *Odes* has perished; what survives is a number of derived forms or states of the text, approximations of varying reliability preserved by tradition. The critic must reduce these approximations as nearly as possible to the first or original state that they imperfectly represent; or if, as sometimes happens for reasons that will be explained below, no single original can beer reconstructed or postulated, he must reduce their number to the lowest possible figure. His methods and the degree of his success will be determined by the nature of the individual problem; *i.e.* the text itself and the circumstances of its transmission. The range of possible situations is vast, as the following survey indicates. The types of text with which the critic is concerned may be classified broadly under three heads.

Books transmitted in print. For practical purposes it is often assumed that the latest edition of a modern book published during the author's lifetime may be treated as the original. This is a simplification. The actual author's original may have been a manuscript or a typescript or a recording; in the process of publication it has passed through several stages of transmission, including possibly storage in a computer, at any one of which errors have necessarily occurred. Experience teaches that some errors will survive uncorrected in the published version. Further errors are likely to occur if a book is reprinted. Even an edition revised by the author is not to be regarded at textually definitive. Errors committed and overlooked by the author himself may be corrected by the critic in appropriate cases. Special problems are posed by an author's second thoughts, whether preserved in his books and papers or incorporated in editions revised by him; recent research has shown that authorial revision in modern printed books has been underestimated. The extent to which a critic is free to choose between authorial variants on awsthetic grounds is a matter of debate.

Books published before the 19th century pose essentially similar problems in a more intractable from, as may be seen in the case of Shakespeare. No manuscript of any of Shakespeare's plays survives, and there were substantial intervals between the dates of composition and th first printed versions, in which unauthorized variation clearly occurred. For Shakespeare's plays, indeed, the very concept of an author's original may be misleading. Elizabethan printers clearly had little regard for strict textual accuracy, so that allowance must be made not only for error but for deliberate alteration by compositors; thus the textual criticism of 16th and 17th century books must include a study of the practices of early printers.

Books transmitted in mansuscript. Nearly all classical and patristic texts, and a great many medieval texts, fall into this category. Every handwritten copy of a book is textually unique, and to that extent represents a separate edition of the text. Whereas the characteristic grouping of printed texts is "monogamous" (*i.e.* in a straight line of descent), that of manuscript texts is "polygamous" or branched and interlocking. The critic is in principle obliged to establish the relationship of every surgiving mansucript copy of a text to every other. The difficulty and indeed the feasibility of this undertaking varies enormously from case to case. The followingextemes embrace awide range of intermediate possibilities. (1) The authority of a text may be a single surviving copy (*e.g.* Menander, *dyscolus)* or a copy that can be shown to be the source of all other copies (*e.g.*, Varro, *De Lingua Latina0* or an edition printed directly from a copy now lost *(e.g.*, the work of the Roman historian Velleius Paterculus); or a text may be transmitted in scores of copies whose interrelationships cannot be exactly determined *(e.g.*, Caudian, *De raptu Proserpinae)*, (2) The interval between the original and the earliest surviving copies may be very short (*e.g.* the Attic tragedians), (3) A tradition may be "dynamic"- *i.e.* the text may have been copied and recopied many times even in a short time (*e.g.*, Dante's *La divina commedta);* or it may be "static"- *i.e.* the number of transmission stages even over a long period may have been few (*e.g.,Eptgrammata Bobiensia,* a Latin translation of Greek epigrams). (4) A text may be a religious or literary work that was respectfully treated by copyists and protected by an exegetical tradition (*e.g.*, the Bible, the Latin poet Virgily); or a popular book that was exposed to correction, glossing, and amplification by readers (*e.g.*, the *regula magistrt* ["Rule of the Master", a Latin work related to the Rule of St. Benedict] and much medieval vernacular literature). (5) A text may have been written and transmitted after the establishment of a scholarly tradition, or it may show signs of "wild" and arbitrary variation dating from an age in which standards of exact verbal accuracy were low. To this extent all Greek books written before the establishment of the Alexandrian library (see below) were exposed to the hazards associated with oral transmission.

Books transmitted orally. Many texts have been orally transmitted, sometimes for long periods, before being committed to writing, and much textual variation may be attributable to this stage of transmission. Often in such cases the fritic cannot attempt to construct an "original" but must stop short at some intermediate stage; thus the edited text of Homer means in practice the closest possible approximation to the text as established by the scholars of Alexandria. The length, complexity, and fidelity of oral traditions varies enormously. The text of the old Indian Rigveda was transmitted orally almost without variation from very ancient to modern times, whereas much old French epic and Provincial lyric has descended in variant redactions fro which a common sources may be postulated but cannot be reconstructed. Sometimes this is attributable not to spontaneous variation but to deliberate reworking, whether by the author, as appears to be the case with the three version of the English poem *piers Plowman,* or by later revisers, as with the four version of *Digenis Akritas* (a Greek epic). The distinction, however, is not always easy to draw. These considerations apply to a wide range of tedts from ancient Hebrew through Old Norse to modern Russian, but they are especially important for medieval literature. In this field perhaps more than in any other the critic's aims and methods will be dictated by the character of the oral tradition, the stage at which it attained a more or less fixed from in writing, and the attitude of copysts in a particular genere to precise verbal accuracy. A problem of particular difficulty and importance is posed by the Greek New Testament. Though the text appears to have been transmitted from the first in writing, the textual variations and it commonly held that the essential task of the critic is not to try to reconstruct the "original" but to isolate those forms of the text that were current in particular centers in the ancient world.

Critical methods. From the preceding discussion it is apparent that there is only one universally valid principle of textual criticism, the formulation of which can be traced back at least as far as the 18th century German historian A. L, von Schlozer; that each case is special. The critic must begin by defining the problem presented by his particular material and the consequent limitations of his inquiry. Everything that is said below about "method" must be understood in the light of this general proviso. The celebrated dictum of the 18th century English classical scholar Richard Bentley that "reason and th facts outweigh a hundred manuscripts" (*ratio et res ipsa centum codicibus potiores sunt)* is not a repudiation of science but a remainder that the ritic is by definition one who discriminates (the word itself derives from the Greek word for "judge"), and that no amount of learning or mastery of method will compensate for a lack of common sense. To study the great critics in action is incomparably more instructive than to read theoretical manuals. As the editor of Manilius, A. E. Housman, wrote.

A man who possesses common sense and the use of reason must no expect to lea5n from treatises or lectures on textual criticism anything that the could not, with leisure and industry, find out for himself. What the lectures and industry, find out for himself. What the lectures and treatises can do for him is to save him time and trouble by presenting to him immediately considerations which would in any case occur to him sooner or later.

Admittedly, the technical advances in textual bibliography mentioned below are not such as would sooner or later occur to any reflective and intelligent person; but bibliography, like paleography, is ancillary to textual criticism proper, and Houseman's words are strictly true. What they imply is that good critics are born, not made.

The critical process can be resolved into three stages: (1) recession. (2) examination, and (3) are in practive performed simultaneously, and even (1) entails the application of criteria theoretically appropriate to (2) and (3).

Recession. The operation of recession is the reconstructing of the earliest from or forms of the text that can be inferred from the surviving evidence. Such evidence may be internal or external. Internal evidence consists of all extant copies or editions of the text, together with versions in other languages, citations in other authors, and other sources not belonging to the main textual tradition. These witnesses (as they may be called) must be identified, dated, and described, using the appropriate paleographical and bibliographical techniques. They must then be collated: *i.e.* the variant readings that they contain must be registered by comparison with some selected from of the text, often a standard printed edition. Where the number of witnesses is large, collation may have to be of selected passages. If there is only one witness to a text, collation and recession are synonymous, and the critic passes straight to examination and emendation. Generally, however, he will be faced with two or more witnesses offering variant forms or states of the text.

Collateral evidence as to the transmission of a text may be supplied from sources external to the direct or indirect textual tradition. Thus the ancient biographers throw light on the circumstances in which Virgil's *Aeneid* was published. Inferred textual stages may be dated on the evidence of copying practices at different periods. or by association with a particular scholar,. or from entries in medieval library catalogues. Generally speaking, information of this sort will contribute more to the history than to the criticism of the text, but the two fields are intimately connected; and the better the textual history is known, the more reliable the control of the critic over conjectural solutions to specific problems. In the case of printed books, such external evidence is as a rule more plentiful: it is often essential, since so much may turn on the accurate dating of editions. Relevant information must besought in the published and unpublished records of stationers, printers, booksellers, and publishers and in other archival material.

Having assembled his evidence, the critic may procced, boradly speaking, in one of two different was, according as he decides to handle the problem of interrelationships "genealogically" or "textually".

In the "genealogical" or stemmatic" approach, the attempt to reconstruct and original text here relies on the winesses themselves regarded as physical objects related to each other chronologically and genealogically, the text and that textual vehicle (the book itself) are treated as a single entity. On the basis of shared variants, ehietly crrors and omissions, a family free of the witnesses *(stemma codicum)* a drawn up. Those witness that repeal the testimony of other surviving witnesses are discarded, and from the agreements of the remainder the textis reconstructed as it existed in the lostcopy from which they descend, the "archetype". Thus in the tradition of the 6th century monk Cassiodorus". *Institutiones* the relationships of the manuscripts of the authentic version of the text of Book II may be represented by the accompanying disagram. The Roman tellers represent extant manuscripts, and th Greek letters represent the lost manuscripts from which they derive, here arbitrarily dated. The tet of the archetype O is established by the agreement of B and Ó. Since B survives, the reading of MUP, which are derived from it, would be of value only where B has suffered damage after and B were copied from it. In such cases the text of B could be inferred from the agreement of UP and the text of B from the agreement of MB (or MU or MP).The text of Ó can be inferred from the agreement of SLo or SL or Sa (or ST or SD) or Lo (or LT or LD). K. being copied from L, would be of value only where I had suffered daimage after was copied from in. An important distinction is here exemplified between "trifid" and "bifid" *stentmata.* Where there are three independent witnesses to a source, as with Ó, its reading is certified by the agreement of all three or of any two, where there are only two witnesses, as with Ù, and they disagree, the reading of the source cannot be certified. Even in the latter situation, however, the number of possible variants existing in the source would have been reduced to two. Thus in theory the genealogical, or stemmatic, method allows the critic to eliminate from consideration all variants that cannot be traced back to the archetype or carliest inferable textual state.

While in principle this method is unassailable, it depends for it practical validity on the assumption that each copyist followed only one model or exempiar and generated only variant peculiar to himself. This is called "vertical" transmission, and tradition of the kind is called "closed". Once the possibility is admitted that a copyist used more than once exemptar or (the more probable supposition) copied an exemplar in which variants from another source or sources had been incorporated *i.e.*, that more than one textual state may coexist in a single witness- the construction of a *stemima* becomes more complicated and may be impossible. This is called "horizontal" transmission, and a tradition of this kind is called "open" or "contaminated". The practice of critics faced with contamination tends to vary, for historical reasons, from field to field. Editors of classical texts generally adopt a controlled eclecticism, classical texts generally adopt a controlled eclecticism, classifying the witnesses broadly by groups according to the general character of their texts and choosing between their readings largely on grounds of intrinsic excellence. Medievalists, following the French scholar Joseph Bedier (see below), sometimes revert to the traditional practice, the which their training may dispose, of selecting a single witness as the main basis of the text. For editors of printed books, contamination is not an important problem.

In the "textual" or "distributional" approach, the text and the textual vehicle are dissociated; the emphasis is on the analysis of the variants themselves and their distribution rather than on the character of the text as presented by individual witnesses. The techniques or models employed include those of statistics, symbolie logic, and biological taxonomy. Two theoretical advantages are suggested for this approach. First, objectivity; no judgments of value are entailed, whereas the genealogical method calls for decisions as to the correctness or readings or textual states. Second, the possibility of mechanization; long and elaborate calculations involving thousands of variants may be performed, by a computer. This possibility is especially attractive to New Testament critics, who are confronted with about 5,000 manuscripts for the Greek text as well as versions in other language and patristic citations. In practice, however, these advantage are to a large extent illusory. An "objective"(*i.e.* undiscriminating) treatment of all variants in a literary text such as Ovid's *Metamorphoses* (of which more than 300 manuscripts exits) without regard to their metrical and stylistic quality would be a self-evident waste of time and produce merely confusion. The critic cannot abrogae his critical function, which implies discrimination, at the very beginning of the critical process. Moreover the preparation of programming of a test for treatment in this ay, whether mechanical aids are used or not, is long and laborious, and one must consider whether is a given case the results justify the expenditure of effort. Texts have been transmitted by a combination of purpose and accident that in any particular instance is both unlaue and unpredictable, and no machine or statistical model exhibits the versatility necessary to unravel the incomplete and tangled skein. Mechanical methods have been most suffcessful in fields other than recession (see below).

Examination. The process of determining whether the transmitted text or any of the transmitted variants of it sis "authentic"- *i.e.* what the author intended - is known as examination The prior process of recenision has reduced the number of textual sttes having a claim to be considered "authoritative". Many different s8ituations are possible. In a completely closed tradition it is theoretically feasible to reconstruct the archetype with such certainly that only single from of the text without variants remains to be edamined. In practice this is extremely unlikely to be the situation. Usually the critic is faced with pairs (some- times triplets) of variants, all with a presumptive claim to be considered authoritative. In some traditions he will confront variant versions of the whole text. Where papyri or other early sources independentofthe main tradition are available, he may have to reckon with "pretraditionsl"(*i.e.* pre-archetypal variants. The process of examination calls upon the critic's full range of knowledge as well as him innate powers of tate and discrimination. The criteria applied must be those appropriate to the particular author (supposing his identity to th known), the period, the genre, and the particular character of the work. The opposing demands of analogy and anomaly must be weighed according to the circumstances. Manyy of the older generation of critics based their decision on aprioristic or rieidly analogical principles of elegance and propriety, while the cannons of moderncriticism are based on historical studies of language and style. It is here that the circularity inherent in the world operation is most evident, for the linguistic and stylistic criteria employed ae themselves based on inductions from texts, probably including the one under examination. There is no escape from this difficulty; as the German philologist Karl Lachmann observed, it is precisely the lask of the critic "to tread that circle deftly and warily."

Emendation. The attempt to restore the transmitted text to its authentic state is called emendation. There will usually be a chronological ga, sometimes of several centuries, between the archetype, or earliest inferable state of the text, and the original: nearly all manuscripts of elassicalauthors date from the Middle Ages. The history of the text during the intervening period may be illustrated from external sources; but if examination has convinced the critic that the transmitted text (orits variants) are notauthentic, he normally has no recourse but to bridge the gap by conjecture. Conjectural emendation has been defined by the American scholar B. L. Gidersleeve as "the appeal from manuscripts we have to a manuscript that has been lost." Theoretically this definition is acceptable, if we interpret "manuscript" as "source", but in practice the making of conjectures, as distinct fromtesting them, is intelligent guesswork.

No part of the thory of textual criticism has suffered more from misunderstanding than has conjectural emendation. Such conjectural, or divinatory, criticism has in the past enjoyed a traditional preeminence; Dr, Johnson observed that William Warburton's correction of "good" to "god" in the second act of *Hamlet* (scene 2, line 182) almost set the critic on a level with the author. That idea is as erroneous as the frame of mind in which the Italian scholar C. Pascal founded the Paravia series of editions in order to purge Latin texts of German conjectures. The best britic is he who discriminates best, whether between varants or between transmitted text and conjecture.

Conjectures as a rule occur to the mind spontaneously or not at all: diagnosis and prescription often present themselves at the same moment. Thisinstinctive process is not under the critic's control, though he can sharpen and regulate is by constant study and observation. The outcome of the process, the emendation itself, can and must be controlled and tested by precisely the same criteria as are used in deciding between variants. This is essentially an exercise in balancing probabilities. These probabilities are historical. The conventional distinction between intrinsic and transcriptional (*i.e.* paleographical or bibliographical) probability tends to obscure a fundamental historical point. If the transmitted from of the text is at few remove or a short distance in time from th original, a conjectural solution which violates transcriptional probability is less likely to be correctthan if the text has undergone a long and complex process of deterioration. In the latter case the critic may attach little or no importance to transcriptional probability. The critic cannot neglect the study of paleography of bibliography, but hemust not give them more than their critical due. That may be depends on the particular historical circumstances. Hewill study carefully the rationale of error in manuscripts and books themselves ratherthan in the schematic classifications of critical manuals; and he will learn from experience to distinguish between the types of error that may be called "psychological"(*i.e.* those committed by a tired or inattentive copyist, whatever language or instruments he uses) and those contingent on the period and the medium of transmission, whether it be the mouth and their, the pen, the hand composing stick, the linotype or typewriter keyboard, the computer or photocopying machine, or the printing pres. Two complementary principles originated by the New Testament critics of the 18th century are often cited as aids to decision: *ulrum in alterum abiturum erat'*(Which reading would be more likely to have given rise to the other ?") and *difficulior lectio potior* ("the more difficult reading is to be preferred").These are no more than useful rules of thumb; it has been suggested that in pracice these another such principles reduce them selvestothe truism *melior lectio potior.*

"the better reading is to be freferred.

"From this discussion it is apparent that the traditional opposition between "conservatie" and "radical" styles of criticism that has haunted textual criticism since St, Jerome has no meaning. The critic does not attack or defend the transmitted text: he asks himself whether it is authentic. How radically he treats it, and how may conjectural readings he substitutes for transmitted readings, depends not on his temperament but on the nature of the problem. If he has studied the history of textual criticism he will know that as a matter of demonstrable fact nearly all conjectures are wrong, and he will accept that many of his solutions are in the nature of things provisional.

Editoral technique. Critical texts are edited according to conventions that vary with the type of text (elassical, medieval, modern) but follow certain general principles. In some cases, as with newly edited papyri and with palimpsests (writing materials re-used after erasure_, the edition will take the from of a diplomatic transcript; (*i.e.* the most accurate possible representation of a particular textual from, Generally, however, the editor constitutes his text in accordance with is own judgment on principles explained in his introduction; and he indicates his sources in critical notes (*apparatus criticus),* preferably at the foot of the page. These notes are usually couched in a special terminology that relies heavily on abbreviation and the use of conventional signs or letters (*sigla*) to identify the witnesses., In classical and patristic texts the language of the notes is usually Latin. Editorial judgment will be influenced by the presumed needs of readers; in and edition intended for scholars, very corrupt passages are often printed as transmitted and marked with a dager (f), whereas in a edition for the student or general reader some compromise may be accepted in the interests or readability.

A much-discussed problem is the treatment of "accidentals"- variations in spelling, capitalization, punctuation, and the like. Few if any ancient text traditions preserve reliable evidence of authorial practice in these matters, so that the editor is concerned only with variants that affect the sense, in preparing his text for printing he will adopt modern conventions of presentation and punctuation and a normalize orthography. The same beholds good for the majority of medieval texts. Printed texts, however, where generally corrected or seen though the press by the author, or at all events by a contemporary, so that the editor may be reasonably confident of reproducing at least a decent approximation to authorial usage, Whether, or to what extent, he should do so is much debated: opinions differ sharply as to the usefulness of "old-spelling" editions of Shakespeare and other early writers.

History of textual criticism. *From antiquity to the Renaissance* Until the 20th century the development of textual criticism was inevitably dominated by classical and biblical studies. The systematic study and practice of the subject originated in the 3rd century BC with the Greek scholars of Alexandria. Literary culture had before that time been predominantly oral, though books were in common use by the 5th century, and many texts had suffered damage because the idea of precise textual accuracy and reproductions was unfamiliar. The aim of the librarians of Alexandria was to collect and catalogue every extant Greek book and to produce critical editions of the most important together with textual and interpretative commentaries. Many such edition and commentaries did in fact appear. Alexandrian editing was distinguished above all by respect for the tradition. The text was constituted from the oldest and best copies available, and conjectural emendation was rigidly confined to the commentary, which was contained in a separate volume. An elaborate battery of critical signs was used to refer from text to commentary. These techniques were applied, though on a less ambitious scale, by Roman scholars to Latin texts. Fidelity to tradition was the chief legacy of ancient textual scholarship to later ages; the copyist was expected to reproduce his exemplars exactly as the cold, and corrections was based on comparison with other copies, not on the unaided contractual sagacity of the scribe. Such was the practice of the best monastic scriptoria such as that of Tours, or of the best scholars, such as Lupus of Ferrieres(fl, 850). From about 1350, however, a change in attitude is evident, particularly in the West. What is often called the revival of learning was in reality a practical movement to enlist the heritage of classical antiquity in the service of the new Christian humanism. In order to make them usable (*i.e.* readable). Texts were corrected freely and often arbitrarily by scholars, copyists and readers (the there categories being in fact hardly distinguishable). At its best, as seen in the activities of a scholar like Demetrius Triclinius. Later medieval and early Renaissance criticism verges on scientific scholarship, but such cases are exceptional. For the most part the correction of tedxts was a purely subjective display of taste, sometimes right but much more often wrong, and resting as a rule on nothing more solid than a superficial sense of elegance. In consequerice, but the (470s, when the first printed editions (*editones principes)* of classical texts began to appear, most Greek and Latin authors were circulating in a textually debased condition. and it was manuscripts of this character that almost always served as copy for the carly printers. Very little editing in any real sense of the word was done; the scholars who any real sense of the word was done; the scholars who saw the *editiones princtpes* though the press generally confined themselves to superficial improvements.

From Politian to Cobet. This state of affairs entailed that down to the 19th century most critics were engaged notin establishing and emending texts on scientific principles but in correcting, in a necessarily unsystematic fashion, a vulgate or received text (*lectio recepta)* that was itself the product of an almost entirely haphazard process of variation and conjecture. The situation was aggravated by the fact that the manuscripts themselves, the basic materials of the investigation, were largely inaccessible to scholars,. The Italian poet and scholar Politian, unlike most of his contemporanes, was aware that only through the identification and comparison of the best manuscripts could texts be improved; his notes and collations show that he understood the problem correctly as essentially one of control of the sources. What might have been done in this held is shown by his work, coot short by his early death, on the Florentine codex of Justinian's Pandects. Many manuscripts were still privately owned, their very existence unknown to scholars public libraries were few and published catalogues fewere; travel was difficult expensive, and often darigerrous. It was not until the twin disciplines of diplomatic and paleography were founded by the great Benedictine monks Mabillon and Montfaucon,and developed their successors, that a critical use of the evidence became possible; and much of the evidence itself did not become aynilable until after the Napoleonic Wars, when most of the private stock of manuscripts passed finally into public collections.

Some advance were taking place, slowly and unsystematically, in both the theory and practice of textual criticism. The history of critical method in this period is most profitably studied in the best editions of the best editors. The accepted method was to correct the text (*i.e.*, the text of the last printed edition) *codicum et ingenti ope: i.e.*, with the aid of the manuscript and printed sources and the critic's own ingenuity. Divination was subordinated to authority, and any reading found in a manuscript or printed text was accounted superior to any conjecture, whatever its intrinsic ments. The first important departure from this pattern is seen in the edition of Catullus by J. J. Scaliger (1577), in which the possibilities of the genealogical method, already understood in principle by polities and other Renaissance scholars, were exemplified by the demonstration that all the extant copies derived from a lost manuscript, whose orthography and provenance Scaliger was prepared to reconstruct. Almost equally significant was Richard Bentley's edition of Horace (1711), in which for the first time the role of conjecture into eh critical and editorial process was recognized and the tradition of producing a corrected version of the text, of previous editors was decisively rejected. Bentley's scholarship was greatly admired in the Netherlands, and the editions of the great Dutch Latinists J.F. Gronovius and N. Hensius were informed by Bentleian principles. Under his influence there grew up that may he called an Ariglo-Ducth school of criticism, the two most typical representatives of which were Richard Person and C. G. Cobet. Its strength lay in sound judgment and good taste rooted in minute linguistic and metrical study; its weaknesses were an excessive reliance on analogical criteria and an indifference to German science and method. Its influence may still be seenin the empiricism that characterizes much critical work by English scholars.

From Bentley to Lachmann. The decisive influence on the editing of secular texts came from the New Testament critics of the 18th common use was still essentially that established in 1516 by Desiderius Erasmus. For his edition, produced in great haste, he had used such manuscripts, neither ancient nor good, as chanced to be accessible to him. Superficially revised, this was the text armed in the Elzevier edition of 1633 "now received by all", *nunc ab omnibus receptum.* Bentley proposed an edition on radical lines in which he engaged to give the text "exactly as if was in the best exemplars at the time of the Council of Nice, So that three shall not be twenty words, nor even particles, difference...". This project never materialized, but editions of the Greek text that did not reproduce the *textus receptuas* were published in England by Daniel Mace (1729). William Bowyer, the Younger (1763), and Edward Harwood (1776). On the Continent, meanwhile. New Testament criticism was being developed on scientific and historical lines by a succession of distinguished scholars, notably J. A. Bengel J. J Wettsten, J. S. Semler, and J. H. Griesbach. They shaped the genealogical method that was latter refined by editors of classical texts. Wettsterin also deserves commemoration as the first New Testament critic to use *sigla* systematically. This was important, since some at least of the deficiencies of classical editions at this time are attributable to the lack of suitable contentions for the presentation of critical information, together with a conservative and belletristic attitude to technical jargon by publishers, scholars, and users of books in general. Though *sigal* occur sporadically in editions as early as the 16th century and were used by S. Haverkamp in his Lucretius (1725) in something like the modern style, they did not become normal until the second half of the 19th century.

The genealogical, or temmatic, method of recession has already been described. It is usually associated with the name of the German Karl Lachmann, but it has its origins in the work of J.A. Bengel and his successors, and almost every essential feature of it was already present in the work of Lachmann's precursors such as J. A. Ernesti. F. A. Wolf, K. G. Zumt. F. W. Ritschl, and J. N. Madvig. Nevertheless Lachmann occupies a central position in the development of textual criticism because of the unusual power and penetration of his scholarship, the range of textual material on which he worked, and his immenswe contemporary and posthumous influence. His edition of the Greek New Testament (1831 M 2nd ed. 1842-50) was intended primarily as a vindication of the principles of Bentley and Bengel and a demonstration that the *textus receptus* must be finally rejected. Similarly his famous edition of Lucretius (1850) is important as an exemplification of the method in action, since the tradition that the *textus receptus* must be finally rejected. Similarly his famous edition of Lucretius (1850) is important as an exemplification of the method in action, since the tradition of Lucretius is peculiarly suitable of the purpose. The demonstration fell short of completeness, for Lachmann had not fully grasped the problem and so failed to exploit the method ully. It has been suggested that Lachmann's best critical work was in his editions of medieval German texts; their influence will be considered below. The Lachmannian model of recession derived added authority from seemingly analogous models in other fields, especially that of comparative philology. as propagated by disciples, notably Moritz Haupt, it dominated textual studies for half a century.

Related developments in the late 19th century. Possibly the mot important technical advancein the latter part of the 19th century was the perfection of photography. Instead of traveling in search of his material, the paleogrpaher or critic could now assemble and study it at relatively little expense and without leaving his desk.

During the last quarter of the 19th century the tempo of archaeological discovery in classical and biblical lands was vastly increased, and many new thexts were unearthed. Some of these were in previously unknown languages, setting new problems of decipherment. Specifically relevant to textual studies are the many Greek papyri recovered from Egypt. These have thrown much light on the history and techniques of ancient book production and scholarship and hence, indirectly, on critical problems. Where the texts they contain are already known, their evidence has tended to emphasize our ignorance of the textual history of classical literature in antiquity itself. Being usually foar older than the manuscripts already known, they often illuminate the "pretraditional" state of the text; by sometimes offering rteadings that agree with those of late and "inferior" medieval copies they justify editors in a policy of cautious eclecticism. Papyrus discoveries have been of particular moment for the text of the New Testament.

Edirors of printed texts, having in variably received a classical education (no other beingavailable), had naturally followed, with minormodifications, the methods of classical editing. They would reprint the text of the last edition with such improvements as editorial taste and learing suggested but with no attempttoinvestigate the sources of the text. Since Lachman's method was inapplicable to printed texts, this procedure continued until, by the end of the 29th century, the text of Shakespeare, for example, was in a sate somewhat analogous to that of most classical writers at the time of the *editiones principles*. Much of the work of modern Shakespearean editors has consisted of undoing the damage inflicted by their predecessors. The early 20th century saw the rise of a new school of "biblio-gextual" criticism, most notably represented by A.W. Pollard, R. B. Mckerrow, and W. W. Greg. Its ject two devise a style of recession appropriate to the special circumstances under which early printed texts were produced and propagated, and its methere those of analytical bibliography. These developmentsare of direct importance forth criticism and editing of a large range of texts of the 16th, 17th and 18th centuries, particularly those of the Elizabethan and Jacobean dramatists. They have also engendered a discussion of general methodological interest on the rold of bibliographical as opposed to historical and literary criteria in the editorial process. This debate continues.

Critics and editors of medieval texts had also inevitably been influenced by developments in the classical field. Before Lachmann in had been usual to choose a single manuscript as the main basis for anedition. Because of the circumstances in which much medieval literature was the circumstances in which much medieval literature was composed and transmitted this was not necessarily unscientific, and the surviving bulk of texts was so large as to dictate that approach inmany cases if they were to be edited at all. This had been the style of editing followed by the Belgian Jesuits known as Bollandists,the French Benedictines called Maurists, and the Italian scholar L. A. Muratori, and perpetuated into eh indispensable *Patrologiae Cursus Completus* (edition of the Church Fathers) of the French priest Jacques-Paul Migne. At its best it is seen in the editions of medieval Latin chronicles by the 18thcentury Oxford antiquary Thomas Hearne, some of which are still standard works. A more scientific approach was adopted in the publications of the *Monumenta Germaniae Historiaca,* the later volumes of which (from about 1880) were produced by editors trained in the school of Lachmann. Similarly, editors of vernacular texts followed the lead that Lachmann had given in his editions so such early German poems as the *Nibelunge Not* (1826) and the *Iwein* (1827). An important development in the application of the method was due to the medievalists G. Grober and G. Paris, who first emphasized the significance of common errors. But in the general uncritical enthusiasm for scientific method, the genealogical approach was too often used without regard for the special conditions under which medieval literature has been handed down.

Reaction against the genealogical method. Haupt had proclaimed in his lectures that his main object was to teach method. But confidence in method led toits misuse. The

Lachmannian formula ofrecension was applied to texts, classical as well as medieval, for which it was unsuitable, often with grotesque results. Commonly this took the from the choosing on "scientific" *(i.e.* stemmatic) ground a "best manuscript"*(codex optimus)* and defending its readings as authoritative even where commonsense whowed that they could not be authentic. This was the type of editing satirized by A. E., Housman in the brilliant prefaces to his editions of Manilius (1903) and Juvenal (1905) and in many reviews and articles. It flourished chiefly between 1875 and 1900, but the dangers of excessive methodloglocial rigidity had already been foreseen. In 1841 H. Sauppe in his *Epistola Critica ad G. Hermannum* had emphasized the diversity of transmission situations and the difficulty or actual impossibility of classifying the manuscripts in all cases. In 1843 Lachmann's pupil O. Jahn. in his edition of Persius, had remann's pupil O. Jahn, in his edition of Persius, had repudiated the strict application of the genealogicval method as unsuitable to the tradition of that poet. The most extreme position was taken by E. Schwzrtz,who in his edition of Eusebius *Historia ecclestatica* (1909) denied that "vertically" transmitted texts of Greek book existed at all. The limitations of the stemmatic method have subsequently been stressed in a more temperate fashion by toerh writers. The modrntendency is to acknowledge the validity of the method in principle while recommending a cautious empiricism in its application. For the editor of a contaminated tradition- and most traditions are probably contaminated- the lesson of recent research is that authoritative evidence may survive even in late and generally corrupt or interpolated sources.

More radical criticism of the method has come from medievalists. In 1913 and again in1928 the French scholar J. Bedier attacked the stemmatic method because the *stemmatea* it produced of medieval texts almost invariably had only two branches. Subsequent investigation has shown that Bedier overrated the inherent improbability of this situation, and it is generally agreed that his criticisms had to do with improper application rather than with the method itself. The point taken by H.Quentin (1922) has already been mentioned: that the method 3entails argument in a circle, since it relies on the identification of errors atthegeginning of a process designed to lead to that very end. This objectiion, more cogent in theory than in practice, applies with greater force to medieval than to classical texts. The linguistic and stylistic cannons of classical Greek and Latin are relatively strict and well defined, whereas the vocabulary, grammar, and usage of many medieval authors (especially when an oral prehistory is in question) is often not ertain enough to allow reliable discrimination between variant and error, Classical texts, moreover, have passed through a series of bottlenecks in their history, which have simplified editorial problems by eliminating a high proportion of the evidence (*cf,* the remarks on papyris above). With a few exceptions, such as the commentary of Servius, only one exceptions, such as the commentary of Servius, only one version of each text remains to be reconstructed, whereas many medieval texts are extant in several redaction that cannot be winnowed by the stemmaticmethod so as toleva only one. Quentin's own method, which depended on the comparison of variants in groups of three, without prejudice as to their correctness, has not been generally adopted. It is immensely laborious and does not in practice possess the objectivity that its inventor claimed for it. Bedier and Quentin have, however, done good serive to textual criticism in enjoining caution. The best critics in all fields now agree in rejecting the "logical" (*i.e.* the illogical) application of any method if the results conflict with common sense, and in stressing the necessity of judging variant readings and forms of a text on their intrinsic merits in the light of the information available.

Mwechanical methods. Quentin also gave a lead to later investigators in calling attention to the possibility of basing recession on the variants themselves, and the more sophisticated methods of Greg (1927). Archibald Hill (1950), Vinton Dearing (1959) and J. Froger (1968) may be seen as a continuation of his work. It has already been suggested that methods of this type, so far as recession in concerned, have been or primarily theoretical interest. But the use of mechanical and computing techniques in this field is in its infancy, and assessment must be provisional. Certain practical applications seem to have proved them selves. Mechanical aids to collation have been successfully used in editing Shakespeare and Dryden. Computer storage and analysis of texts can provided information about authorial usage, such as stylistic and metrical patterns, and facilitate the production of concordances. These aids are more relevant to conjectural emendation (as shown by their application to the Dead Sea Scrools0 and the "higher" criticism (*e.g.* determination of authenticity) than to the recession of texts. The formula or machine that will do the critic's essential work for him still awaits discovery; the best texts are produced by the best scholars, whatever their method or lack of method. Lachmann observed that the establishment of a text according to its tradition is a strictly historical undertaking. Twentieth-century research into the composition and transmission of ancient, medieval, and modern texts has confirmed the truth of his pronouncement.

BIBLIOGRAPHY

Historiography; c.v. LANGLOTS and c. SEIGNOBOS. *Introduction aux etudes historiques* (1898); HAROLD TEMPERLEY (ed.). *Selected Essays of J.B. Bury* (1930, reprinted 1964); JAMES T. SHOTWELL, *The History of History* (1939); JAMES W. THOMPSON and BERNARD J. HOLM. *A History of Historical Writing,* 2 Vol, (1942); ROBIN G. COLLINGWOOD. *The Ideat of History* (1946); HERBET BUTTERFIELD. *Man on His Past* (1955); JOHN W. MILLER. *The Philosophy of History with Reflections and Aphorisms* (1981); AGNES HELLER. *A Theory of History* (1982).

J. B. BURY, *The Ancient Greek Historians* (1909, reprinted 1958); M. L. W. LAISTNR. *The Greater Roman Historians* (1947, reprinted 1963); MOSES 1, FINLEY (ed.). *The Greek Historians* (1959), selected passages in translation with a valuable introduction; MAURIC PLATNAUER (ed.). *Fifty Years of Classical Scholarship* (1954 : rev. ed. with appendixws. *Fifty Years (and Twelve) of Classical Scholarship,* (1968), a selection from his vast collection of valuable articles in *Contributo alla storia degli studi classici e del mondo antico,* 5, vol. (1959-69); T. A. DOREY (ed.), *Latin*

Historians (1966) and *Latin Biography* (1967); JOHN BARKER. *The Superhistorians : Makers of Our Past* (1982).

GYULA MORAVCSIK. *Bycantinoturcica,* 2nd ed., vol. 1 (1958), not always reliable in its judgments. There is no satisfactory study in English. There is much useful information in the appendixes to J. B. BURY's edition of *The History of the Decline and Fall of the Roman Empire,* 7 vol.(1896-1900, reprinted 1909-14).

THOMAS F. TOUT. "The Study of Medraeval Chronicles". *Bulletin of the John Rylards Library* : 6:414-438 (1921); reprinted in *The collected Papers of Thomas Frederick Tout.* 3 vol. (1932-34); REGINALD L. POOLE, *Chronicles and Annals* (1926). M. L. W. LAiSTNER. *Thought and Letters in Western Europe. A.D. 500 to 900,* new ed. (1957): CHARLES H. HASKINS. *The Renaissance of the Twelfth Century* (1927); RALPH H.C. DAVIS and JOHN M. WALLACE-HADRILL (eds.). *The Writing of History in the Middle Ages* (1981).

WALLACE K. FERGUSON. *The Renaisance in Historical Thought* (1948); DENYS HAY, "Flavio Biondo and the Middle Ages", *Proceedings of the British Academy,* 45:97-128 (1960); MYRON GILMORE. *Humanists and Jurists* (1963): PAUL O. KRISTFLLER. *Eight Philosophers of the Italian Rendissance,* ch. 2 (1964), on Valla: FELIX GILBERT. *Machiavelli and Guiectardini: Politics and History in Sixteenth Century Florence* (1965): IDA MAIER. *Ange Politien* (1966) : L. D. REYNOLDS and N. G. WILSON. *Scribes and Scholars: A Guide to the Transmissiono of Greek and Latin Literature* (1968): ROBETO WEISS. *The Renaissance Discovery of Classical Antiquity* (1969): E. J. KENNEY. "The Character of Humanist Philology", In R. R. BOLGAR (ed.). *Classical Influences on European Culture, A. D. 500-1500*(1971).

J. G. A. POCOCK. *The constitution and the Feudal Law : A Study of English Historical Thought in the Seventeenth Century* (1957), also valuable for France: HERBERT BUTTERFIELD. "The History of Historiogrpahy and the History of Science". *Melanges Alexandre Kovre.* vol. 2 (1964); and "Delays and Paradoxes in the Development of Historiogrpahy", in KENNETH BOURNE and D. C. WATT (ed.). *Studies in International History Essay Presented to W. Norton Medicott* (1967): GLAnmor WILLIAMS. *Reformation views of Church History* (1970): DONALD R. KELLEY. *Foundations of Modern Historical Scholarship: Language, Law, and History in the Tudor lge* (1971); G. STRAUSS. "The Course of German History: The Lutheran Interpretation," in

ANTHONY MOLHO and JOHN A. TEDESCHI (eds.), *Renaissance: Studies in Honor of Hans Baron* (1971).

DAVID C. DOUGLAS, *English Scholars, 1660-1730*, 2nd rev.ed. (1951): MARTIN L. CLARKE, *Greek Studies in England, 1700-1830* (1945); DAVID KNOWLES. "Jean Mabillon", *Journal of Ecoclestdstical History*, vol. 10, no. 2 (1959), and *Great Historical Enterprises* (1962); CHRISTOPHER DAWSON, "Edward Gibbon", *Proceedings of the British Academy*, 20M159-180 (1934); and EDWARD GIBBON. *The History of the Decline and Full of the Roman Empire*, 6 vol. (1776-86, best modern edition by J. B. BURY, *op. cit.)*; HUGH TREVOR-ROPER. "The Historical Philosophy of the Enlightenment," in *Studies on Voltaire and the Eighteenth Century*, 27:1667-87 (1963), and "The Idea of the Decline and Falol of the Roman Empire", in *The Age of the Enlightenment* (1967).

J. G. D. CLARK. *Prehistoric Europe: The Economic Basts, rev. ed.* (1962):; O. G. S. CRAWORD. *Archaeology in the Field* (1953); J. G. D. CLARK. *World Prehistory* (1960); CHARLESSAMARAN (ed.), *L. Historre et ses methodes*, vol. 11 of the *Encyclopedie de la Pleiade* (1961): VIVIAN H. GALBRAITH. *An Introduction to the Study of History* (1964).

ARTHUR M. SCHLESINGER (ed.). *Historical Scholarship in America* (1932): WILLIAM T. HUTCHINSON (ed.), *The Marcus W. Jernegan Essays in American Historiogrpahy* (1937):HUGH H. BELLOT. *American History and American Historians* (1952): DONALD SHEEHAN and HAROLD C. SYURETT (eds.). *Essays in American Historiogrpahy: Papers Presented in Honor of Allan Nevins* (1962): JOHN HIGHAM (ed.), *The Reconstruction of American History* (1962): THOMAS J. PRESSLY. *Americans Interpret Their Civil War*, 2nd ed. (1962); RICHARD HOFSTADTER. *The Progressive Historians. Turner, Beard, Parrington* (1968): MARCUS CUNLIFFE and ROBIN W. WINKS (eds.), *Pastmasters : Some Essays on American Historians* (1969); C. L. SONNIGSEN. *The American West* (1983).

LORD ACTON. *Historical Essays and Studies* (1907), see especially "German Schools of History", J. B. BURY. *The Idea of Progress: An Inquiry into Its Origin and Growth* (1920, reprinted 1960): EDMUND WILSON. *To the Finland Station* (1940), especially for French historiogrpahy; IPETER GEYL. *Napoleon. voor en iegen in de Franse geschiedschrijving* (1946; Eng. trans., *Napoleon. For and Against*, 1949): *Some modern Historians of Britain: Essays in*

Honour of R. L. Schuyler (1951): G. P. GOOCH. *History and Historians in the Nineteenth Century*, 2nd rev. ed. (1952): FERDINAND SCHEVILL. *Six Historians* (1956), particularly interesting on Ranke in American and German Historical Thought", in *History and Theory, 2: 17-123* (1962); and *The German Conception of History* (1968); HENRY E. BELL. *Maitland: A Critical Examination and Assessment* (1965); FREDERICK M. BARNARD, *Herder's Social and Political Thought: From Enlightenment to Nationalism* (1965): JOHN CANNON (ed.), *The Historian at Work* (1980): J. W. BURROW. *A Liberal Descent : Victorian Historians and the English Past* (1981).

EI:GENE N. ANDERSON. 'Meinecke's *Ideengeschichte* and the Crisis in Historical Thinking", in *Medieval and Historiogrpahical Essavs in Honor of James Westfall Thompson* (1938): MARC BLOCH. *Apologie poar A'histoire; ou, Metier d'historien* (1949; Eng. trans., *The Historian's Craft.* 1953); *Architects and Craftsmen in history: Festschrift fur abbott PaysonUsher* (1956), biogrpahis of leading historians; JACK H. HEXTER. *Reappraisals in History* (1961): RICHARD PARES. *The Historian's Business. and Other Essays* (1961), particularly valuable for the works of ARNOLD TOYNBEE: FRIEDRICH MEINECKE, *Die Idee der Staatsrdson in der neueren Geschichte* (1957: Eng. trans;, *Machiavellism: The Doctrine of Raison d Etat and Its Place in Modern History,* (1957): DONALD C. WATT (ed.), *Contemporary history in Europe* (1968); LAWRENCE STONE. *The Past and the Present* (1981).

On Russian historiogrpahy there is no satisfactory general survery in English. The following can be useful for particular periods or historians: ANATOLE G. AMZOUR. *Modern Russian Historiogrpahy;* 2nd ed. (1958): ALEXANDER S. VUCINICH. *Science in Russian Culture: A History to 1860* (1963): and RICHARD IPPES (trans). *Karamzin's Memoir on Ancient and Modern Russia* (1966); JOHN S. CURTISs (ed.). *Essays in Russian and Soviet History, in Honor ofGerold Tanquary Robinson* (1962), especially on Semevsky; ALAN D. FERGUSON and ALFRED LEVIN (eds.). *Essays in Russian History: A Collection Dedicated to George Vernadsky* (1964): JOHN KEEP and LILIANA BRISBY (eds.), *Contemporary History in the Soviet Mirror* (1964).

FRANZ ROSENTHAL. *A History of Muslim Historiogrpahy,* 2nd rev. ed. (1968).

WILLIAM G. Good general introduction to the aims and methods of archaeology are LEONARD WOOLLEY, *Digging Up the Past*

(1930): SIR MORTIMER WHEELER., *Archaeology from the Earth* (1954); and GRAHAME CLARK. *Arcacology and Society*, 3rd rev. ed. (1957). For the history of archaeology and its relation to the development of anthropology, sec C. W. CERAM. *Gotter, Graber und Gelehrte* (1949 : Eng. trans., *Gods, Graves and Scholars. 1951);* G. BIBBY. *The Testimony of the Spade* (1956); and GLYN DaNIEL. *A Hundred and Fifty Years of Archaeology* (1974). Anthologies of archaeological writings that relate both to the history of the subject and its present methods are many. The following are recommended : R. F. HEIZER. *The Archaeologist at Work* (1959), and Man's *Discovery of his Past.* 2nd ed. (1963). For the devlopment of American archaeology, see G. WILLEY and G. SABlOFF. *The History of American Archaeology* (1973). Special aspects of the development of archaeoology are dealt with in D. BROTHWELL and E. HIGGS. *Since in Archaeology,* 2nd ed. (1969): GEOREG F. BASS. *Archaeology Cnder Water* (1967): W. F. LIBBY, *Radiocarbon Dating,* 2nd ed. (1955): KENNETH HUDSON. *A social History of archacology* (1981): MYRA SHACKLEY. *Environmental Archaeology* (1981); and M. G> L. BAILLIE, *Tree-Ring Dating in Archaeology* (1982).

Bibliography : THEODORE BESTERMAN. *The Beginning of Systematic Bibliogrpahy;* 2nd ed. rev. (1936); A. ESDAILE. *A Student's Manual of Bibliogrpahy,* 3rd rev. ed. (1954); L. N. MALCLES. *Les Sources du travil bibliogrpahique.* 3 vol. (1950-58); GEORG SCHNEIDER. *Handbuch der Bibliogrpahie.* 4th ed. (1930), reprinted 1969); J. H. SHERA and M. E. EGAN (eds.). *Bibliogrpahic Organization* (1951); RONALD STAVELEY. I. C. MCILwaINE, and JOHN H.ST. MCILWAINE. *Introduction to Subject Study* (1967); R. STOKES. *The Function of Bibliogrpahy* (1969); CURT F. BUHLER *et al., Standatds of Bibliogrpahical Description* (1949); J. D. COWLEY. *Bibliogrpahical description and Cataloguing* (1939); R. B. MCKERROW. *An Introduction to Bibliogrpahy for Literary Students* (1927); F. T. BOWERS. *Bibliogrpahy and Textual criticism* (1964) and *Principles ofBibliogrpahical Description* (1949); O. M. BRACK. JR. and W. BARNES (eds.). *Bibliogrpahy and Textual Criticism: English and American Literature. 1700 to the Present* (1969); ROBERT B. HARMON, *Elements of Bibliogrpahy* (1981).

Chronology: JAMES C. MACDONALD. *Chronologies and Calendars* (1897): ALFRED E. STAMP, *Methods of Chronology* (1933); R. L. POOLE. *Studies in chronology and History,* collected and ed. by A. L. POOLE (1934, reprinted 1969).

On the astronomical basis of Chinese calendrical systems, see JOSEPH NEEDHAM. *Science and Civilisation in China.* vol. 3 pp. 390-408 (1959). A standard reference for conversion between Chinese and Western calendars is MATHIAS TCHANG. *Synchronismes chinois* (1905).

ROBERT SEWELL and S. B. DIKSHITA, *The Indian Calendar* (1896), describes the various systems of calendars in India, with tables of concordance and a useful index: ROBERT SEWELL, *The Siddhantas and the Indian Calendar* (1924), a study of the Hindu astronomical system as a basis for the traditional calendar: JEAN FILLOZAT. "Notions de chronologie," in LOUTS RENOU and JEAN FILLIOZAT. *Inde classique,* vol. 2 (1953), a general summary and list of different eras used in India.

RICHARD A. PARKER, *The Calendars of Ancient Egypt* (1950), a basic work providing valid solutions to most of the problems of Egyptian chronology; "Lunar Dates of Thutmose III and Ramesses II." *J. Egyptian Archaeol.,* 34:57-74 (1948), and "Comparative Chronology at the Time of Dynasty XIX," *J. Near Estern Stud.* 19:15-22 (1960), two articles that deal with the date for the accession of Rameses II (1290 or 1304 BC); ERIK HORNUNG. *Cntersuchungen zur Chronologie und Geschichte des Neuen Retches* (1964), the most up-to-date synthesis of the chronological problems of the New Kingdom: L. E. S. EDWARDS, "Absolute Dating from Egyptian Records and Comparision with Carbon-14 Dting." *Phil, Trans. R. Soc.* Series A. 269:11-18 (1970), includes a complete list of all radiocarbon dates taken from Egyptian samples.

The most complete general work on the chronology of Western Asia, including Mesopotamia, is P. E. VAN DER MEER. *The Chronology of Ancient Western Asia and Egypt.* 2nd rev. ed. (1955): however, is should be used with caution. For the general chronology of ancient Western Asia, with special reference to Mesopotamia, see M. B. ROWTON in *The Cambridge Ancient History,* 3rd ed., vol. 1. pp. 193-237 (1970), and the extensive literature quoted there (up to 1959). For a discussion of the gap in the 23nd millennium BC. see A. GOETZE, "the Kassites and Near Eastern Chronology". *J. Cuneiform Stud.,* 18M97-101 (1964); and B. L. VANDER WAERDEN, *Die Anfange der Astronomie,* pp. 28-49 (1966). For the chronology of the late 2nd millennium BC and the chronological gap in the 1st meillennium BC, see J. A. BRINKMAN. *A Political History of Post-Kassite Babylonia. 1158-722 BC.,* pp. 37-85 (1968).

B. RATNER. *Seder Olam Rabba: Die grosse Weitchronktk* (1897), the authoritative edition, carefully annotated and with a detailed introduction, of the oldest rabbintc chronology extending from the earliest records to the first century of the current era; E. MAHLER. *Handbuch der fudischen Chronologie* (1916), the ony comprehensive work on Jewish chronology, covering all aspects and summarizing most previous works on the subject; S. ZEITLIN. *Megillat Taanit As a Source for Jewish Chronology and History in the Hellenistic and Roman Periods* (19220, removes all discrepancy in I and II Maccabees'and Josephus' chronological data in the Hasmonean phase of Jewish history, thus reinvesting their statements with historical significance and authority.

ALAN E. SAMUEL. *Greek and Roman Chronology; Calendars and Years in Classical Antiquity* (1972), a fundamental work; HENRY FYNES CLINTON. *Fast Hellenict.* 3 vol. (1834), still useful in providing the sources for the framework of Greek chronology; W. KUBITSCHEK. *Grundriss der antiken Zeitrechnung* (1928), the standard handbook but unreliable; A. E. SAMUEL, *Ptolematic Chronology* (1962); E. J. BICKERAMN. *Chronology of the Ancient World* (1968), a summary survey to be used judictously; W. DEN BOER. *Laconian Studies.* pt. 1, "The Struggle for the Chronological Pattern" (1954), on ancient attempts to systematize archaic chronology: A. G. WOODHEAD. *The Greeks in theWest.* pp. 69-72 (1962), on dates in the archaic period.

E. J. BICKERMAN. *Chronology of the Ancient World* (1968), an excellent short manual, unfortunately marred by a number of factual errors: AGNES KIRSOPP MICHELS. *The Calendar of theRoman Republic* (1967), contains much valuable information on chronology as well as the calendar-probably the best book ever written on the Roman calendar: F. K. GINZEL, *Handbuch der mathematischen und technischen Chronologie das Zeitrech nungswesen der Volker.* 3 vol. (1906-14), the standard work of reference on its subject.

F. K. GINZEL. *Handbuch der mathematischen und technischen Chronologie das Zeitrechnungswesen der Volker,* 3 vol. (1906-14), still the fundamental work; JACK FINEGAN, *Handbook ofBible Chronology* (1964), the best for its subject: E. J. BICKERMAN. *Chronology of the Ancient World* (1968), very thorough and complete.

AL-BIRUNI. *The Chronology of Ancient Nations.* Eng. trans. by C. EDWARD SACHAU (1879), useful source material on the

Muslim knowledge of chronology down to the 10th century AD: see especially pp. 16-82. For actual tables of Muslim chronological information and comments, the following may be consulted; E. LACOINE. *Tables de concordance des dates des calendriers* ...(1991); C. L. IDELER. *Handbuch der mathematischen und technischen chronologie.* 2 vol. (1825-26): S. LANE-POOLE. *The Mohammedan Dynasties* (1894); and C. E. BOSWORTH. *The Mohammedan Dynasties* (1967). See also articles on calendar, chronology, and "Hidijra" in the *Encyclopaedia of Islam.* An extensive collection of conversion tables is given in FRANK PARISE (ed.). *The Book of Calendars* (1982).

S. G. MORLEY. "An Introduction to the study of the Maya Hieroglyphs," *Bull. U. S. Bur, Am. Ethnol.* no. 57 (1915. reprinted 1968), a clear exposition of Maya chronology; J. ERIC s. THOMPSON. *Maya Chronology: The Correlation Question* (1935) and *Maya Hieroglyphic Writing: Introduction* (1950, reprinted 1971): H. H. SPINDEN. *The Reduction of Maya Dates* (1924), a presentation of earlier correlation; L. SATTERTHWAITE and E. K. RALPH. "New Radiocarbon Dates and the Maya Correlation Problem." *Am. Antiq.* 26M165-184 (1960).

Diplomatics: HARRY BRESSLAU. *Handbuch dr Urkundenlehre far Deutschland und Italien*, 2nd ed., vol. 1 (1912), vol, 2 pt. 1 (1914), vol. 2. pt. 2 ed. by H. W. KLEWITZ (1931, all reprinted 1958, with separate index), although somewhat out of date, still the best handbook by far for Germany and Italy; OSWALD REDLICH. *Die Privaturkunden des Mittelalters* (1911, reprinted 1967), an excellent work on the private documents of the Middle Ages; LED SANTIFALLER, *Beitrdge zur Geschichte der Beschreibstoffe im Mittelalter.* pt. 1 (1953), the ost up-to-date account of the history of writing materials during the Middle Ages; FRANZ DOLGER and JOHANNES KaRAYANNOPULOS, *Byzantinische Urkundenlehre die Kaiserurkunden* (1968), the only study of the documents of the Byzantine emperors; C. R. CHENEY, *The Study of the Medieval Papal Chancery* (1966), an excellent general survey of modern research; R. L. POOLE. *Lectures on the History of the Papal Chancery down to the Time of Innocent III* (1915), the best book in English on this subject, though now out of date: PETER HERDE, *Beitrdge zum papstlichen Kanzlei und Urkundenwesen im 13. Jahrhundert,* 2nd ed. (1967): and *Audientia Litterarum contradictarum.* 2 vol. (1970), on papal letters of justice; WILHELM ERBEN, *Die Kaiser- und Konigsurkunden des*

Mittelalters in Deutschland. Frankreich und Italien (1907, reprinted 1967), an excellent supplement of Bresslau on the imperial and royal documents of the Middle Ages in Germany. France, and Italy: GEORGES TESSIER. *Diplomatique royale francaise* (1962), the best and most up-to-date handbook on the royal French diplomatic: ALAIN DE BOUARD, *Manuel de diplomatique francaise et ponuftcale* (1929), a handbook on French and papal diplomatic: F. M. STENTON. *The Latin Charters of the Anglo-Saxon Period* (1955), a good brief survey on research since the 18th entury; P. H. SAWYER. *Anglo-Saxon Charters* (1968), the most up-to-date annotated list and bibliogrpahy; R. C. VAN CAENEGEM. *Royal Writs in England from the Conquest to Glanvill* (1959), the best book on writes: V. H. GALBRAITH. *An Introduction to the Use of the Public Records* (1934) and *Studies in the Public Records* (1948), two works especially useful for the later periods:C. R. CHENEY. *The Records of Medieval England* (1956) and *English Bishops Chanceries 1100-1250* (1950); T. F. TOUT. *Chapters in the Administrarive History of Medieval England*, 6. vol. (1920-33), the basic work on the subject, including the chancery: HARRY BRESSLAU, Ïnternational Beziehungen im Urkunden wesen des Mittelalters."*Archiv fur Urkundenforschung*, 6:19-76 (1918), the only survey on international relations in the documentary system of the Middle Ages; HORST ENZENSBERGER, *Bettrdge zum Kanzlert und Urkundenwesen der normannischen Herrscher Unteritaliens und Siziliens* (1971), the most up-to-date account of the chancery and documents of the Norman rulers in southern Italy and Sicily; H. O. MEISNER, *Archivalienkunde vom 16. Jahrhundert bis 1918* (1969), the best study of records from the 16th century through 1918 for central Europe, especially Germany: CHARLES CARTER. *The Western European Powers. 1500-1700* (1971), a very useful survey on archives and their records. All the cited works have comprehensive bibliographies, with some of them also containing bibliogrpahies of editions and facsimiles of documents, H. THOMAS HICKERSON. *Archives and Manuscripts; An Introduction to Automated Access* (1981), discusses specific concern of the contemporary archives business.

Epigrpahy: J.B. PRITCHARD (ed.). *Ancient Near Eastern Texts Relating to the Old Testament*, 3rd ed. (1969), gives translations of inscriptional material, especially from Egypt. Mesopotamia, Palestine, and Asia Minor. J. FRIEDRICH, *Entzifferung verschoilener Schriften und Sprachen* (1954: Eng. trans. *Extinct Languages,* 1957), deals especially with the decipherment of inscriptions, while his *Kleinasiatische Sprachdenkmaler* (19320, transiterates a veriety of epichoric texts from Asia Minor. R. G. KENT. *Old Persian.* 2nd ed. rev. (1953), is a comprehensive work including grammar. texts ,and lexiconW. HINZ. *Altiranische Funde und Forschungen* (1969), includes a number of important recent inscriptional finds from ancient Iran. J. BLOCH. *Les Inscriptions d'Asoka* (1950), gives texts and translations of all *Inscriptions* (1962), provides a transliterated selection of later Indic epigraphy as well. L. DEROY, *Initiation a l'epigraphie mycenienne* (1962), provides a comprehensive survey of the study of Mycenaean tablets, E. s. ROAERTS. *An Introduction to Greek Epigraphy,* 2 vol. (1887-1908), remains the classic compendium of its kind; while more recent, shorter surveys of its subject are found in G. KIAFEENGACH, *Griechische Epigraphik* (1957); and A. G. WOODHEAD. *The Study of Greek Inscriptions* (1959). A more elaborate recent treatment is that of M. GUARDUCI, *Epigrafta greaca,* 2 vol. (1967069). The Cretan laws have been sumptuously edited and cominented in R. F. WIUETTS. "The Law Code of Gortyn", *Kadmos,* suppi, 1 (1967). The old standard works on Latin inscriptions, J. E. SANDYS, *Latin Epigraphy,* 2nd ed. rev. (1927); and R. L. V. CAGNAT. *Cours depigraphie latine,* 3rd ed. rev. (1927); and R. L. V. CAGNAT.*Cours depigraphie latine,* 3rd ed. (1998), are updated only in such summary surveys as R. BLOCH. *Lepigraphie Latine,* 3rd ed. (1964). The elaborate edition of the principal Umbrian inscription by J.W. POULTNEY, *The Bronze Tables of Iguvium* (1959), gives text, translation, grammar, extensive commentary, and facsimiles of the tables themselves, R. W. V. ELLIOTT, *Runes: An Introduction* (1959), is especially thorough on the side of British runes; while W. KRAUSE, *Runen* (1970), is a compact but comprehensive survey of the entire field of runology.

Genealogy: For an outline of the sources and methods of procedure, see L. G. PINE, *Heraldry and Genealogy,* 4th ed. (1974). Also useful is A. J. WILLIS, *Genealogy for Beginners,* 3rd ed. (1976), J. UNETT, *Making a* Pedigree, *2nd ed. (1961), contains information on medieval records. G. HAMILTON EDWARDS,* In Search of Ancestry (1966), is a larger work with more detail, especially on naval and military sources. On American genealogy, see G. H. DOANE and J. B. BELL, *Searching for Your Ancestors: The How and Why of Genealogy,* 5th ed. (1980); and J. S. SWEET, *Genealogy and Local History: An Archival and Bibliogrpahical Guide*, 2nd rev. ed. (1959). See also L.G. PINE, *American Origins* (1960, reprinted 1980), on sources of genealogical research in Europe, and *The Genealogist's Encyclopedia* (1969). A good starting point in genealogical quests is P. WILLIAM FILBY, *American and British Genealogy and Heraldry : A Selected List of Books*, 3rd ed. (1983).

Paleogrpahy: The most compreshensive work, certainly in English, is still e. MAUNDE THOMPSON, *An Introduction of Greek and Latin Palaeogrpahy* (1912). Also valuable, and in print, is his shorter version. *Handbook of Greek and Latin Pataeogrpahy* (1893, reprinted 1966). For Greek paleogrpahy, see B. A. VAN GRONINGEN, *Short Manual of Greek Palaeogrpahy*, 3rd rev. ed. (1963); and C. H. ROBERTS, *Greek Literary Hands, 350 B.C.- A.D. 400* (1956). The article "Handwriting" in C. G. CRUMP and E. F. JACOB (eds.), *The Legacy of the Middle Ages* (1926), is an important account of Latin book hands. Essential for the study of abbreviations in medieval Europe is ADRIANO CAPPELLI, *Lexicon abbreviaturarum: dizionario di abbreviature latine ed italiane*, 6th ed. (19610. a standard textbook for medieval English cursive hands is CHARLES HOHNSON and HILARY HENKINSON. *English court Hand A. D. 1066 to 1500* (1915), continued in Jenkinson's *Later Court Hands in England from the Fifteenth to the Severiteenth Century* (1927), L. C. HECTOR. *The Handwriting of English Documents*, 2nd ed. (1966), contains a valuable introduction to the paleogrpahy of English administrative manuscripts. Very many classical, biblical, and liturgical texts have now been published in facsimile, often with colour plates. Large collection in facsimile comprise E. A. LOWE, *Codices Latini antiqutores.* 12 vol. (1934-71); CHARLES SAMARAN and ROBERT MARICHAL, *Catalogue des manuscrits en ecriture latine, portant des indications de date* (1959-); BERTRAM COLGRAVE (ed.), *Early English Manuscripts in Facsimile* (1951-); and the "Oxford Palaeogrpahical Handbooks", a series designed to deal with various aspects of the subject, such as C. H. ROBETS (see above); C. E. WRIGHT, *English Vernacular Hands from the Twelfth to the Fifteenth Centuries* (1960); M.B. PARKES. *English Cursive Book Hands, 1250-1500* (1969); and T. A. M. BISHOP, *English Caroline Minuscule* (1971). See also MARC DROGIN, *Medieval Calligrpahy, Its History and Technique* (1980); and DONALD JACKSON. *The Story of Writing* (1981).

Sigillogrpahy: The best general account is SIR HILARY JENKINSOn.

Guide to Seal in the Public Record Office (1954). JOSEPH H. ROMAN, *Manuel de sigillogrpahie francaise* (1912), is a longer study mainly on French seals.The basic catalog for European seals and impressions is WALTER DE GRAY BIRCH. *Catalogue of Seals in the Department of Manuscripts in the British Museum,* 6 vol. (1887-1900). Seal matrices are discussed by ALEC B. TONNOCHY in the *Catalogue of British Seal Dies in the British Museum* (1952). ALFRED B. WYON, *The Great Seals of England from the Earliest period to the Present Time* (1887), provides a systematic and well-illustrated account of English Great Seals. A full discussion of Classical seal use, with bibliogrpahy and occasional reference to Near Eastern sources, is given in the article "Signum", by WENGER in *Pauly-Wissowa Real_Encyclopadie.*vol 2, col. 2361-1248 (1923); and details of use in of use in the Aegean and Greece are conveniently given in JOHN BOARDMAN. *Greek Gems and Finger Rings* (1970). No adequate study exists of the uses of seals in ancient western Asia See at present, however. ELENa CASSIN, "Le sceau; un fait de ctvilisation dans la Mesopotamie ancienne", *Annales,* pp. 742-751 (1960); and M. I. ROstOVTSEFF, "Seleucid Babylonia : Bullae and Seals of Clay with Greek Inscriptions", *Yale Classical Studies* 3:1-114 (1932). A very full bibliography of ancient Eastern seal publications from which information on use may be gleaned is given by HANS H. VON DER OsteN in *Ancient Oriantal Seals in the Collection of Mr. Edward T. Newell.* pp. 168-190 (1934); and in *Altorientalische Siegeisteine der Sammlung Hans Silvius von Aulock,* pp. 156-219 (1957), but to more recent convenient bibliogrpahy exists; systematic study of use must depend mainly on the examination of sealed texts. For Egypt, P. E. NEWBERRY, *Scarab-Shaped Seals* (1907), provides a brief account, now much in need of revision. Books on Chinese and Japanese seals deal mainly with those of painters, calligraphers, and collectors, ROBERT H. VAN GULIK, *Chinese Pictorial Art As Viewed by the Conoisseur* (1958), has the most illuminating discussion of the artist's use of seals. See also VICTORIA CONTAG and WANG CHI_CHIEN, *Seals of Chinese Painters and Collectors of the Ming and Ch'ing Periods,* rev. ed. (1966); and CH'EN CHIH-MAL. *Chinese Calligraphers and Their Art* (1966).

Textual criticism: For oral transmission the fundamental work is H. M. and N. K. CHADWICK. *The Growth of Literature,* 3 vol. (1932-40, reprinted 1969). Classical, biblical, and medieval texts are all covered (but somewhat unevenly) by H. HUNGER *et al., Geschichte der Textuberlieferung der antiken und mittelalterlichen Literature,* 2 vol. (1961-64). For classical texts in general the best introduction is L. D. REYNOLDS and N. G. WILSON, *Scribes and Scholars* (1968): more specialized are A. C. CLARK. *The Descent of Manuscripts* (1918); and A. DAIN, *Les manuscrits,* 2nd rev. ed. (1964). For special areas, see B. A. VAN GRONINGEN, *Traite d'historie et de critique des textes grecs* (1963); R. D. DAWE. *The Collation and Investigation of Manuscripts of Aeschylus* (1964); L. HAVET. *Manuel de critique verbale appliquee aux textes latins* (1911), an exhaustive catalogue raisonne of scribal error; E. G. TURNER, *Greek Papyri: An Introduction* (1968), important for the history of Greek texts in antiquity. For biblical texts, in addition to Hunger *(op. cu.),* the standard work on the New Testament is B. M. METZGER. *The Text of the New Testament,* 2nd ed. (1968). For patristic texts an excellent case study raising important general issues is M. BEVENOT, *The Tradition of Manuscrpts; A Study in the Transmission of St. Cyprion's Treatises* (1961). For medieval texts a good exposition of typical problems may be found in D. A.S. AVALLE, "Die Liederhandschriften und die Textkritik." in Hunger (*op. cit.),* 2M273-290; see also J. A. ASHER, "Truth and Fiction: The Text of Medieval Manuscripts", *Aumla,* 25:6-16 (1966). For printed books the standard work is F. BOWERS, *Bibliogrpahy and Textual Criticism* (1964); while a useful collection of essays may be found in O.M. BRACK and W. BARNES (eds), *Bibliogrpahy and Textual Criticism; English and Amertcan Literature. 1700 to the Present* (1969).

For the history of the stemmatic method and the contribution of Lachmann, s. TIMPANARO, *La genestdel metodo del Lachmann* (1963), is definitive. For its application, P. MAAS, *Textual Criticism* (Eng. trans. 1958), an austere theoretical exposition; and G. PASQUALI, *Storia della tradizione e critical del testo,* 2nd ed. (1952), brilliant but discursive, are complementary and fundamental. The reaction to the stemmatic method may be studied in H. QUENTIN. *Memotre sur L'etablissement du texte de la Vulgate* (1922), *Essats de critique textuuelle-ecdotique* (1926); H. BURKE SEVERS, "Quentin';s Theory of Textual Criticism", *English Inst. Annual 1941,* pp. 65-93 (1942); J. BEDIER, "La tradition manuscrite du Lai de L'Ombre: Reflexions sur I'art d'editer les anciens textes", *Romania,* 54:161-96, 321-56 (1928). A. CASTELLANI, *Bedier avail-il raision ?* (1957); W. W. GREG,

The Calculus of Variants (1927); A. A. HILL, "Some Postulates for Distributional Study of Texts, "*Stud, in Biblphy,* 2M63-95 (1950). For further discussion of these developments, see W. P. SHEPARD, "Recent Theories of Textual Criticism", *Mod, philol.,* 28:129-141 (1930); J. ANDRIEU, "Principes et recherches en critique textuelle", in *Memorial des etudes latines ...J. Marouzeau,* pp. 458-74 (1943): E. B. HAM. "Textual Criticism and Common Sense", *Romance Philol..,.* 12:198-215 (1959). For mechanized techniques, see V. A. DEARING, *A Manual of Textual Analysis* (1959); J. FROGER, *La critique des textes et son automatisation* (1968). For the taxonomic approach, see J. G. ÇRIFFITH. "A Taxonomic Study of the Manuscript Tradition of Juvenal", *Mus, Helv.* 25:101-138 (1968); "Numerical Taxonomy and Some Primary Manuscripts of the Gospels", *J. Theol, Stud.,* 20:390-406 (1969).

For classical texts on textual criticism the standard works are still; O. STAHLIN, *Editionstechnik,* 2nd ed. (1914); and A. deLATTE and A. SEVERYNs, *Emploi des signes critiques* (1938).For medieval texts, see A. DONDALNE, "Abbreviations Latines et signes raccommandes pour l'apparat critique des editions des textes medievaux". *Bul, de la soc, int. pour l'etude de la philosophie med..,* 2:142-149 (1960); and for papyri, see Turner *(op. cit.);* and H. C. YOUTIE. *The Textual Criticism of Documentary Papyrt: Prolegomena* (1958).

Many of the works cited above include discussion of general principles of textual criticism. In addition the following workds may be mentioned: H. KANTOROWIcz, *Einfuhrung in die Text kritik* (1921), sound emphasis on the roles of probability and common sense; A. E. HOUSMAN, "The Application of Thought to Textual Criticism", *Proc. Class, Assoc,* 18:67-84 (1922), a brilliant polemic against hard-and-fast "rules" of criticism; L. BIELER, "The Grammarian's Craft", *Folia,*10:3-42 (1956), a useful summary discussion of modern developments; and A. H. MCDONALD. "Textual Criticism", in *Oxford Classical Dictionary,* 2nd ed. (1970), a sound and up-to-date exposition for classical students, JEROME J. MCGANN, *A Critique of Modern Textual Criticism* (1983), is a study of the role of non-literary contexts in textual criticism.

SOURCE

The New Encyclopaedia Britannica, Vol. 20 (15ht edition), (chicago, Ency.Brit Inc, 1988 A.D.), Page 621-685

CHAPTER 2

The Nature of History

Adapted from Henry Steele Commager : The Study of History

The first thing to be said about History is that the word itself NAS two quite distinct MFANINGS. It means the past and all that happened in the past. It means, too, the record of the past-all that men have said and written of the past, or, in the succinct words of Jacob Burckhardt, "what one age finds worthy of note in another."

Sometimes it is said that these two things are in fact much the same : that the past exists only in our record of it, or our awareness of it, and that without such a record, there would be no meaningful past at all. Thus the great Italian philosopher-historian, Benedetto Croce, asserted that all history was contemporary history. There is, as we shall see, a germ of truth here. But this view is not so much wrong as confused. The past is not dependent on us for its existence, butexists in its own right. It happened even though historians failed to record it, just as the tree fell in the forest even though no one was there to hear the sound of its fall. History does not suddenly spring to life when some historian gets around to discovering it or recording it. The historian who clears up some puzzle about the past, or who discovers new material and fills income gap in our knowledge of the past, does not infect create the past, though he may recreate it. What happened, happened independently of him, and the consequences of whatever happened ensued independently of him. James Madison's Notes on the Federal convention, for example, was not published until 1836; only then were historians able to penetrate into the very chamber of the Convention, to know, andtoexplain, what had occurred. Yet what had happened at the Convention- what delegates had said, for example- had in fact happened, and had made history. The consequences of the debates in the Convention did not wait upon the publication of Madison's Notes.

But if the debates in the Federal Convention were history, so was Madison's Notes. Just as what happened at the Convention had consequences, so the publication of the Notes fifty years later had consequences. It clothed with flesh and blood the skeleton of formal resolutions and conclusions with which historians had previously CONSOLED themselves, and STARTED but a more realistic and a more nationalistic interpretation of the American Constitution.

What this suggests is that the historian, by discovering some lost ingredients in the past, or by illuminating dark areas of the past, can in a real way re-make the past. History is there-there in the fact that it did occur; there, too, in the consciousor the unconscious memories of men. The memory can be jogged, the consciousness can be stimulated, the image of the past can be changed. When the historian does these things he makes history.

History, then, is the past, History is also the memory of the past. Needless to say it is with the second of these meanings that we are concerned.

Let us consider history as memory.

For a people to be without history, or to be ignorant of its history, is as for a man to be without memory- condemned forever to make the same discoveries that have been made in the past, invent the same techniques, wrestle with the same problems, commit the some errors; and condemned, too, to for feitthe rich pleasures of recollection. Indeed, just as it is difficult to imagine history without civilization, so it is difficult to imagine civilization without history. As Frederic Harrison has written :

Suppose that all knowledge of the gradual steps of

civilization, of the slow process of perfecting the arts of life and the natural sciences, were blotted out; suppose all memory of the efforts and struggles of earlier generations and of the deeds of great men, were gone; all the land-marks of history; all that has distinguished each country, race, or city in past times from others; all notion of what man had done or could do; of his many failures, of his successes, of his hopes; suppose for a moment all the books, all the traditions, all the buildings of past ages to vanish off the face of the earth, and with them the institutions of society, all political forms, all principles of politics, all systems of thought, all daily customs, all familiar arts; suppose the most deep-rooted and sacred of all our institutions gone; suppose that the family and home, property, and justice were strange ideas without meaning; that all the customs which surround each of us from birth to death were blotted out; suppose a race of men whose minds, by a paralytic stroke of fate, had suddenly been deadened to every recollection, to whom the whole world was new. Can we imagine a condition of such utter helplessness, confusion, and misery ? (The meaning of History and Other Historical Pieces, New York, 1914, p. 5)

Clearly the concept of history set forth here embraces rather more than most historians would claim; the total record of the past- literature, law, art, architecture, social institutions, religion, philosophy, all indeed that lives in and through the memory of man. We need not embrace this total definition of History in order to agree that man without memory would be bewildered and lost. But memory, as we all know, Disorganized and confused. History is organized memory, and the organization is all important. As organized memory, history takes almost innum-erable forms, serves almost innumerable purposes. Let us consider some of the forms with it assumes and some of the purposes which it serves.

First, and if not most important, then most elementary, history is a story. That was its original character, and that has continued to be its most distinctive character. If history forgets or neglects to tell a story, it will always lose much of its appeal and much of its authority as well. With the Iliad and the odyssey story-telling and history are so completely joined that we do not to this day know whether to classify them as literature or as history; they are of course both. "The Father of History", Herodotus, had a story to tell-the struggle between the Greeks and the Persians- and he told it well. So, too, his great successor Thucydides, who gave us the story of the Peloponnesian War. Livy and Tacitus, the greatest of the Roman historians, were both excellent story-tellers, as are most of the leading modern historians, Voltaire and Gibbon, Carlyle and Macaulay, Prescott and Motley and Parkman. For, as Lord Macaulay wrote, "the art of history is the art of narration, the art of interesting the affections and presenting pictures to the imagination. by skillful selection and disposition without indulging in the license of invention."

Here we come to the second quality of history. History is a story, yes, but it is not a made-up story; history draws on and excites the imagination, but it is not a flight of the imagination. It is a story of what happened in the past, or what the historian is able to recover and reconstruct of what actually happened. In short, history is a record. It collects and organizes such facts as are available and relevant, provides some kind of framework for them, and lay down the guidelines for the presentation. It supplies order, harmony, direction, for what might otherwise be a confused collection of miscellaneous facts.

There are of course, serious limitations on the record, as well as on the ability of history to organize the record; we have to accept this without getting too disturbed about it. First, the record is, and is bound to be, fragmentary and incomplete. That is particularly true of the several thousand years of history before the invention of the printing press, and of the history of many of the peoples who even after the mid-fifteenth century did not know threat of printing the American Indians, for example, or the peoples of Africa, whose history is largely unrecorded. For much of modern history the record appears to be more nearly complete witness the miles of filing cabinets filled with documents from the Second World War. Yet even here, the record is incomplete. How can we know what happened, during the war years, to each of the forty million or fifty million men and women who fought in the war ? How can we know what happened to the hundreds of millions of civilians who were involved in the war, as participants, as victims, or as spectators ? The energies, the intelligence, and the practical and technical resources of historians. No individual historian, not even the largest committee of historians, can read all those miles of documents, all the newspapers, all the personal records of the combatants of all the countries involved in the Second World War.

The record is not only irremediably incomplete, it is also lopsided and biased. How can it be otherwise ? Much of it is wholly by chance . Our knowledge of the past depends pretty much on what happened to be preserved, and what happened to be preserved is only a small part of the total record. Much of the record has been destroyed by fire and sword-from the burning of the Alexandrian Library to the bombings of World War II; much of it has been destroyed by fanaticism, religious or national; much or it has simply been lost : thus of the forty volumes of Polybius' Histories only five survived, or the 142 books of Livy's History of Rome only thirty-five have survived ! There is no logic here, no pattern; what has survived is largely a matter of luck.

Largely but not wholly; for what has survived- or rather what has failed to survive is also to some degree a matter of power. Justice Holmes used to say that Truth was the majority vote of that nation which could defeat all others,. history, too, is in part the verdict of the nation which defeats others. Over the centuries history has been written by the winners, not the losers. It is the Romans who have written the history of the Punic wars, not the Carthaginians; the Spaniards who told the story of the conquests of Mexico and Peru, not the Aztecs and the Incas. One of the less likeable traits of winners, in the past, has been the deliberate destruction of enemy records and the silencing often by death of enemy historians.

The record which has come down to us, then, is not only

fragmentary and selective, it is also biased. To be biased is as human as to err. Everyone knows that bias enters into even the simplest statement of events. No two stories of a family quarrel are ever alike; how should we expect that a dozen accounts of the war of 1851,orof the beginnings often First World War, should be alike ? History is, after all, not something which exists independently of man; it is something that comes to us filtered through the mind and the imagination of men.

More about all this, later, when we consider some of the problems of history. History as a record consists of three states, or processes, usually so skillfully blended that they appear to be a single one. The first is the collection of what are thought to be relevant facts; but remember, what seems relevant to one person may not appear relevant to another. The second is the organization of these facts into some coherent pattern; but remember, no two patterns are ever quite alike. The third is the interpretations of the facts and of the pattern; and certainly no two interpretations are ever quite alike. Now, all of these processes flow into each other. The practiced historian is not ordinarily conscious of these separate steps any more than a skillful baseball player is conscious of the separate steps that go into a decision to strike at a ball. It is impossible to collect the facts in the first place without some theory of relationships among them; after all, what are you looking for ? It is impossible to organize them into a pattern without some theory that dictates the pattern. And it is impossible to interpret them except on the basis of the material that has been selected and the pattern that has been drawn.

Neither collection nor organization is entirely under the control of the individual historian who is, in fact, wholly dependent on others for the material which he uses. No individual scholar can go very far in the collection of his material; mostly it has been done for him, over the years and the centuries, by earlier scholars; by archivists who have preserved manuscripts and records; by devoted librarians who have assembled manuscripts and books, organized them, classified them, and protected them; by government officials who have provided for the preservation of court or legislative or diplomatic records; and by editors who have organized these. Imagine trying to write on the history of modern Parliament without hansard's Debates; imagine trying to write on the American constitutional system without the 375 or so volumes of the Supreme Court Reports, to say noting of the thousands of volumes of lower court decisions; imagine trying to reconstruct the history of the French in Candad without the Jesuit Relations; imagine trying to interpret Thomas Jefferson without the help of nay without total dependence on the devoted editors who have collected his papers and made them available to other scholars.

It is interpretation- the third step in the organization of the record which is most nearly individual and which therefore makes the highest demands upon the historian. Industry will go far towards solving the first problem, that of collecting the materials; common sense and judgment will contribute much to the second, the organization of the materials. But intelligence of a high order is required for the interpretation of the facts. The greatest of historians, certainly in modern times, have been the interpreters; and all the major modern historians have tried to be interpreters that is they tried to extract some meaning out of the raw materials o history, or to impose some philosophy upon it. Thus the grea English historians; Clarendon and Gibbon and Hume Macaulay and Froude and Lecky, Buckle and Freeman Maitland and Lord Acton, and in our own day Namier an Butterfield, and Father David Knowles and Veronic Wedgwood, and Denis Brogan and Winston Churchill. Thu in France, Montesquieu and Voltaire and Michelet and Tain and Tocqueville and Aulard; thus in Germany, Niebuhr an Ranke, and von Sybel and Treitschke and Lamprecht, an Burckhardt, and more recently, Meinecke and Rothfels. Thu in the United States Francis Parkman and John Lothrc Motley, henry Adams and Vernon Parrington, Lawren Gipson, S. E. Morison, and Allan Nevins.

Yet while interpretation depends on the accumulation

facts and their skillful organization, even the most prodigious industry and the most painstaking analysis do not guarantee a profound interpretation. That requires judgment, originality, imagination, and art. And this brings us to the third form, or character, of history as art. As Arthur Schlesinger, Jr. has said :

All the elements of artistic form are as organic in historical as in any other kind of literary composition. There are limits on the historian's capacity for invention, but there need be none on his capacity for insight. Written history, after all, is the application of an aesthetic vision to a welter of facts; and both the weight and the vitality of an historical work depend on the quality of the vision. ("The Historian as Artist.")

This is another way of saying that history is a branch of literature and that it serves some of the purposes and is governed by some of the principles of literature. Certainly most of the historical writing which we call great, and put into the category of the "classics", has literary distinction.

Literary history is not just a matter of fine writing. That can easily be overdone, and often is; the best style is plain and straightforward, as with Lincoln or Churchill in the realm of politics, or Trevelyan and Brogan among English historians, Douglas Freeman and Allan Nevins among American. Listen to an example from a master of literary style who was also a master of historical fact, Francis Parkman, calling to our attention one of the paradoxes of Franco-American history :

The French dominion is a memory of the past; and when we invoke its departed shades, they rise upon us from their graves in strange, romantic guise. Again their ghostly camp-fires seem to burn, and the fitful light is cast around on lord and vassal and black-robed priest, mingled with wild forms of savage warriors, knit in close fellowship on the same stern errand. A boundless vision grows upon us: an untamed continent; vast wastes of forest verdure; mountains silent in primeval sleep; river, lake, and glimmering pool; wilderness oceans mingling with the sky. Such was the domain which France conquered for civilization. Plumed helmets gleamed in the shades of its forests, priestly vestments in its dens and fastnesses of ancient barbarism. Men steeped in antique learning, pale with the close breath of the cloister, here spent the noon and evening of their lives, ruled savage hordes with a mild parental sway, and stood serene before the direst shapes of death. Men of courtly nurture, heirs to the polish of a far-reaching ancestry, here, with their dauntless hardihood put to shame the boldest sons of toil. (Pioneers of France in the New World, preface.)

While it is true that unless history is reasonably accurate and fair it should not be read, it is equally true that unless history is well written it will not be read. "The world at large", writes Allan Nevins, himself a distinguished practitioner of literary history,

will sooner forgive lack of scientific solidity than lack of literary charm. The great preservative in history, as in all else, is style. A book of consummate literary art may abound in passages of bad history, but nevertheless carry generation after generation before it. It is useless to protest that Lord Clarendon was far too biased on the English Civil War; he will be read for centuries by all who savor a close-packed, pithy, elopquent style, full of graphic sketches of men and events. Motley is unscientific in his treatment of Spanish misrule in the Netherlands, but the world will continue to read Motley. If and historian were compelled to take his choice, fame might urge him to select the winged pen, rather than the Aristotelian mind, to choose Apollo against Minerva; but he may choose both. (The Gateway to History, Garden City, N. Y. : Doubleday & Company, Inc., 1962 ed., p. 379.)

Justice Holmes used to say, finely, that "life is painting a picture, not doing a sum." So we may say that writing history is painting a picture, not taking a photograph. It is not enough to give photographic exactness; not even a photograph by Brady carries the impact of a painting by Goya, the "Massacre" for example. It is not enough to compile statistics; if it were, the latest census report would be our best historical volume. It is not enough to pile up mountains of historical and social details; if it were, the raw materials of newspapers would suffice for historical literature. It is not enough to put together strings of episodes and anecdotes, no matter how dramatic; picture magazines which do this dull rather than excite the mind. History must rest on statistics, embrace details, use drama, but it should control all of these ingredients as an artist controls the ingredients of his materials and the elements of his subject-control them, master them, penetrate them with meaning and suffuse them with imagination.

Yet we must keep ever in mind that literary history, or history as literature, is not merely a matter of style- the winged word, the happy phrase, the brilliant epigram, the dramatist's art. The historian does not enroll, automatically, in the literary school when he writes well, nor suffer expulsion from that school when he writes in a flat or wooden style. Literary history is something more than a matter of style; it is something more than a matter of emphasis; it is a matter of philosophy.

The literary historian is primarily interested in recreating the past. He is, in sense, a painter, and who can deny a Rembrandt, a Goya, a Longhi or Canaletto, a Reynolds, a George Catlin a place among historians ? he is, in a sense, a dramatist, and who would deny Shakespeare or Moliere or Holberg the title of historian ? The literary historian employs his talents to conjure up what was once real and is now no more, and to excite the imagination of the beholder to see the past through his eyes. Like the painter, or the dramatist, he seeks to capture, for a moment, a brilliant, a famous, an endearing scene, to recreate a picturesque tableau, to paint a familiar portrait. He is Motley admitting us to the bedside of the dying Philip II of Spain; he is Prescott making us spectators of the bold attack across the causeway on Montezuma's great city; he is Michelet bringing us to our knees as we look on the tragic scene of the burning of the Maid of Orleans; he is Carlyle involving us in the heat of the battle of Rossbach.

All this is a far cry from the more prosaic and realistic purposes of the scientific historian. The gap between the literary and the scientific is not stylistic; it is deeper and more fundamental, a difference in the philosophy of history itself. The scientific historian is not really interested in recreating the past for its own sake, nor at pains to stir the imagination of the reader; indeed he is rather inclined to distrust the picturesque or the dramatic and even the individual. It is reason he wants to excite, not imagination, and as for the past he does not want to recreate it but to explain it. a great "technical" historian- Frederic Maitland, for example, who "turned the dust of archives into gold", or a Hastings Rashdall who made the medieval university as familiar as the contemporary, or Father Knowles, or S. E. Morison, can write with a style that sings and soars. But their primary purpose is not to stir the imagination but to solve problems. Was the "Mirror of Justices", upon which Lord Coke relied, authentic ? How did St. Bernard triumph over the Cluniacs ? why did the students of medieval Bologna and Padua organize into Nations ? Were the Puritans really hostile to music and the arts ? Each of our historians has illuminated these problems with literary grace, but it was the problem that was important, not the grace.

Let us see how two distinguished historians, one "literary," the other "scientific", deal with the same situation. Here is Van Wyck Brooks, of all historians of American literature the most evocative, conjuring up for us the image of Nathaniel Hawthorne confronted by the spectacle of the New England Puritan in Rome :

was Hawthorne right in feeling that "it needs the native air" to give a writer's work reality ? Rome had provided him with a fairy setting for the last of his own romances, the last he was ever to finish, the tale of Hilda, Miriam and Donatello, the dusky Miriam of the shrouded past and the delicate wood-anemone of the Western forest. This dance of Yankee girls and fauns and specters was like a Pompiian fresco or something immobilized on a Grecian urn. A bituminous light suffused it, as of an afternoon in the realm of shades. One caught in the shifting groups the magical, mythological grace of Poussin. One heard Mignon's song rising from the depths in the fitful measure of a wind-harp. Hawthorne had drawn enchantment from the Roman air; and yet, for all the spell of The Marble Faun, it was hardly comparable with The Scarlet Letter or The House of the Seven Gables. The orchidaceous existence of most of the exiles seemed to bear him out in his distrust. One could dream forever in these Roman gardens, under the cypress and ilex, while all one's mental muscles atrophied. Norton, with his acute social conscience, his sense of a mission at home, probed under the surface of Italian life. The repressive political system disturbed him, and he had understood, from his own observation, the sorrows of Petrarch, Dante and Alfieri, who had mourned over their country and its degradation. Norton's critical faculties were alert; he had ridiculed the old romantic guide-books and the cold and pretentious work of the German painters who were dominant in modern Rome. He had cared for the realities of Italian life, as Gereenough and Margaret Fuller had cared before him. The others did not wish to care. It was to escape from the prose of existence that they had left America. If their writing lost all grip and bottom, was not this the reason and the explanation ? (The Flowering of New England, New York : E. P. Dutton and Co., 1936, p. 477.)

Here is what Francis Matthiessen has to say in his brilliantly written interpretation of the American Renaissance:

The danger of Brooks' impressionism is even more marked in the half paragraph which ...is the only space he has left for the Marble Faun. When he says that Rome had provided Hawthorne with "a fairy setting", and speaks of "the dusky Miriam of the shrouded past, the delicate wood-anemone of the Western forest,' the flower that he envisages has nothing to do with Hawthorne's maturely bitter fruti ...As a result of letting his attention be deflected from the work itself, he has made one of our few major artists seem less male and robust, much less concerned with important issues, than he was. Of all Hawthorne's heroines, Miriam leaves a impression least like the fragility Brooks describes ... Her quick response to Kenyon's statue of Cleopatra (which is Hawthorne's response to Story's) is owing to her feeling within herself the operation of qualities equally fierce and turbulent ...She is more deeply involved in a background of ambiguous guilt than any other of Hawthorne's characters; and his method of conveying this should be observed as a final aspect of his tragic technique, since it leads directly into the practice of James and Eliot. (American Renaissance, New York : Oxford University Press, 1941, P. 352.)

The differences here go to the very heart of the problem of the nature of history. Why does the literary historian want to salvage, to resurrect, to recreate, the past ? It is because he is interested in the past for its own sake, interested in the drama, the spectacle, the pageant, interested in the actors and actresses. His is the view expounded by george Macaulay Trevelyan : "It is not man's evolution but his attainment that is the greatest lesson of the past and the highest theme of history."

The scientific historian is not interested in history for its own sake. He studies it because it is part of the evolutionary process, and it is that process which concerns him. He behaves, as Herbert Butterfield observes, "as though only those things are worthy of attention which gain importance from the fact that they led to something else." Like a good scientist, the technical historian wants to solve problems.

If the scientific historian has done much to illuminate the processes of history, it is the literary historian who has done most to expand its boundaries. For if we are to conjure up the past, not only its drama and its heroisms but its everyday simplicities, we cannot ignore the commonplace. To be sure, literary historians do yield to the seduction of the dramatic-witness a Prescott or a Motley, or, in our own time, a Guedalla or a Rowse. But Carlyle- who was himself irresistibly tempted by the dranmatic warned against this a century ago : "Mournful it is to behold what the business called 'History' in these so enlightened and illuminated times, still continues to be, can you gather from it ...any dimmest shadow of an answer to that great question: how men lived and had their being ?, were it but economically, as what wages they got and that they bought with them ?" Carlyle did try to tell this, and so did his contemporary, John R. Green; somewhat later, so did the Dane Troels-Lund and the German Karl Lamprecht and the Frenchman Eli halevy, and so did the American John Bach McMaster, who wrote clumsily enough. But we conclude as we began: "literary" history is not a matter of fine writing; it is a matter of the center of intellectual and historical gravity.

History is art; history is also philosophy. Lord Bolingbroke put is for all time when, drawing on the ancients, he defined History as "philosophy teaching by examples". So almost all the great historians have thought, from Thucydides to Toynbee. History was philosophy in Thucydides, Polybius, Plutarch, Livy, and Tacitus among the ancients. Most modern historians accepted the Bolingbroke dictum as a matter of course : Montesquieu in his Spirit of the Laws and The Grandeur and Decadence of Rome, Voltaire in the Age of Louis XIV, Gibbon in The Decline and Fall of the Roman Empire, the Abbe raynal in his many-volumed History of the Indies, designed, really, as an "instrument of war" against the Church and the Empire, and David Hume in his History of England. It is only recently that historians have attempted to discard this traditional function of history, and without much success. For philosophy, ousted from the front door, creeps back in through the side door. The public still wants philosophy with its history, and it is not accident that the most popular historians of our time- H. G. Wells and Winston Churchill and Arnold toynbee, Georg Brandes and Oswald Spengler, Benedetto Croce and Andre Malraux, Salvadore de Madariaga and Raymond Aron, all wrote history as philosophy.

Yet few historians have been philosophers in any formal sense. They have relied on history, most of them, to teach simple moral lessons : the dangers of infidelity; the triumph of virtue over vice, or, in more sophisticated times, the futility of religious intolerance, the wickedness of kings, the depravity of man and the necessity of restraints upon his passions, the rise and fall of empires and the causes of these and other lessons equally simple and equally dubious.

No one can seriously question the claim of history to be story, record, literature, and philosophy. What of her claim-or the claim of some of her more infatuated disciples to be a science ? History is invariably embraced in that loose term, "the social sciences," but we do not know what that term really means. Are the social sciences in fact sciences at all, or is the word "science" used here rather in its original sense as "knowledge" ?

It was the Victorians who first asserted that history was a science; that generation, so confident of its ability to create a science of man, embraced within this concept the science of society, economy, politics, law, and history. Thomas Buckle was sure that he had reduced history to a science by bringing it under the dominion of "one glorious principle of universal and undeviating regularity"- the law of Nature; while across the Channel August Comte announced that "History has now been for the first time systematically considered, and has now been for the first time systematically considered, and has been found, like other phenomena, subject to invariable laws." And at the turn of the century two Regius Professors at Cambridge University, Lord Action and J. B. Bury, intimated that if history was not yet a science it would inevitably become one. No modern Regius Professors now speak in such confident tones, yet the habit of thinking and speaking of history as a science is deeply engrained.

Clearly history is not a science in the sense that chemistry or biology are sciences. It cannot submit its data to scientific experiments; it cannot repeat its own experiments; it cannot control its materials. Wanting these, it will be said that of course history is not a science in any useful sense of the word. Yet it is equally clear that history uses or aspires to use the scientific method. That is, it tests all things which can be tested, and holds fast to what it finds to be true, in so far as it is able to make any findings at all. But how does history "test" things ? what are the techniques of testing ? How does it know when it has arrived at "truth" or even when it has achieved agreement of "facts" ? The chemist does not inject his personality, his beliefs and prejudices, into the chemicals which he uses in his experiments; how does the historian rid his materials of such foreign ingredients ? Indeed can the term "scientific method" ever mean the same thing in history that it means in the exact sciences ? Should it perhaps give place to a more realistic term such as "critical method", and should "scientific" history yield to "technical" history ?

For there is this further, and sobering, consideration that the scientific method is valid if at all only in what might be called the formal and somewhat elementary realms of history, never in the really fundamental realms. Thus we can prove scientifically if you will that John Wilkes Booth did in fact shoot President Lincoln in Ford's Theater in Washington, on the night of the fourteenth of April, 1865. So far so good-but how far, and how good ? For beyond that our science does not take us. Why did Booth do it ? Who, or what, was responsible for his action ? What were the consequences of the act ? These, the really interesting questions, cannot be answered scientifically; they can hardly be answered at all.

Disillusioned with the claims of scientific history, some modern historians settled for what we maycall Technical History- a term coined by Professor herbert Butterfield of Cambridge University. Let us not aspire too high, let us not try to formulate laws of history, let us not try to don the mantle of science ! Let us rather take problems, one by one, as a biogogist or a philologist takes problems one by one, the smaller the better, and works them out. If enough historians work tirelessly at enough problems, we may in time obtain a firm foundation upon which future historians can somehow rear the grand fabric of history.

The characteristic, of technical history are by now sufficiently familiar. It distrusts the dramatic and prefers to catch history in a chemical solution, as it were, in a moment of arrested development, and to analyze it and dissect it. It pays little attention to the narrative butturns instead to Problems, though it does not really believe that nay problems can be finally solved. It detests generalizations and is revolted by Laws; it delights in the minute and the specific, and its characteristic from is the monograph. It has little interest in ideas and none at all in individuals, looking upon them as aberrations from some norm to be arrived at by the study of statistics, or distractions from the consideration of impersonal institutions. It is impatient with the notion of history as literature and rejects out of hand the idea of history as philosophy. And it has an irresistible fascination for the academic mind.

In all this, technical history has obvious association with modern development in literature, art, criticism, and philosophy. In the second and third quarters of the twentieth century, literature too turned from its traditional concern with the narrative and the dramatic to the analytical and the descriptive, abandoned interest in plot and in characters and entangled itself instead with the impersonal, the subconscious, and the amorphous. "Let us record the atoms as they fall upon the mind in the order in which they fall", wrote Virginia Woolf.

"Let us trace the pattern, however disconnected and incoherent in appearance, which each sight or incident scores upon the consciousness." Art, too, became increasingly abstract and impersonal, disdaining to tell a story and reluctant to present anything dramatic, heroic, or colorful : historical paintings and portraiture declined with historical narratives and biographies. Criticism addressed itself increasingly to the explanation of texts, while philosophy turned away from the great problems with which it had traditionally been preoccupied to problems so semantics. In the circumstances it was not surprising that the historian, bemused by the intricacies of technical history, should look with suspicion on history in the grand manner-history as narrative, as philosophy, as art- and settle for something that seemed to offer intellectual security.

CHAPTER 3

Judgment in History

To judge or not to judge, that is the historical question. Should the historian sit in judgment over the great dram of the past and the men and women who performed on that vast and crowded stage, exposing evil and celebrating virtue and damning and praising famous men? Or should he observe the historical processes with scientific detachment, and record them as automatically as a tape-recorder, rigorously excluding personal, national, or religious considerations? Is he competent to perform either of these functions- the function of the judge, or the function of the impartial reporter ?

The problem is difficult and perhaps insoluble. It raises hard questions about purpose of history, the duties and responsibilities of the scholar, the nature of historical judgment. It raises questions, too, about the competence of any historian to judge the past, and the sanctions, if any, behind such judgment as are rendered. And it requires us to weigh the dangers implicit in moral neutrality against those inherent in moral arrogance and intellectual parochialism.

Earlier generations of historians, were not seriously troubled by this problem of judgment. The Greek historians, Herodotus and Thucydides, were surprisingly free from the urge to judge, but their successors in the ancient world took for granted that their function was to edify, to instruct, and to judge. Livy invited his readers to ponder the moral lessons taught by the history of Rome-as he presented it-and to observe how Rome rose to greatness through her virtues, and how the decay of these virtues brought ruin. Tacitus thought the highest function of history was to ''rescue merit from oblivion,'' and "to hold out the reprobation of posterity as a warning and a rebuke to all base conduct." Plutarch, who wrote some sixty Moral Essays, compiled his famous parallel Lives not to adorn a take, but to point a moral, and succeeded beyond his farthest imagination.

Medieval historians knew perfectly well the moral standards to which history was obliged to conform, and knew, too, the penalties of non-conformity, for what was history but the working out of cod's will with man? Even the great eighteenth century historians, Gibbon and Hume and Robertson, Rollin and Voltaire and Raynal, accepted Bolingbrook's aphorism that history was "philosophy teaching by exampled," and they assumed that its lessons were moral and that it was the duty of the historian to point them. Only with the rise of "historicism" in the nineteenth century-there were antecedents, to be sure, in such historians as Machiavelli and vico-did the question of the propriety and the validity of moral judgment come to the fore. Ranke, and his successors and disciples in almost every country, abjured moral judgment, or said that they did, minimum of comment, and eighth henry Adams later found so futile: "To satisfy himself whether, by the severest process of stating, with the least possible conswquement, he could fix for a fam9iliar moment a necessary sequence of human movement." (The Education of Henry Adams, p.382.)

There was bound to be a reaction away from this austere principle, especially as so few of its protagonists actually lived up to it. the Victorian, which in Germany saw the triumph of historicism, in politics and in history, as in art and in literature. It is difficult to know whether such historian as frond in England, Michelet in France, Teritschke in Germany of Motely in America considered themselves prmarily sharply between the two roles, "The eternal truths and rights of things," said James Anthony Froude in his Inaugrul Address as Rctor of st. Andrews University," exist independent of our thoughts or wishes, fixed as mathematics, inherent in the nature of man and the world."

To the American, Joohn L. Moley, historian of the heroic struggle of the Dutch against the Spanish rulers, and of the creation of a United Netherlands, this was the story of the struggle of Protestantism against Catholicism, of the principle of liberty against the principle of tyranny. motley did not pronounce moral judgement; Listen to his final verdict on Philip II of Spain:

There have been few men known to history who have been able to accomplish by their own exertions so vast an amount of evil as the king who had just died. If Philip possessed a single virtue it has eluded the conscientious research of the writer of these pages. If there are vices-as possibly there are-from which he was exempt, it is because it is not permitted to human nature to attain perfection even in evil. The only plausible explanation-for palliation there is none-of his infamous career is that the man really believed himself not a king but a God. He was placed so high above his fellow creatures as, in good faith perhaps, to believe himself incapable of doing wrong; so that whether indulging his passions or enforcing throughout the world his religious and political dogmas, he was ever conscious of embodying divine i9nspirations and elemental laws, when providing for the assassination of a monarch, or commanding the massacre of a townful of protestants; when trampling on every oath by which a human being can bind himself then laying desolate with fire and sword during more than a generation the provinces which he had inherited as his private property or in carefully maintaining the flames of civil war in foreign kingdoms which he hoped to acquire; while maintaining over all Christendom a gigantic system of bribery, corruption and espionage...he ever feltn that these base or bloody deeds were not crimes. but the simple will of the godhead of which he was a portion, but the simple will of the godhead of which he was a portion.(United Netherlands, New York, 1868, V, pp.74-75.) And, in case his readers might think that he had stepped out of his province in thus condemning the Spanish monarch, Motley added a word on the responsibility of the historian:

When an humble malefactor is brought before an ordinary court of justice, it is not often, in any age or country, that he escapes the pillory or the gallows because, from his own point of view, his actions, instead of being criminal, have been commendable, and because the multitude and continuity of his offenses prove him to have been sincere. And because anointed monarchs are amenable to no humans tribunal, have to that terrible assize which the people, bursting its chain from time to tome in the course of the ages, sets up for the trial of its oppressors, and which is called Revolution, it is the more important for the great interests of humanity that before the judgment-seat of History a crown should be no protection to its wearer. There is no plea to the jurisdiction of history, if history be true to itself. As for the royal criminal called philip Ii, his life is his arraignment, and these volumes will have been written in vain if a specification is now required. (Ibid., p. 79.)

In a Carlyle or a Motley moral judgment was a from of self-indulgence. But there was more to than this, there was high Duty! The clearest and most persuasive statement of the moral function of the historian came from Lord Action himself. In 1895 Lord Action was appointed Regius professor of History at Cambridge University. In his Inaugural Address he exhorted his listeners, and all student of history,

Never to debase the moral currency or to lower the standard of rectitude, but to try others by the final maxim that governs your own lives, and to suffer no man and no cause to escape the undying penalty which history has the power to inflict on wrong. The plea in extenuation of guilt and mitigation of punishment if perpetual. At every step we are met by arguments which go to excuse, to palliate, to confound right and wrong and reduce the just man to the level of the reprobate.....Opinions alter, manners change, creeds rise and fall, but the moral law is written on the tablets of eternity.

"We have the power," he concluded,"... to learn from

undisguised and genuine records to look with remorse upon the past, and to the future with assured hope of better things; bearing this in mine, that if we lower our standard in history, we cannot u[hold it in Church or State."

We cannot glibly ascribe Action's philosophy to his Catholicism; he was after all, not a very orthodox Catholic. Such diverse contemporary historians as veronica Wedgwood, Isaiah Berlin, and Arnolds Toynbee-None of them Catholic-all come out for the obligation, of the necessity, of moral judgment in history. This miss Wedgwood, who has so much to illuminate the great political and religious issues that stirred England in the seventeenth century, warns us against

the confusion into which historians fall when they make allowances for "the standards of the age." Their intention is to understand and be just to the past, but the result in the long run may be unfair to the present, because this outlook steadily and stealthily fosters the conviction to its surroundings... The aspiration to understand and to forgive is noble and valid in personal relationships between the living but / she concludes/ the application of the principle of... forgiveness to historical personages is a sentimental fallacy. (Truth and Opinion, new York: The Macmillan Company, 1965, pp. 48-49.)

Arnold Toynbee, who has concerned himself more consistently with the universal and the eternal than any other modern historian, has remained throughout his distinguished career a Christian moralist, ready to judge the quick and the dead; his assertion that the expulsion of the Arabs from Palestine by the Israelis was no less a crime than the Nazi murder of some six million Jews precipitated an international controversy.

All of thus constitutes what might be called a moral argument in favor of moral judgment. The moral laws were universal, and timeless; murder is always murder and betrayal is always betrayal, cruelty and intolerance are always the same, the historian cannot stand above the moral laws, or stand aside from them, but must acknowledge them and participate in them and apply them. If he does not, he will fail the cause of morality- and of History as well-and forfeit the confidence and respect of his peers.

There is, however, another and perhaps more persuasive argument for moral judgment in history, one that rests not so much on moral as on psychological grounds. It is this: that the historian cannot, in any event, help himself, and that he might as well acknowledge what is inherent and implicit in his condition, He is, after all, a creature of his time, his society, his faith. Even if he resolutely refrains from overt moral judgment, he well surely be guilty of covert judgment: his choice of subject, his selection of facts, his very vocabulary, will betray him. How much better, then, how much fairer and more honest, to acknowledge his position in advance; how much better to call his book=it is Charles A. Beard who makes the point-An Economic Interpretation of the Constitution rather than to fall back on a title like The Making of the Constitution, one which "does not advise the reader at the outset concerning the upshot to be expected." History is not a science, and the historian is not a scientist. "The supreme command,"therfore, "is that he must cast off his servitude to the assumptions of natural science and return to his own subject matter- to history as actuality."

This is the argument, too, of the distinguished oxford philosopher, Sir Isaiah Berlin, who sees in the passion for scientific impartiality yet another expression of the misguided and pernicious belief that history is a science. "The case against the motion of historical objectivity," he writs, "is like case against international law, or international morality; that it does not exist." And he adds the warning that:

Except on the assumption that history must deal with human beings purely as material objects in space, must, in short, be behaviouristits method can scarcely be assimilated to the standards of an exact natural science. The invocation to historians to suppress even that minimal degree of moral of psychological evaluation which is necessarily involved in viewing human being as creatures with purpose and motives... seems to me rest with those of natural science. It is one of the greatest and most destructive fallacies of the last hundred years. (Historical Inevitability, oxford, oxford University Press, 1954, pp. 52-53.)

But the stout champions of moral judgment do not have things with all their own way. Not at all. Here comes a whole phalanx of historians with a formidable arsenal of counter-arguments.

First, while it is true that history tries to observe something like historical "due process," it cannot in the nature of the case do so. The past is not there to defend itself. We cannot recall the witnesses, put them on the stand, question and cross-examine them. It is difficult enough to render a moral verdict on anything so recent as, let due say, Hoover's dispersion of the "Bonus army," or the conduct of the Vichy government, or the resort to the atomic weapon at Hiroshima; how much more difficult, then, to suit in judgment of the character of Alibiades, the justification for the murder of Caesar, the conduct of the Norman invaders of England, or of the Spanish conquistadores.

Second, while technical judgment is essential, in the law, in the civil service, in the university, in athletics, if society is to function, such judgment does not pretend to be moral but professional. A university professor who permitted his moral views of a candidate to dictate his grades, a referee whose decision were based on moral considerations, even a judge who allowed hid private moral convictions to influence his decisions on questions of contracts, wills, liability, or bankruptcy proceedings, would be regarded as not only incompetent but expendable. There are reasonably clear standards for such practical judgments as society requires-laws, moral judgments present questions of labyrinthine complexity even when all the relevant evident appears to be available. Where history is concerned, the conduct of men or of nations in past centuries, all the relevant evidence is never available, and there are no universal standards. What the historian does, when he judges, is merely to identify his own "can't-help-but-believes" with entities. Herodotus made this point twenty-five centuries ago: When Darius was the throne, he summoned.

into his presence the Hellenes at his court and asked them for what price they would to make a meat of their fathers when they died. The Hellenes replied that all the money in the World would not induce them to do such a thing, whereupon Darius summoned the Collation Indians, who do eat their parents, and asked them (in the presence of the Hellenes, who were kept informed, through an interpreter, of the tenour of the conversation) for what price they would be willing to burn their fathers when they died. The Indians shrieked aloud and begged him not to pursue an unmentionable subject-a story which illustrates the habitual attitude of Mankind towards this question, and which, in my opinion, justifies Pindar's poetic question, and which, in my opinion, justifies Pindar's poetic aphorism that "Custom is king of all."

Justice Holmes made the point with even greater succinctness. "I prefer champagne to ditch-water," he said. "but I see no reason of suppose the cosmos does."

If history "tells us" anything, it tells us that standards, values, and principles have varied greatly from age to age and from society to society; indeed, that they have varied greatly from one generation to another within the same society. Popes chosen for their learning and their virtue were certain that morality required that they put down heresies with fire and award, cruelty and torture; sixteenth century Europeans head no compunction about killing Indians, because the Indians had no souls; learned and century Christians in the American south regarded slavery as a blessing. The Hellenes of whom Herodotus tells us were no more shocked at the notion of eating their dead fathers than we are at Hellenic notions of love. Consider, for example, Plato's defense of a practice which most of our contemporaries regard not only as immoral but as pernicious, and which our military and civil authorities combat with sleepless zeal:

I cannot say what greater benefit can fall to the lot of a young man than a virtuous lover and to the lover than a beloved youth...If then there were any means whereby a state or army could be formed of lovers and favorites, they would administer affairs beater and all others, provided they abstain from all disgraceful deeds and compete with one another in honest rivalry, and such men, together with others like them, though few in number, so to speak would conquer the world. (Symposium, p.178.)

A problem which has confronted, and perplexed, American historians for a hundred years is slavery. Surely if anything is wrong, slavery is wrong. No social institution more dee-ply offends our moral sensibilities than this; no other collective experience induces in us a comparable sense of sham. Slavery, we are all agreed, corrupts alike the slave and the master; slavery corrupts the body politic, the poison still infects us.

This is the vocabulary of morality, and it is this vocabulary which we invoke, almost instinctively, whenever we discuss what was long euphemistically called the "peculiar institution."

Yet when we come to pronounce judgment on slavery we are met, at the very threshold, with the most intransigent consideration-that generation after generation of good, human, Christian men and women not only accepted it, but considered it a blessing. What are we to say when confronted by the fact-a formidable body of evidence permits us to use that word-that our own forebears, only two or there generations back, embraced slavery rejoiced in it fought to defend it, and gave up their lives confident that they were dying in a good cause.

Clearly, we cannot fall back on the simple explanation that all these men and women-these who owned slaves and those who sustained the slave system-were bad. These beneficiaries of and defenders of livery were neither better nor worse than their cousins north of the mason and Dixon line who had managed to get rid of the "peculiar institution" one or two generations earlier; they were neither better nor worse than we are whatever may be said, on practical grounds, for the moral righteousness and self-righteousness of Abolitionists who fought slavery, it can be said that no comparable pressures weigh upon us as historians. It is absurd for us to pass moral judgment on slave-holders, absurd to indict a whole people or to banish a whole people to some historical purgatory where they can expiate their dins. Lincoln sea this, Lincoln who sea so much. The people of the North and the South, he said in his Second Inaugural Address, "read the same Bible and pray to the same God, and each invokes His aid a just god's assistance in wringing their bread from the sweat of other men's faces. But let due judge not, that we be not judged."

We can agreé now, most of us, that slavery was an unmitigated evil, but we cannot there from conclude that those who inherited it, were caught in it and by it, supported it and fought for it, were evil men, what we can say is that but for the grace of God, for the accident of history, we might ourselves have been caught up in slavery, and bound by it, and habituated to accepting it, just as our forebears were. What we can say is that if earlier generations-north and South alike-bore the burden and the guilt of slavery, we have born the burden, and the guilt, of racial discrimination, and that morally there is not much to choose between the two.

Clearly, different generations have different moral standards; it is a from of intellectual arrogance for us to impose ours upon the past. We do not accept ex post facto laws, bills of attainder, or guilty by association in our legal system; we should not apply these concepts or rules retroactively to the past. Far better to refrain from the folly and the vanity of moral righteousness about the past; far better to accept Lincoln's admonition to judged. The historian's task is not to judge, but to understand. How did it happen that men dedicated to carrying out the precepts of the Sermon on the Mount Couldsend those who disagreed with them to the stake? How did it happen that men dedicated to the expansion of European civilization could carry fire and sword to the hapless inhabitants of the American continents? How did it happen that men and women who dearly loved their own children and whose daily lives were bound each to each with natural piety could bitterly oppose laws designed to protect little children from the awful burden of work in factory upon slavery as a blessing? how did it happen that a people who boasted a high civilization, who had produced Leibniz and Kant, Beethoven and Mozart, Goethe and Heine, Rilke and Thomas Mann, could stand by while six million Jews were done to death?

Tout comprendre, tout pardonner. But it does not follow that the historian who understands all forgives all. It is the historian's business to "understand"; it is not the historian's business either to condemn or to forgive. He is not God.

For here is a third argument against moral judgment in history-that the historian is not God. He is not called upon to judge the quick or the dead; indeed he is not called upon to judge. If he sets up as a judge he changes the whole pattern of his intellectual and professional role from one dedicated to objective inquiry to one devoted to prosecution or defense. As the distinguished historian of the Russian Revolution, E.H. Carr, unhistorical and contradicts the very essence of history, It provides a dogmatic answer to questions which the historian who accepts answers n advance to these questions, goes to work with his eyes blindfolded, and, renounces his vocation."

The historian is not god; he is a man and like other men. He confesses most of the failings, responds to most of the pressures, succumbs to most of the temptations that afflict his fellow men. Consciously, or unconsciously, he is a almost always tasking sides. Can we really trust Carlyle on Cromwell, or "Motely of philip II, or Charles A. Beard of the causes of the civil war or Vernon Arrington on John Marshall? can we trust either Macaulay iron Winston Churchill to write impartially about the Duke of Marlborough? Can we trust Lord Acton or benedetto Croce on a subject so close to their hearts as the history of liberty? Clearly we cannot. The historian, like the judge, the priest, or the statesman, is a creature of his race, nationality, religion, class, of his inheritance and his education, and he can never emancipate himself from these formative influences and achieve Olympian impartiality. Where he undertakes to judge he does not even have the prop of professional training and traditions to sustain him, as he does when he records and reconstructs. His judgments are, therefore, as herbert butterfield has observed, but "pseudo-moral judgments, masquerading as moral omens, mixed and muddy affairs, part prejudice, part political animosity, with a dash of ethical flavoring wildly tossed into the concoctio0n." And because not even a Ranke, not even a Mommsen not even a Toynbee, an survey the whole of history, his forays into the past are bound to be haphazard and fortuitous as well. for purposes of reconstructing the past, that is not a fatal handicap; others will fill in the gaps. But for purposes of formulating a moral code and code and applying it systematically and impartially, it is a fatal handicap.

We may, then accept the findings of the historian in maters of fact-always subject to subsequent revision, to be sure-but why should we accept his conclusions in matters of morality? "I beseech you in the bowels of Christ," wrote Oliver Cromwell in his Letter to the Church of Scotland, "think it possible you may be mistaken they have stood ready to pronounce judgments which differ little from the tainted and tarnished judgments of statesmen, soldiers, and priests. Catholic historians have sustained the persecution of protestant heretics, and protestant historians looked with equanimity upon the persecution of Catholics. national historians have almost invariably defended and justified the conduct of their own their nation; more, they have themselves provided the arguments for chauvinistic nationalism, imperialism, and militarism. No wonder that the chief professional preoccupation of the historian in our day is revision!

There is no special dispensation for the historian, He is not exempt from the prejudices, the ambitions, the vanities, the fears, that afflict his fellow men. When he dons his professional robes he is an impressive and sometimes a majestic figure; when he is persuaded to put on the robes of the moral judge, he is as naked as the unhappy Emperor of Hans Andersen's story.

We come then to a fourth consideration, practical rather

than philosophical: the futility of moral judgment in history. Surely, say those who insist that the historian be a judge, it is proper that the historian reprobate the Inquisition and exalt tolerance, that he deplore slavery and celebrated freedom, that he forces of liberation. But why should the historian go out of his way to condemn or to praise these thing? the assumption behind this expectation is that the reader has no mind of his own, no moral standards, no capacity to exercise judgment; that he is incapable of distinguishing between slavery and freedom, persecution and tolerance, but depends upon the historian to do this for him. are those mature enough to read serious histories really so obtuse that they cannot draw conclusions from the facts that are submitted to them? Is there really any danger that students will yearn for slavery or rejoice in the inquisition or admire philip II or Adolph Hitler if the historian does not bustle in and set them right? Alas, if the reader does not know that Hitler was a moral monster and that the murder of six million Jews was a moral outrage, nothing the historian can say will set him right, if se does not know in his bones that slavery corrupts both sale and master, nothing the historian can say will enlighten him. Is there not, indeed, some danger that if the historian continually usurps the role of judge, the reader may react against his judgments; that if the historian insists on treating his readers as morally incompetent, they may turn from history altogether to some more mature from of literature?

There is a further consideration, which might be called a plea in abatement. It is this; that the problem of judgment may be trusted to take care of itself. No reader comes wholly unprepared to the contemplation of a chapter of history ; he brings with him his own education, his own moral and philosophical outlook. Nor is the student ever confined to a single account of any important cheaper of history. We can be confident that historians will differ in their interpretation of the past and that these differences will be available and familiar to readers. Errors will be corrected; wrong opinions will be set right. For every historian who defends British policy in Ireland there will be one to expose it and reprobate it; for every historian who paints slavery in sunlight terms, there will be one to expose its darkness and cruelty; for every historian who places responsibility for the First World War Squarely at the door of the Germans, there will be one ready to make clear it was the Russians or the French who were really to blame. Let the historian learn humility: the reader is not dependent upon him for the whole of his history; he is not dependent upon him for moral instruction.

That is what the great Italian historical philosopher Benedetto Croce meant when he wrote that "those who, on the plea of narrating history, bustle about as judges, condemning here and giving absolution there, because they think that this is the office of history, are generally recognized as devoid of historical sense."

One final observation is appropriate. We should not confuse moral with professional judgment. In the field of his professional competence the scholar has the same obligation as the judge, the teacher, the physician, the architect. The judge who pronounces sentence, the teacher who condemns a building, is not indulging in moral but exercising professional judgment. So the historian who, after painstaking study of all available evidence, and after cleansing himself of all the perilous stuff which might distort his vision, concludes that Lee did right to surrender at Appomattox rather than fight it out in the west, that conduct of the Crimean war was characterized by criminal folly, that the violation of Belgian neutrality in 1914 was an error of the first magnitude, that cavort rather than Garibasi deserves credit for Italian unification, that Shakespeare and not Bacon wrote Hamlet, that only the stone and not the inscription on the Kensington rune stone is genuine, and that the protocols of Zion are forgeries, is performing his professional duty. He may be mistaken-but so may the judge, the teacher, the physician-that is a chance society takes. His judgments may have moral overtones-it is difficult to keep those out, and we have learned to discount them. But if it is exasperating to fond a Carlyle or a Motley laying down the moral laws for us, it is equally exasperating to discover that when you lay all the scholarly investigators of a subject end to end, they do not reach a conclusion.

CHAPTER 4

The Trouble with Facts

These are some of the limitations on the historian. But there are limitations inherent in the facts of history, as well.

Poor, despised facts, they have a hard time. Nobody believes in them; nobody has any faith in them. With almost a single voice historians say that there are no facts, none that can be relied upon anyway; there are only some agreed-on assumptions which we choose to call facts so we can get on with the job. But do not be misled by them, do not take them seriously, or they will betray you. Facts are subjective, they exist in the mind of the historian, they change their character with each historian. The facts of the Franco-Prussian War are one thing to a French historian, another to a German; the facts about the creation of the state of Israel read very differently in the eyes of Jews and Arabs. Facts are like the Cheshire cat, in Alice in Wonderland; as we look at them they fade away, all but the grin.

What is the trouble with facts?

First, a paradox. There are too few facts, and there are too many. There are far too few facts about immense areas of past history. How little we know, after all, about most of mankind- about the people of Asia, of Africa, or pre-Columbian America; how little we know about lost people like the Carthaginians and the Etruscans, the early Colts and the Basques. How little we know about the remote past, as contrasted with the recent past. How do we dare reconstruct the ancient world with any assurance, when our knowledge is confined to small areas around the Mediterranean; yet we confidently call this Ancient History. How can we write with any assurance about the history of the American continents when except for what ethnology and archeology may tell us- our knowledge embraces only five centuries out of a possible twenty-five thousand years ? How little we know- even in modern times- of the lives of the poor, of those vast majorities of each generation about whom we have no reliable fact.

And, at the other end of the scale, we know almost too much about the modern history of the west America, Britain, France, Germany, Italy in the nineteenth or twentieth centuries. We are overwhelmed by mountains of evidence; it accumulates faster than even computers can records it, and we still have to process the material from the computers. We do not and cannot have all the facts about the Second World War, but it is safe to guess that historians will never get through the miles of filling cases of historical records now resting in warehouses throughout the country. Inevitably our vision of the past is distorted by this disproportion in our evidence; inevitably we translate this disproportion into historical distortions.

We have already noted the role of chance in the historical records, and the influence of modern-mindedness and of subjectivity. There are still further limitations on "facts". There is for example the elementary consideration that we can rarely attain factual accuracy about the past, even about the recent past. The uninitiated take factual accuracy for granted in history as they take it for granted in chemistry or physics, but as soon as they try to reconstruct any chapter of past history they spedily discover that accuracy is unattainable. The science or statistics is new, and even such statistics as we have are rarely reliable. We do not know such fundamental things as the populations or the birth and death rates of ancient peoples; we do not know the numbers in armies or in battles, or the casualties in war. We do not know the value or the volume of farm production or of domestic industries or of trade. Even in modern history, statistics often fail us : we do not and probably cannot know with any accuracy the number of soldiers in the Union or the Confederate armies, or the losses, or the cost of the war; the ascertainable "facts" do not go very far in explaining why Britain did not intervene on the side of the Confederacy. Even so apparently elementary a matter as the total acreage of public lands granted by state and federal governments to American railroads has long been and still is a matter of conjecture and debate. On these, and a hundred other important questions of history, we can only make educated guesses.

There are, to be sure, some matters about which we can be accurate and certain, but alas, these turn out to be matters of no great importance. We can be accurate about the succession of American Presidents, or of the kings of England of France, and we prefer an historian who know that Buchanan succeeded Pierce, and not the other way around, and who can list the Richards and the Henrys, the Philips and the Louis in their proper order. This is too elementary to be helpful. We can be accurate about the dates of the Buchanan administration, but no about Buchanan's role in the coming of the Civil War; we can be accurate about the dates for Louis XVI, but there is no agreement on his contribution to the breakdown of the ancient regime.

Finally, the facts of history turn out to be not hard and objective but impalpable and subjective. Ranke and his successors taught us to realy speak of themselves. Alas, they do not speak for themselves. The speak, rather, for us, and with a hundred different voices. They tell us not what actually happened but, more often than not, what we want to hear. Take, for example, the two most famous documents of American history- the Delaration of Independence and the federal Constitution. Even the textual history of the Declaration is an intricate affair, but look aside form the textual history to the political and philosophical. Here are the immortal words- their immortality, note, not inherent, but conferred upon them by later generations what do they mean?

What did Jefferson and the members of the Continental congress mean when he wrote, and they endorsed, the statement that "all men are created equal" ? What id he mean when he wrote, what did they mean when they endorsed, the sentiment that the "pursuit of happiness" is an unalienable right ?

No two people read quite the same thing into these words. Certainly the generation of Thomas Jefferson (even the term "generation" is an artificial one, and if we accept Jefferson's own calculation of a generation as twenty years, he belonged to four) and our own generation read different meanings into terms like "equality" and "happiness". Certainly, too, in our own day, men and women read different meanings into the word "happiness", and northerners and southerners, whites and Negroes, read different meanings into the term "equality". It requires a lifetime of study to understand these words, and after a lifetime of study different historians come up with very different explanations. Clearly this famous document does not speak for itself.

Contemplate, then, the Constitution of the United States, a document of some six thousand carefully chosen words, simple, lucid, logical. Does the Constitution speak for itself ? Clearly it does not; if it did we should not need the 375 volumes of Supreme Court Reports to explain and interpret it, nor would learned and upright judges on the Supreme Court so frequently disagree about the meaning of such phrases as "commerce among the several states", "the executive power", "impair the obligation of contracts," "common defense and general welfare", "necessary and proper", and "due process of law."

Or take another kind of document: a painting. Does the meaning of the painting inhere in the painting itself ? Not entirely. You can look at it and see a great deal which you have missed; an art historian or art critic can look at it through the eyes of history and see many things which escape the rest of us and some, perhaps, which were not in the mind of the artist when had painted the picture.

Take for example, the various paintings by Poisson on the theme Et in Arcadia Ego, which Edwin Panofsky has dealt with in a fascinating essay on that subject. To the onlookr it is a simple matter- shepherds and maidens stumbling on a tomb with that touching inscription are struck into sober contemplation by the realization that others before them had lived in Arcadia and now were dead and gone. But is that really what the paintings mean, or what the phrase and the concept originally meant ? Not at all, says Panofsky. What they mean in not "I too have lived in Arcadia", but "Death, too, is in Arcadia". That reverses the moral of the pictures completely; it is no longer a reminder that every generation has known happiness, but a reminder that death is ever present, even in Arcadia. But wait, it is not that simple, either, for eighteenth century painters did in fact reverse the original meaning. Unwilling to contemplate the presence of death in Arcadia, they turned the whole thing into a pastoral scene, one designed to show that generation was liked to generation by happiness, not by death.

Contemplate another, and more familiar, artistic document: Dnanuel Leutze's painting of "Washington Crossing the Delaware". Clearly this is not a contemporary record: There were no artists present to record that famous crossing. It was painted three-quarters of a century after the event; the river was the Rhine, not the Delaware, and Washington was Worthington Whittredge, a young American artist studying in Dusseldorf. The scene it self was a product of leutze's romantic imagination. If Washington has stood up in that rowboat the would have fallen overboard; the flag was quite incorrect; and as the crossing was made before dawn of a winter night, neither Washington nor the sailors who rowed him would have been visible in the dark. But all that was of no importance. The painting had a life of its own. It was accepted with rapture as an authentic representation; it made its way at once into the minds and hearts of the American people; it has come to be, for all practical purposes, the authentic representation of the historic event. If it does not reproduce an historical fact it is, itself, an historical fact.

A document, then, may mean many things. Its meaning is to be understood in the light of its own contemporary history; it is to be understood in the light of the reason, temperament, and prejudices of the historian who uses it; it is to be arrive at and interpreted through the symbolism it communicates. Even that is not the end of it. For the historian has to communicate with each individual reader, and each one will read the document or the analysis in his own way, just as each individual looks at a Whistler painting or listens to a Mozart sonata in his own way.

The facts of history are fragmentary, elusive, and subjective. But that is true of most of these studies which engage the minds and the passions of men art and letters, morals and ethics, even law and politics, as every judge and statesman knows. We must no expect things to be easier for the historian than they are for those many others who try somehow to reconcile the heritage of the past its laws and principles and monuments with the imaginations, the passions, the emotions, and the facts of their own time. It is not of history, but of the whole cargo of thought and character and habit that William Vaughn Moody wrote those moving lines :

This earth is not the steadfast thing
We landsmen build upon;
From deep to deep she varies pace,
And while she comes is gone.
Beneath my feet I feel,
Her smooth bulk heave and dip;
With velvet plunge and soft upreel
She swings and steadies to her keel
Like a gallant, gallant ship.
("Gloucester Moors")

Yet though we admit the limitations and difficulties of history, item by item, if we take them too hard, we will find ourselves out of a job. If the limitations really are so severe, and the facts really are so elusive, we may be forced to give up history altogether. If we are to get on with the job, we must agree upon some kind of dactual foundation or framework for our histories, if only that Washington was in fact the first President of the United States, or that the United States did in fact fight a war with Mexico which brought her Texas and California, or that Lincoln was in fact assassinated. For, treacherous as they no doubt are, facts are like syntax and grammar; we need them as a framework and a mechanism if we are to make ourselves clear. There is nothing sacred about grammar, and a wide latitude is permitted in its usage, but if we are perpetually to stop and question the authority of our grammar we will never finish what we are saying or writing.

Historians have, after all, surmounted the difficulties that crowd about them, and given us famous and affluent histories. Gibbon was aware of the difficulties, and Macaulay, Ranke and Mommsen, Maitland and Holdsworth, Parkman and Henry Adams, yet all of them managed to write histories which have enlarged the thoughts and lifted the spirits of generations of men. Let they young historian take to heart the lines of the Greek Anthology:

A shipwrecked sailor, buried on this coast
Bids you set sail;
Full many a gallant bark, when we were lost
Weathered the gale.

CHAPTER 5

Writing History

Let is be said at once that there is no mystery about writing history. There is no formula for historical writing. There are no special techniques or special requirements, except the technique of writing clearly and the requirements of honesty and common sense. It is useful to ha e special training, as it is useful to have special training for almost anything you wish to do well driving a car, or cooking, or painting but special training is by no means essential and most of the great historians have been innocent of formal training. Professional history is, indeed, a very recent affair it came in with "technical history" in the nineteenth century and, except in Germany, the near-monopoly of historical writing by academicians is even more recent. Almost all the great historians of the past were men involved in one way or another in public affairs- Thucydides, Livy, Tacitus, Plutarch and, in modern times, Bolingbroke, Voltaire, Hume, Macaulay, Bancroft, Guizot, Grundtvig. Most of them, too, were amateurs, at least in the sense that they were not professional teachers: thus in the United States Bancroft, Prescott, Motley, Parkman, and Henry Adams. The amateur tradition is now almost a thing of the past, but it lingers on in Europe more tenaciously than in America : witness the contributions of such public figures as Croce, Madariaga, Malraux, De Gaulle, George Lukacs, and Winston Churchill.

Integrity, industry, imagination and common sense these are the important, indeed the essential, requirements. They are by no means familiar commonplace qualities. The requirement of integrity is of course implacable, in history as in all other forms of scholarship or science, admitted that standards of "integrity" are not universal, and that honest men differ on the nature of truth in history as in all other realms of thought. Perhaps it is sufficient to say that the historian must be honest according to his lights; that he should never consciously distort his evidence, even by literary artistry; that he should ever be on guard against religious, racial, class or national preconceptions; that he should try to see every problem from all possible points of view; that he should search diligently for all the evidence, and not be content until he has exhausted the available resources; that he should always remember that he is not God and that final judgment is not entrusted to him.

The requirement of industry, too, is elementary and rigorous. You need not, perhaps, emulate the great historian of ancient Rome, Theodore Mommsen, who customarily worked eighteen hours a day and complained that on his wedding day he managed only twelve hours work, or that other German phenomenon, Leopold von Ranke, who kept working and writing well into his eighties, and who at the age of eighty-five launched a History of the World, seven volumes of which appeared in the next five years of his life. But, as with most things that are important, the writing of history requires patience, devotion, and indefatigable industry, much of it tiresome. You will have to accustom yourself to spending long hours and days tracking down some source with as often as not will prove quite useless, reading through newspapers or journals which as often as not yield only a scanty return, working patiently through ill-scrawled manuscripts in the hope, often vain, of hitting on something that is relevant to your inquiry, fighting your way stubbornly through the jungles of verbiage in the Congressional Globe or the Reports or royal commissions, or the decisions of courts. If you are going to come up with something that is new, original, fresh, and valuable, you cannot avoid these exercises; if you are not prepared for them, you will do well to abandon history for something less arduous.

As for imagination, that is in all likelihood something that cannot be cultivated; either you have it or you do not. If you do not have it you may be a worthy compiler of facts, a good analyst, a safe guide through the labyrinths of the past, but you will never be able to recreate the past, never set the blood coursing through the veins of your readers, or ideas tumbling over each other in their heads. As for "common sense" alas it is by no means as common as the phrase implies. It is an allinclusive term which embraces such disparate qualities as moderation, balance, judiciousness, critical intelligence, open mindedness, tolerance, proportion, and good humor, and doubtless other qualities as well. Without it the most scholarly and interesting works misfire for example as with William crosskey's two learned volumes designed to prove that the Founding Fathers of the United States meant something quite different from what they said and wrote, or Otto Eisenschiml's elaborate proof that Secretary Stanton master minded the plot to assassinate Lincoln, or Charles Tansill's well documented volume designed to prove that Franklin Roosevelt instigated the Second World War, or to take a more extreme example those many volumes deducted to the proposition that Lord Bacon or the Earl of Oxford, or somebody else wrote the plays hitherto attributed to Shakespeare.

Let us turn, then, to some practical considerations in the writing of history: first, the choice of a subject. That seems almost too elementary a matter to justify comment, but alas it is not. Again and again otherwise sensible young historians choose poorly when they select a subject for their investigation. Here is where common senses comes in. Your subject should not be too ambitious, or too petty. It should be something you can manage within the time you have available, the time and the space. It should be something which has not been chewed up by generations of historians; at the same time it should not be something so strange and rare that it will be of interest only to you. Take care, too, that the materials you will need to use are not only available but available to you. Do not select some subject for which the materials are scanty and unreliable, or theressential documents inaccessible some chapter in the history of the Secret Service, for example, or the CIA- or in the possession of a family which preserves them for its own purposes, or in the archives of Spain or Austrialia unless indeed you happen to be bound for Spain or Australia. If you live in Nepal do not select a subject which has to be studied in the files of German newspapers; if you live in Pokhara do not select a subject which has to be studied through materials scattered throughout a dozen European historical societies. If your command of languages is shaky, avoid subjects which has to be studied through materials scattered throughout a dozen European historical societies. If your command of Languages is shaky, avoid subjects which require a knowledge of half a dozen foreign languages; if your eyesight is poor avoid subjects which are to be studied in seventeenth or eighteenth century manuscripts or for that matter in the manuscripts of horace Greeley or Charles Summer or others whose handwriting was notoriously indecipherable.

All of this is purely negative this elimination of subjects that do not lend themselves to orderly treatment. There is one affirmative consideration equally basic and imperative: select a subject the way you would select a friend. It is something you are going to live with for a long time, perhaps for years; select therefore a good companion for the journey. Ideally you should find a subject which so interests and excites you that you cannot resist it. On the whole it is desirable to choose a subject which enlists your sympathy, though that is by no means essential, you can write effectively about the Massacre of St. Bartholomew even though you disapprove in principle of religious intolerance; you can write intelligently of Hitler without approving of Nazism; yet it is perhaps best to avoid the first if you are of Huguenot descent and the second if you are Jewish.

For biographical subjects it is particularly important to find a figure who enlists your sympathy as well as your interest. As you would not want to live intimately with someone you heartily disliked, so you will not want to live on terms of intimacy with some historical character whom you heartily dislike. There are example of biographers who have disliked or come to dislike their subject: Froude certainly appeared to dislike Carlyle though in fact he did not and Lytton Strachey had no use for his Eminent Victorians, while Paxton Hibben scarcely tried to conceal his contempt for William Jennings Bryan. But these are exceptions. The best biographers confess admiration and sympathy for their subjects, and some of them deep personal affection- Boswell's famous biography of Dr. Johnson, for example, or William Dean Howells tender interpretation, My Mark Twain, or George Otto Trevelyan's spirited biography of his uncle, Lord Macaulay.

Once you have found a sympathetic subject, and ascertained that there is something new to be said about it and that the materials on which to base your study are ample and readily available, you can get started. And from now on common sense really does take charge.

Even here there are some practical observations that are relevant. The first is this : do not was to time and energy in what is amiably called "reading around" a subject. Reading around, or reading for background, is more often than not an excuse for not getting on with the job: it is pleasant, it is edifying and it is inexhaustible. A chemist concerned with a specific problem does not stop to "read around" the law. Plunge into the subject itself; get your problem by the throat and grapple with it. The closer you come to it, and the deeper your understanding of it, the more surely you will become familiar with all the surrounding landscape. Gradually everything will fall into place. That, after all, is the natural way: you come only gradually to know the background of a friend, and even children do not fill in the background of parents and grandparents until they themselves have children. In short, start with the particular, not with the general; read deeply in the history of the particular, and you will find that the general takes care of itself.

A second practical rule is to begin almost at once collecting the essential materials for your essay or monograph and organizing them into some coherent pattern. Granted you do not really know what is "essential", or just what the pattern is to be; the sooner you get started, the sooner you will find answers to these questions. Do not think you have to read everything, take notes on everything, track down every reference, look at every piece of manuscript before you begin to write. The sooner you begin the better, for only s you write will you discover the lacunae in your knowledge, and fill them.

There is a third practical consideration here that has to do with the compilation of your materials. For most purposes that means "taking notes" that arduous and never ending process with ca, unless you are careful, become something of an opiate, a pleasant substitute for the real work of thinking and writing. There is more to be said for note taking than merely copying mountains of material. This your could hire someone to do. The great literary historian Van Wyck Brookes, author of the most interesting of literary histories of America, did all his own copying and, what is more, did it all by hand. He could, do course, have employed copyists, or bought himself a copying machine. He preferred to do his own work because he knew what every scholar comes to know: that if you copy things yourself, you remember them. He knew, too, another important lesson: that the by-product of copying is often more important than the product, namely the ideas you get as you go. No copyist can get those ideas for you, and there is no substitute for the inspiration which comes from your own direct, fresh, and uncomplicated relation with your materials.

When it comes to writing history, keep in mind that there are almost as many ways of writing as there are historians. There is no formula; you will have to find your own formula. There is no pattern; you will have to work out your own pattern. But this is not to suggest that there are no models. There are models by the score. You will doubtless be influenced by them, just as a painter is influenced by

Rembrandt or Goya, Whistler or Picasso. That does not mean that you can successfully adopt for your own the lordly style or a Gibbon, the rhetorical style or a Carlyle, the balanced cadences of a Macaulay, the strong masculine style of a Mahan, the brilliant style of a Parrington, the epigrammatic style of a Philip Guedalla, the allusive style of a Denish Brogan, the intimate style of a Paul Hazard. All of these are available, but in writing, as in other matters, the style reflects the man and your style must reflect you.

But style is not a single or a static thing; you will want to vary your style, to adapt it to the subject matter. You would not think of using the same pattern of organization, the same style of presentation, for all subjects, any more than you would clothe all men and women alike at all times. A style suitable, let us say, to a history of the Tariff of 1890 it no a good style for a history of the conquest of Peru or for a biography of Herman Melville. Each subject makes its own claim upon you; each one demands individual treatment. Practiced historians know this almost instinctively, and very their styles, as do professional couturiers or photographers. Thomas Beer, for example he was a novelist as well as an historian used very different styles in his biography of Stephen Crane and his essay on The Mauve Decade; John Morley varied his style to suit the different requirements of Voiltaire and of Gladstone; Henry Adams had one style for the History and a quite different one for the Education, more subtle, more allusive, though not more brilliant.

CHAPTER 6

Some Problems of History

Limitations on the Historian

"The historian", writes Veronica Wedgwood", ought to be the humblest of men; he is faced a dozen times a day with the evidence of his own ignorance; he is perpetually confronted with his own humiliating inability to interpret his material correctly; he is, in a sense that no other writer is, in bondage to that material." In bondage ! Most sophisticated historians would readily agree with this. They are ever conscious of the limitations and handicaps under which they work, and of the temptations and dangers to which they are exposed. But the public tends to overlook these limitations, and some historians are even innocent enough, or brash enough, to gloss over the difficulties inherent in their profession.

History is in fact far more complex and disorderedly than the amateur suspects. To most laymen it is all simple and straightforward. What is it, he asks, that you want to know ? It is the writing of the Magna Carta, the consolidation of Germany under Bismarck, the triumph of Communism in China ? Got your facts, put them together in some sensible order, and Presto ! there is your history. The great historian Henry Adam's has made the classic observation on this notion of history. "He had even published a dozen volumes of American history," he recalled, "for no other purpose than to satisfy himself whether, by the severest process of stating, with the least possible comment, such facts as seemed sure in such order as seemed rigorously consequent, he could fix for a familiar moment a necessary sequence of human movement." The result, he confessed, was failure, "Where he saw sequence other man saw something quite different, and no one saw the same unit of measure," and he concluded that "the sequence of men led to nothing and that the sequence of their society could lead no further, while the mere sequence or time was artificial, and the sequence of thought was chaos." (The Education of Henry Adams, Boston : Houghton Mifflin Company, 1918, P. 382).So he abandoned history altogether and asserted, somewhat perv3ersely, that any nine pages of his novel,, Esther, were worth more than the nine volumes of his History. Posterity does not agree with this verdict, but that is another matter.

What, then, are some of these limitations which have discouraged so many historians, and which, Miss wedgood admonished us, should induce humility?

First, there are the many and sobering limitations on historical materials. There is, for example, the role of chance. The chemist or biologist can command whatever materials he needs for his experiments, but the historian works with what happens to come to hand. What we are permitted "to know" is not only but a small part of "what happened in history", but it is a collection which has come to us in large part by chance rather than by choice. It is lost because it was never compiled; it is lost because of the erosion of time fire and water and weather and carelessness; it is lost because it was deliberately destroyed. How do we know that what has come down to us is other the most important or the most authentic representation of any chapter of past history ?

Another limitation is that of distortion. Thus we know a great deal of the history of some European peoples, and because this record is available we confuse it with History and write as if it embraced the whole of the past. It is not morely that the records for most non-European societies are non-existent or lost the African, for example, or the American Indian or the Carthagenian but that even where records are available in China, or in India for example western historians have not used them. This is easy to understand, but we should not call what we choose to interest ourselves in History, and formulate broad, even universal, generalizations on the basis of such fragmentary and arbitrary evidence.

The very fact that history is based so largely on the written record introduces a note of unbalance, and distorts our view. For what it inevitably means is that we exaggerate the role of the written record and of those peoples who did keep records at the expense of those who did not, or whose records are poorly kept. Almost every historian has an unconscious bias in favor of the literary history-conscious, western European, and against the others: in favor of the Jews and against the Babylonians, in favor of the Greeks and against the Persians, in favor of the Romans and against the "barbarians" Even in highly sophisticated societies such as our own we must acknowledge a distortion induced by the charms of the written record.

The tyranny of the written records introduces another element of distortion, namely, that what attracts the record-keeper and the historian is the dramatic, the spectacular, and the catastrophic. This has always been true, and it emains true today, as reference to any daily newspaper will make clear. The monks who bequeathed us so many records id not usually record the daily routine of life, but only events which they considered out of the ordinary or miraculous : comets and earthquakes and plagues and wars; and millions of families have endorsed this view of history by recording in their family records only births, marriages, and deaths. The historian too is attracted by whatever is dramatic or unusual or romantic; he writes the annals of the rich and the great; for the annals of the poor, as we know, are short and simple. How natural it is for us, how inevitable perhaps, to believe that history is, by its very nature, the records of what is dramatic and astonishing. A great statesman, a soldier, an explorer, we say "makes history"; or a particular people at a particular time the Athenians of the fifth century BC, on the French during their Revolution, "make history". This is, of course, nonsense; everybody makes history all the time, the Slave as well as the Master, the South sea Islander as well as the Parisian. What we mean is that these people make the kind of history that appeals to us, that we happen to know about, and that we like to write about; if follows very easily that what appeals to us and what we write about is history.

Closely associated with the enchantment of the dramatic is the spell of the familiar. So accustomed are we do the formal patterns of history that it requires an effort for us to remember that these are not history's patterns, but ours. We have already considered the dangers latent in familiar chronological and regional patterns the habit of dividing history into neat packets labelled Ancient, Medieval, and Modern, or of carving up American history into Colonial, Revolutionary, Middle Period, and so forth. There is a further refinement on these divisions which is even more artificial, the habit of forcing history into the straitjackets of monarchical or presidential patterns. Thus we write of the Age of Louis XIV or of Napoleon, of the Jeffersonian era, or the era of Franklin D. Roosevelt.

Of all patterns which we have imposed upon history, it is the national which is the most powerful and the most pervasive, and perhaps the most mischievous. The limitations which nationalism imposes upon history go far beyond those of providing convenient but misleading patterns; we shall deal at greater length with these further limitations.

The narrowness of nationalism or of race is familior, and most of us try to guard against it. We are less aware of and more vulnerable to another form of narrowness, the narrowness of time.

Present mindedness is, perhaps, the most difficult of all the limitations on history- our instinctive habit of looking at the past through our own eyes, judging it by our own standards, recreating it in our own words or reading back into the language of the past our own ..assuming that whatever happened, happened in some "past" and ...that every past was once a present. As that wise counselor, ... reminds us :

If we speak, we must speak with words; if we think we must think with thoughts. We are moderns, and our words and thoughts cannot but be modern. Perhaps ...it is too late for us to be early English. Every thought will be too sharp, every word will imply too many contrasts. We must, it is to be feared, used many words and qualify our every statement until we have almost contradicted it. ("Township and Borough.")

It is probable that we are, to a large degree, helpless in this matter; try as we will we cannot "think ourselves back into a twilight, "to use Maitland's wonderful phrase. We cannot really put ourselves inside the minds, or skins, of Cyrus, or Brutus, or Joan of Arc, or the Indian chief Pontiac. That we do try is a tribute to our historical conscience, and a few great histories and biographies are monuments to the fact that we are not always unsuccessful, though in the nature of the case we are not permitted to know even this. But the difficulty of present mindedness is really deeper. It is that we almost instinctively assume that the past was made just for us, that it is interesting only insofar as it caters to our current interests, and significant only when it has consequences for us. How easily we fall into what might be called the fallacy of "quaintness" the fallacy of supposing that Medieval People were medieval in their own eyes as well, or that Renaissance Man betrays us if he does not live up to our notion of what he should be, or that the Forefathers knew that they were Forefathers. How hard it is for us to realize that the past was as aeal to those who lived in it as the present is to us and that they no more lived for our edification than we live for the edification of distant future generations.

There is another danger implicit in present mindedness, one, again, which we cannot, in the nature of things, escape, but against which we must everlastingly guard ourselves. That is what we may call the danger of the fait accompli. We know what happened in history and because we know that the Athenian expedition to Syracuse is going to fail; that Rome will humble Carthage, and the Roman Republic change into an empire; that the Moslems will eventually be driven out of western Europe; that it is the English who will win the struggle for the American continent; that no matter how dark the outlook Washington will lead his ragged army to victory at Yorktown. We are, all of us, in the position of the reader of mystery stories who reads the last chapter first. But we should remember that we do not know how our own history is going to come out, and neither did earlier generations of men.

Our inability to divorce ourselves from knowing how history is going to come out almost guarantees that our view of the past will be near-sighted. We always read back into the past what we know occurred and adopt, a past hoc propter hoc attitude toward history. As Rome is bound to fall to the barbarian invaders we find explanations of that fall in the corruption and immorality of public life; as Britain is doomed to lose her American colonies, we accept Tom Painc's observation that it is absurd for a continent to belong to an island; as the Confederacy is predestined to defeat we confidently find the causes of that defnt. But if we adopt these positions, we render ourselves incapable of understanding the past in its own terms. As David Donald has said, historians are comp-followers of victorious armies. Knowing which side is going to win the Romans, the Union, the Atlantic powers they instinctively ally themselves with the winning side; they look for explanations of what triumphed and ignore the evidence on the other side. Some of them see the hand of God, of Progress, of Evolution, in whatever triumphed and whatever failed.

Nothing, surely, is more fatal to the integrity of historical investigation than the doctrine of inevitability implicit in this attitude. For if whatever happened in history was inevitable, whether because it expressed the will of God or the force of evolution or of progress, then there is little point in conducting any investigation whatsoever into the causes or the consequences of things. Felix qui potuit retum cognoscere causes, but if the causes of things re predestined, there is no happiness, and no value either. As Charles A. Beard warned us :

If all human affairs were reduced to law, to a kind of terrestrial mechanics, a chief end of the quest, that is, human control over human occurrences and actions, would itself become meaningless. Should mankind discover the law of its total historical unfolding, then it would be imprisoned in its own fate, and powerless to change it; the past, present and future could be revealed as fixed and beyond the reach of human choice and will. Men and women would be chained to their destinies as the stars and tide are to their routine. (The Open Door at Home, New York : The Macmillan Company, P. 14).

But, as far as we know, the course of history is not predestined. Life has always been, as it is now, "a roar of bargain and of battle", and the intellectual challenge to understand the past is no less compelling than the challenge to understand the present and the future. There is, to be sure, one sobering difference here. If we understand the present we may be able to command it, but there is no way by which we can command the past.

CHAPTER 7

Interpretation and BIAS

Let us admit at once that history is neither scientific nor mechanical, that the historian is human and therefore fallible, and that the ideal history, completely objective and dispassionate, is an illusion. There is bias in the choice of a subject, bias in the selection of material, bias in its organization and presentation, and, inevitably, bias in its interpretation. Consciously, or unconsciously, all historians are biased: they are creatures of their time, their race, their faith, their class, their country creatures, and even prisoners.

Most historians strive manfully to avoid bias and achieve objectivity when they teach or write history, but here have always been some who have accepted the fact of bias and tried to make a virtue of it. The famous German historian, Heinrich von Treitschke, represents the first attitude. Writing in 1865 he asserted that a "bloodless objectivity which does not say on which side is the narrator's heart, is the exact opposite of the true historical sense," and in his own many volumed History of Germany in the Nineteenth Century he left no one in doubt about what side his heart was no, or his mind and his temper either. The American Charles A. Beard represents the second attitude. "Any selection and arrangement of facts", he said in his address on "History as an Act of Faith", "pertaining to any large area of History, either local or world, race or class, is controlled inexorably by the frame of reference in the mind of the selector or arranger." As long as this was true, he concluded, it was only honorable for the historian frankly to acknowledge his "frame of reference" that is, his bias. And, as history is, inevitably, an instrument of propaganda, peace and progress, for justice and truth, and not for bad.

Piety the poor historian. He is the victim, the prisoner, or circumstances, or Nature and of human nature. Is he a modern man: then how will he ever understand medieval man ? Is he a European : can he ever really understand and do justice to the world of Asia and of Africa- or even of America ? Is he a white man : can he really understand the colored peoples who constitute three quarters of the human race ? Is he a Christian : can he do justice to the non-Christian ? Is he a Catholic : can he be fair to Protestants ? Is he a Protestant : can he be fair to the Papacy and the Inquisition ? It he and he almost certainly is a member of the middle or the upper classes, can he really understand the point of view of the workingman and the peasant ? Can a liberal like Macaulay do justice to the Stuarts ? Can a Marxist like Albert Mathiez do justice to the ancient regime or even to the Gironde ? Can a Republican like Albert Beveridge understand Jefferson or a Democrat like Claude Bowers understand Hamilton or a New Dealer like Arthur Schlesinger, Jr. , be fair to Herbert Hoover ? Can a Georgia gentleman like Ulrich B. Phillips ever really understand slavery ? can a Negro Marxist like W. E. B. Du Bois write dispassionately of slaveholders or of southern Bourbons ? Can and Englishman or an Irishman, a German or a Frenchman be expected to emancipate himself from his national predilections, and write history that gives no bint of national affiliations or loyalties ?

It was the hope of Lord Acton that a new generation of historians could answer all these questions in the affirmative. When, in 1896, he launched the co-operative Cambridge Modern History, he told potential contributors that "we shall avoid the needless utterance or opinion or service of a cause. Contributors will understand that our Waterloo must satisfy French and English, Germans and Dutch like; that nobody can tell, without examining the list of authors, where the Bishop or Oxford laid down the pen and whether Fairbairn or Gasquet, Liebermann or Harrison, took it up." But few historians have over really managed to live up to these austere standards; and it is doubtful whether Action did himself.

It is easy enough to discern bias in history, easy enough to recognize a great deal of what passes for history as propaganda of varying degrees of subtlety. Much of this propaganda does not rise to the dignity of history- the histories, put out by Nazi historians, designed to prove the superiority of the Aryan race and the virtue of Hitlerian Germany; the "new-think" put out by Communist historians to justify every turn and twist of Communist policy. But we should remember, too, that some of the most influential works of history have been propaganda : Clarendon's classic History or the Rebellion, for example, or the Abe Raynal's Philosophical History of the Indies- an "instrument of war" against the Church- or Frederic Masson's adulatory but learned biography of Napoleon, or Henry Wilson's Rise and Fall of the Slave Power in America. In our own day we can readily discern elements of propaganda, or partisanship, in such major works as Charles A. Beard's studies of American foreign policy between the wars, or Parrington's brilliant Main Currents of American Thought, or Winston Churchill's World Crisis, but we do not really think the worse of them for that.

Actually partisanship often adds zest to historical writing; for partisanship is an expression of interest and excitement and passion, and these can stir the reader as judiciousness might not. Certainly Macaulay lives, while Stubbs and Gardiner are read only by the specialists; Motley's thrilling story of the Rise of the Dutch Republic has inspired generations of readers with enthusiasm for liberty and detestation of tyranny which cannot be wholly misguided; Parrington, for all his faults, excites an interest in American literature that no other historian or critic has been able to equal; Winston Churchill's splendid tributes to English courage had consequences to history that no other histories of this century could match. As that immaculate historian

Lord Action himself observed, "the stronges and most impressive personalities.. project their own broad shadows upon their pages. This is a practice proper to great men, and a great man may be worth several immaculate historians."

Let us, then, not be too distressed that history is unscientific, partisan and hopelessly subjective; that is lends itself so readily to misrepresentation and even to propaganda; that it reflects, for better or for worse, the personality, the prejudices, the idiosyncrasies of historians. The subjectivity is inevitable; the partisanship is regrettable, it carries with it a kind of built-in discount; the idiosyncrasy is almost always interesting. And let us remember, too, that nothing which deals with human beings can approach scientific objectivity, that there is no wholly impartial justice, no wholly impartial political, economic, or social theory, no impartial education.

There is one bias, one prejudice, one obsession, so pervasive and so powerful that it deserves special consideration: nationalism. History, which should be the most cosmopolitan of studies, most catholic in its sympathies, most ecumenical in its interests, has, in the past century and a half, become an instrument of nationalism.

Nationalism is, no doubt, the most powerful force in modern history, and it is scarcely surprising that it should have captured historiography and enslaved historians. The historian no longer writes in a universal language latin for example, or, in the eighteenth century, French- but in the national vernacular; he adapts his history to a national framework, depend on national archives and similar sources for materials, and almost inevitably expresses a national point of view. In the eighteenth century the ardors of nationalism were moderated by rationalism and cosmopolitanism, and if such books as humc's England, Robertson's Scotland or Muller's Switzerland threw history a bit out of focus, they did no serious violence to historical truth. Very different was the nationalist history which came in, as on flood tide, with the French Revolution and napoleon, and with modern, chauvinistic, nationalism. The new history reflected national interests, prejudices, and passions or, worse, stimulated them. It is a far cry from the cool rationalism of Robertson's Scotland to the romantic lyricism of Michelot's France, the savage chauvinism of Treitschke's Germany, the patriotic passion of Francis Palacky's History of the Bohemian People, or even the ardent enthusiasm of George Bancroft's History of the United States.

Nationalism, as we know it, is both recent and parochial. It was invented by western Europeans- British, French, Germans and has flourished forless than 200 years. For historians to confuse it with universal history of as some do with the cosmic system, to read into it absolute values and absolute virtues, to identify themselves and truth passionately with one nation rather than another, is to betary history itself. It is to violate what should be the historical categorical imperative : never to subordinate the whole to the part, the prmanont to the transient, the end to the means.

Overt bias, such as that which responds to nationalism, is easy to detect and into difficult to discount. There is a more subtle form that present mindedness which we considered earlier. This is sometimes called the problem of nunc pro tunc : the now for the then, the present for the past. What point of view should the historian adopt when he deals with the past, or with societies and civilizations very different from his own ? Should he maintain hisown standards and values, or should he try to adopt the standards and values of the peoples and the age with which he is concerned ?

At first glance this problem seems easy enough : the right and proper thing to do it to adopt the measure and the standards of the era and the people we are trying to understand and to explain. How absurd, after all, to judge the Persians, or even the Egyptians or the Greeks, by the standards of modern England; how absured to judge the American Indian by the standards of eighteenth century Europe; how misguided to apply our own artistic standards to ancient China or India, our intellectual and scientific standards to the Middle Ages. No, let us rather enter into the minds and the spirits of the people we are studying. So said Ranke, and all those who, after him, developed what it is fashionable to call Historicism, Let us so immerse ourselves in the past that we can see with their eyes, hear with their cars, think as they thought, and feel as they must have felt: only by emancipating ourselves from the present and re-entering into the pastcan we be true to history; only by this renunciation of our own personalities canwe hope to recover the character of the past.

This ideal was hopefully advanced in a recent biography of the "Great American Preacher" Theodore Parker :

I have tried to know and to feel what Parker and his friends knew and felt, to accept the limitations of their minds, and, perhaps, of their characters. I have tried to see men and measures with Parkor's eyes, to react to the events of the time as he did, or as I think that he did. I have permitted Parker to act as he chose to act, to render such judgment as he wished to make, to love those friends whom he did love, and to disparage those persons whom he disliked, whether he was wise in all this, or unwise. Where he was wise in all this, or unwise. Where he was vain I have not sought to rebuilt his vanity, where he was inconsistent I have not thought it necessary to remark his inconsistency, where he was ungenerous I have not taken him to task, where he was violent I have not tried to abate him violence, where as was mistaken I have not attempted to set him right; all of these things he confessed in his own words and actions and they appear without my intervention (H. S. Commager, Theodore Parker, Boston : Little, Brown and Company, 1936, preface.)

Douglas Freeman,. the distinguished biographer of Robert E. Lee, attempted to achieve this goal by the somewhat mechanical method of limiting himself, quite rigorously, the knowing only what Lee Knew, and writing entirely within that framework of knowledge or of ignorance. Still another methods of recreating the past is that used by two mastes of intellectual history, the American, Van Wyck Brooks, and the Franclman, Paul hzard; it is the technique of literary intimacy. Here is Mr. Hazard describing the adventurers of the eighteenth century :

In those days no one would stop in one place. Here was Montesquieu, off on the search for political constitutions; diderot, after holding out against the idea for along time, at length made the journey to Russia. Then, one fine day, the youthful goldsmith resolves to set out for the Continent, and set out he does, without a penny to his name, with no one to fall back on in case of need, and with no definite itinerary in view. However, off he goes, playing his flute at cottage doors in the hope of getting, maybe, a bowl of soup or a shake-down in a barn. Holberg says good-bye to Denmark, and takes to the road, relying on his fine voice, as Goldsmith on his flute-playing, to get him along. On he goes, from country to country, learns French in Paris, and teaches it at Oxford. He was not a man to be baulked by trifles. All these inquiring gentlemen, indeed, are as mobile as can be, and they are never satisfied, they've never seen enough. Exile brings them no repining. They don't mind knocking at strange doors, and the bread of the stranger leaves no bitterness in the mouth. Tossed by fate far beyond their native land, they profit by the occasion to improve their knowledge and shape their minds anew. Voltaire has no bad time of it in London...Nor does the Abbe Prevost fare so badly in Holland. Anyhow, that's where he sows this wild oats, and pretty plentifully, withal ...And Bolingbroke soon made himself at home as a noble lord of France, with his mansion and his ornamental gardens. he gathers a flowing about him, and wields the intellectual scepre. Wincklemann finds his spiritual home in Italy. Look at the host of persecuted philosophers that crowded around Frederick in Berlin. No fugitives craving sanctuary, these; no more exiles; now we call them cosmopolites. (European thought in the Eighteenth Century, London : Hollis and Carter, 1954, Pp. 249-250)

This is all admirable, but does it really cable us to recapture the past ? We may believe that we can think as therefore Parke thought, o know only what General Lee knew, or live and feel with the philosophers, but perhaps we fool ourselves.

For when we turn to the past and use the literature or the monuments of the past as a means of ontering into its mind and spirit, how do we know that we have chosen correctly ?The philosophers whom Hazard celebrates left an immense and entrancing literature, but did they really speak for France or for Germany in the eighteenth century ? The Abolitionists of New England were incomparably articulate, but they were few in number and of feeble influence; they speak for themselves, to be sure, but do they speak for New England ? We can, of course, confine ourselves to single individuals; we can spend a lifetime immersing ourselves in the writings of Jofferson of Edmund Burke or Napoleon until we come, at last, to think as these men thought. Ah, but do we ? How odes it happen that men who have in fact spent a lifetime with these figures come up with such different reports ?

We can doubtless do quite well in understanding the past where the literature is voluminous, where the society is familiar, and where the past is recent. But what shall we say of the attempt to enter into the minds and thoughts of a distant or unfamiliar past of the Spartans, for example, who differed so profoundly from the Athenians; or the Aztecs or the Incas whose records are fragmentary; of the Dances who invaded and harried England in the ninth century ? Perhaps we can manage to understand Jefferson or Burke; can we manage to understand the Persian Cyrus, or Eric the Red ?

There are many things to be said for accepting our limitations and looking at the past through the eyes of the present, but this is the most persuasive : no matter how hard we try, that is what we do anyway. We see the past through our own eyes, translate its language into our own, find interesting the things that interest us, and find significant the events that have had consequences for us. All this helps explain why each generation rewrites the history of the past : the view depends upon the point of view.

There is a final commentary on what is called Historicism. Even those who are most anxious to avoid imposing their own standards on the past and strive most sincerely to see the past in its own storms are tempted to make one exception to their principle. That is in the realm of moral judgment. Let us not force the past into the straitjacket of the present, they say, but at the same time let us not suspend the cternal rules of right and wrong.

And this brings us to the troublesome problem of moral judgment in history.

CHAPTER 8

History as Law and as Philosophy

THE USE OF HISTORY

We are acquainted with the young man who earnestly assures us, with a mixture of vanity and zeal, that he has always "hated history." It is all dates, he tells us, or it is all a lot of rather tiresome problems- the problem of the "fall" of Rome, the problem of the French Revolution, the problem of Secession and Civil War. And it never gets you anywhere; you are no better off when you have finished than when you began.

Some of this attitude may be confidently set down to poor and uninspiring teaching-teaching which never challenged the interest nor excited the imagination of students. Some of it-perhaps a good deal may be put down to the same kind of uninspired teaching embodied in textbooks in which the authors try to please everybody, avoid the "controversial," ignore the dramatic, concentrate on problems which are never solved or whose solution is of no interest, and , like so may of the novels and drams of our time eschew narrative and leave out heroes and villains. Some of it can be ascribed to the drama of the past. In all likelihood he is one of those of whom Wordsworth wrote:

A primrose by the river's brim,
A yellow primrose was to him,
And it was nothing more.

But after we have done all this explaining, there remains

a stubborn residuum of intelligent and open-minded students who still find nothing to nourish them in history. They may agree with Gibbon that history is "the register of the follies and misfortunes of mankind," or with Napoleon that it is a "lie agreed upon," or with Carlyle that it is "a great dustheap," and they do not stop to read those marvelous volumes in which Gibbom recorded the "follies and misfortunes" of man, or discover how Carlyle proved that history was charged with life and passion, nor are they excited by the challenge to separate truth from lies about Napoleon himself.

What are we to say to all this? Why should the young study history Why should their elders read history, or write it?

That is a question which recurs again and again: What use is history? Let us admit at once that in practical way history has no use, let us concede that it is not good for anything that can be weighed, measured, or counted. It will not solve problems; it will not avoid wars, or how to win them; it will not provide scientific explanations of depressions or leys to prosperity; it will not contribute in any overt way to progress.

But the same can be said, of course, of many other things which society values and which men cherish. What use, after al, is a Mozart sonata or a painting by Renoir, or a statue by Milles? What use is the cathedral of Siena or the rose windows of Chartres or novel by Flaubert or a sonnet by Wordsworth? What use, for that matter, are a great many mundane things which society takes for granted and on which it lavishes thought and effort; a baseball game, for example, or a rose garden, or a brocade dress, or a bottle of port?

Happily, a civilized society does not devote all of its thought and effort to things whose usefulness can be statistically demonstrated. There are other criteria than of usefulness, and other meanings to the term "useful" than those acknowledged by the Thomas Gradgrinds of this World.

History, we can confidently assert, is useful in the sense

that art and music, poetry and flowers, religion and philosophy are useful. Without it-as without these-life would be poorer and meaner; without it we should be denied some of those intellectual and moral experiences which give meaning and richness to life. Surely it is no accident that the study of history has been the solace of many of the noblest minds of every generation.

The first and doubtless the richest pleasure of history is that it adds new dimensions to life itself, enormously extending our perspective and enlarging our experience. It permits us to enter vicariously into the past, to project our vision back over thousands of years and enlarge it to embrace all the races of mankind. Through the pages of history we can hear pedicles deliver his Funeral oration, look with wonder as Scipio and Hannibal lock forces ten that desperate field of Zama, trek with the crusaders to the Holy land, sail with Columbus past the gates of Hercules and to a new world, sit with Diderot as he edits the Encyclopedia, share the life of Goethe and Schiller at the little court of Weimar, stand and listen to those stirring debates in those dusty prairie towns which sent Douglas to the Senate and Lincoln to the White House, share the agony of general Lee as he surrenders the Army of Northern Virginia at McLean's Court House, stand beside Winston Churchill as he rallies the people of Britain to their finest hour. History supplies to us all those elements which Henry jams thought essential to the knife of the mind: density, variety, intricacy, richness, in the pattern of thought and of action and with it "the sense of the past."

This immense enlargement of experience means, of course, that history provides us with great companions on our journey through life. This is so familiar a consideration that it needs no collaboration. Wherever the historian or biographer has been, he has given new depth and range to our associations. We have but to take down the books and we are admitted to the confidence of Voltaric and Rousseau, Johnson and Boswell, Thomas Jefferson and John Adams, Justice Holmes and William James. We can know them with more of an intimacy than their contemporaries knew them, for we can read their letters, journals and diaries. This is not just one of the pleasures of history, it is one of the indispensable pleasures of life.

A third, and familiar, pleasure of history is the experience of identifying the present with the past, and thus adding a new dimension to places and events. It was Macaulay who observed that "the pleasure of History is analogous in many respects to that produced by foreign travel. The student is transported into a new state of society. He sees new fashions. He bears new modes of expression. His mind is enlarged by contemplating the wide diversities of laws, of morals, and of manners." George Macaulay Trevelyan-himself a grand-nephew of Macaulay-has conjured up this pleasure for us in one of his most glowing passages:

Places, like books, have an interest of a beauty of association, as well as an absolute or aesthetic beauty. The garden front of St. John's Oxford, is beautiful to everyone; but for the lover of history its outward charm is blent with the intimate feelings of his own mind, with images of that same college as it was during the Great Civil War. Given over to the use f a Court whose days of royalty were numbered, its walks and learning to accept sorrow as their lot through life, the ambitious abandoning hope of power, the wealthy hardening themselves to embrace poverty, those who loved England preparing to sail for foreign shores, and lovers to be parted forever. There they strolled through the garden, as the hopeless evening fell, listenning, at the end of all, while the siege guns broke the silence with ominous iteration. Behind the cannon on those low hills to northward were ranked the inexorable men who came to lay their hands on all this beauty, hoping to change it to strength and sterner virtue. And this was the curse of the victors, not to die, but to live, and almost to lose their awful faith in god, when they saw the Restoration not of the old gaiety, that was too gay for them, and the old loyalty that was too loyal for them, but of corruption and selfishness that had neither country nor kind. The sound of the Roundhead cannon has long ago died away died away, but still the silence of the garden is heavy with unalterable fate, brooding over besiegers and besieged, in such haste to destroy each other and permit only the vile to survive. St. John's College is not mere stone and mortar, tastefully compiled, but an appropriate and mournful witness between those who see it now and those by whom it once was seen. (Clio, A muse and Other Essays, New York, 1913,p.26.)

Everyone who has visited historic towns, in the old world or the New, knows that when he looks at them through the eyes of history they cease to be museum pieces and pulse with life and with vigor. Nestling between its ancient hills, bisected by the gleaming Arno, its domes and towers piercing the skies, Florence is beautiful to the eyes of even the purblind . But how it springs into life when we people its piazzas and narrow streets with the men and women o the past: when we conjure up the spectacle of Savonarola burned at the stake in the great piazza deal Signori where the mighty David now stands: Bruneleschi cresting the giant Duomo: Ghiberti carving the great bronze doors of the Baptistery, a lifetime work, this: Giotto and Fra Filippo Lippi and Raphael and Leonardo and Michelangelo painting those pictures which now hang in such lavish profusion from the glittering walls of the Uffizi and the pitti palaces: Machiavelli pondering the history of the condottieri while he writes the Prince, and Galileo seeing a new universe through his telescope and opening up a new universe of the mines as well. Did ever a city boast a comparable galaxy of genus; did ever a city publish itself more generously in its monuments, or impress itself more richly on the mind?

Nor is it only the great centers of art and letters, like Florence or Venice or Salzburg, that take on new dimensions when seen through the eyes of the history; the same miracle transforms even the most modest of towns. Henry James observed, somewhat condescendingly, that Emerson had "dwelt for fifty years within the undecorated walls of his youth"; but to Emerson those rooms were redolent of the past, as was the little village of Concord. And as for

Hawthorn, how, wrote James, Could he have found materials for his stories, living where he did, where "the coldness, the thimess, the blankness..present themselves so looking for subjects in such a field," But Hawthorne himself looked out of his attic window on a Salem rich in history and tradition and found in it the ingredients for The Scarlet Letter and The House of Seven Gables, and a dozen other stories that are a precious part of our literature.

Consider the little town of Salem in Massach32usetts, now no more than a suburb of Boston. It is a lovely town in its own right, there by the sea and the rocks, its handsome old houses still standing sedately along Chestnut and Federal streets, As we look at it through the eyes of history we conjure up a straggling village busy with fishing and with theological disputes and remember that Roger Williams preached here those heresies which brought him banishment from the Bay Colony, and so too Mistress Anne Hutchinson. We look at Gallows Hill and recall the dark and terrifying story of Salem witchcraft which haunted Nathaniel Hawthorne, who grew up here, and whose sprit still broods over the town. We recreate it in its heyday, when its captains sailed all the waters of the globe and its flag was thought o be the flag of an independent nation, and the splils and rewards of the Chins trade glittered in every drawing room. For at the turn of the century Salem was like one of the famous city states of Italy-Florence or Venice of Pisa. It had its own architects. like Samuel Mcintyre who built the stately mansions of the sea captains and the merchant princes, mansions which still stand; its own preachers, like the famous William Bentley of the East Church, reputed to be the most learned man in America; its own jurists, like Samuel Puttnam and Samuel Sewall who became Chief Justices of the Commonwealth, and Joseph Story who joined the Surpreme Court of the United Sattes at thirty-two. Samuel Bowditch was a boy here, watching the sailing ships come in to India wharf and learning celestial mathematical and navigation from a library which had been captured from a British ship during the war for Independence; he sailed on a Salem merchantman, and grew up to write the practical Navigator. So was George Crowninshield who built the magnificent Cleopatra's Barge and sailed it through the Mediterranean, and the dour Timothy Pickering who lived in the oldest house in town-which still stands-and grew up to be the most reactionary politician in the country; so too the astonishing Benjamin Thompson who grew up to be Count Rumford of the Holy Roman Empire and to live in state in Munich and found the Royal Institution in London, and so too William Prescott who played as a boy along India Wharf and Derby Wharf. and swam in the cold waters of the harbor and picnicked on Hog Island, and who became the historian of Mexico and of Peru-Then another generation, and Salem entered its long decline, its harbors silted up and its wharfs falling into decay and grass growing up between the cobblestones of its ancient streets, while the paint peeled off the proud Mcintyre house. It is all there-in Nathaniel Hawthorne's stories, in the reminiscences of Joseph Story and Rufus Choate, in the historical romances by Joseph Hergesheimer and Esther Forbes, so faithful to the spirit and the reality of the old town-all there for us to recapture through the pages of history.

Needless to say , all this makes great demands upon the imagination' the imagination of the historian and of the student alike. "At bottom," George Macaulay Trevelyan has said," the appeal of history is imaginative," and be gives us, as an example of this, one of Carlyle's recreations of the past-it is in his essay on Boswell's Johnson:

Rough Samuel and sleek wheedling James were, and are not, their life and whole personal environment has melted into air. The Mitre Tavern still stands in Fleet Street; but where now is its scot-and-lot pay beef-and -ale loving, cocked-hatted, pot-bellied Landlord; its rosy faced assiduous Landlady, with all her shining brass-pans, waxed tables well-filled larder-shelves; her cooks and boot jacks, and errand boys and watery-mouthed hangers-on? Gone! Gone! The becking waiter, who, with wreathed smiles, was wont to spread for Samuel and Bozzy their supper of the gods, his long since pocketed his last sixpence; and vanished, sixpences and all, like a ghost at cock-crowing. The Bottles they drank out of are all broken, the Chairs they sat on all rotted and burnt; the very knives and Forks they ate with have rusted to the heart, and become brown oxide of iron, and mingled with the indiscriminate clay. All, all has vanished; in very deed and truth, like that baseless fabric of Prospero's air-vision. of the Mitre Tavern nothing but the bare walls remain there; of London, of England, of the World, nothing but the bare walls remain; and these also decaying (where they of adamant), only slower. The Mysterious River of Existence rushes on; a new Billow there of has arrived, and lashes wildly as ever round the old embankments; but the former Billow with its loud, mad eddying, where is it?-Where?-

Now this Book of Boswell's, this is precisely a revocation of the edict of Destiny; so that Time shall not utterly, not so soon by several centuries, have dominion over us. (critical Essays, p.4.)

A dangerous thing, this, for once we introduce the element of imagination we imperil the integrity of the historical record. yet how can we possibly exclude it? what is history, after all, without imagination? Imagination comes to our aid at every moment; it is what permits us to clothe the bare bones of history with life. It throws a glow over the most impersonal, the dullest, of the data of history. It infuses even a statistical table with color and life; who can read the statistical of the population growth of the western territories and states of the United States in the nineteenth century without seeing, in his mind's eye, the Conestoga wagon, and the canal boats on the Eric canal, the railroad puffing its way across the Appalachians, weather-beaten men their wives and children and cattle, beating out a trail to Oregon or to the Mormon utopia at the Great Salt Lake?

Imagination brings home to us that the names in the history books represent real people, that the decisions which were made involved the same fears and hopes and uncertainties and courage as those which we ourselves make that latimer at the stake and Lord Nelson at Trafalgar

Suffered the same agonies and exaltations which we ourselves experience, that to a man like Robert E. Lee the decision to stay with his state was no abstract "problem" of secession, but just such a spiritual and moral crisis as would plunge us into despair if we confronted it today. Alas, many historians are like the preacher of whom Emerson writes:

A snow-storm was falling around us. The snow-storm was real, the preacher merely spectral, and the eye felt the sad contrast in looking at him, and then, out of the window behind him into the beautiful meteor of the snow, He had lived in vain, he had no one word intimating that he had laughed or wept, was married or in love, had been commended, or cheated, or chagrined. If he had ever lived and acted, we were none the wiser for it .The capital secret of his profession, namely to convert life into truth, he has not learned...This man had ploughed and planted and talked and bought and sold; he had read books; he had eaten and drunken; his bead aches, his heart throbs; he smiles and suffers; yet was there not aches, his heart throbs; he smiles and suffers; yet was there not a surmise, a hint, in all the discourse, that he had ever lived at all. (Divinity School Address, July 15,1838.)

It might be thought that imagination like-let us say- an ear for music, is something you either have or have not. If you have it, well and good; if not, there is nothing to be done about it. But the imagination, like a taste for music, or for [painting, an be cultivated. How can the historical imagination be cultivated? It can be cultivated thought drama and poetry. Shakespeare suffused? It can be cultivated through drama and poetry. Shakespeare suffused the stuff of history with his glorious imagination; no wonder Winston Churchill said that he had learned all of his English history out of Shakespeare! How history comes alive in the novels of Walter Scott-such varied historians as Prescott and Carlyle and Trevelyan have acknowledged his historian as Prescott and Carlylw ant Trevelyan have acknowledged his inspiration. With what insight does Wordsworth read its moral lessons, in the sonnet "On the Extinction of the Venetian Republic," for example, or in "To Toussaint L,Ouverture," or in The prelude. Imagination can be cultivated, too, by the study of art and architecture. Who can wander through the National portrait Gallery in London and not feel stirred by the spectacle of these men and women who have made England; how exhilarating to visit such great Palladian palaces as the Villa Rotonda and the Villa Malcontenta outside Vicenz, and to see Jefferson's Monticello emerge out of these models.

This does not exhaust the pleasures of history; they are, indeed, inexhaustible. We may, without too gross and impropriety paraphrase Dr. johnson's observation on London, that anyone who is tired of history is tired of life.

Can we go beyond the pleasures of history to Laws of history, or even to the philosophy of History? That all depends on what you mean by "laws" and by "philosophy."

CAUSATION IN HISTORY

One of the liveliest pleasures of history is that, more continuously and more persuasively that almost any other study, it nourishes and enlists the reflective faculties. nowhere are those faculties more busily engaged than in seeking for causes.

"Happy is he who knows the causes of things." But if this is true then it can be said that historians are forever pursuing happiness, but never quite attaining it. The search for the causes of things is, and has long been, the chief preoccupation of thoughtful historian what happened; he wants to explain why it happened. Off all problems of history. causation so the most urgent, the most fascinating, and the most baffling.

Why did history turn out the way it did ? Why were the Chinese ahead of the West in civilization; why did civilization flourish so spectacularly in Greece at a time when most of Europe was lost in what we think of as barbarism; why were Europeans so far in advance of Americans for so many centuries? Why did the Roman Empire "Decline and fall"; why were the Moslems able to conquer so much of Europe, and why did Moslem power ebb? what explains the amazing vitality of the caking and then of the Norsemen who swarmed over seas and over land. and carried their culture to the shores of Ireland and France and Sicily, and then fell back into obscurity? How did to happen that a little fog-bound island off the north coast of Europe came to be one of the greatest of world powers, and that the English language-of all unlikely languages-came to be spoken from London to Singapore and from Toronto to the Cape of Good Hope? Why did the American colonies break away from the Mother Country, and why were they American colonies break away from the Mother Country, and why were they successful in their reclusion; why did the Southern States break way from the American Union had why was their resolution unsuccessful? why did British American become two great countries, while Latin America fragmented into more that twenty? why do only English-speaking peoples have a two-party system while all others have a one-or a multi-party syatem ? what caused the two great wars of the twentieth century; what explain the spread and the triumphs of Communism? How explain the change in styles, from classical to romantic from age to age- the changing attitude forwards slavery, for example, or towards child labor, or towards sex?

For over two thousand years philosophers and historian have tried to answer these and similar questions about course of history, though it is only in the last two or there centuries that the inquiry has been both open-minded and independent. Socrates. in one of the most famous of his discourses, asserted the validity of inquiry: "That we shall be better and braver and less helpless if we think that we ought to enquire that we should have been if we indulged in the idle fancy that there was no knowing and no use in seeking to know what we do not know- that is a theme upon which I am ready to fight in word and deed to the utmost of my power."

yet most ancient historians did, in fact, indulge in something very like "idle fancy." The great Greek and Roman historians rarely inquired into the caused of things; it was enough for them that whatever happened was bound to happen, that it was all in the hands of the gods of fate:

The things men looked for cometh not,
And a path there is where no man thought-
So hath it fallen here.

Even so great an historian as Thucydides does not seek the deeper causes of the Peloponnesian War or the defend of Athens, nor does a moralist like Plutarch inquire into the explanation for the virtues and the vices which he describes.

Christian historians, too, had an easy time of it. Everything that happened in history, from the sparrow that fell to the earth to the fall of empires, had a cause: I it was all the working out of a divine plan. St. Augustine had made this clear, once and for all, in The City of God, and thereafter it was accepted without serious question. It is hard for us to realize, now, how this simplistic theory dominated historical thinking for more than a thousand years, how it persisted, even, well past the Renaissance and Reformation and down to the Age of Reason. Thus is was in the seventeenth century that the great French historian, Jacques Dossuct prepared his Discourse on universal History to demonstrate that the whole course of history was but the working out of a divine plan which happened, also, to be the plan of the catholic popes. And at almost the same time, Bossuet's American contemporary, Edward Johnson, explained the planting of the Bay Colony under the title The Wonder-Working providence of Sion's Saviour in new England. Or consider the great debate over the meaning and the explanation of America which raged from the fifteenth to the eighteenth centuries. How explain the New World? How explain its primitive state, the backwardness of its native races , the absence of organized society, or government? Every historian and philosopher who addressed himself to this problem started with the Flood, postulating for the New World a later Flood or a greater Flood, postulating for the New World a later Flood or a greater Food or a series of Floods; all, too, with few exceptions, took for granted that mankind in every continent was descended from a common set of ancestors , Adam and Eve.

The mental habit of ascribing historical events, great and

small, to the caprice of the gods or to the inscrutable will of god, persisted even into the eighteenth century; thus the popularity of Cyclical theories of history or of what might be called the "ebb and flow" theory, as illustrated by The Grandeur and Decadence of Rome, or the Decline and Fall of the Roman Empire, Westward the Star of Empire, and other books with titles of a like nature. So, too, did the habit of acknowledging the authority of impersonal law, only now it was secular, not divine law, now it was "the law of Nature" as well as of "Nature's God." This was the Newtonian theory applied to the affairs of men, and it had the immense advantage of making history not only a secular but a rational affair. soon all the historians and philosophers were explaining history in terms of Nature, and in one way of another this has persisted sown to our own time. The eighteenth century concept of nature and Nature's law was, however, very different from ours; Nature was orderly, rational, and, in a curious way, anthropocentric. The universe, as men knew it, was ruled by Law that operated harmoniously and implacably, like some great universal law. Oddly enough this did not turn out to be deterministic in any malign sense. For the laws which controlled the universe were harmonious and rational. For the laws which controlled the universe were harmonious and rational. That meant that they applied to society and government as well as to the courses of the stars or the ebb and ebb flow of the tides, and it meant that they could be apprehended and adopted by the reason of man. If men could but confront to these laws of Nature instead of ignoring them of flouting them, the miseries and agonies that has so long afflicted man would disappear, and peace, prosperity, and progress would usher ion a millenium.

Curiously enough, though the faith in reason evaporated, reliançe on Force persisted in a more sophisticated from down to our own tome. Montesquieu had argued the importance of "climate" in history-a term which he used much as we would use the term "environment," and since his day climate or geography has been one of the most popular of all explanations of history. The Abbe Raynal used it to explain the backwardness of the Americas; and after him a host of scholars and scientists as diverse as Alexander von Humboldt and Henry T. Buckle, Richard Green and Friedrich Raetzel, Frederick Jackson Turner and Brooks Adams celebrated the predominant role of climate and geography in guiding the destinies of man. But climate and geography were by no means the only impersonal forces which won the allegiance of historians. Karl Marx founded a school of history, and not o history alone, which interpreted most of the activities and ideas of men in terms of economic interests and force. Admiral Mahan worshipped sea power as a kind of brooding omniscience in history; Henry Adams insisted quite simply on force-first-and for many centuries- the force of religion, then, in modern times, coal, steam, and electricity as symbolized in the dynamo. "The historians' business," wrote Henry Adams," was to follow the back of energy" wherever it led, and that is what he did, until he came at last to radium and to atomic power. "power leaped from every atom, and enough of it to supply the stellar universe showed itself running to waste at every pore of mater. Man could mo longer hold to off. Forces grasped his wrist and flung him about as though he has hold of a live wire." (The Education of Henry Adams, p. 494.)

The "forces of the stellar universe" were impersonal and aimless; if history was indeed controlled by such forces, there was no possibility of reducing it to law-just what Adams concluded when he somewhat perversely hit upon the law of the dissipation of energy as the sovereign law of history. But the eighteenth century had invented and the nineteenth had perfected a new and more benign force. progress was the new idea and the new force; progress first within the framework of Natural Law and then within the framework of Evolution. Turgot had announced it in a memorable address in 1750; the Encyclopaedists had embraced it, and with Conduced it became well-nigh official. We are all children of the age of progress, all heirs to the belief that

through the ages one increasing purpose runs,

And the thoughts of men are widened with the process of the suns,

(Tennyson, "Locksley Hall")

and it is unnecessary to elaborate upon anything so familiar.

The doctrine of progress was confirmed by faith rather than by observation , and sometimes-as Voltaire made clear in Candide or Dr.johnson in Rasselas-faith gave way to scepticism. It lacked historical support-had there really been progress in the oldest societies such as China or Egypt or Greece?-and it lacked scientific support, as well. How fortunate, then that the doctrine of evolution appeared to provide it with the strongest scientific support, a t least the doctrine of evolution according to herbert Spencer. For Spencer made Clear that the great, transcendent laws of organic evolution which regulated the animal world, regulated the world of man as well. As evolution assured the survival of the fittest in the world of Nature, so it guaranteed that man, too, would progress towards perfection by the elimination of all imperfections. "progress is not an accident," said Spencer, "but a necessity. It is a part of Nature." And his American disciple, John Fiske, wrote raptly that "The creation of man is the goal towards which Nature tended from the beginning. Not the production of any higher creature, but the perfecting of Humanity, is to be the glorious consummation of nature's long and tedious work."

All this was gratifying enough, but as an explanation of history it was not very helpful. For to be told, when we ask Rome declined, or why the Spanish Armada foundered, or why the Confederacy lost the Civil War, that it was all in harmony with the law of progress, or that it was part of Evolution, leaves us pretty much where we were in the beginning. Granted progress, granted evolution, why should they manifest themselves in one way rather than in another? Was the decline of the Roman Empire progress? Is it certain that Britain and not Spain was destined to be the beneficiary of the evolutionary process?

No, the search for an explanation could not be satisfied

that easily. If we were to explain the past, if we were to predict the future, we needed something at once more rigorous and more specific than the windy doctrine of progress or the impersonal doctrine of evolution. Mathematics, biology, chemistry, physics, these things had provided laws which explained so much that had heretofore been mysterious; surely history, too, could provide laws which would explain the past and illuminate the future. So said Auguste Comte, in France, who worked out an elaborate scheme of the social sciences; so said Herbert Spencer in England, who created a science of society on the basis of biology and anthropology and psychology, so said the American john Fiske whose outlines of Comic philosophy drew on the whole body of social and philosophical thought to find the laws which regulated the moral world, and whose many histories proved that these laws had operated in America from the beginning. Other social sciences boasted laws-Malthus' law of population growth, Gresham's law in ensconces, Ferdinand LaSalle's law of wages, Henry Buckle's law of geography, which was "one glorious principle of universal and undeviating regularity"-why should not history, too, have her laws?

LAWS IN HISTORY

"Four out of five students who are living today," wrote Henry Adams some sixty years ago,

> have, in the course of their work, felt that they stood on the brink of a great generalization that would reduce history under a law as clear as the laws which govern the material world...He seemed to have it, as the Spanish say, in his ink stand. Scores of times he must have it, as the Spanish say, in his ink stand. scores of times he must have dropped his pen to think how one short step, one sudden inspiration, would show al human knowledge; how in these thickest forests of history, one corner turned, one faint trail struck, would bring him on the high road of science.

Alas, when Adams himself hit on a law-it was the law of entropy, or the degradation of energy-it did not clear a way through thickest forests, but put up a permanent barrier to further historical research. Twenty years later Edward p. Cheyney sounded the same note:

I look forward /he said in his presidential Address to the American historical Association in 1923/ to some future meeting of this Association when the search for the laws of History and their application will have become the principal part of their procedure..The most conspicuous part on the program will be assigned to some g9ifted young historical thinker who, quite properly disregarding the earlier and rude efforts of his predecessors, will propound and demonstrate to the satisfaction of all his colleagues, some new and far-reaching law or laws of history.

Alas, again, for human hopes; forty years later the sessions of the Historical Association were given over almost exclusively to "technical history," and philosophical speculations were looked upon with disfavor.

Professor Cheyney himself propounded six "laws of history" and it may be useful to recite them, foe they reveal, as well as anything of their kind, some of the difficulties inherent in the formulation of such laws. They are: 1. The law of continuity; 2. The law of mutability: 3. The law of interdependence; 4. The law of democracy; 5. The law of the necessity for free consent; 6. The law of moral progress. Now it can be said of these-as of almost every attempt to formulate laws of history-the either they do not deal with history, but with life in general, or that they are not laws but expressions of hope and of faith. Take, for example, Cheymey's law of continuity. If this means that we have constructed an historical chronology and that in this chronology one event appears to follow another, then it is valid but meaningless. If it means that everything that happens grows out of some antecedent. If it means that everything that happens grows out of some antecedent cause which we can discover, then it is not so. The voyages of Columbus and the discovery of America doubtless grew out of a omplez of antecedent causes which yield a logical pattern, but can it be said that the destruction of the Azrec and the Inca empires grew out of recognizable causes and followed a pattern which the natives of Mexico and Peru would have regarded as logical? Scholars who trace the history of Negro slavery ion America construct a neat and logical pattern which almost makes us think that slavery was inevitable, but is there a comparable logic which would persuade Africans kidnapped and transported to America that slavery was inevitable for them? One manor trouble with the principle of continuity and of causation is that it assumes a single line of continuity, a single chain of cause, instead of a hundred or a thousand.

Or consider Cheyney's law of mutability: it is a law is permanent in history. But that is not a law of history, it is a law of life, and poets and moralists had proclaimed it more than two thousand years before Cheyney took it over for history. what is important- amt what the historian wants to know-is that some things appear to be more permanent than others. Which seem to be more permanent, and why? To this urgent question the law of mutability says nothing. it is as if we should submit, as a "law" of history, that all men are mortal and that all flesh is grass.

And what of Cheyney's other laws-democracy, morality? clearly these are the formulations of a Victorian liberal. How many Chinese or Russian historians would subscribe to the "law" of democracy; how many american Negroes would subscribe to the "law" of liberty; how many German Jews would endorse the "law" of moral progress, or for that matter how many of the survivors of Hiroshima or of Dresden?

Confronted by the seemingly insuperable difficulty of formulating laws or solving the problems of causation. some historians have thrown in the sponge, as it were, and taken refuge in the principle of fortuity. Thus H.A.L. Fisher, whose History of Europe is something of a classic, confessed in his preface to that work that:

One intellectual excitement has been denied me. Men wiser and more learned than I have discovered in history a plot, a rhythm, a predetermined pattern. these harmonies are concealed from me. I can see only one emergency following upon another as wave follows upon see only one emergency following upon another as wave follows upon wave; only one great fact with respect to which, since it is unique, there can be no generalizations; only one safe rule for the historian: that he should recognize in the development of human destinies the play of the contingent and the unforeseen. (preface to A History of Europe, Boston: Houghton Mifflin Company, 1935-36.) In its most uncomplicated form this becomes the "Cleopatra's nose" theory of history first stated by no other than Blaise Pascal: "Had Cleopatra's nose been shorter, the whole face of the earth would have been different." Voltaire embraced the same theory and so too did his friends Frederick the Great: "The older one becomes, the more clearly one sees that king Hazard fashions three-fourths of the events in this miserable world."

"The passion for tidiness," Arthur Schlesinger, Jr., has written, "Is the historian's occupational disease." It is, indeed, though we should add in all fairness that it is a kind of historical necessity, as well. organization always does some violence to the stream of thought or the chaos of conduct that is life- the organization of melody into music, the organization of color into painting, the organization of inspiration into poetry, and of ideas into philosophy, and the organization of facts into history. Granted that history is a record of disorderly conduct; it does not follow that it is to be reported in a disorderedly fashion, and it is the mark of a great judge that he is able to bring order and coherence out of conflicting evidence and arguments. History is a jangle of accidents, blunders, surprises and absurdities, and so is our knowledge f it, but if we are to report it at all we must impose some order upon it, Literature is able to compensate for this necessity by falling back on the "stream of consciousness" technique, but history cannot do this.

The danger is that in tidying up history the historian will convey the impression (he may even convince himself) that everything was tidy from the beginning. A battle, for example, is often a nightmare of blunder and confusion; then the historian comes along and tidies it all up, tells us just how the battle was planned, how the center struck at this moment and the left flank moved in next, how the artillery joined in, or the cavalry charged, and there is your victory, all nicely explained. Or he looks back upon a diplomatic incident, or upon an election, and explains it all very neatly, leaving out all the contingencies, all the unforeseen events, all the hesitations and fears and confusions. He presents us with the logic of some historical <u>fait accompli</u> -the Monroe Doctrine, or the open Door policy, or Truman's point Four, and we can indeed of point Four, that it was all a series of accidents, and that far from being a deliberate policy it came even to president Truman himself as a happy surprise.

But while we must avoid assuming that history is a kind of chess game with every gambit logical and planned, we must avoid, equally, the other extreme, that of ascribing everything to accident or luck; we must avoid giving too much prominence to untidiness and disorder. For disorder is, in a since, itself orderly; it is at once a principle of life and a rule of life. Birth is a very disorderly business, but we forget the disorder (or assume that it is taken for granted) and celebrate the birthday. The whole of life is disorderly- our growing-up, our education, our falling in love, our jobs or careers, our relations with friends or enemies. Our societies are disorderly- physically disorderly in their cities, institutionally disorderly in their economies, their polities, their social relationships. Intelligence tries to bring order out of all of this, and thereby to decrease the disorder, or to master it. So, too, in history, the intelligence of the historian is directed to bringing some order out of the chaos of the past.

And there is too, a further and consoling consideration, that though accidents often change the pace or the pattern of history, they rarely change it in any fundamental way. for the sophisticated historian remembers what is, after al, the common sense of the matter, that there are always enough accidents to go around at a football game knows that there are enough fumbles to go around and that a particular fumble rarely changes the course of a game, or of a season of games.

It is immature and almost perverse to assign too much importance to what we denominate the accidents of history, The wind scattered the Spanish Armasa helped the English sedtroy it, but that was not the reason why Spain failed to conquer England; Sjpain had never conquered England, wind or no wind, nor had any other power. Washington surprised the Hessians at Trenton on Christmas of 1776, and the American cause looked up; but that was not the reason the Americans finally won their independence. Even had the Hessian repulsed Washington's ragged troops the Americans would, in al likelihood, have won sooner or later. A federal soldier picked up Lee's plan of battle for Antietam and took it to McClellan; that was not the reason Lee lost the battle of Antietam or the Confederacy lost the war Even had Lee won the bayyle of Antietam it is highly improbable that the Confederacy would have won the war. president Wilson suffered a fateful breakdown on his train outside Wichita, Kansas, in the midst of his crusade for the ratification of the League of Nations, and the League was defeated. But that is not the reason that the S3enate rejected the League or that the republicans won the election of 1920; these things would have come about in any event, regardless of the fate of president Wilson.

Yet in every one of these instances, and in a hundred others which we could readily conjure up, fortuity did play a part, and an important part. It changed things; it meant that some men who might have lived, died; it meant that some battles had to be fought over again; it meant that what we call the course of history was slowed up of speeded up or temporarily deflected.

May we not conclude that fortuity itself is predictable, and that the mature historian takes it into account in his explanations, just as the wise general or statesman takes it into accounting his calculations? An earthquake, a drought, the discovery of a new continent, or of gels and silver mines, an epidemic, an assassination, all of these are in a sense fortuitous, yet al of them are in a since normal, as well, for such as these recur in the history of every country and every century.

Perhaps the most useful lesson the student of history can learn is to avid oversimplification, and to accept the notion of multiple causation or to resign himself to the fact that as yet we do not know enough to explain the causes of things. To yearn for a single, and usually simple, explanation of the chaotic materials of the past, to search for a single thread in that most tangled of all tangled skeins, is a sign of immaturity. More, it is a practice which encourages dangerous intellectual habits, fot is leads, almost inevitably, to a simplistic view of the present as well as of the past. Any historian who invities us to accept some single explanation of the great events of the past excites our distrust; all too often such men find the explanation of prodigious events in some fortuitous occurrence, in some lurid conspiracy, or in some naïve observation of character. They tell us that for want of a nail a kingdom was lost; they explain the Reformation in termed of Luther's desire to marry, or the Spanish coquets of Mexico top traitors in the United states Department of State! They are those men of maxims against whom George Eliot has warned us:

All people of strong, broad sense have an instinctive repugnance to men of maxims; because such people early discover that the mysterious complexity of our life is not to be embraced by maxims, and that to lace ourselves up in formulas of that sort is to repress all the divine promptings and inspirations that spring from a growing insight and sympathy. And the man of maxims is the popular solely by general rules, thinking that these will lead them to justice by ready-made patent method, without the trouble of exerting patience, discrimination, impartiality, without any care to assure themselves whether they have the insight that comes from a hardly-earned estimate of temptation, or from a life vivid and intense enough to have created a wide fellow-feeling with all that is human.

CHAPTER 9

History always Alive, always Challenging

HISTORY, To read history is like visiting strange far-off lands. Like travel, it takes us out of the narrowness and commonplace ofeveryday life and shows us the wonderful panorama of man in his slow ascent from earliest savagery to modern civilization. The stupendous story goes back to "the times of the old patriarchs with their flocks and herds, the keen-eyed greek, the stately Roman, the watching Jew, the uncouth Goth, the horrid Hun, the settled picture of the unehanging East, the restless shifting of the rapid West, the rise of the eold and elassical eivilization, its fall, the rough impetuous Middle Ages, the vague warm picture of ourselves and home."

In prehistoric times, primitiye peoples learned of their past through legends and myths. Soothsayers and priests passed these tales on by word of mouth. Fathers told them to their sons. Faneiful and full of supernatural explanations, these stories changed with each telling. Their picture of past events is romantic rather thean accurate. Our modern knowledge of prehistoric peoples has been gained chiefly from the remains of their homes and possessions uncovered by archaeologists (See Archaeology).

Recorded history could not exist until men has invented methods of writing and has developed an accurate ealendar to measure the passage of time (See Calendar; Writing). Even then, the early records of ancient civilizations told little about the lives of the people. They were mainly inscriptions on temples and palaces, made to glorify the exploits of rulers.

Modern history uses all this material and calls upon astronomy, geology, chemistry, and other sciences to help interpret the evidence. Using all the findings, it tells us how men struggled out of savagery, how nations and laws came into being and why we find human life organized as it is today.

Greeks Were First Historians

History, as we think of it now, orginiated with the ancient Greeks. After they had beaten off ...attempts at conquest, they were immensely interested in the Persians, the Egyptians, the Babylonians, and even the barbarians of distant lands. In the 5th century B.C., Herodotus spent perhaps 17 years traveling and gathering information about these strangers. The athenians were so delighted with his 'History' that they voted him a reward of ten talents, a sum sufficien to make him a wealthy man.

Thueydides, the great historian of the Peloponnesian War, has been called the first scientific historian. As a Athenian general, he grasped the significance of this war. He wrote a careful record of events to help people who might face similar problems later. He was the first to recognize that a study of the past might serve as a guide to the future.

He also realized the need to be careful and to consider each side of a question. As an Athenian he was inclined at first to take the Athenian view of the wars between Athens and Sparta. But the Athenians exiled him.Then for years he studied the Spartan viewpoint. By studying both sides in trying to reach the truth, he set an example for later historians.

History Calls for an Open Mind

Thueydides is quoted as saying that "history is philosoply teaching by example". Certainly to be "historically minded" is to see things in relation and in perspective, and to judge tolerantly. We must remember how differently men have thought and acted in different times. We must always keep an open mind, ready to receive and weigh new evidence. If we grasp this idea, we will never think that a historian is someone who can remember dates. That childish idea is like calling a man a statesman because he can remember the names of voters in his districts. A waiter could remember more names and a telephone operator more numbers than the greatest historian.

The true historian is not content to take all his facts from other historians. Today he makes sure that his statements are based on sound "documents" or "Sources" which go back to the time of the facts themselves. Those sources are of all kinds ruined monuments, old tombs, and other material remains; legal papers, letters, diaries, newspapers, and written or printed narratives of eyewitnesses, even my the and fables; contemporary pictures, drawings, photographs, and the like. Sometimes the discovery or the finding of the key to new sources- such as the hieroglyphs of ancient Egypt or the cuneiform tablets of Babylonia and Assyria adds whole new realms to our historical knowledge.

But the historian needs continually to be on his guard not to be misled by his sources. A document may be entirely forged. Its author may be deliberately lying. He may be so prejudiced by national, religious, party, or personal bias as to be grossly unfairto the other side. If honest, he may be misinformed as to the facts and mistaken in his inferences. Scores of pitfalls must be avoided by the research worker in this fascinating field.

Anyone who reads the accounts published in the different countries concerningthe causes and results of wars, or who sees how widely the reports of political affairs in Republican newspapers differ from those in Democratic ones today, will realize that the historian needs caution and training in handling his sources. The trained historian asks first : "Did this writer mean to tell the truth ?" and second : "Was he in a position or frame of mind to tell the truth even if he eanted to ?" Every statement must be patiently weighed and tested and combined with all other available imformation in order to get at the truth.

Formerly history was regarded chiefly as a branch of literature. Today emphasis is placed upon accuracy and soundness and breadthof understanding.

Periods of Western Civilization

Histor is realy a ceaselessly flowing stream, ever widening and deepening its course. For convenience we divide it into more or less artificial periods. This does no harm if we remember that changes in history, like changes of the seasons, are gradual, and each period passes into the nxt as smothly as winter into spring.

Ancient history covers more than half the span of our recorded knowledge. It stretches frm the beginonings of Sumerian and Egyptain inscriptions, through "the glory that was Greece and the grandeur that was Rome," to the coming into the Roman Empire of the Germanic barbarians who overthrew classical civilization (about 3100 B.C. to about A.D. 375).

The Middle Ages extend from A.D. 375 to about 1500. The period starts with an epoch of confusion and transition which lasted to about A.D. 800. To it the term Dark Ages is sometimes applied. Then comes the height of the Middle Ages, from Charlemagneto Dante 800 to 1300. In this period feudalism, monasticism, scholasticism, the Crusades, and Gothic architecture flourished, and a world empire and a world papacy confronted each other and strove for mastery (see Middle Ages). The period closes with a second epoch of transitin (about 1300 to 1500), called the renaissance (see Renaissance).

Since 1500 we have th modern period, characterized by the organization of national states, European settlement of the New World, the progress of science and inventions, and the rise of democracy.

We give the name Prehistoric Age to the long periodbefore writen record began, when man was taking his first steps in the arts which make up civilization (see Stone

Age). Writen records go back only about 5,000 years. But geologists believe that the earth may be 2 billion years old, and man has lived on it for perhaps a million years. To give some idea of the shot duration of recorded history compared with this vast expanse of time, Prof. J. H. Robinson asks us to imagine a library of many volumes of a thousand pages each, one page for every 5,000 years that the earth has existed. The whole of recorded history from the earliest Sumerian and Egyptian inscriptions to the present day would scarcely over the last page of this enormous journal.

Today's Social History

If history as a study is often dull and dry, a mere catalog of names and dates of rulers and battles and treaties, it is the fault of the writer. Nothing is more fascinating than the true story of how people lived in the past-their houses, food and clothing; how they cultivated teir fields, manufactured goods, God and the world of nature; their laws and manner of government; the songs their poets sang, and the beautiful things their artists made. All this is included in the social history taught today.

Even wars and political struggles are interesting when we once knw what they were about and how they were carried on and become well enough acquainted with the heroes and leders to feel that the wee real men and women dealing with things the were of vast importance to their peoples. The great historian Edward A. Freeman once wrte the "history is past poltics, and poltics present history. "But this view is too narrow. Arnold J. Toynbee writes not about nations or races but about the great drama of human experience since civilization began.

(For Reference- Outline, see World History).

CHAPTER 10

Ready Reference to World History

HISTORICAL, charts are to history what maps are to geography. They help us to visualize the facts- to fix them in *time* as maps do in *space*- and so aid both the understanding and memory. When the history of the chief countries is shown in paralled columns, as here, there is the added advantage of "synchronizing" the events.

A glance across these pages will enable one to see what was happening in the different countries in any period. Thus a student will quickly find that when the Greeks were beseging Troy, Samuel was ruling in Israel, and Tiglath-Pileser I and his armies were conquering to the Mediterranean. He will learn that some of the Norman knights who invaded England with William to Conqueror lived to take part in the First, Crusade, and that shortly before that the Northmen had discovered America. In the same century that the puritans we settling Plymouth and Boston, there was revolution and civil war in England, Huguenot were persecuted in France, a religious war was fought in Germany, and the Dutch won their independence from Spain. This graphic arrangement of contemporaneous events is valuable in teaching the student to regard history, not as a collection of disconnected incidents, but as a series of related movements, each contributing to the story of civilization.

PREHISTORIC PERIOD

Old Stone Age Began About 500,000 Years Ago. Neolithic (New Stone) Age Began About 6000 B.C.

HISTORIC PERIOD —— I. ANCIENT HISTORY

B.C.	EGYPT	PALESTINE	BABYLONIA AND ASSYRIA	AEGEAN REGION AND GREECE	ITALY
4000	Predynastic period in Nile Valley. 3100. Beginning of historical period with unification of country under the first dynasty of kings.		3100–2340 (about). **Sumerian** city kingdoms (non-Semitic). Development of **cuneiform writing.**	New Stone Age in Crete.	New Stone Age in Italy.
3000	2700–2200. **OLD KINGDOM** (Dynasties III–IV): high cultural development; capital at **Memphis**, in Lower Egypt; **Great Pyramids** at Gizeh. 2200–2050. **First Intermediate Period** (Dynasties VII–X): monarchy weakened; **rise** of independent feudal lords.	**Canaanites** are settled in Palestine and have many flourishing cities.	2340–2180 (about). Semites under dynasty of **Sargon of Akkad** rule **Sumeria.**	3000–2800. **Transition** from Stone to Bronze Age. Dawn of European civilization in Crete. 2800–1200. **Minoan Age in Crete**; high civilization with capital at **Cnossus.** 2500–2000. Second city of Troy flourished.	
2000	2050–1800. **MIDDLE KINGDOM** (Dynasties XI–XII): capital moved to Thebes, in Upper Egypt; strong monarchy and flourishing culture. 1800–1570. **Second Intermediate Period** (Dynasties XIII–XVII). **Hyksos** rule Egypt (Dynasties XV–XVI). 1570–1090. **NEW KINGDOM** (Dynasties XVIII–XX): **The period of empire.** 1501–1450. **Thutmose III** conquers Palestine and Syria. 1405–1370. **Amenhotep III**: magnificent palace and temple at Thebes. 1370–1352. **Amenhotep IV (Akhenaton)** tries to reform old religion; builds new capital at Tell el-Amarna. Nefertiti his queen. 1292–1232. **Rameses II** completes great hall of Temple at Karnak.	1300 (about). **Israelites** conquer Palestine. 1200–1000 (about). **Rule of Judges. Samuel** the last judge. Wars against Philistines. **Saul** becomes first king of the Israelites. Dies in battle against Philistines.	1800 (about). **Hammurabi** founds first dynasty of Babylon; **Code of Laws** issued. Assyria, in the north, under Shamshi-Adad I, becomes independent of Babylonia. 1600–1200 (about). **Kassite** immigrants from **Elam** gradually gain power in Babylonia and establish Kassite dynasty. 1400. Babylonia has well-established diplomatic and commercial relations with Egypt. 1100. **Tiglath-Pileser I** of Assyria conquers to the Mediterranean.	2000–1500. 3d, 4th, 5th, and 6th cities of Troy. 1500–1450. **GOLDEN AGE OF CRETE.** 1500–1200. 7th city of Troy (Homeric city). 1500–1100. Greatness of **Mycenae**, Tiryns, etc. 1500–1000. Greek (Achaean) **colonization of Greece** and islands. Dorian and Ionian conquests and colonization follow. 1450–1200. **Hittite Empire** in Asia Minor. 1200. **Fall of Troy** following siege by Greeks; gradual growth of hero songs about the siege.	2000. Lake dwellers occupy Italian lakes.
1000	1090–950. **Dynasty XXI** rules at **Tanis**, and **priest kings at Thebes.** 950. **Beginning of Dynasty XXII of Libyan kings.** 925 (about). **Sheshook I, first king of Libyan dynasty, invades Palestine.**	**King David** defeats Philistines and establishes capital at **Jerusalem.** **King Solomon** builds **Temple.** After Solomon's death kingdom divided into **Israel** and **Judah.** 925 (about). **Egyptians** invade Palestine.	930 (about). **Brilliant period of Assyrian history begins.** (Great activity in architecture, literature, and sculpture as well as in military conquests.)	1000–900. **Greek colonization** of Aegean islands and Asia Minor extended.	1000. **Etruscans** come into Italy (probably from Asia Minor by sea). 1000. Latin villages established along Tiber.
900	Dynasty XXII continues through century.	Dynasty of Omri at Samaria. Prophets **Elijah** and **Elisha.** 853. **Ahab** takes part in battle of Karkar.	884–859. Ashurnasirpal II restores the empire of Tiglath-Pileser I; marches to Mediterranean.	900–800. '**Iliad**' and '**Odyssey**' composed (by Homer?). 820. **Lycurgus** frames laws for Sparta.	
800	730. **Dynasties XXIII and XXIV,** weak and short-lived, end with conquest of Egypt by **Ethiopians**; beginning of Dynasty XXV (Ethiopian).	**Prophets Amos and Hosea.**	750–606. **ASSYRIAN EMPIRE** at its height. 745–727. **Babylonia subjugated by Tiglath-Pileser III** of Assyria. Assyrian rule extended to Egypt.	800–700. **Rise of aristocracies** in Greece. 776. **Traditional date of first record of Olympic games (1st Olympiad).** 750–650. **Sparta** conquers **Messenia**; becomes a military power.	753 (traditional date). **Rome founded.** 750. Etruscan kings invade Latin towns.

I. ANCIENT HISTORY (*Continued*)

B.C.	EGYPT	PALESTINE AND SYRIA	BABYLONIA, ASSYRIA, AND PERSIA	GREECE	ITALY AND ROME
		722. **Israel destroyed; people carried to Assyria.** 701. **Sennacherib invades Judah. Prophet Isaiah.**	722-705. Conquests of **Sargon II.** 722. Conquest of Israel; people made captive. 705-681. **Sennacherib; great palace at Nineveh; destruction of Babylon.**	734 (traditional date). **Syracuse founded in Sicily.** 708. **Tarentum founded in Southern Italy.**	
700	671. **Assyria conquers Egypt.** 663. Assyrians plunder Thebes and withdraw; native Egyptian rulers restored; Dynasty XXVI (Saite); revival of power and art.	621. **Josiah reforms religion of Judah. Prophet Jeremiah.**	681-668. **Esarhaddon; Babylon rebuilt.** 668-626. **Ashurbanipal.** 606-539. **CHALDEAN (NEW BABYLONIAN) EMPIRE.** 604-561. **Nebuchadnezzar**; wars in Palestine and Syria; **Hanging Gardens of Babylon built.**	650-600. **Rise of tyrannies** in Ionia; established in Corinth, Megara, etc. 630. Cyrene founded in Africa. 621. Code of Laws for Athens issued by **Draco.** 594-593. **Solon,** archon of Athens, **reforms Athenian constitution.** 560-527. **Pisistratus tyrant of Athens.**	700. **Greek colonies in Sicily and Southern Italy.**
600	525. **Persia conquers Egypt** and makes it a Persian province.	**Prophets Haggai and Zechariah.**	586. **Capture of Jerusalem.** Jews carried to Babylon. 546. **Cyrus the Great defeats Croesus,** king of Lydia; captures Sardis. 539. **Babylon taken by Cyrus the Great;** becomes Persian province. 533-330. **MEDO-PERSIAN EMPIRE.** 525. Cambyses II conquers Egypt. 522-486. **Darius I** rules from Aegean and Egypt to India; advances to Danube against Scythians (513).	514. Hipparchus, son of Pisistratus, slain by Harmodius and Aristogiton; his brother Hippias expelled, 510. 509. **Reforms of Clisthenes** at Athens.	510 (traditional date). **Kings (Etruscans?) expelled from Rome; republic founded.**
500	404. Egyptians revolt and throw off Persian rule.	444. **Nehemiah** returns to Jerusalem and rebuilds city and temple. **Prophet Malachi.**	499. Revolt of Greeks in Asia Minor; two expeditions against Greece (492, 490). 486-465. **Xerxes.** Great expedition against Greece (480). Internal decay of Persian Empire: frequent revolts of Egypt, etc. 401. Unsuccessful revolt of Cyrus the Younger against his brother, Artaxerxes II: **retreat of Xenophon** and the 10,000 Greeks.	500. Athens aids Greeks of Asia Minor against Persia. 493-492. **Themistocles** archon of Athens. 493-479. **Persian Wars.** Darius sends expedition into Thrace and Macedonia (493); attacks Greece (**Marathon,** 490); **Xerxes invades Greece (Thermopylae** and **Salamis,** 480; **Plataea,** 479). 478. An **Athenian Empire** founded by Confederacy of Delos, against Persians; **Athens and Sparta at head of rival leagues.** 444-429. **AGE OF PERICLES,** height of Athenian culture. (Aeschylus, Sophocles, Euripides, Aristophanes, Herodotus, Thucydides, Phidias, Ictinus, Socrates, **Zeno.**) Acropolis developed; Parthenon built. 431-404. **Peloponnesian Wars** between Athenian and Spartan alliances; Athenian expedition to Syracuse unsuccessful (415-413); Spartans besiege Athens (413-404); Athenian fleet destroyed at Aegospotami (405); **surrender of Athens.**	494. **Struggle** between **Patricians** and **Plebeians;** tribunes created. 450. **Roman laws made** public (12 tables).
400	341. **Egyptian independence ends with new Persian conquest of Egypt** by Artaxerxes III.	397. **Ezra returns to Jerusalem.**	362-338. **Artaxerxes III** king of Persia; in 346 suppresses with great cruelty revolt of Sidon chief city of Phoenicia.	399. **Socrates put to death in Athens.** 379-362. War between Sparta and Thebes (**Epaminondas**); Leuctra (371); **leadership passes to Thebans.** 357-355. **Revolt** of Athens' allies **destroys Athenian Empire.** 359-336. **Rise of Macedon** to power under **Philip** (power of Thebes destroyed at Chaeronea, 338). **Macedonian supremacy** in **Greece.** 336-323. **Alexander the Great.** Invades Asia and founds Greek (Hellenistic) power of far-reaching influence.	396. **Romans take Veii** after 10 years' **siege; end danger from Etruscans.** 390. **Gauls plunder Rome (Battle of the Allia).** 367. **Licinian laws passed to equalize Patricians and Plebeians.** 343-341. **First war against Samnites** (kindred mountain tribes southeast of Rome). 340-338. Revolt of Latins crushed; Latin League dissolved.

MACEDONIAN EMPIRE

334. **Alexander attacks Persian Empire** (Battle of the **Granicus,** 334; of **Issus,** 333; of **Arbela,** 331).
332. **Palestine** conquered by Alexander.
332. **Alexander conquers Egypt** from Persia and founds **Alexandria.**
330. Darius III slain while fleeing after Arbela; **end of Persian Empire.**
323-276. **Wars among the successors of Alexander (Diadochi),** who divide the Macedonian Empire.

EGYPT	PALESTINE	SYRIA AND ASSYRIA	GREECE	ITALY AND ROME
323-30 B.C. **Ptolemies** (descendants of one of Alexander's generals) rule Egypt; great library at Alexandria.	323-276. Ptolemies rule Palestine.	312-281. **Seleucus,** son of one of Alexander's generals, rules from Syria to **the Indies** (his descendants called Seleucids).	323-146. **Macedonia** and Greece under Demetrius Poliorcetes and his descendants. 323-322. Greek states fail in revolt against Macedonians.	326-304. Second Samnite War. **Roman army defeated in the Caudine Forks and sent "under the yoke"** (321). Victories of Romans at Vadimonium Lake (310) and Bovianum (305) end the war. **Rome becomes the dominant power of Italy south of the Rubicon River.**

I. ANCIENT HISTORY (*Concluded*)

B.C.	EGYPT	PALESTINE	SYRIA AND ASSYRIA	GREECE	ROME
300	285–247. Ptolemy II (Philadelphus); brilliant court at Alexandria; Egypt's navy rules eastern Mediterranean.	276. Antiochus of Syria conquers Palestine from Egypt.	250. Parthians under Arsaces revolt. 223–187. Antiochus the Great; defeated by Romans at Magnesia (190); Seleucid rule curtailed in west.	280–183. Aetolian and Achean Leagues prevent Macedonia securing complete power in Greece.	282–272. War with Tarentum aided by King Pyrrhus of Epirus. 264–241. First War with Carthage (over Sicily). Rome becomes a naval power, invades Africa and Sicily, and defeats Carthage in numerous battles at sea. Rome gains Sicily. 218–202. Second War with Carthage. Hannibal invades Italy over the Alps; defeats Romans at Cannae (216). Scipio carries the war into Africa (204), and defeats Hannibal at Zama (202). Carthage becomes a vassal state. 215–206. First Macedonian War.
200	Decline of Egypt: frequent wars of Ptolemies with the Seleucids of Syria.	167–130. Maccabees (kings) rule Palestine as Roman vassals.	174–136. Mithridates I founds Parthian Empire (Media, Persia, Babylonia, etc.).	197. Macedonians defeated at Cynoscephalae by Romans, and Greece freed from Macedonian rule. 146. Achean League defeated by Romans and Corinth destroyed. Greece passes under Roman rule.	200–197. Second Macedonian War; Greece freed. 190. Antiochus of Syria overthrown (western Asia Minor under Roman control). 171–168. Third Macedonian War; end of Macedonian monarchy. 149–146. Third War with Carthage; Carthage destroyed. 146. Macedonia becomes a Roman province. 133. Practically all Spain under Roman rule. 133–123. Tiberius and Caius Gracchus attempt to reform the land laws and are slain. 113–101. Cimbri and Teutones (Germanic invaders) defeated by Marius.
100	Civil wars among degenerate Ptolemies pave way for fall. 47. Cleopatra made ruler of Egypt under Roman supremacy. 31. Cleopatra and Antony defeated at Actium. Egypt becomes a Roman province.	63. Pompey makes Jews tributary to Rome. 40. Herod (the Great) recognised by Rome as dependent king of Judaea. 4. Birth of Christ.	88–64. Mithridates VI (the Great) defeated by Romans; Syria and Armenia submit to Rome.		90. Roman citizenship granted to all Latins and most other Italians, following revolt of Rome's allies ("Social War," 90–88). 88–82. Civil War between Sulla (wealthy classes) and Marius (poorer classes). Reactionary reign of terror under Sulla as dictator. 73–71. Revolt of gladiators and slaves under Spartacus. 66–62. Catiline's conspiracy (Cicero's speeches). 60. Caesar, Pompey, and Crassus form first Triumvirate. 58–51. Caesar conquers Gaul; two expeditions to Britain (55–54 B.C.). 49–48. Civil war between Caesar and Pompey (Battle of Pharsalus; Pompey slain). Under forms of the republic, Caesar gets all power into his own hands. 44. Assassination of Caesar by Brutus, Cassius, and others. 43–42. Mark Antony, Octavian (Augustus), and Lepidus form second Triumvirate and defeat Cassius and Brutus at Philippi. 31–30. War between Octavian and Antony; Antony and Cleopatra of Egypt defeated at Actium. 31 B.C.–14 A.D. Octavian rules as Emperor Augustus. Beginning of ROMAN EMPIRE. (Golden Age of Roman culture; Livy, Horace, Vergil, Seneca, Pliny the Elder.)
TIME B.C. / TIME A.D.	Under Roman rule Egypt enjoys a period of industrial and commercial prosperity.	6. Judaea becomes part of Roman province of Syria. 70. Jerusalem destroyed by Titus following revolt. Dispersal of survivors.			14–37. Tiberius emperor (stepson of Augustus). 37–41. Caligula (great-grandson of Augustus). 41–54. Claudius; Britain added to Roman Empire. 54–68. Nero; his crimes and excesses; great fire in Rome; Christians persecuted. 69–79. Vespasian proclaimed emperor by his troops in Syria; good rule. 79–81. Titus (son of Vespasian). 79. Eruption of Vesuvius destroys Pompeii and Herculaneum. 98–117. Trajan, a Spaniard by birth and a great general (conquest of Dacia; defeat of Parthians in Syria; Empire reaches greatest extent).
100	Revolt of native troops begins decline of Egypt.	132–135. Revolt of Jews suppressed by Hadrian; survivors dispersed.	114–116. Armenia, Mesopotamia, and Assyria made Roman provinces. 193–211. Northern Assyria conquered by Rome.		117–138. Hadrian adopted by Trajan; frontiers strengthened; Asia east of Euphrates given up; magnificent buildings. 138–161. Antoninus Pius. 161–180. Marcus Aurelius, adopted son of Antoninus and a renowned Stoic philosopher. Wars with barbarians along Danube. 193–284. Emperors elected by the army. 193–211. Septimius Severus; war in Mesopotamia; northern Assyria conquered.
200	270. Egypt occupied by Zenobia of Palmyra. 273. Egypt reconquered by Rome.		226–241. New Persian Empire under Sassanids. 267–273. Zenobia, queen of Palmyra, defeated by Aurelian.		212. All freemen in the Empire made citizens (to get more taxes). 270–275. Aurelian; recovers Palmyra and subdues revolt in Gaul; new walls about Rome. 284–305. Diocletian (resides in East); empire divided into four administrative prefectures; great persecution of Christians; abdicates.
300	Quarrels between branches of the Christian Church lead to persecution of the Arians.				311. Christianity made legal. 323–337. Constantine the Great sole ruler; capital removed to Constantinople; empire reorganized. 325. Council of Christian church at Nicaea. 375. Beginning of TEUTONIC MIGRATIONS into the Empire. 378. Visigoths defeat Roman army at Adrianople. 379–395. Theodosius the Great, last ruler of united empire. 395. Empire divided into Eastern and Western parts.
400					395–476. WESTERN EMPIRE. 410. Alaric the Visigoth captures Rome. 455. Vandals from Africa sack Rome. 476. German leader Odoacer deposes last Roman emperor in West. 395–1453. EASTERN OR BYZANTINE EMPIRE. For nearly 1,000 years a defense against Asiatic invasions.

II. MEDIEVAL AND MODERN HISTORY

	WESTERN EUROPE		ENGLAND	EASTERN EUROPE AND OTHER COUNTRIES
	383-394. Wars for power among claimants of Empire in West ended by recognition of Theodosius (*see* Eastern Europe). 395-423. Honorius receives Western Roman Empire on permanent division (Stilicho, his minister).		Romans rule Britain since about 43-81 A.D.; Christianity introduced; Hadrian's wall begun (121).	375. Visigoths cross Danube; defeat Romans at Adrianople (378). 395. Death of Theodosius the Great, last ruler of united Roman Empire. 395-1453. EAST ROMAN EMPIRE (Arcadius emperor, 395-408).
400	410. Sack of Rome by Visigoths under Alaric; Visigoths move into Spain (414). 429. Vandals cross from Spain into Africa; under Genseric plunder Rome. 451. Attila the Hun defeated at Châlons (in Gaul). 476. Odoacer, German mercenary, displaces Roman emperor; end of Western Roman Empire. 481-511. Clovis founds kingdom of Franks in Gaul (Merovingians); becomes Christian (496). 493-555. Ostrogoths (Theodoric the Great) rule Italy.		410. Roman legions withdrawn. 449-700. Angles, Saxons, and Jutes conquer Britain ("Angleland" or England).	474-491. Zeno eastern emperor.
500	511-751. Decline of Merovingian kings of Franks and rise of Mayors of Palace. 568-774. Lombard kingdom in Italy. 590-604. Pope Gregory I (the Great); Rome the head of Christendom.		577. Battle of Deorham; West Saxons reach Bristol Channel. 597. Augustine reintroduces Christianity.	527-565. Justinian emperor; Roman law codified; Vandals in Africa and Ostrogoths in Italy overthrown.
600	613. Queen Brunhilde of Austrasia (Eastern Frank-land) captured, tortured, and dragged to death by wild horses in Merovingian quarrels. 687. Pepin of Heristal becomes Mayor of Palace for whole Frankish kingdom (Battle of Testry).		607. Chester sacked and left desolate for 300 years.	622. Mohammed's flight from Mecca (the "Hegira"); founding of Mohammedan religion.
700	711. Mohammedans from Africa overthrow Visigothic kingdom in Spain. 732. Franks (Charles Martel) defeat Mohammedans at Tours (in France). 751. Pepin the Short (Mayor of the Palace) deposes last Merovingian king and takes the crown (Carolingian rule).		755-794. Offa king of Mercia.	750. Mohammedans rule all western Asia, northern Africa, and Spain—from Indus River to the Pyrenees.
800	800. Charlemagne, king of the Franks and ruler of most of western Europe (768-814), crowned emperor at *Rome*. 843. Partition of Verdun. Charlemagne's empire divided; separation of France and Germany.		827. Egbert of Wessex unites England. 871-899. Alfred rules southern England; Danes checked.	809. End of brilliant reign of Harun-al-Raschid, calif of Bagdad. 862. Russian kingdom founded by Rurik the Northman (Kief, capital).
900	FRANCE	GERMANY AND ITALY		
	911. Normandy ceded to Rolf (Rollo), the Northman; decline of Carolingians in France. 987. Hugh Capet chosen king (Capetian line); Feudalism at height of its power.	911-918. Conrad I (Franconian) first non-Carolingian king. 936-973. Otto I, the Great (Saxon), ends anarchy in Italy; defeats Hungarians (955); revives Empire (962).	910-954. Northern England ("Danelaw") reconquered from Danes. 980. Danish invasions renewed.	905-959. Constantine VII ("Born in the Purple") emperor, patron of literature.
1000	1095. Council of Clermont; Pope Urban II calls First Crusade.	1002-24. Henry II (the Saint), last of the Saxon line. 1075. Investiture conflict begun by Pope Gregory VII (Hildebrand) and Emperor Henry IV (1056-1106).	1016-1035. Canute of Denmark king. 1042-66. Edward the Confessor king. 1066. Norman conquest (William I).	1000. Northmen discover America (Greenland discovered, 984).
	PERIOD OF THE CRUSADES—TO RESCUE PALESTINE FROM MOHAMMEDAN RULE—1096-1291 1096-99. First Crusade. People's crusade under Peter the Hermit fails. Crusade of nobles under Godfrey of Bouillon and others takes Jerusalem (1099) and establishes a feudal kingdom of Jerusalem.			
1100	1108-37. Louis VI (the Fat) establishes order in crown possessions.	1122. Concordat of Worms ends investiture conflict.	1100-35. Henry I ("the Lion of Justice"); a charter issued.	1144. Edessa taken by Mohammedans.
	1147-49. Second Crusade. Preached by St. Bernard of Clairvaux; led by Conrad III of Germany and Louis VII of France without results.			
	1180-1223. Philip Augustus; recovers Normandy, etc., from England.	1152-1190. Frederick Barbarossa (Hohenstaufen); quarrel with pope; defeated by league of Lombard towns.	1154-89. Henry II (Plantagenet) holds Normandy, Anjou, Maine, etc., in France. Conquest of Ireland begun.	1187. Capture of Jerusalem by Saladin.
	1189-92. Third Crusade. Led by Richard Coeur de Lion of England and Philip Augustus of France; Emperor Frederick Barbarossa drowned on way. Armistice with Saladin permits pilgrimages to Holy Places.			
1200	1209-29. Albigensian crusade. 1214. Battle of Bouvines: defeat of English and enemies of Frederick II. 1226-70. Louis IX (St. Louis); good rule. Crusade to Egypt (1248-54); to Tunis (1270). 1285-1314. Philip IV (the Fair). Power of king increased; quarrels with pope.	1200-1450. Hanseatic League between German cities promotes commerce. 1215-50. Frederick II; rules Naples and Sicily as well as Empire; quarrels with pope; Fifth Crusade (1228-29). 1254-73. Interregnum in Empire. 1273-91. Rudolph of Hapsburg king of Germany. 1295. Marco Polo returns from 20 years' travels in China and the East.	1204-06. King John loses Normandy and Anjou; forced to grant Magna Carta (1215). 1272-1307. Edward I; conquest of Wales (1282); wars with Scotland begun. 1295. Model Parliament called.	1202-04. Fourth Crusade directed against Constantinople by Venetians. 1206-27. Genghis Khan conquers China, Persia, Turkestan, and Southern Russia. 1291-1499. Growth of Swiss Confederation (Battle of Morgarten, 1315; Sempach, 1386). 1297. Fall of Acre; end of Crusades.
1300	1302. First meeting of Estates-General. 1302. Battle of Courtrai; Flemish townsmen defeat French knights. 1305-77. "Babylonian captivity of Popes" (papal residence at Avignon, France). 1328. Philip VI (Valois) becomes king. 1337-1453. Hundred Years' War with England (Peace of Bretigny, 1360; war renewed, 1369). 1364-80. Charles V (the Wise). Most of English possessions in France won back by Du Guesclin.	PERIOD OF ITALIAN RENAISSANCE 1300-1500. Dante, Petrarch, Boccaccio, Giotto, Michelangelo, Da Vinci, Raphael, Titian. 1347-1437. Emperors of Luxemburg-Bohemian line. 1348. Black Death appears in Florence and spreads over Europe. 1356. Charles IV issues Golden Bull. 1377. Papacy returns from Avignon to Rome. 1378-1417. Great Schism (two, later three, claim to be pope). 1380. Venice crushes Genoa at Chioggia.	1314. Edward II defeated at Bannockburn by Scots under Bruce. 1327-77. Edward III. 1337-1453. Hundred Years' War with France. English victories at Crécy (1346) and Poitiers (1356). 1381. Peasants' revolt led by John Ball and Wat Tyler. 1399. Henry IV (Lancaster) overthrows Richard II.	1331-55. Stephen Dushan rules an extended Serbian Empire. 1354. Ottoman Turks gain foothold in Europe (Gallipoli). 1389. Serbs defeated by Turks in great battle at Kossova.

II. MEDIEVAL AND MODERN HISTORY—(*Continued*)

	FRANCE	GERMANY	ITALY AND PAPACY	GREAT BRITAIN	OTHER COUNTRIES
1400	1415. Hundred Years' War renewed in reign of Charles VI (insane after 1392). 1429–31. **Joan of Arc saves France.** (War ends in 1453: England loses all its possessions in France except Calais.) 1461–83. **Louis XI strengthens** France. 1477. **Charles the Bold** of Burgundy overthrown; his duchy annexed to France. 1494. **Charles VIII invades Italy** (Italian wars begun).	1410–37. Sigismund emperor. 1419–36. **Hussite Wars.** (Ziska blind leader against Germans.) 1440–93. **Frederick III** (Hapsburg) emperor. 1450. Gutenberg invents printing. 1493–1519. **Maximilian I** emperor.	1414–18. **Council of Constance;** schism ended; **John Huss** burned as heretic (1415). 1469–92. **Lorenzo de Medici** rules Florence. 1494–98. **Savonarola** attempts reform in Florence.	1415. **Henry V invades** France (**Agincourt, 1415**). 1450. Jack Cade's rebellion. 1455–85. **Wars of the Roses** (Houses of York and Lancaster claim crown). 1485. **Henry VII** (Tudor) defeats Richard III (York) at Bosworth and ends war. Strong monarchy established.	1453. **Turks take Constantinople;** end of Eastern Empire. 1492. **Columbus discovers America.** 1492. Conquest of Granada; Moors expelled from Spain. 1497–98. **Vasco da Gama reaches India by sea.**
1500	1515–47. **Francis I; wars with** Charles V over Milan; Renaissance encouraged in France. 1562. **Huguenot Wars begun** (St. Bartholomew's Massacre, 1572). 1589–1610. **Henry IV** (Bourbon). Edict of Nantes ends Huguenot wars (1598).	1517. Luther begins **Protestant Reformation; Diet of Worms** condemns Luther (1521). 1519–56. **Charles V rules Spain, Germany, Netherlands, parts of Italy and America.** Opposes Luther; wars against Turks (1526–32); abdicates (1555–56). 1555. **Religious peace of Augsburg** (toleration of Lutherans). 1556–64. Ferdinand I. 1563. **Council of Trent ends** (beginning of Catholic recovery).	1503–13. **Pope Julius II** (Italian wars; patron of Michelangelo and Raphael). 1508. League of Cambrai (Pope, Austria, France, and Spain) against Venice. 1513–21. **Pope Leo X** (Medici) patron of arts and letters. 1542. Pope Paul III establishes the Inquisition in Rome. 1571. League of Papacy, Spain and Venice against Turks (**Battle of Lepanto,** 1572).	1509–47. **Henry VIII; separation of English Church from Rome.** 1547–53. Edward VI. 1553–58. **Queen Mary** restores Catholic Church. 1558–1603. **Elizabeth establishes Church of England.** Growth of sea power; industrial development. Elizabethan period of literature (**Shakespeare**). 1588. **Spanish Armada** destroyed.	1518. **Zwingli** begins Reformation in Switzerland. 1519–1522. **Magellan** circumnavigates the globe. 1536. **Calvin** begins Reformation at Geneva. 1540. **Jesuit order founded** by Loyola. 1556–98. **Philip II** succeeds his father Charles V in Spain, Italy, Netherlands, and the New World. 1568. **Revolt of Netherlands** against Spain; siege of Leyden (1574); Union of Utrecht (1579); declaration of independence by the Dutch (1581).
1600	1610–43. Louis XIII; political power of the Huguenots crushed. (**Richelieu** chief minister of the crown.) 1643–1715. **Louis XIV;** numerous wars of conquest; extravagant court at **Versailles;** brilliant period of French literature. 1685. Edict of Nantes revoked and toleration of Huguenots ended.	1618–48. **Thirty Years' War.** Imperialist (Catholic) generals, **Tilly** and **Wallenstein; Gustavus Adolphus,** Protestant king of Sweden, victorious at **Leipzig** (1631); **Lützen** (1632); **Peace of Westphalia** (1648). 1640–88. **Growth of Prussia** under the **Great Elector.** 1683. **Vienna besieged for last time by Turks;** rescued by **King John Sobieski of Poland.**	1629. War over Mantua between Spain (which possessed Milan) and Austria. 1684. Venice joins Austria and Poland in attack on Turks: makes conquests in Morea.	1603–25. **James I** (Stuart); personal union of England and Scotland. 1607. Virginia colony founded (Jamestown). 1620. Plymouth colony settled (Boston, 1630) by Puritans fleeing persecution in England. 1642–49. **Civil war** between Crown and Parliament; Marston Moor (1644); Naseby (1645). Charles I executed (1649). England a commonwealth. 1653–58. **Cromwell rules** England, Scotland, and Ireland as Lord Protector. 1660. **Stuart restoration** under Charles II. 1688. **"Glorious Revolution"** expels James II and seats William and Mary; Protestant succession established.	1611–32. **Gustavus Adolphus** king of Sweden. 1644. Manchu rule begins in China. 1648. Spain recognizes independence of the Dutch Netherlands. 1672–1715. **Peter the Great;** introduction of western culture in Russia; St. Petersburg founded (1703). 1697–1718. **Charles XII of Sweden.**
1700	1701–13. **War of the Spanish Succession.** Treaty of Utrecht seats French prince (Philip V) on Spanish throne. 1715–74. **Louis XV;** debauchery at court; France aids Prussia in Austrian Succession War. 1756–63. **Seven Years' War;** France aids **Austria** against Prussia, loses **Canada** and India to British. 1774–92. **Louis XVI** (Marie Antoinette of Austria, queen); reform measures defeated. 1789–95. **French Revolution.** Estates-General becomes National Assembly (1789); constitution accepted by king (1791); kingship abolished (1792); **Louis XVI** executed (1793); **Reign of Terror** (1793–94); **Directory** established (1795). 1796–99. Rise of **Napoleon Bonaparte** to be First Consul.	1701. Elector of Brandenburg receives title of **King of Prussia.** 1701–13. Austria takes part in **War of Spanish Succession.** 1713–40. Frederick William I develops Prussian army. 1740–80. **Maria Theresa** queen of Bohemia and Hungary, archduchess of Austria; **War of Austrian Succession** (1740–48). 1740–86. **Frederick II** (The Great) seizes Silesia from Austria and retains it in **Seven Years' War** (Battles of **Rossbach** and **Leuthen,** 1757); builds up **Prussia** in peace time. 1765–90. **Joseph II** emperor; attempts **reforms** in Hapsburg lands. 1790–92. Leopold II emperor.	1714. Milan, Naples, etc., given to Austria by treaty. 1715. Turks drive Venetians from the Morea and Crete. 1735. Spanish Bourbons established in Naples. 1738. Tuscany given to Francis of Lorraine (husband of Maria Theresa). 1796. **Napoleon** invades Italy; siege of Mantua. 1797. Cisalpine Republic set up by Bonaparte.	1701–13. England takes part in War of Spanish Succession (**Blenheim,** 1704). 1702–14. Anne queen. 1714. **George I** (Hanover) **becomes king;** growth of cabinet government. 1741–48. England aids Austria in Austrian Succession War. 1745. Jacobite rebellion (Stuart supporters). 1756–63. **Seven Years' War; England aids Prussia; Canada acquired;** supremacy established in **India; British Empire founded.** 1764. **Industrial Revolution begun;** Hargreaves invents spinning jenny. 1775–83. **Revolt of the American colonies.** 1788. British colonization of **Australia** begun.	1709. Battle of Pultowa: forces of Charles XII crushed by Russia. 1763–96. **Catherine II** empress of Russia. 1772–95. **Poland partitioned** among Russia, Prussia, and Austria.

WARS OF THE FRENCH REVOLUTION AND BONAPARTE—1792-1815

1796. **Bonaparte's Italian Campaign.**
1798. **Egyptian expedition fails** (Battle of the Nile).
1800. **Napoleon's victory at Marengo.**
1805. Nelson victorious at **Trafalgar.**
1805. **Bonaparte wins at Austerlitz.**

1806. Prussia crushed at **Jena.**
1807. Napoleon defeats Austrians at **Wagram** and Russians at **Friedland.**
1807. **Peace of Tilsit;** hard terms for Prussia. Alexander I of Russia becomes Napoleon's ally.

1812. **Napoleon invades Russia;** sack of Moscow; retreats with heavy losses.
1813. Napoleon defeated in three-day battle at **Leipzig.**
1815. Wellington victorious at **Waterloo.**
1815. Treaty of Vienna.

II. MEDIEVAL AND MOD

	FRANCE	GERMANY	AUSTRIA-HUNGARY	ITALY
1800	1804. **Napoleon made emperor.** 1814. **Napoleon** abdicates; returns from Elba (1815); exiled after Waterloo (1815). 1814. **Bourbons restored** under Louis XVIII. 1824–30. **Charles X**; reactionary policy. 1830. **July Revolution**; Charles X abdicates; **Louis Philippe becomes king** ("citizen king"). Conservative policy. 1848. **February Revolution**; Louis Philippe abdicates; republic proclaimed. 1848–52. **Second Republic** (Louis Napoleon, president). 1851. Coup d'état of Louis Napoleon; proclaimed emperor (**Napoleon III**, 1852–70). 1854–56. **Crimean War.** 1859. **War with Austria** in behalf of Italy. 1861–67. Attempt to found a monarchy in Mexico fails (Maximilian). 1870–71. **Franco-Prussian War**; France loses **Alsace-Lorraine.** 1870. **Third French Republic** proclaimed. 1875. Republican constitution adopted. 1891. **Dual Alliance** of France and Russia. 1894–1906. Trials of Dreyfus for treason. 1896. Annexation of Madagascar.	1806. **Confederation of the Rhine formed.** 1806. **Holy Roman Empire dissolved.** 1819. **Carlsbad decrees** passed by German Diet suppress liberalism. 1834. German Customs Union (**Zollverein**) formed, a first step toward unity. 1840–61. **Frederick William IV** king of Prussia. 1848–49. **Frankfort Parliament** to unite Germany fails; liberal uprising fails. 1861–88. **William I** king of Prussia. 1862. **Bismarck** becomes chief minister. 1864. **Schleswig** and **Holstein** taken from Denmark by Prussia and Austria. 1866. **Austro-Prussian War** over Holstein. 1867–71. **North German Confederation** under Prussian leadership. 1870–71. **Franco-Prussian War.** 1871. **German Empire** proclaimed; **William I** emperor; Bismarck chancellor (1871–90). 1882. **Triple Alliance** with Austria and Italy. 1884. Germany begins African colonization. 1888–1918. **William II** emperor. 1899. Germany obtains Baghdad railway concession from Turkey.	1805. **Holy Roman Empire dissolved;** Francis II becomes Francis I of Austria. 1809. **Metternich** becomes minister of foreign affairs; reactionary leader of Europe (1815–48). 1815. **Congress of Vienna**; treaty of Vienna signed; "**Holy Alliance**" formed by Russia, Prussia, and Austria. 1835–48. Ferdinand I; reactionary rule. 1848. Revolution expels Metternich. **Francis Joseph I** begins long reign. 1849. **Hungarian war for independence** fails (**Kossuth**). 1859. **War with France and Italy.** 1866. **War with Prussia.** Austria withdraws from German Confederation and loses Venetia. 1867. **Dual Monarchy of Austria-Hungary** established. 1876–90. Count Tisza, liberal leader, pursues policy of "Magyarization" in Hungary; economic development. 1882. **Triple Alliance** formed by Austria, Germany, and Italy.	1815. Italy a group of small states under Austrian domination. 1830. **Revolution** fails. 1850. **War with Austria**; Austrian control broken. 1860–61. **Garibaldi conquers and unites Italy** (except Rome) under Victor Emmanuel; kingdom of Italy proclaimed. 1870. **Rome** taken from pope and made capital. 1882. **Triple Alliance** with Austria and Germany 1896. **Abyssinia** repels Italian attack at Adowa.
1900	1904. **Entente Cordiale between France and** Great Britain settles disputes over colonies. 1905–06. **Algeciras Conference** upholds French policy against Germany's challenge. 1911. War with Germany narrowly averted over **Moroccan question.**	1900. **Great naval development** begins. 1911. **Enormous growth** of Germany in population, industry, and trade. 1911–13. German standing army increased from 515,000 to 866,000 men. 1912. **Socialists make gains in Reichstag.**	1907–12. Reform blocked in Austria. 1908. Austria annexes **Bosnia** and **Herzegovina.** 1914. **Archduke Francis Ferdinand** assassinated in Bosnia by Serbs.	1900. **Victor Emmanuel III** becomes king. 1911–12. **War with Turkey; Italy takes Tripoli.** 1912. **Universal suffrage** introduced.

THE FIRST WORLD WAR AND

	WESTERN FRONT	EASTERN FRONT	OTHER FRONTS AND EVENTS
1914	Aug. 24. Naval battle at Helgoland; **German navy bottled up.** Sept. 6–10. **German invasion of France** stopped at the **Marne.** Entrenched line established from channel to Switzerland. Oct.–Nov. Germans held at Ypres.	Aug. 26–31. Hindenburg stops Russian offensive at **Masurian Lakes** (Battle of Tannenberg). Aug.–May, 1915. Russians invade **Galicia** and capture Carpathian passes. Nov.–Dec. German attacks on **Warsaw** fail.	July 28. **Austria declares war on Serbia.** Aug. 1. **Germany declares war on Russia** over mobilization. Aug. 3. **Germany declares war on France**, Russia's ally. Aug. 4. **Germany invades Belgium. England declares war.** Aug. 23. **Japan** joins the Allies. Oct. 29. **Turkey** openly joins Germany and Austria.
1915	Repeated attempts to break the line by the Allies at **Neuve-Chapelle** (Mar. 10); by the Germans at **Ypres** (Apr.–May); by the Allies above **Arras** (May–June); by the Germans in the **Argonne** (July).	May–Sept. **Mackensen's** drive expels Russians from Galicia. June–Oct. **Austro-German** drive into **Russian Poland**; capture of **Warsaw** (Aug. 5); Brest-Litovsk (Aug. 25); Vilna (Sept. 18).	Feb.–Dec. Anglo-French attacks on **Dardanelles** fail. May 7. **Lusitania** sunk; 1,198 lives lost. May 23. **Italy declares war on Austria.** Oct. 13. **Bulgaria** joins Teutonic allies. Oct.–Dec. **Austro-German army conquers Serbia.** Dec.–Jan., 1916. Allies abandon **Gallipoli** expedition.
1916	Feb.–July. Terrific **German attacks on Verdun fail.** ("They shall not pass".) July–Nov. Allies gain in the **Battle of the Somme** at heavy cost in lives.	June–Aug. Russian counterattack on Galicia. Aug.–Dec. **Rumania invades Transylvania**; Germans, Austrians, Bulgarians counterattack, **take Bucharest, crush Rumania.**	Jan.–Feb. Austro-Bulgarian invasion of **Montenegro** and **Albania.** Mar. 9. **Portugal** joins the Allies. May 31. **Naval battle of Jutland**; German fleet withdraws. Aug. 4. **Italians take Gorizia** (Aug. 9). Aug. 27. **Rumania** joins the Allies.
1917	Mar. **Germans withdraw to Hindenburg Line**; lay waste to country on 50-mile front. Apr.–Dec. **Repeated Allied attempts to break line at Arras** (Apr.–June); **Vimy Ridge** taken (Apr. 9–12); Allies attack along **Aisne** (Apr.–Nov.); in **Flanders** (July–Dec.); at **Cambrai** (Nov.–Dec.).	Mar. 15. **Russian revolution** destroys effectiveness of Russian army. July. **Russian offensive** on Eastern front fails. Sept. 3. **Riga** captured by Germans. *(Continued on next page)*	Jan. 31. **Germany announces unrestricted submarine war.** Feb. 3. **United States severs diplomatic relations with** Germany. Mar. 15. **Czar of Russia dethroned**; Kerensky sets up government. Apr. 6. **United States enters war**; Panama, Cuba, Liberia, Brazil follow. June 12. King Constantine deposed and **Greece** joins Allies. Oct.–Dec. Italian disaster at **Caporetto**; **Allenby's Palestine campaign takes Jerusalem** (Dec. 10).

III. MODERN HISTORY BETWEEN

WESTERN EUROPE	EASTERN EUROPE	OTHER COUNTRIES
1918. Oct. 31. **Hungary declares itself independent republic.** 1918. Nov. 12. **Republic of Austria** proclaimed. 1919. **Treaty of Versailles; France regains Alsace-Lorraine.** 1919. **Irish** declare **independence.** 1920. Danzig and Saar Valley put under **League of Nations.** 1922. **Irish Free State** inaugurated. 1922. Fascists control Italy; **Mussolini prime minister.** 1924. British Labor Government; Italy annexes Fiume. 1925. President Ebert of Germany dies; Hindenburg elected. 1926. Herriot and Poincaré premiers of France, **Germany admitted to League of Nations.** 1927. Italian government curbs labor. 1928. **Fascist Grand Council supreme power in Italy.**	1918. **Republic of Poland** proclaimed. 1918. **Czechoslovakia established.** 1919–20. Greece obtains Thrace, Smyrna from Turkey. 1921. Polish constitution adopted. 1922. King Constantine of Greece abdicates; Prince George king of Greece. 1924. **Lenin dies**; King George of Greece deposed and republic proclaimed. 1926. Pilsudski dictator of Poland. 1927. President Masaryk of Czechoslovakia re-elected; Socialist riots in Vienna. 1928. **Trotzky banished from Russia.**	1920. **League of Nations established.** 1920. Treaty with Yugoslavia gives Istria and Gorizia to Italy; Fiume a free state. 1921. Limitation of Armaments Conference in Washington. 1922. British end protectorate over Egypt. 1924. Pictures sent over wire and by radio. 1927. Radio-telephone between England, United States. 1927. Motion pictures sent by radio ("television"). 1927. Lindbergh makes nonstop flight New York to Paris.

(Continued on next page)

ERN HISTORY (*Concluded*)

GREAT BRITAIN	RUSSIA	TURKEY AND THE BALKANS	OTHER COUNTRIES AND GENERAL PROGRESS
1801. **Irish Parliament abolished;** Irish members seated in British Parliament. **United Kingdom** of Great Britain and Ireland. 1806. **Cape Colony** conquered; beginning of British rule in South Africa. 1812-15. **War with the United States;** Treaty of Ghent (1814). 1820-30. **George IV** king. 1830-37. **William IV** king. 1832. **Reform Bill;** political power to middle classes. Other legislation abolishing slavery, reforming labor conditions, etc. 1837. **Victoria** begins her long reign (1837-1901). 1854-56. **Crimean War** with Russia. 1857. **Indian Mutiny;** British government assumes **rule of India** (1858). 1867. Second parliamentary reform act; political **power** extended to **workingmen;** beginning of **democratic rule.** 1868-74. First ministry of **Gladstone** (Liberal). 1870. Beginning of **Home Rule** agitation. 1874-80. Disraeli ministry (Conservative). 1882. British occupy **Egypt.** 1899-1902. **Boer War. Union of South Africa** formed (1909).	1801-25. **Alexander I** emperor. 1809. Russia gains **Finland** after war with Sweden (1807-09). 1815. Czar grants a constitution to Poland. 1825-55. **Nicholas I** emperor. 1830-32. Revolution in Poland fails; **Poland** made a **Russian province.** 1854-56. **Crimean War;** western powers against Russia. Peace of Paris (1856). 1855-81. **Alexander II** emperor. 1861. **Czar frees Russian serfs.** 1863. **Polish insurrection** suppressed. 1877-78. **Russo-Turkish War.** 1881. Alexander II assassinated. 1881-94. **Alexander III pursues** strong **reactionary** policy. 1891. **Dual Alliance** with France. 1894-1917. **Nicholas II** exercises **absolutism;** suppression of intellectual progress. 1899. Finnish constitution abrogated.	1821-29. **War for Greek independence** (Philhellenic movement; Lord Byron). **Greece** gains **independence** (1829). 1828-29. **Russo-Turkish War** (Treaty of **Adrianople;** Greek Independence acknowledged; **Moldavia** and **Wallachia** partially independent). 1830. **Serbia** secures **autonomy.** 1833-62. **Otto I** (House of Bavaria) king of Greece. 1854-56. **Crimean War.** Western Powers aid Turkey against Russia. 1866. **Rumania formed** as self-governing state by union of Moldavia and Wallachia (Charles I, 1866-1914). 1877-78. **Russo-Turkish War** (siege of **Plevna,** 1877). **Treaties** of **San Stefano** and **Berlin** make Serbia, Montenegro, and Rumania independent; Bulgaria partly autonomous.	**Industrial Revolution.** The application of **steam power** opens new era. 1807. **Steamboat** service established by **Fulton.** 1830. Independent **monarchy** established in **Belgium** (**Leopold I,** 1833-65). 1830. Manchester and Liverpool railroad opened; Baltimore and Ohio railroad begun. 1837. Patent granted to S. F. B. **Morse** for **electromagnetic telegraph.** 1840. **China opened** to foreigners. 1854. **Japanese ports opened** to foreigners. 1858. **Transatlantic** telegraph **cable** laid. 1859. Publication of Charles **Darwin's** 'Origin of Species' setting forth doctrine of evolution. 1864. Beginning of **International Red Cross.** 1869. **Suez Canal** opened. 1885. Congo Free State formed. 1894-95. **War between China and Japan.** Expansion of Japan begins. 1899. **First Hague Peace Conference.** 1899. **Wireless telegraphy** by **Marconi** between France and England.
1901-10. **Edward VII** king. 1901. **Commonwealth of Australia** formed. 1907. **Anglo-Russian agreement** over **Persia.** 1910-36. **George V** king. 1911. **Power of House of Lords limited.** 1914. **Irish Home Rule Bill** passed; suspended.	1902. **Trans-Siberian railroad** opened. 1904-05. **Russo-Japanese War.** 1905. **Russian Revolution** begins; first Duma meets (1906). 1907. Anglo-Russian agreement.	1908-09. Successful **revolution in Turkey** by **"Young Turks."** 1911-12. **Turco-Italian War.** 1912-13. **Balkan Wars;** Balkan allies conquer most of Turkey in Europe.	1903. **First airplane** flight, by **Wright** brothers. 1905. **Union of Sweden and Norway dissolved.** 1907. **Second Peace Conference** at The Hague. 1910. **Portugal** becomes **republic.** 1912. **Republic** proclaimed in **China.** 1914. **Panama Canal** opened to traffic.

THE PEACE SETTLEMENT—See Also Chronology in Fact-Index

	WESTERN FRONT	EASTERN FRONT	OTHER FRONTS AND EVENTS
	(*Continued from preceding page.*)		
1918	Mar.-July. **German drives stopped:** Picardy (Mar. 21); Lys River (Apr. 9); Aisne and Marne (May 27); Oise (June 9); Marne (July 15). July 18. **Allied counteroffensive begun:** second battle of the Somme (Aug. 8); Americans take **St. Mihiel** (Sept. 12); **Meuse-Argonne attack** (Sept.-Nov.); **"Hindenburg Line"** broken (Oct.); Germans driven from Belgium (Sept.-Nov.); **Germans surrender on Armistice Day** (Nov. 11.)	Jan.-Feb. **Breakup of Russia;** Finland, Lithuania, Ukraine, Crimea, Armenia, Siberia **set up independent governments.** Mar. 3. **Russia accepts** humiliating peace **of Brest-Litovsk.** Feb.-Mar. **Germany moves forces to west.** Sept. Allies defeat **Bulgarian armies** in Macedonia, and **Bulgaria sues for peace.** Oct.-Nov. **Montenegro and Serbia recovered by Allies.**	Jan. 8. **President Wilson** lays down his **"Fourteen Points."** Sept. 30. **Bulgaria signs armistice.** Oct. 30. **Turkey signs armistice.** Nov. 3. **Austria signs armistice.** Nov. 9. **Polish republic announced.** Nov. 10. German emperor flees to Holland; abdicates Nov. 28. Nov. 11. **Germany signs armistice.** Nov. 12. **Emperor Charles abdicates** Austrian throne. Nov. Unitary Kingdom of Serbs, Croats, and Slovenes (Yugoslavia) established.

THE PEACE SETTLEMENT

1919 Jan. 18. **Peace Conference** of 27 Allied and Associated Powers **meets at Versailles.** Treaties drawn up with five enemy nations.
June 28. **Treaty with Germany** signed **at Versailles;** includes **Covenant of the League of Nations.** Germany loses her overseas colonies, Alsace-Lorraine, parts of Posen and West Prussia, and lesser European territories; armament reduced; reparations settlement undertaken. Ratified by all the Powers except the United States, whose Senate rejects the treaty on Nov. 19, 1919, and Mar. 19, 1920.
Sept. 10. **Treaty with Austria** signed **at St. Germain.** Austria reduced from 115,000 to 32,000 square miles, and from 30,000,000 to 6,500,000 population, by territorial cessions to Czecho-Slovakia, Hungary, Poland, Rumania, Serbia, and Italy.
Nov. 27. **Treaty with Bulgaria** signed **at Neuilly.** Bulgaria loses her conquests of the Balkan Wars of 1912-13 and of the World War to Rumania, Serbia, and Greece.

1920 June 4. **Treaty with Hungary** signed **at Trianon.** Hungarian boundaries established with territorial concessions to Rumania, Jugo-Slavia, and other border states.
Aug. 10. **Treaty with Turkey** signed **at Sèvres.** Turkey loses half her population and two-thirds of her territory; the Straits internationalized; much of Asiatic Turkey distributed among the Powers as mandataries. (Not ratified by Turkey; replaced in 1923 by **Treaty of Lausanne.**)

TWO WORLD WARS

WESTERN EUROPE	EASTERN EUROPE	OTHER COUNTRIES
(*Continued from preceding page*)		
1929. Italy ends quarrel with pope; **Vatican State established.** 1932. Briand of France dies; President Doumer assassinated; succeeded by Lebrun. Hindenburg re-elected President of Germany. 1933. **Nazi Revolution in Germany; Hitler** becomes **Chancellor** of **"Third Reich";** Germany leaves League of Nations. 1934. Hindenburg dies; **Hitler supreme** in Germany. 1935. The **Saar** rejoins **Germany. Italy attacks Ethiopia** in war of conquest.	1928-29. Russia begins Five Year Plan for industry and farming. 1930. Carol of Rumania resumes throne. 1933. Dollfuss makes Austria semi-fascist. 1934. Russia admitted to League of Nations. King Alexander of Yugoslavia assassinated. 1935. Marshal Pilsudski of Poland dies. Monarchy restored in Greece.	1928. Many nations sign **Kellogg-Briand** peace pact. 1929. German dirigible, **Graf Zeppelin,** flies around the world. 1931. **Spain becomes republic;** King Alfonso flees. 1931-32. **Japan sets up new state of Manchukuo.** 1933. **United States** recognizes Soviet Russia. **Japan announces withdrawal from League of Nations.** 1934. **Leopold III king of Belgium.** Chancellor **Dollfuss** of Austria assassinated by **Nazis.** 1935. **Transpacific air route established. League of Nations sanctions against Italy fail.**

413

MODERN HISTORY BETWEEN TWO WORLD WARS (Concluded)

WESTERN EUROPE	EASTERN EUROPE	OTHER COUNTRIES
1936. **George V of England dies; Edward VIII abdicates after 11 months; George VI becomes king.** 1937. Chamberlain English premier. Germany aids Spanish fascists. 1938. **Germany annexes Austria**; France and England abandon Czechoslovakia by accepting Munich Pact with Germany. 1939. England and France guarantee Polish independence.	1936. New Russian constitution. 1937. Russia aids Spanish loyalists. 1938. Czechoslovakia loses one third of area to Germany, Poland, Hungary. 1939. **Russia signs nonaggression pact with Germany.**	1936–37. **Civil war in Spain. Transatlantic air plane service begins.** 1936. **Italy annexes Ethiopia.** Germany reoccupies Rhineland; Italy, Germany, Japan combine against Communism. 1937–38. Japan attacks China in undeclared war. 1938. Austria becomes a German state. 1939. **Italy annexes Albania. Germany seizes all of Czechoslovakia. Fascists win Spanish civil war.**

THE SECOND WORLD WAR— See Also Chronology in Fact-Index

	EUROPE AND AFRICA	PACIFIC OCEAN AND ASIA (Dates Refer to Local Time)
1939	**Sept. 1.** Germany invades Poland. **Sept. 3.** Britain, France declare war. **Sept. 17.** Russia occupies East Poland. **Sept. 27.** Warsaw surrenders to Germans. **Oct. 14.** German U-boat sinks British battleship **Royal Oak**. **Nov. 4.** Roosevelt signs Neutrality Act. **Nov. 30.** Russia invades Finland. **Dec. 2.** Russia captures Finnish port of Petsamo. **Dec. 17.** Germans scuttle **Admiral Graf Spee** in harbor of Montevideo, Uruguay. First Canadian troops land in England.	"Undeclared war" continues between China and Japan.
1940	**Mar. 2.** Russians crack Finnish defense. **Mar. 12.** Finland and Russia sign peace treaty. **Apr. 9.** Germany occupies Denmark, invades Norway. **May 3.** Allies evacuate Norway. **May 10.** Germany invades Belgium and Netherlands. **May 14.** The Netherlands surrenders. **May 28.** King Leopold surrenders Belgian army to Germans. **May 29–June 4.** British and French troops flee from Dunkirk to England. **June 5.** Battle of France begins. **June 9.** Norway surrenders; British withdraw from Narvik. **June 10.** Italy declares war on France and Britain. **June 14.** Germans enter Paris. **June 22.** France signs armistice with Germany. **Aug. 8.** Germany begins air attack on England. **Aug. 25.** First British planes bomb Berlin. **Sept. 27.** Japan joins Rome-Berlin Axis. **Oct. 8.** Germany ends large-scale daylight raids on England. **Oct. 10.** Germany occupies Rumania. **Oct. 27.** DeGaulle sets up "Free French" government. **Dec. 9.** British strike back at Italians in Egypt.	"Undeclared" Chinese-Japanese war continues.
1941	**Feb. 5.** British drive Italians from Egyptian Sudan. **Apr. 3.** British yield Bengasi, Libya, to Axis attack. **Apr. 30.** British forces leave Greece. **June 22.** Germany invades Russia. Italy declares war on Russia. **Oct. 31.** U-boats sink U.S. destroyer **Reuben James** off Iceland. **Nov. 22.** Germans take Rostov, key to Caucasus. **Dec. 11.** Germany, Italy declare war on United States. United States declares war on Germany, Italy.	**July 21.** French give military control of Indo-China to Japan. **Oct. 18.** Tojo appointed premier of Japan. **Nov. 20.** Japanese submit "last proposals" to United States. **Dec. 6.** Roosevelt appeals to Hirohito to intervene for peace. **Dec. 7.** (Dec. 8 in Far East.) Japanese attack Pearl Harbor, Wake, Guam, Philippines, Hong Kong; invade Siam. **Dec. 8.** United States declares war on Japan. **Dec. 23.** Wake Island surrenders to Japanese.
1942	**Jan. 29.** German **Afrika Korps** recaptures Bengasi, Libya. **Mar. 28.** British Commandos raid U-boat base at St. Nazaire. **May 12.** Russia counterattacks on Kharkov front. **July 1.** British stop German drive in North Africa at El Alamein. **Aug. 24.** Nazis advance on Stalingrad in Russian Caucasus. **Nov. 8.** American troops invade North Africa. **Nov. 14.** Allied troops enter Tunisia. **Nov. 27.** French scuttle fleet at Toulon to prevent Axis seizure.	**Jan. 2.** Japanese enter Manila. **Jan. 23.** Japanese invade Solomons, capture Rabaul on New Britain. **Feb. 15.** Singapore falls to Japanese. **Apr. 18.** Doolittle fliers from **Hornet** raid Tokyo. **June 3–6.** Japanese invade Aleutian Islands; Americans repel attack on Midway. **July 21–22.** Japanese land at Gona and Buna in New Guinea. **Dec. 9.** Allies take Gona in northern New Guinea.
1943	**Jan. 18.** Russian army lifts siege of Leningrad. **Feb. 2.** Russians defeat Germans at Stalingrad. **May 12.** German resistance ends in North Africa. **July 9–10.** Allies invade Sicily. **Sept. 3.** Allies invade southern Italy. **Oct. 1.** Allies take Naples; Germans retreat to Volturno River. **Oct. 18.** Allies force Germans from Volturno defenses. **Nov. 6.** Red army liberates Kiev during winter offensive.	**Feb. 8.** U.S. forces completely occupy Guadalcanal. **Mar. 2–4.** Allies bomb Japanese convoy in Bismarck Sea. **May 30.** Americans capture Attu in the Aleutians. **Aug. 5.** Americans take Munda on New Georgia Island. **Aug. 25.** Japanese evacuate New Georgia. **Sept. 16.** MacArthur's forces capture Lae, New Guinea. **Nov. 24.** Americans conquer Tarawa and the Gilberts. **Dec. 26.** Marines land at Cape Gloucester, New Britain.
1944	**Jan. 22.** Allies land at Anzio beachhead in Italy. **May 9.** Russians recapture Sevastopol after 24-day siege. **May 18.** Allies capture Cassino. **June 4.** American 5th Army enters Rome. **June 6.** Allies invade France at Normandy coast. **Aug. 15.** Allied armies invade southern France. **Aug. 25.** Americans march into Paris. **Sept. 5.** Russia declares war on Bulgaria. **Nov. 22.** American 3d Army takes Metz. **Dec. 16.** Germans counterattack in Ardennes (Battle of the Bulge).	**Feb. 1.** Americans land on Kwajalein in Marshall Islands. **Apr. 3.** American forces occupy Bikini atoll. **June 15.** U.S. Marines invade Saipan in the Marianas. **July 21.** American Marines invade Guam. **Sept. 15.** U.S. Marines invade Peleliu in the Palaus. **Oct. 20.** Americans begin Philippine campaign; invade Leyte. **Oct. 23–26.** American Navy defeats Japanese in Leyte Gulf. **Dec. 15.** U.S. forces invade Mindoro in Philippines. **Dec. 26.** MacArthur announces end of resistance on Leyte.
1945	**Jan. 17.** Red army takes Warsaw. **Jan. 20.** Hungary signs armistice with Allies. **Mar. 7.** Americans cross Rhine River. **Apr. 8–13.** Russians capture Vienna. **Apr. 21.** Russians enter Berlin. Allies take Bologna, Italy. **Apr. 22.** British enter Hamburg. **Apr. 26.** British capture Bremen. **Apr. 29.** Germans in northern Italy surrender. **May 2.** Berlin surrenders. **May 4.** Nazis surrender Denmark, Netherlands to British. **May 7.** Germans surrender unconditionally at Reims.	**Jan. 9.** Americans invade Luzon in Philippines. **Feb. 4.** Americans enter Manila. **Feb. 15.** Americans land on Bataan Peninsula in Philippines. **Feb. 19.** U.S. Marines land on Iwo Jima, conquer island Mar. 16. **Apr. 1.** U.S. Army, Marines land on Okinawa. **June 21.** Americans complete conquest of Okinawa. **July 5.** MacArthur announces final liberation of Philippines. **Aug. 6.** American fliers drop atomic bomb on Hiroshima. **Aug. 8.** Russia declares war on Japan. **Aug. 27.** American occupation force enters Japan. **Sept. 2.** Japan surrenders aboard U.S.S. **Missouri** in Tokyo Bay.

RECONSTRUCTION AFTER THE WAR

WESTERN EUROPE	EASTERN EUROPE	OTHER COUNTRIES
1946. **Fourth French Republic proclaimed. Allies and Russia occupy Germany, Austria. Italy becomes a republic.** 1947–48. **Britain grants India independence; Moslem state of Pakistan created.** 1949. Ten democracies of Western Europe ratify **North Atlantic Treaty with Canada and United States.** 1952. George VI of Great Britain dies; succeeded by elder daughter. **Elizabeth II** crowned 1953. 1955. West Germany becomes **sovereign nation**; joins NATO. 1958. Six-nation duty-free **common market** becomes effective. 1959. **Charles de Gaulle takes office as president of Fifth French Republic.** 1960. Seven-nation **European Free Trade Association** established.	1946–47. Russia opposes United States, Britain, France in postwar policies; begins "cold war." 1947. Poland elects Russian-dominated government. 1949. Tito of Yugoslavia defies Russia. 1950. Communist-controlled Eastern Germany recognizes Poland's postwar frontiers. 1952. **Turkey, Greece** join **NATO.** 1953. **Stalin**, premier of **Russia**, dies. 1957. **Hungary** in unrest after 1956 revolt. 1958. Russia's **Khrushchev** becomes premier. 1959. **Cyprus** dispute settled.	1946–48. Disorder and civil war in Palestine, China, French Indo-China, East Indies. 1949. Chinese Communists overrun China. Palestine becomes Israel. 1950. Communist North Korea invades South Korea. 1955. **Argentina** ousts dictator Juan Perón. 1956. **Sudan** becomes a republic. 1957. Gold Coast becomes nation, **Ghana.** 1958. Egypt, Syria form **United Arab Republic. Iraq** and **Guinea** become republics. 1959. Twelve French territories in Africa become self-governing states.

IV. CANADIAN HISTORY

	PERIOD OF DISCOVERY—1000-1500	OTHER COUNTRIES
1000	**1000. Northmen discover America.** **1497. John Cabot discovers Newfoundland.**	
	FRENCH RULE	1515–47. **Francis I king of France.** 1539–43. **De Soto's expedition in southern United States.** 1555–64. Coligny attempts to found Huguenot colony in Florida.
1500	1534. **Cartier** coasts along Newfoundland; **explores the St. Lawrence** (1535, 1540).	
1600	1604. **Port Royal** (Annapolis, Nova Scotia), first permanent French settlement, founded. 1608. **Quebec settled** by French colonists led by **Champlain.** 1610. **Hudson discovers Hudson Bay** while searching for the Northwest Passage; England claims Hudson Bay region. 1613. **English colonists** from Virginia **capture Port Royal; Quebec** captured by the British (1629); New France and Acadia restored to the French by the treaty of St. Germain (1632). 1615. **Champlain explores Lake Huron.** 1623–32. War between English and French. English attack Acadia (Nova Scotia); capture Quebec. Canada restored to France by treaty. 1627. St. Lawrence valley granted to Richelieu's company of **"One Hundred Associates"**; control New France (1627–63). 1642. **Montreal founded** by Maisonneuve as a religious colony. 1658–60. **Groseillers** and **Radisson** reach the Mississippi and Great Plains. 1663. Charter of the company of "One Hundred Associates" revoked; **New France a royal colony.** 1666. **Allouez** founds a mission on Lake Superior. 1670. **Hudson's Bay Company founded** in England to carry on trade in the new territory. 1672. **Frontenac** becomes governor of Canada. 1673. **Marquette and Joliet discover the Mississippi.** 1682. **La Salle descends the Mississippi** and takes the country for France. 1689–97. **"King William's War"; Acadia captured** by the British; attack on Quebec fails: conquest restored at the Peace of Ryswick (1697).	**1607. Jamestown, Virginia, settled** by English colonists. **1618–48. Thirty Years' War** in Europe. **1620. Plymouth Colony founded** by English Puritans. 1643–1715. Louis XIV king of France. 1688. William III of Orange ascends English throne. 1689–97. War of Louis XIV over succession in the Rhenish Palatinate. 1699. French settle in Louisiana
1700	1701. **Detroit** founded as French post; **Forts Frontenac and Duquesne,** and other posts on the British frontier follow. 1701–13. **"Queen Anne's War."** Unsuccessful attack on Quebec; **Acadia seized; France cedes Hudson Bay region, Newfoundland, and Acadia to Great Britain** (Treaty of Utrecht, 1713). 1743. The **Verendryans** reach the foothills of the Rocky Mountains. 1744–48. **"King George's War." Louisbourg** captured by **English colonists** (1745); restored to French by treaty of Aix-la-Chapelle. 1749. English **settlement of Halifax founded**; colonization of Nova Scotia begins. 1755–63. **"French and Indian War."** French deported from Nova Scotia (1755); British under **Wolfe capture Quebec** (1759); **New France ceded to England** by Peace of Paris (1763).	**1701–13. War of the Spanish Succession** in Europe. 1702–14. Anne queen of England. 1727–1760. George II king of England. 1740–48. War of the Austrian Succession. 1756–63. **Seven Years' War** in Europe.
	ENGLISH PERIOD	
	1774. **Quebec Act** passed by British Parliament **to organize** government for Canada. 1775–83. **American Revolution;** Loyalists flee to Canada: colonists' attack on Quebec repulsed. 1791. Canada divided into **Upper** and **Lower Provinces** by the **Constitutional Act** passed by British Parliament; popular assemblies established with limited powers. 1793. **Sir Alexander Mackenzie** reaches the Pacific Ocean.	1789–95. **French Revolution.** 1792–1815. Wars of the French Revolution and Napoleon.
1800	1812–15. **War with the United States;** American attempts to invade Canada repulsed: surrender of **Detroit** (1812); naval **battle of Lake Erie** (1813). 1812–20. Earl of **Selkirk** founds settlement in Red River Valley. 1837–38. **Rebellions** against officialdom; French Canadians led by **Papineau** attempt to found a republic in lower Canada; **William L. Mackenzie** heads armed rebellion in Upper Canada. 1838. **Lord Durham** sent out from England to determine conditions in Canada; famous report to colonial office leads to changes in Canadian policy. 1840. **Act of Union** joins the two provinces under a royal governor. 1842. Webster-Ashburton treaty between Great Britain and United States settles Maine boundary dispute. 1854. Reciprocity treaty with the United States; abrogated by United States (1866). 1858. Capital removed to **Ottawa.** 1864. **Quebec Conference** held to consider question of confederation.	1803. United States buys Louisiana territory from France. 1832. **Parliamentary Reform** Act passed by the British Parliament. 1837. Victoria ascends the British throne. 1846. Boundary between the United States and Canada settled at 49th parallel. **1861–65. Civil War** in the United States.
	DOMINION PERIOD	
	1867. **British North America Act** establishes the **Dominion of Canada** (Confederation of Ontario, Quebec, New Brunswick, Nova Scotia), with self-government. 1867. Conservative government organized by **Sir John Macdonald** (premier 1867–73, 1878–91). 1869. Hudson's Bay Company's land purchased by Canadian government. 1870. **Rebellion of Red River** half-breeds **against** extension of Dominion control over Manitoba; led by **Louis Riel.** Province of **Manitoba** formed. 1871. Treaty of Washington between Great Britain and the United States provides for the settlement of the Nova Scotia fisheries dispute and the Oregon boundary question. 1871. **British Columbia joins the Union.** 1872. Anti-Unionist agitation in Nova Scotia ended by defeat of the party in general elections. 1873. **Prince Edward Island admitted** to the Union. 1873. Conservative government overthrown because of Canadian Pacific Railroad scandal; **Alexander Mackenzie** forms Liberal government. 1878. Conservatives restored on protectionist platform. 1885. **Riel** leads half-breed rebellion in Saskatchewan to obtain squatter rights. 1885. **Canadian Pacific Railroad finished.** 1893. Bering Sea controversy with the United States settled. 1896. Conservatives defeated on question of reëstablishment of Roman Catholic schools in Manitoba. 1896–1911. **Sir Wilfrid Laurier** premier (Liberal).	1866. Atlantic cable laid. 1870–71. **Franco-Prussian War.** **1887. First British Colonial Conference.** 1899–1902. **Boer War** in South Africa.
1900	1903. Alaskan boundary dispute settled. 1905. **Alberta** and **Saskatchewan organized as provinces.** 1914–18. First World War (see separate outline). 1921. **W. L. Mackenzie King** premier after Liberal victory in **general election.** 1930. **Richard B. Bennett premier** after Conservative victory. 1935. Liberal victory makes **Mackenzie King** premier. 1939. British King and Queen make good-will tour; **Canada enters second World War.** 1940. **Mackenzie King** government returned in general election; re-elected 1944–45. 1948. **St. Laurent** succeeds Mackenzie King as premier. 1949. **Newfoundland** becomes Canada's **tenth province. Canada gains right to amend constitution.** 1950. Canada's **Supreme Court** replaces **British Privy Council** as Canada's final tribunal. 1952. First native governor-general, Vincent Massey; 1956—lifts arms embargo to **Middle East.** 1958. Conservative party, led by **John Diefenbaker,** wins second election in 11 months. 1959. **St. Lawrence Seaway,** a joint United States-Canada project, is formally opened to navigation.	1901. Commonwealth of Australia formed. 1914. Panama Canal opened. 1926. **Imperial Conference creates British Commonwealth of Nations.** 1939. **War** breaks out in Europe. 1945. United Nations established. 1947. India divided into independent India (Hindu) and Pakistan. 1956. Israel, Arab nations clash. Egypt seizes control of **Suez Canal.** 1958. United States joins Canada in a joint air defense command.

V. AMERICAN HISTORY—COLONIAL AND REVOLUTIONARY

PERIOD OF DISCOVERY—1000-1600

1000

1000. Leif the Lucky (Northman) discovers America.
1492. Columbus discovers America.
1497. John Cabot discovers Newfoundland, etc.
1513. Ponce de Leon discovers Florida.
1513. Pacific Ocean discovered by Balboa.
1519–21. Conquest of Mexico by Cortez.
1528–36. Narvaez and De Vaca explore the Gulf Region.
1534–43. Cartier discovers and explores the St. Lawrence.

FOUNDING OF THE THIRTEEN COLONIES

1600

VIRGINIA

1607. Jamestown founded (first permanent English settlement). Captain John Smith.
1611–16. "Dale's Rule."
1619. House of Burgesses meets (first representative assembly in America).
1619. First negro slaves introduced.
1624. Virginia becomes a royal colony.
1642. Berkeley becomes governor.
1652–58. Self-government under the Protectorate.
1676. Bacon's rebellion.
1693. William and Mary College founded.

1700

1710–22. Spotswood governor.

MARYLAND

1632. Maryland granted to Lord Baltimore.
1634. St. Mary's settled by English Catholics.
1647. Representative assembly established.
1649. Act of toleration for all Christians passed.
1691. Maryland becomes a crown colony.
1729. Baltimore founded.

NEW YORK

1609. Hudson discovers the Hudson River.
1614. Dutch trading post established on Manhattan Island.
1626. New Amsterdam founded.
1629. Patroon system organized.
1638. Swedes settle along the Delaware.
1655. Dutch seize Swedish colony.
1664. New Amsterdam captured by English fleet; becomes New York.
1683. First assembly in New York.
1688. New York united to New England under Andros.

NEW JERSEY

1664. New Jersey granted to Berkeley and Carteret.
1674. Colony divided into East and West Jersey.
1682. Penn purchases East Jersey.
1702. Two Jerseys reunited as a royal province.

DELAWARE

1623–64. Dutch and Swedes settle west side of Delaware Bay and River.
1682. Delaware included in Penn's grant.
1703. Delaware becomes a separate colony.

MASSACHUSETTS

1620. Pilgrims land at Plymouth. ('Mayflower' voyage.)
1623. New Hampshire settled at Dover.
1630. Boston (Massachusetts Bay Colony) founded.
1636. Roger Williams expelled from Salem.
1636. Harvard College founded.
1643. New England Confederation formed.
1645. Free school at Roxbury.
1652. Massachusetts extends control over Maine.
1675. King Philip's War in New England: Indian uprising against settlers suppressed.
1684. Massachusetts charter annulled.
1686. Andros becomes governor of New England.
1691. Plymouth unites with Massachusetts.
1692. Salem witchcraft cases.

NEW HAMPSHIRE

1680. New Hampshire separates from Massachusetts.

RHODE ISLAND

1636. Roger Williams founds Providence.
1638. Newport settled.
1663. Rhode Island obtains a charter.

CONNECTICUT

1635. Hartford, Windsor, etc. settled.
1637. Pequot War.
1638. New Haven founded.
1662. Charter granted to Connecticut.

STRUGGLE BETWEEN FRANCE AND GREAT BRITAIN FOR SUPREMACY IN

1689–97. King William's War: New England colonists under Sir William Phips seize Port Royal, Acadia; attack on Quebec fails; Peace of Ryswick restores conquests on each side (1697)
1701–13. Queen Anne's War: frontier raids by French and Indians (Deerfield, 1704; Haverhill, 1708); English capture Port Royal; expedition against Quebec unsuccessful. France cedes Hudson Bay region, Newfoundland and Nova Scotia (Acadia) to Great Britain (Treaty of Utrecht, 1713).
1744–48. King George's War: Colonists capture Louisburg (1745); restored to France by Treaty of Aix-la-Chapelle (1748).
1755–63. French and Indian War: expedition against Fort Duquesne fails (Braddock)

CONFLICT BETWEEN COLONIES AND PARLIAMENT—

1763. British ministry adopts rigid colonial policy; Navigation Acts restricting colonial commerce to England strictly enforced; renewal of Sugar Act taxing importations from foreign colonies.
1764. Stamp Act resisted in the colonies. Virginia resolutions (1765); Stamp Act Congress protests against colonial policy (1765); Act repealed.
1767. "Townshend Acts" to enforce trade laws and taxing tea, paper, etc. Boston riot (1770); Boston Tea Party (1773).

REVOLUTIONARY WAR—1775-1783

1775. Skirmishes at Lexington and Concord; Capture of Ticonderoga and Crown Point: Battle of Bunker Hill.
1775. Second Continental Congress meets.
1776. British evacuate Boston; naval attack on Charlestown fails.
1776. July 4. Declaration of Independence adopted.
1776–77. Washington retreats across New York and New Jersey (Battles of Long Island, White Plains, Trenton, and Princeton).
1777. British attempt to cut the colonies in two: Burgoyne's and St. Leger's campaign from Canada fails (Oriskany, Bennington, Saratoga). Howe's campaign against Washington (Battle of Brandywine, occupation of Philadelphia, Germantown).
1777. Congress adopts Articles of Confederation (ratified by states, 1777–81).
1777–78. Washington winters at Valley Forge.
1778. France recognizes independence of the colonies; arrival of French army under Rochambeau.
1778. British evacuation of Philadelphia and retreat toward New York (Monmouth).
1778–79. George Rogers Clark marches through Illinois territory; captures Kaskaskia and Vincennes.
1779. British defeat Americans and French near Savannah; British occupy Georgia.
1779. Naval battle between the 'Bonhomme Richard' and the 'Serapis' (John Paul Jones).

CRITICAL PERIOD—1783 TO 1789

1785. Maryland and Virginia delegates meet at Alexandria to consider commercial relations of the two states.
1786. Annapolis Convention to consider commerce of the country calls general convention at Philadelphia.
1786–87. Shays' rebellion in Massachusetts, caused by heavy taxes and general poverty, suppressed with difficulty.
1787. Northwest Ordinance organises government in the Northwest Territory.

ARY PERIODS—TO 1789

-42. Coronado explores the Southwest.
De Soto discovers the Mississippi River.
Spanish found St. Augustine.
-90. Raleigh attempts to establish a settlement on Roanoke Island.

NIES

OTHER EVENTS IN NORTH AMERICA

Port Royal founded (first permanent French settlement).

Quebec founded by Champlain.

Hudson discovers Hudson Bay; England claims the Hudson Bay region.

Marquette and Joliet explore the Mississippi.

La Salle descends the Mississippi to its mouth.

Detroit founded as French fort and trading post.

French settle New Orleans.

CAROLINA

Charter for Carolina granted to Lord Clarendon and others.

Fundamental constitution drawn up by John Locke.

Charleston settled.

-31. Overthrow of proprietary government.

-31. Division into North and South Carolina.

SOUTH CAROLINA | NORTH CAROLINA

PENNSYLVANIA

1651. Charter for Pennsylvania granted to William Penn.

1682. Philadelphia founded.

GEORGIA

1733. Georgia settled by Oglethorpe.

1752. Georgia a royal colony.

NORTH AMERICA—1689-1763

...dock's defeat); expedition against French at Crown Point (Battle of Lake George, 1755); capitulation of French frontier posts (Duquesne, Frontenac, etc.); capture of Quebec by Wolfe (1759). France cedes Cape Breton, Canada, etc., to Great Britain (Treaty of Paris, 1763).

1763-1774

1774. Boston Port Bill closing the port, and other acts to punish Massachusetts.

1774. First Continental Congress draws up Declaration of Rights.

British victory at Camden.

-81. War in the South: Charleston captured by the British; battles of King's Mountain, Cowpens, Guilford, Eutaw; Cornwallis retreats to the north.

Siege of Yorktown; surrender of Cornwallis.

Evacuation of Savannah and Charleston; hostilities cease.

Treaty of Paris: Great Britain recognizes the independence of the colonies.

1787. Federal Constitution framed by the Constitutional Convention; ratified by 11 states by end of 1788.

VI. UNITED STATES—1789 TO PRESENT

1789

1789–97. George Washington, President, John Adams, Vice-President.

1789. First Congress meets at New York; State, Treasury, and War departments organized.

1789. First 10 Amendments to the Constitution adopted by Congress and sent to states.

1790. First census: population, 3,929,214.

1790. National debt funded; state debts assumed by federal government.

1790–95. Indian war in the Northwest Territory.

1791. First national bank chartered by Congress.

1791. Vermont admitted; Kentucky (1792); Tennessee (1796).

1793. Eli Whitney invents the cotton gin.

1794. Genet, minister from France, recalled for unneutral acts.

1794. Whisky rebellion in western Pennsylvania against internal revenue law.

1794. Jay treaty of amity and commerce with Great Britain.

1797

1797–1801. John Adams, President (Federalist); Thomas Jefferson, Vice-President (Democratic-Republican).

1797. X Y Z Affair with France leads to naval war; Alien and Sedition Acts passed against French partisans.

1798. Virginia and Kentucky resolutions directed against Alien and Sedition Acts assert right of nullification.

1798. Eleventh Amendment adopted.

1800. Presidential election: Republicans holding democratic ideas of strict construction and "states' rights" defeat aristocratic Federalists advocating strongly centralized government.

1801. John Marshall made Chief Justice.

1801

1801–09. Thomas Jefferson, President (Democratic-Republican): Aaron Burr (1801–05), George Clinton (1805–09), Vice-Presidents.

1801–05. War with Tripoli; end of tribute to Barbary states.

1803. Ohio admitted.

1803. Louisiana Purchase from France extends U. S. boundary to Rockies.

1804. Twelfth Amendment provides separate ballots for president and vice-president.

1807. Fulton's steamboat makes successful trial voyage.

1807. Dispute with Great Britain over neutral commerce and the impressment of seamen (Chesapeake Affair).

1807–09. Embargo against Great Britain and France in retaliation for their blockade of European ports.

1808. Importation of slaves prohibited.

1809

1809–17. James Madison, President (Democratic-Republican); George Clinton (1809–13), Elbridge Gerry (1813–17), Vice-Presidents.

1811–14. Indian war in the West (Tippecanoe).

1812. Louisiana admitted; Indiana (1816).

1812–15. War with Great Britain. Unsuccessful invasions of Canada (1812, 1814); British take Washington (1814); Battle of New Orleans (1815). Numerous naval duels; Perry's victory on Lake Erie (1813). Treaty of Ghent (1814).

1814. Hartford Convention protests against embargo and war.

1816. Second national bank chartered.

1816. Mildly protective tariff passed.

1817

1817–25. James Monroe, President (Democratic-Republican); D. D. Tompkins, Vice-President (1817–25).

1817. Mississippi admitted; Illinois (1818); Alabama (1819); Maine (1820); Missouri (1821).

1817. Seminole Indian War in Florida.

1818. Great Britain and the United States agree upon joint occupation of Oregon territory.

1819. Florida acquired from Spain.

1820. Missouri Compromise on question of slavery in territories.

1823. Monroe Doctrine advanced against the aggression of the Holy Alliance in America.

1824. Protective tariff passed.

1824. Internal Improvements Bill passed.

1825

1825–29. John Quincy Adams, President (Democratic-Republican); John C. Calhoun, Vice-President.

1825. Erie Canal completed.

1828. "Tariff of Abominations"; tariff becomes a live issue.

OTHER COUNTRIES

1789. French Revolution begins.

1793. War between France and England.

1793–94. Reign of Terror in France.

1799. Napoleon made First Consul.

1804. Napoleon becomes emperor.

1806. Napoleon establishes Continental ("paper") Blockade.

1806. England issues Orders in Council blockading French territories.

1810–25. Spanish and Portuguese colonies in Central and South America become independent.

1815. Battle of Waterloo.

1815. Treaty of Vienna; Holy Alliance formed.

1821. Russia attempts to restrict trade on North Pacific coast.

VI. UNITED STATES HISTORY (*Continued*)

		OTHER COUNTRIES
1829	1829–37. Andrew Jackson, President (Democrat); John C. Calhoun (1829–33), Martin Van Buren (1833–37), Vice-Presidents. 1829. "Spoils system" appointments to office. 1830. Webster-Hayne debate on "state rights." 1830. Baltimore and Ohio Railway opened, first steam locomotive in America. 1831. William Lloyd Garrison establishes The Liberator, a journal advocating abolition of negro slavery. 1831. McCormick invents the reaper. 1832. New tariff bill reduces duties but retains principle of protection. 1832. South Carolina passes ordinance "nullifying" the tariff; Jackson's proclamation denounces nullification; "Force Bill" passed (1832); Compromise tariff (1833); nullification ordinance repealed. 1832. Jackson reëlected; system of national nominating conventions begins. 1832–37. Jackson's war on the National Bank: act for renewal of charter vetoed. 1835–42. War against Seminole Indians in Florida. 1836. Arkansas admitted; Michigan (1837). 1836. "Specie circular" issued requiring the payments for public lands to be made in specie.	1830. Independent monarchy estab[lished] in Belgium. 1830. Louis Philippe ascends [the] throne. 1832. English parliamentary Reform [Bill] passed. 1835. Texas secedes from Mexico [and] establishes an independent state.
1837	1837–41. Martin Van Buren, President (Democrat); R. M. Johnson, Vice-President 1837. Financial panic, due to over-speculation and unsound financial policies. 1840. Independent treasury established. 1840. "Hard cider" campaign results in a Whig victory.	1837. Queen Victoria of England [begins] her long reign.
1841	1841. William Henry Harrison, President (Whig); John Tyler, Vice-President. 1841. Death of Harrison.	
	1841–45. John Tyler, President (Whig). 1841. Tyler vetoes bill to reëstablish the national bank (1841) and bill for a "Fiscal Corporation"; break between Tyler and the Whigs; entire cabinet resigns. 1842. Webster-Ashburton treaty with Great Britain settles the Northeast boundary dispute 1842. Dorr Rebellion in Rhode Island secures liberal constitution. 1844. First telegraph, between Washington and Baltimore, completed. 1844. James K. Polk (Democrat) elected President. 1845. Florida admitted.	
1845	1845–49. James K. Polk, President (Democrat); George M. Dallas, Vice-President. Texas annexed, 1845. 1846. Iowa admitted; Wisconsin (1848). 1846. Northwest boundary line settled at 49th parallel by treaty with Great Britain. 1846. Low tariff enacted. 1846–48. Mexican War. American victories at Buena Vista (1847); Cerro Gordo (1847); capture of Mexico City (1847). Treaty of Guadalupe Hidalgo (1848), Mexico relinquishes claims to Texas; cedes New Mexico and Upper California to United States. 1846. Wilmot Proviso prohibiting slavery in territories acquired from Mexico defeated. 1848. Territory of Oregon organized without slavery. 1848. Presidential election results in Whig victory. Formation of the Free Soil Party.	1846. Great Britain repeals corn [laws;] free trade established. 1848. Revolutions in France and [the] second French Republic founded.
1849	1849–50. Zachary Taylor, President (Whig); Millard Fillmore, Vice-President. 1849. Rush of gold seekers to California. 1850. Clayton-Bulwer treaty with Great Britain provides that neither country should have exclusive control over any canal built across Nicaragua or Panama isthmus. 1850. Death of President Taylor.	
	1850–53. Millard Fillmore, President (Whig). 1850. "Clay's Compromise": California admitted as a free state; other territory acquired from Mexico left open to slavery; slave trade abolished in the District of Columbia; new Fugitive Slave Law enacted. 1850. Maine adopts prohibition. 1851. Rail connection established between New York City and Lake Erie at Buffalo. 1852. 'Uncle Tom's Cabin' published; stimulates growth of abolition sentiment in North. 1852. Franklin Pierce (Democrat) elected president.	1852. Louis Napoleon proclaimed [em]peror of France.
1853	1853–57. Franklin Pierce, President (Democrat); William R. King, Vice-President. 1853. Gadsden Purchase settles boundary dispute with Mexico. 1854. Kansas-Nebraska Bill repeals Missouri Compromise and organizes Kansas and Nebraska on the principle of "squatter sovereignty." Civil war in Kansas between free state and slave state settlers (1855–57). 1854. Treaty with Great Britain establishes reciprocity with Canada. 1854. Admiral Perry secures the opening of Japanese ports to foreign trade. 1854–55. "Know Nothing" Party, a secret party opposed to foreigners participating in American politics, at the height of its power. 1854–55. Movement to add slave territory to the United States; Ostend manifesto favors annexation of Cuba (1854); filibustering expedition to Nicaragua (1855). 1856. First Republican national convention adopts anti-slavery platform.	1854–56. Crimean War.
1857	1857–61. James Buchanan, President (Democrat); J. C. Breckenridge, Vice-President. 1857. Dred Scott decision maintains that neither negro slaves nor their descendants can become citizens; that a slave does not become free by being carried to free territories. 1858. Minnesota admitted; Oregon (1859); Kansas (1861). 1859 John Brown's raid on the United States arsenal at Harper's Ferry. 1860. Abraham Lincoln (Republican) elected president; South Carolina secedes from the Union. 1861. Ten other Southern States secede and form the Confederacy.	1861. Italy united under [Victor] Emmanuel.
1861	1861–65. Abraham Lincoln, President (Republican); Hannibal Hamlin (1861–65), Andrew Johnson (1865), Vice-Presidents. 1861–65. Civil War. 1861. Apr. 12. Fort Sumter fired upon by the Confederates. 1861. July 21. Union army defeated at Bull Run. 1861. Seizure of Confederate commissioners (Mason and Slidell) from British steamship nearly leads to war. 1862. Apr. 6–7. Grant's victory at Shiloh; McClellan's peninsular campaign (Mar.–July); naval battle (Mar. 9) between Monitor and Merrimac; New Orleans captured by Farragut (Apr. 23). 1862. Slavery abolished in the District of Columbia. 1863. Jan. 1. Lincoln issues the Emancipation Proclamation. 1863. July 1–3. Union victory at Gettysburg; Vicksburg captured (July 4). 1863. West Virginia admitted as a free state. 1864. Grant made commander-in-chief of the Union armies. Sheridan's raid up the Shenandoah Valley; Sherman's march to the sea; capture of Mobile. 1864. Nevada admitted. 1864. Lincoln reëlected. 1865. Apr. 9. Lee surrenders at Appomattox Court House. 1865. Apr. 14. Lincoln assassinated.	1861–88. William I king of Prussia. 1863–67. Maximilian attempts to [establish] monarchy in Mexico.

VI. UNITED STATES HISTORY (*Continued*)

		OTHER COUNTRIES
1865	1865–69. **Andrew Johnson**, President (Republican administration, but Johnson a Democrat). 1865. Proclamation extending amnesty to the South (14 classes excepted). 1865. **Thirteenth Amendment** prohibits slavery in the United States. 1865–67. President quarrels with Congress over the reconstruction policy; Congress passes over his veto **Civil Rights Bill** to extend citizenship to freedmen (1866), act continuing **Freedmen's Bureau, Reconstruction Act** (1867), and **Tenure of Office Bill** (1867). 1867. **Alaska** purchased from Russia; **Nebraska** admitted to the Union. 1867. Johnson forces French to withdraw army from Mexico. 1868. President impeached; conviction fails by one vote (two-thirds of Senate required) 1868. **Fourteenth Amendment extends citizenship to freedmen.**	1866. **Austro-Prussian War.** 1866. **Permanent Atlantic cable laid.** 1867. **Dual monarchy** of Austria-Hungary established.
1869	1869–77. **Ulysses S. Grant**, President (Republican); **Schuyler Colfax** (1869–73), **Henry Wilson** (1873–77), Vice-Presidents. 1870. **Fifteenth Amendment extends franchise to the negroes.** 1871. **Treaty of Washington** with Great Britain provides for a clearer definition of the Oregon boundary, settlement of disputes over the Canadian fisheries, and arbitration of the "Alabama claims." 1872. **General Amnesty Act** restores most of the ex-Confederates to their civil and political rights. 1872. Grant reëlected; **National Reform-Labor Party** adopts platform of labor and economic reform; **Prohibition Party** names presidential candidates. 1873. Financial panic. 1873. Grant vetoes bill to increase paper money; Congress decides to **resume specie payments** (1875). 1872–74. Political scandals: **"Credit Mobilier"** implicates public men in Union Pacific scandal; **"Salary Grab" Act** greatly increasing congressmen's salaries (1873); **Whiskey Ring conspiracy** to defraud government of internal revenue on distilled liquors (1874). 1876. **Colorado** admitted. 1876. Election returns disputed; commission declares Republican candidate elected (Rutherford B. Hayes). 1876. Custer Indian massacre in Montana. 1876. **Alexander Graham Bell** invents the telephone.	1869. **Suez Canal opened.** 1870–71. **Franco-Prussian War.** 1870. **Third French Republic proclaimed.** 1870. **Union of Italy completed.** 1871. **German Empire established.**
1877	1877–81. **Rutherford B. Hayes**, President (Republican); **William A. Wheeler**, Vice-President. 1877. **Federal troops withdrawn from the South.** 1877. Railroad and miners' strikes contribute to **widespread industrial depression.** 1878. **Greenback Party** favoring "cheap money" at height of power. 1878. **Bland-Allison Act** for purchase and coinage of silver passed over Hayes' veto. 1879. **Specie payments resumed.** 1879. **Thomas A. Edison** invents the electric light. 1880. Hayes fails of renomination because of his differences with party politicians.	1877–78. **Russo-Turkish War.**
1881	1881. **James A. Garfield**, President (Republican); **Chester A. Arthur**, Vice-President. 1881. Garfield assassinated (July 2).	
	1881–85. **Chester A. Arthur**, President (Republican). 1883. **Pendleton Civil Service Reform Bill** passed. 1884. Civil government established in Alaska. 1884. Bitter presidential election campaign; independent Republicans ("Mugwumps") swing to Democratic support.	1882. **Triple Alliance** formed between Germany, Austria, and Italy. 1884. **Partition of Africa.**
1885	1885–89. **Grover Cleveland**, President (Democrat); **T. A. Hendricks**, Vice-President. 1885. Immigration of contract laborers forbidden. 1887. **Interstate Commerce Act** passed; beginning of national regulation of railroads. 1888. Bill for tariff for revenue only fails to pass Congress. 1889. **Department of Agriculture** established.	1888–1918. **William II** emperor of Germany.
1889	1889–93. **Benjamin Harrison**, President (Republican); **Levi P. Morton**, Vice-President. 1889–90. Admission of **North and South Dakota, Idaho, Montana, Washington, and Wyoming.** 1889. **Oklahoma** thrown open to settlement. 1890. **McKinley tariff** establishes protectionist principle. 1890. **Sherman Anti-Trust Act** passed to prevent monopolies by corporations. 1890. **Silver Purchase Act** provides for monthly purchases of silver to be paid for in treasury notes. 1890. Controversy with Germany over the **Samoan Islands** settled by the **Treaty of Berlin.** 1891. **People's Party** (Populists) formed. 1892. Cleveland (Democrat) elected again on tariff issue. 1892–1896. Development of the automobile. 1893. **Bering Sea controversy** with Great Britain referred to arbitration.	1891. **Dual Alliance** of France and Russia announced.
1893	1893–97. **Grover Cleveland**, President (Democrat); **Adlai E. Stevenson**, Vice-President. 1893. Financial panic; **Silver Purchase** Act repealed and **gold standard supported.** 1894. Tariff duties reduced; **Pullman railroad strikes** suppressed by Federal troops. 1895. United States demand for arbitration of **British-Venezuelan controversy** acceded to by Great Britain. 1896. **Utah** admitted to the union.	
1897	1897–1901. **William McKinley**, President (Republican); **Garret Hobart** (1897–1901), **Theodore Roosevelt** (1901), Vice-Presidents. 1897. **Dingley tariff** reëstablishes high protection. 1898. United States battleship **Maine** blown up in Havana harbor. 1898. **Spanish-American War**; Spanish fleets destroyed at **Manila Bay and Santiago**; invasion of Cuba. Spain recognizes **Cuban independence; Puerto Rico, Guam, and the Philippines** ceded to United States; Cuba occupied by United States until 1902. 1898. **Hawaii** annexed to the United States. 1899. Insurrection in the Philippines suppressed; civil government established. 1899. Secretary **Hay** obtains recognition of the **"Open Door" policy** toward China. 1900. Currency law adopts **gold standard**; McKinley reëlected on the "full dinner-pail" platform. 1901. McKinley assassinated (Sept. 6).	1897. **Marconi perfects the wireless telegraph.** 1899–1902. **Boer War in South Africa.** 1899. **First Hague Peace Conference.** 1900. **Boxer uprising in China.**

VI. UNITED STATES HISTORY (*Concluded*)

		OTHER COUNTRIES
1901	1901–9. **Theodore Roosevelt**, President (Republican); **Charles W. Fairbanks**, Vice-President (1905–9). 1901. **Hay-Pauncefote treaty** with Great Britain allows United States to build **Panama Canal** on condition that it be open to all nations on equal terms. 1902. French interests in **Panama Canal purchased**; canal zone obtained from Panama by treaty (1904). 1903. **Alaska** boundary dispute with Great Britain settled. 1903. Beginning of **stricter government regulation of transportation and trade**; **Department of Commerce and Labor** created, railroad rebates abolished (1903); jurisdiction of Interstate Commerce Commission extended (1905); suits brought against trusts under Sherman Anti-Trust Law; **Hepburn Act** regulating railroad rates passed (1906); Meat Inspection and Pure Food Acts passed (1906). 1903. **Development of democratic government**; state-wide **primary election** law in Wisconsin followed by widespread adoption in other states; **initiative and referendum** adopted by Oregon (1902). 1903. **Wright brothers make first airplane flight** at Kitty Hawk, N. C. 1906–9. **Intervention in Cuba** to restore order following armed revolt. 1907. **Oklahoma** admitted as a state.	1901–10. **Edward VII** king of Eng... 1902. **Trans-Siberian railway** opene... 1903. **Panama** declares itself an inde**pendent republic; immediate recogni**tion by President Roosevelt. 1904–1905. **Russo-Japanese War**; me**diation of Roosevelt results in the Peace of Portsmouth.** 1907. **Second Hague Peace Conference** 1907. **Triple Entente** formed betw... Great Britain, France, and Russia. 1908–9. **Naval Conference** at Londo... **adopts rules for naval warfare.**
1909	1909–13. **William Howard Taft**, President (Republican); **James S. Sherman**, Vice-President. 1909. Dispute with Venezuela arbitrated. 1909. **Payne-Aldrich tariff** passes; rules of the House of Representatives reformed. 1910. Postal savings bank created; parcel post, 1912. 1912. **Arizona and New Mexico** admitted as states; territorial government established in Alaska. 1913. **Sixteenth Amendment** gives Congress power to levy **income tax**.	1909. **Peary reaches North Pole.** 1910. **George V** king of England. 1911. **Revolution in Mexico.** 1911. **Amundsen reaches South Pole.** 1912–13. **Turkish-Balkan wars.** 1912. **Chinese republic proclaimed.**
1913	1913–21. **Woodrow Wilson**, President (Democrat); **Thomas R. Marshall**, Vice-President. 1913. **Seventeenth Amendment** provides for **election of senators by the people**. **Department of Commerce and Labor** becomes two separate departments. **Underwood-Simmons tariff** lowers duties; **Federal Reserve system** of banks created; graduated **income tax law passed**. 1914. **Federal Trade Commission** created; **Clayton Anti-Trust Act** passed. 1914. **Panama Canal opened.** 1914. Dispute with Mexico over "Tampico incident"; **American troops occupy Vera Cruz.** 1914. **Neutrality in European war proclaimed.** 1916. Tariff Commission created; **Adamson Law** establishes eight-hour day for railway employees. 1916. Punitive **expedition sent into Mexico.** 1916. **Wilson re-elected on a peace platform.** 1917. **War declared against Germany** (see Chart II for First World War). 1918. **Armistice** signed by Germany (see Chart II for First World War). 1919. **Eighteenth Amendment establishes nationwide prohibition.** 1919. **Treaty of Versailles fails** to receive two-thirds majority **in the Senate.** 1920. **Nineteenth Amendment establishes nation-wide woman suffrage.**	1914. Direct wireless communicati... established between Germany an... United States. 1914–18. **First World War.** 1917. Denmark sells Virgin Islands t... United States. 1919. **Treaty of Versailles signed.** 1919. First transatlantic flights, b... airplane and dirigible. 1920. **League of Nations established**
1921	1921. **Warren G. Harding**, President (Republican); **Calvin Coolidge**, Vice-President. 1921. Budget Bill passed establishing **budget system** in national finance. 1921. Treaty with Colombia ratified paying her $25,000,000 to settle Canal Zone dispute. 1921. Bill passed **restricting immigration.** 1921. President signs joint Congressional resolution declaring **peace with Germany** and Austria (July 2). 1921–22. **Limitation of Armament Conference** at Washington prepares **Four Power Treaty** between U. S., Great Britain, France, and Japan, for maintaining peace in the Pacific, and **Five Power Naval Treaty** between U. S., Great Britain, France, Italy, and Japan limiting naval tonnage. 1922. Strikes of coal miners and railroad shop workers keep a million men idle. 1922. **Fordney-McCumber Tariff Act** passed, raising duties to high level. 1923. President Harding dies (Aug. 2).	1921. Famines in Russia and China. 1921. Ex-Emperor Charles unsucces**s**fully attempts to regain throne o... Hungary; exiled to Madeira. 1922. European economic conferenc... including German and Russian dele**gates, at Genoa.** 1922. Tomb of King Tutankhamen i... Egypt (about 1350 B. C.) discovered near Luxor.
1923	1923. **Calvin Coolidge**, President (Republican). 1924. Investigation of **leasing of government oil reserves** to private interests creates national scandal. 1924. Immigration law passed **greatly limiting immigration.** 1924. Army aviators make **round-the-world flight.** 1924. **Coolidge re-elected; Charles G. Dawes**, Vice-President. 1927. Greatest Mississippi River flood ever known causes immense crop and property losses. 1928. **Secretary of State Kellogg** negotiates **Pact of Paris** by which nations renounce war.	1926. **British dominions** recognized a... autonomous units in the empire. 1927. Controversy between Mexico and United States over oil and lan... laws. 1927. United States intervenes to s... civil war in Nicaragua.
1929	1929. **Herbert Hoover**, President (Republican); **Charles Curtis**, Vice-President. 1929. President calls special session of Congress to consider problems of **farm relief** and changes in the **tariff.** 1929. President Hoover appoints **Federal Farm Board.** 1929. **World-wide economic depression** begins; stock markets collapse; banks fail; millions unemployed. 1930. **Hawley-Smoot bill** raises tariff. 1932. Relief measures to meet depression adopted.	1930. United States, Great Britain, an... Japan agree on new naval reductio... **at London Naval Conference.** 1931. Great Britain drops gold standard 1931–32. Japan invades Manchuria, se... up **Manchukuo.**
1933	1933. **Franklin D. Roosevelt**, President (Democrat); **John Nance Garner**, Vice-President. 1933. Congress enacts first **"New Deal" program** (NRA for business, AAA for agriculture; abandonment of gold standard); Soviet Russia recognized. Prohibition (18th) amendment repealed. 1935. Congress passes **Wagner Labor Act** and **Social Security Act**. Huge appropriations for work relief. Supreme Court kills NRA. Philippine independence voted. New neutrality policy established. 1936. Supreme Court kills AAA. **Veterans' bonus paid. Roosevelt and Garner re-elected.**	1936. **Edward VIII**, king of England abdicates; **George VI** becomes king 1937–38. Japan conquers much of China 1938. Nazi Germany annexes Austria and most of Czechoslovakia.
1940	1940. Huge rearmament program, **peacetime conscription, adopted.** 1940. **Roosevelt re-elected with Henry A. Wallace**, Vice-President. 1941. **Lend-lease** aid enacted. **Japanese attack Pearl Harbor; U. S. goes to war against Japan, Germany, and Italy** (see Chart III for Second World War). 1944. **Roosevelt elected for fourth term, with Harry S. Truman**, Vice-President. 1945. **Roosevelt dies** (April 12), **Truman is President.** 1947. Army, Navy, Air Force put **under one Cabinet member.** 1948. Congress votes ERP; **Truman re-elected, A. W. Barkley**, Vice-President. 1949. United States signs **North Atlantic Treaty.**	1940–41. Twenty-one American repub**lics resolve to act jointly for defense o**... Western Hemisphere. 1942. Twenty-six **United Nations pledge mutual assistance against Axis.** 1945. **Second World War ends.** 1946–47. **Allies draft peace treaties** with Finland, Bulgaria, Hungary, Rumania, Italy.
1950	1950. United States sends arms to non-Communist nations; **hydrogen bomb ordered.** 1950–51. United States troops fight with United Nations forces in **Korean war.** 1953. **Dwight D. Eisenhower**, President (Republican); **Richard Nixon**, Vice-President. 1956. **Eisenhower-Nixon re-elected.** 1957. **Eisenhower Doctrine** for Middle East announced. 1958. United States launches **earth satellites.** 1959. **Alaska** becomes 49th state; **Hawaii** is proclaimed 50th state. 1961. **John F. Kennedy**, President (Democrat); **Lyndon B. Johnson**, Vice-President.	1951. France promotes Schuman P... 1952. **Elizabeth II** queen of England 1952. **Japan signs peace treaties.** 1957. **Russia launches earth satellite** 1958. **Fifth French Republic** pro**claimed.** 1959. **Twelve world powers sign treaty to demilitarize Antarctica.**